Mental Health Handbook for Schools

Mary Atkinson and Garry Hornby

LONDON AND NEW YORK

First published 2002
by RoutledgeFalmer
11 New Fetter Lane, London EC4P 4EE

Simultaneously published in the USA and Canada
by RoutledgeFalmer
29 West 35th Street, New York, NY 10001

Reprinted 2003

RoutledgeFalmer is an imprint of the Taylor & Francis Group

Typeset in Goudy by Taylor & Francis Books Ltd
Printed and bound in Great Britain by TJ International Ltd, Padstow, Cornwall

British Library Cataloguing in Publication Data
A catalogue record for this book is available from the British Library

Library of Congress Cataloging-in-Publication Data
Atkinson, Mary, 1954–
A mental health handbook for schools / Mary Atkinson and Garry Hornby.
Includes bibliographical references and index.
1. Children–Mental health–Handbooks, manuals, etc. 2. Teenagers–Mental
health– Handbooks, manuals etc. 3. Students–Mental health
services–Handbooks, manuals, etc. I. Hornby, Garry. II. Title.
[DNLM: 1. Mental Disorders–Adolescence. 2. Mental Disorders–Child. WS 350
A877m 2002]
RC454.4 .A86 2002
618.92'89–dc21 2001040809

ISBN 0–415–20829–7

Mental Health Handbook for Schools

This handbook is a p lth in schools. It provides t scent mental health probler stions for identifying and su

The book focuses on d the circumstances which

- ADHD
- suicidal behaviou
- eating disorders
- obsessive–compu
- anxiety disorders
- autism
- substance abuse
- parental separatic
- depression
- bullying
- schizophrenia
- bereavement.

The handbook is an inv ation about child and adolescent mental health services and outlines a whole-school approach to the promotion of good mental health. It will prove indispensable for all teachers, special educational needs co-ordinators, heads of year, PSHE co-ordinators, education welfare officers and educational psychologists.

Mary Atkinson is a Senior Research Officer with the National Foundation for Educational Research (NFER). **Garry Hornby** is a Reader in Education at the Institute for Learning, University of Hull, and co-author of *The Special Educational Needs Co-ordinator's Handbook* (Routledge, 1995).

Contents

Foreword

Peter Wilson, Director, Young Minds

Schools are such an ordinary part of our everyday experience that it is all too easy for us to overlook how extraordinary they are. Entrusted implicitly with the well-being of our young, they are required to take on the formidable task of enriching, cultivating and educating the minds of increasingly diverse groups of human beings. They are first and foremost places of learning, of building competencies and academic achievement; but they are also places of safekeeping, of care and encouragement in creating the health and the confidence necessary for future independence in adulthood. Schools have many functions, meeting a wide range of needs in a broad spectrum of young people. A Department of Education circular in 1994, called *Pupils with Problems*, made it clear that 'schools … play a vital part in promoting the spiritual, cultural, mental and physical development of young people … the emotional development of children must continue to be a concern of mainstream education'. More recently, in a consultation document, entitled *Schools: Building on Success*, the department has emphasised the importance of 'establishing Education with character in schools'. Amongst other things, it states that schools should provide opportunities for pupils to 'develop as well-rounded, creative, self-reliant individuals, who know right from wrong, who can work in teams, who respect their fellow pupils whatever their background, who are able to manage their own learning …'. All of this is to be much commended, but we do need to acknowledge how much it adds up to a very tall order – and the teachers who work in the schools need all the training and support they can get to meet such high and important aspirations. At the heart of this book is a deep concern for this need and a full recognition of the breadth of responsibility that the teachers carry for both the mental health and education of their pupils.

'Mental health' and 'education' – these are words and concepts that over time have rarely sat comfortably with each other. The word 'mental' has had its immediate popular association with madness, giving rise to all kinds of fears about loss of control and self-coherence and of stigmatisation. 'Education' has had a more favourable reception, but for many it has too rapidly been linked to academia, with little reference to 'health'. A crude divide has occurred in our thinking about emotion and intellect, to a large extent fostered in the histories, trainings and preoccupations of those who engage in the separate world of schools and mental health services. Much of this may well have been necessary in the past, but increasingly it is being seen as unhelpful, serving only to obscure one or two simple truths that, if more fully accepted, would be of inestimable value in child development. It is, for example, in the very process of education that physical and mental health are enhanced; equally it is out of physical and mental health that the learning potential of individuals is increased.

It is with this sense of integration in mind, that Mary Atkinson and Garry Hornby have written this important and innovative book. They clearly understand the meaning of mental health – that it is more than merely the absence of illness; and they well recognise the pivotal and unique role that teachers play in promoting mental health in general throughout their schools, as well as preventing mental health problems from arising, and also dealing with them when they have become established. The authors are not, of course, suggesting that teachers become specialist therapists or quasi psychiatrists; nor are they losing sight of the teacher's primary educational purpose. They are, however, highlighting the major contributions that teachers can make – through their day-to-day knowledge of their pupils; through their ways of being with and responding to them; through their experience, expertise and sheer familiarity and availability – to the emotional and social well-being of their pupils.

This book honours this contribution by providing a remarkably coherent and comprehensive manual that will enable teachers to understand better the extraordinary complexity of the children and young people who come to them – in all the different shapes and sizes of their minds and experiences, from such diverse family and social backgrounds and with such variety of ability, talent and expectation. The manual will help teachers find their bearings, make better use of their own perceptions and form clearer judgements about the problems that they face. It will equip them with the knowledge to make more effective and appropriate decisions – how best to teach children with certain kinds of mental disorder or special need, how to alert parents and others quickly to emerging problems and how to make effective referrals for help elsewhere.

The value of this book lies in its readiness to hold together the particular and the whole. It is unequivocal in its determination to draw into the field of education a full and detailed account of the different forms of mental disorder – using the language and understanding of formal psychiatric classification. This is a bold move, crossing the waters from one domain to another, but absolutely essential, if teachers are to recognise and differentiate between the symptoms and behaviour of the children they meet, with different kinds of personalities and problems. At the same time the book keeps alive the context in which these disorders and problems occur and in which teachers, parents and others can work together. The potential of a school – through its ethos, its whole school policies and its pastoral provision and classroom management – to build a community of people in which everybody, young and old, feels fundamentally respected and encouraged, their differences welcomed and their difficulties understood, is enormous. All of this is very much captured in the realistic optimism, clear thinking and writing and sustained sense of endeavour in this book. It sets a standard and offers an invaluable guide to reaching that standard, in the best interests of improving the quality of school life in general and of strengthening the capacities of teachers, who, let's face it, are crucial to the development of the minds of our children.

References

Department for Education (DFE) (1994) *Pupils with Problems, Circulars 8–13/94*. London: HMSO.
Department for Education and Employment (DfEE) (2001) *Schools: Building on Success*. Norwich: Stationery Office.

Preface

The idea for this book arose from our own experience of working alongside mainstream teachers in supporting them to address the needs of children and adolescents with mental health problems. On the one hand, in the first author's case, this was as a teacher within a child and adolescent mental health unit offering advice to mainstream teachers on pupils' return to school. On the other, in the second author's case, this was as an educational psychologist providing guidance to teachers on dealing with pupils with emotional and behavioural difficulties.

In addition, our experience in the early days of our teaching careers led us to believe that many mainstream teachers lacked awareness of children's mental health problems and, at times, even experienced teachers felt out of their depth when confronted with pupils with such problems. When working as a teacher in a class for children with learning difficulties, for example, the second author's own lack of knowledge was highlighted when a pupil developed symptoms of schizophrenia and he was uncertain how to help. Through our own experience and training we became aware of many pupils whose emotional or behavioural needs were unmet because teaching staff lacked the necessary knowledge, understanding and skills. In these situations they appeared uncertain about the approach they should adopt and were concerned that they might exacerbate these children's difficulties. This was not helped by the fact that mental health professionals were often reluctant to share information with teachers or to acknowledge the constraints that teachers were under when working with these children in a mainstream school setting. It was evident that teachers required more knowledge and understanding of children's mental health problems and of the potential strategies for addressing such difficulties. Our training and experience have led us to believe that teachers can do a lot more to improve children's mental well-being if they have greater knowledge and understanding of the mental health problems they are likely to encounter.

The central message in this handbook is a hopeful one. Whilst not all children recover fully from serious mental health disorders, as Clarke and Clarke (2000: 19) state, in their review of research evidence for the long-term effects of early experiences: 'There is no known adversity from which at least some children had not recovered if moved to something better.' For many children, therefore, despite adverse circumstances, there is much hope. They state too that: 'The whole of the life path is important, including the early years.' It is never too late to help children with mental health problems, no matter how serious their symptoms and how adverse their circumstances may seem. This is poignantly illustrated by the recent international best selling book *A Child Called It* by Dave Pelzer (2000). Despite appalling circumstances of child abuse and neglect throughout his childhood, Dave went on to live a happy and satisfying life. Whilst this must in part be credited to his own strength and resilience, the central role that teachers played in his survival is confirmed by the fact that he dedicated the book to his teachers.

The need for a book that bridges the divide between mental health and education is long overdue. In writing the book, we set out to:

- raise teachers' awareness of the importance of mental health in children and adolescents, how this may impact on their learning potential, and the link between mental health and special educational needs;
- increase teachers' knowledge of the range of mental health problems and disorders they may encounter, the criteria by which they can be identified, and strategies they might employ to address them;
- present teachers with a range of strategies aimed at preventing mental health problems;
- raise teachers' awareness of the way in which liaison between Child and Adolescent Mental Health Services and schools can be improved and how both services can work together to address the mental health needs of children and young people.

It is envisaged that the handbook will be a useful guide for practising teachers to dip into when mental health difficulties are encountered and will also inform aspects of whole-school development, both policy and practice. In addition, it will be of assistance to professionals involved in supporting teachers and pupils with emotional and behavioural difficulties, such as special educational needs co-ordinators, educational psychologists, education welfare officers and behaviour support teachers. Finally, it will provide a useful text for students on post-graduate courses in education. The handbook is divided into four parts.

Part I is an introductory section. The first chapter provides a general introduction to children's mental health problems. The second chapter focuses on the distinction between abnormal and normal child development, particularly emotional development, theories of mental health and classification systems. Both chapters were considered important to include as a background against which to discuss more specific mental health problems.

Part II includes detailed accounts of most of the common childhood and adolescent mental health problems which teachers are likely to encounter. The decision about what to include and what not to include was very much based on the authors' own experiences of the children and young people they had encountered in mainstream school settings. Each chapter is divided into two sections. The first section provides an overview of the current information with regard to diagnosis, features, incidence, causes, treatment and outcome of the disorder in question. The second section of each chapter discusses strategies teachers can employ by way of prevention and early identification, as well as intervention for pupils recognised as having the disorder.

In Part III specific circumstances that pupils may encounter that are likely to lead to mental health problems are discussed. Again, the first section in each chapter deals with current information with regard to definition, features, incidence, effects, causes, treatment and outcome. The second section focuses on ways in which teachers can help to alleviate and address the difficulties associated with these circumstances in order that more serious mental health problems might be prevented.

Part IV focuses on mental health services and the prevention of mental health problems in children. In the penultimate chapter information about Child and Adolescent Mental Health Services is provided, together with a discussion of some of the issues that may arise in collaboration between teachers and mental health professionals. The final chapter outlines a whole-school approach to the promotion of mental health in schools and discusses the role that teachers can play in this.

References

Clarke, A. M. and Clarke, A. D. B. (2000) *Early Experience and the Life Path*. London: Jessica Kingsley.
Pelzer, D. (2000) *A Child Called It*. London: Orion.

Acknowledgements

There are a lot of people who have contributed to this handbook, many without knowing it. It is impossible to thank them all here. However, the first author would personally like to thank all the children and families encountered during her time as a teacher at the West End Adolescent Unit in Kingston upon Hull, for the inspiration to embark on this book. She would like to thank the staff at the unit, from whom she learned so much. Both authors are indebted to Dany Wlodarcyk, Marcia Pilgrim and Jennifer Karn for taking the time and trouble to read and comment on drafts of chapters of the book. Their feedback was most helpful. We would like to thank Mandy Maull for her contribution to the cameos of children at the beginning of each chapter. These are based on actual cases with the names changed to preserve anonymity. In addition, thanks go to Steven Morris for the support received throughout the production of this book.

We are grateful to the American Psychiatric Association and all diagnostic criteria is reprinted with permission from *Diagnostic and Statistical Manual of Mental Disorders*, Fourth Edition. Copyright 1994 American Psychiatric Association.

Part I

Mental health in context

1 Introduction

A leading authority on mental health in children in the UK has estimated that, in the average secondary school of around a thousand pupils at any one time there will be fifty students who are clinically depressed, a further hundred with significant emotional difficulties, ten affected by eating disorders and up to ten who will attempt suicide in the next year (Mind, 1997). The importance of mental health in children and young people is highlighted by recent concern about increases in:

- children with disruptive behaviour being excluded from schools;
- violence in schools and juvenile crime;
- psychosocial disorders in young people;
- suicides and incidences of self-harm among children and adolescents;
- the numbers of children affected by marital breakdown;
- the numbers of children involved in substance abuse;
- the incidence of children subjected to abuse or neglect.

Despite these factors, children's mental health has so far been paid insufficient attention in schools. Teachers are uniquely placed to influence the mental health of children and young people. As well as being in a position to recognise the symptoms of mental health difficulties at an early stage, they can enhance the social and emotional development of children and foster their mental well-being through their daily responses to pupils. According to the Mental Health Foundation (1999), schools have 'a critical role to play' in these aspects of mental health. In addition, Rutter (1991) provides evidence that school experiences are important for children's psychological, as well as their intellectual, development and asserts therefore that schools need to concern themselves with children's self-esteem and their social experiences, as well as their academic performance. So, to suggest that schools need to focus on mental health issues 'is not simply to add yet another demand to a teacher's already impossible workload; effective social and affective education is directly beneficial to academic attainment and can therefore help teachers be more effective' (Weare, 2000: 6).

The majority of children with mental health problems never reach specialist services so their needs have to be addressed by mainstream institutions, such as schools. At the same time, current pressures on schools, such as the demands of the National Curriculum, make it more difficult for teachers to address the emotional and social needs of pupils. Whilst it is desirable that children achieve academic success, personal and social development are also vital if they are to grow into well-adjusted adults. The inclusion of children with a wide range of special needs in mainstream schools means that today's teachers must also support many troublesome and troubled children, whose needs are not easily met. Although some teachers may consider that meeting the mental health needs of children does not fall within their remit, unmet emotional needs inevitably impact on children's learning and make the task of teaching more difficult. So it is therefore important for teachers to directly address children's mental health needs.

Many mainstream teachers lack awareness of children's mental health issues. They lack the necessary knowledge, understanding and skills for addressing the needs of children with mental health problems. At times, even very experienced teachers can feel out of their depth when faced with such pupils. They may be uncertain about the approach they should adopt or have concerns that whatever they do may exacerbate these children's difficulties. This dilemma is sometimes reinforced by the reluctance of health professionals to share information with teachers and their failure to acknowledge the constraints that teachers are under when working with these children in a mainstream school setting. It is important that teachers have more knowledge and understanding of children's mental health problems and that they are aware of potential strategies for addressing them. With increased knowledge, training and experience, teachers can do a lot more to improve children's mental health.

This handbook spans the boundary between mental health and education. In doing so, it is hoped that it will provide the information and guidance teachers need to help pupils with mental health problems. They must also be able to recognise, however, the limits of what they can achieve alone, as well as the indications that children should be referred for more specialist help. When working with pupils with diagnosed mental health disorders, a teacher's role should be complementary to that of mental health workers, with whom they will need to liaise closely.

Definitions

Most teachers will be aware of pupils with emotional and behavioural difficulties (EBD), but there is often considerable uncertainty about the boundaries between 'normal' misbehaviour, emotional and behavioural difficulties, and mental illness. Within DFE Circular Number 9/94 (DFE, 1994a: 4) children with EBD are described as being on a continuum, with their difficulties lying between 'occasional bouts of naughtiness' at one end and 'mental illness' at the other. When assessing children, whether they have EBD will depend on 'the nature, frequency, persistence, severity, abnormality or cumulative effect of the behaviour' compared with normal expectations for children of their age. EBD can take a wide variety of forms. The Special Educational Needs Code of Practice (DFE, 1994b) refers to withdrawn, depressive or suicidal attitudes, obsessional preoccupation with eating habits, school phobia, substance misuse, disruptive, antisocial and uncooperative behaviour, as well as frustration, anger and threats of violence.

Teachers, however, are rarely able to articulate a clear definition of EBD (Daniels *et al.*, 1999). Hyperactive children, for example, are frequently described as naughty. Teachers may find it difficult to assess where on the continuum between 'occasional bouts of naughtiness' and 'mental illness' children lie. They need, however, to be able to distinguish between them in order to be able to take appropriate action. The relationship between EBD, mental health problems and mental health disorders can be conceptualised as on a continuum (Weare, 2000), as illustrated in Figure 1.1.

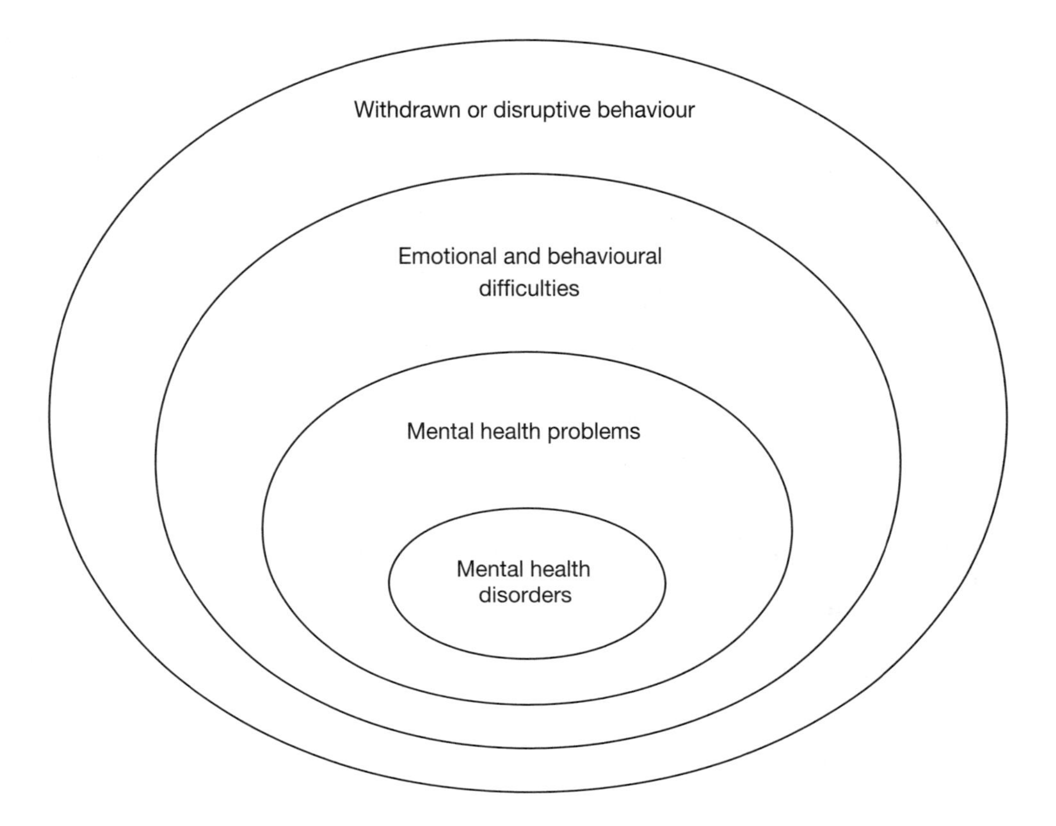

Figure 1.1 The relationship between EBD and mental health disorders

Many children exhibit occasional episodes of disruptive or withdrawn behaviour, but for some children these episodes will be severe enough and persistent enough to be considered as evidence of EBD. The difficulties of a proportion of the children with EBD will also be sufficiently severe to constitute a mental health problem, for example children who are diagnosed as clinically depressed. Similarly, some of these children's difficulties will be considered so extreme that they warrant classification as a mental health disorder, such as schizophrenia. Therefore, whilst EBD affect a relatively large number of pupils, mental health disorders affect a relatively small, but still a significant, number of children. One would also expect to find a far higher degree of mental health problems within a group of children already identified as having EBD than in a randomly selected group of children, which is in fact the case. Mental health problems and EBD also share common risk factors, which are discussed in more detail later in this chapter.

A mental health problem is defined as 'a disturbance of function in one area of relationships, mood, behaviour or development of sufficient severity to require professional intervention' (Wallace *et al.*, cited in the Department of Health, 1995: 10). A mental health disorder is defined as 'a severe problem (commonly persistent), or the co-occurrence of a number of problems, usually in the presence of several risk factors' (ibid., 1995: 10). The Department of Health (1995) stated that the significance of a mental health problem could be determined by:

- its severity
- its complexity
- its persistence
- the risk of secondary handicap
- the child's stage of development
- the presence or absence of protective and risk factors
- the presence or absence of stressful social and cultural factors.

An understanding of the distinction between occasional withdrawn or disruptive behaviour on the one hand and EBD, mental health problems and disorders on the other is a crucial one. The severity and persistence of the problem need to be taken into account otherwise inappropriate responses may be adopted. A child who is persistently withdrawn following bereavement and has difficulty concentrating on his or her schoolwork, for example, may be perceived as lazy, or a child with a conduct disorder may be rejected because of his or her disruptive behaviour. As a result, vulnerable children may be further alienated from those who could provide them with the understanding and support that they need to help alleviate their problems. Educational policies that focus mainly on children defined as having EBD may result in children who have more internalising disorders, such as depression and anxiety, being neglected (Mental Health Foundation, 1999). This is because their difficulties are less obvious and cause teachers and other pupils fewer problems than children with externalising problems, such as behavioural difficulties.

The importance of children's mental health

A high priority has recently been placed on addressing the mental health needs of children and adolescents (Department of Health, 1995) because:

- mental health difficulties cause distress and may impact on many or all aspects of children's lives and, as well as affecting children's emotional development, they may affect their physical and social development and their educational progress;
- children's mental health difficulties have implications for all those involved in their care, as well as those who come into contact with them on a daily basis, such as teachers and other pupils;
- problems unresolved at this early stage can have long-term implications and may lead to a disrupted education, poor socialisation and a lack of mental well-being in adulthood;
- mental health problems in children increase demands on other services, such as social services, educational and juvenile justice services.

There is growing awareness of the impact of school experiences on children's mental well-being. School years are a vital period in children's lives, particularly for their emotional development, and a safe and secure environment is essential for them to grow up happy and confident. Teachers, among others, should encourage children to form healthy and effective relationships, help them to achieve their potential and should prepare them for increasing independence. Children can, however, experience a variety of pressures and difficulties during their school years. Some have difficulty coping with these challenges and this can have a serious effect on their lives in the future.

The prevalence of mental health problems

Mental health problems are relatively common in children and adolescents, although severe mental illness is rare. It has been suggested that 20 per cent of children display some sign of poor mental health and a proportion of these may require professional help for mental health problems at some time (Department of Health, 1995; Mental Health Foundation, 1999). The prevalence rates of specific disorders are discussed in more depth in individual chapters. There is good evidence to suggest that the prevalence of psychiatric disorders in children and adolescents is similar in all developed countries. Within most ethnic minority groups in the UK the rates of psychiatric problems are generally similar to those of the general population, although the circumstances that lead to them may differ. In the African–Caribbean population, however, higher rates have been found.

The prevalence of mental health disorders varies with the type of problem and the age and sex of the child. The most common mental health disorders are conduct disorders and emotional disorders, which are found in about 10 per cent of 10-year-old children. Some problems, such as feeding and sleep difficulties, appear to be relatively common in young children, whilst others, such as bed wetting and temper tantrums, although still found in a significant proportion of children, appear to be relatively less common. Some problems, such as obsessive–compulsive disorder, eating disorders, suicide and attempted suicide and substance misuse, are particularly prevalent during adolescence, whilst others, such as soiling, become less common with increasing age. This highlights the relevance of a developmental approach to tackling mental health problems. Developmental issues are discussed in some depth in Chapter 2 of this handbook.

A Europe-wide increase in the incidence of a range of psychosocial disorders, including depression, suicide, delinquency, eating disorders, and drug and alcohol abuse, has been reported (Fombonne, 1998). Several studies also suggest an earlier age of onset for these disorders. This has implications for all professionals working directly with children and young people, especially teachers. Society is becoming more complex and families are less able to cope. Parents may be unavailable, whether through bereavement, divorce, illness or deprivation, to promote their children's growth and development and this can have serious consequences. Children respond to these difficulties in various ways – they may become aggressive or withdrawn, they may feel anxious or afraid. These reactions can manifest themselves through sleep and eating problems, difficulties in learning, difficulties in forming relationships, depression or even attempted suicide.

Factors influencing the mental health of children

There is no easy way of telling whether children will develop mental health problems or not. Some children maintain good mental health despite traumatic experiences, whilst others develop mental health problems even though they live in a safe, secure and caring environment. There are, however, some common risk factors that increase the probability that children will develop mental health problems. These include individual factors, such as a difficult temperament, physical illness or learning disability, family factors, such as parental conflict and inconsistent discipline, and environmental factors, such as socio-economic disadvantages or homelessness (Mental Health Foundation, 1999). Risk factors are cumulative. If children are exposed to one risk factor the likelihood of developing a mental health problem is between 1 and 2 per cent, but with four or more risk factors this increases to 20 per cent.

Stressful life events will affect some children more than others. An important key to promoting children's mental health is a greater understanding of the protective factors that result in some children being more resilient than others. Factors that protect children against mental health problems also include individual factors, such as being more intelligent and having an easy temperament, family factors, such as good relationships with parents and an educationally supportive family, and environmental factors, such as a good support network and positive school experiences (Mental Health Foundation, 1999). The more protective factors the child experiences the greater the likelihood of mental well-being.

There is a complex interaction between the range of risk factors, their interaction with each other and with any protective factors, and this relationship is not clearly understood. However, children's risk is greatly increased when adverse environmental circumstances, adverse family relationships and their personal characteristics reinforce each other. Research clearly suggests that as the disadvantages and the number of stressful circumstances accumulate, more protective factors are needed to compensate for this. Whilst biological factors may predispose children to some types of mental health difficulties, social circumstances, such as unemployment, divorce and stressful life events, and educational factors, such as their achievement and the school environment, are an important influence. An understanding of the main influences on children's mental health can lead to effective treatment measures at child, family and environmental levels. There is also considerable correlation between these influences and later mental health difficulties, poor education outcomes and antisocial behaviour. These influences, therefore, are the concern of teachers, as well as health professionals, and by enhancing positive influences on mental health in schools, educational achievement, as well as emotional well-being, can be promoted.

Mental health and learning

The impact that emotions can have on children's learning potential was emphasised by Greenhalgh (1994: 2), who stated that:

> Awkward, irritating and painful feelings can play a powerful role in getting in the way of learning. The realm of feelings, of our subjective experiences, can indeed both facilitate and inhibit growth, development and learning.

Attention to children's emotional development not only helps them to become responsible citizens, but also enhances their motivation to learn and helps them to see the relevance of education. Teachers need to understand how emotions, such as fear, anxiety and anger, can lead to withdrawn or difficult behaviour that inhibits learning. How many children, for example, have become adept at avoiding learning situations because of their overwhelming feelings of inadequacy, frustration and fear of failure? How many children fail to concentrate on the task in hand because they are worried and concerned about circumstances at home? In addition, rejection by peers can lead to low self-esteem, poor motivation and poor academic performance, increased vulnerability to bullying and increased likelihood of school refusal and depression. Techniques and practices which enhance emotional competence have a lasting impact on pupils, so social and emotional awareness are as important, if not more important, than intellectual ability in achieving success (Goleman, 1996). Yet, attention to children's emotional competence has so far been omitted from the school curriculum. There is thus a powerful argument for teachers to have a role in educating all children about their emotions and in enhancing pupils' emotional well-being, as well as having a role in identification, assessment and intervention with children with recognised mental health difficulties.

The role of teachers in addressing mental health problems

Children's mental health problems cannot be tackled in isolation. They may manifest themselves in the school environment and experience suggests that parents often turn to teachers first for help with children's difficulties. It may be more appropriate for mainstream services, such as schools, to help these children because of the relationship they have developed with them, because the resources required are readily available or because their problems may not be severe enough to warrant referral to more specialist services. Teachers can often, therefore, find themselves in the 'front line' having to deal with these issues. The overall increase in mental health problems in children and young people means also that Child and Adolescent Mental Health Services (CAMHS) find it difficult to cope and specialist resources are increasingly stretched. Service cuts, growing waiting lists and delays in referral have been highlighted. Many children with mental health problems are not seen by specialist services and professionals working directly with children and adolescents in schools and in the community are forced to deal with these problems themselves. In addition, the promotion of children's mental health needs to be carried out in a range of settings, including schools, since school and educational factors can impact on children's emotional development and well-being (Mental Health Foundation, 1999).

The Department of Health (1995) emphasised the need for all agencies working with children and adolescents to recognise the importance of mental health and to work together to address children's needs. A four-tier model of service was recently proposed for CAMHS (NHS Health Advisory Service, 1995). The tiers each represent a different level of specialist service. Tier 1 involves non-specialists, such as teachers, and school nurses, who have direct contact with children and young people and whose role is to promote mental health, offer general advice and identification of mental health problems. Tier 2 involves individual community child and adolescent mental health workers who network with other professionals and non-specialists, such as support teachers and educational psychologists. These professionals offer intervention, assessment and access to more specialist levels of service provision, as well as consultation and training for professionals in Tier 1 services. Tier 3 provides specialist services for children and adolescents with more severe, complex and persistent mental health disorders, whilst Tier 4 provides highly specialised and intensive interventions, such as residential psychiatric treatment, for those who are severely mentally ill or at suicidal risk.

In reality, there is a dynamic relationship between the four tiers. Where pupils are in receipt of specialist mental health services within Tiers 3 and 4, the teacher's role is one of close liaison with mental health professionals and maintaining contact with the pupil, so that continuity of education is maintained and reintegration into mainstream school is facilitated. Within Tiers 2 and 3, teachers have a role to play in providing information towards the assessment of children with mental health problems. They may also receive training and consultation from professional colleagues in mental health services. As non-specialists working on a day-to-day basis with children and young people, however, they have a particularly key role to play in Tier 1, in the prevention of mental health problems and the promotion of children's general mental well-being through early identification and intervention with children and families.

Prevention and the promotion of children's emotional well-being

The term mental health encompasses physical and emotional well-being as well as the absence of mental illness. It is about the capacity to live a full and active life and the flexibility to cope with life stresses when they arise (Weare, 2000). In children, it also involves being able to make the most of their abilities and relationships. Increasingly, the remit of CAMHS has expanded to involve a more proactive approach and a role in the promotion of emotional well-being, in addition to addressing the needs of those with severe mental health problems. Encouraging children's emotional competence and developing their social skills can help them to build up resilience to mental health problems, as well as enhancing their learning potential. Schools have a primary role in helping children develop these skills (Mental Health Foundation, 1999) and, in this way, teachers can make a major contribution to addressing both the mental health and learning needs of the children and young people with whom they come into contact. The Foundation recommends the appointment of mental health co-ordinators in schools, school-based mental health services, peer support schemes and out of school activities to foster children's emotional and social skills and to combat growing concern about widespread psychological and psychiatric problems among children. Strategies for accomplishing this are discussed further in the final chapter of this handbook.

Whilst some children's mental health difficulties may have a distinct biological cause, in the majority of cases environmental factors and children's interactions with those around them can greatly enhance or hinder their progress. An interactive view is now widely accepted and, increasingly, greater emphasis is placed on the impact of the school environment on children with problems (DES, 1989). School influences are very often important contributing factors, for example, in pupil behaviour (e.g. Galloway *et al.*, 1982; Rutter *et al.*, 1979) and the importance of the teacher's interaction with pupils is well recognised (Greenhalgh, 1994). The school environment is of paramount importance and it is widely acknowledged that schools and teachers can have an enormous influence on shaping children's emotional development and behaviour.

This has led to greater consideration of whole-school approaches to children's mental health problems. By creating a positive ethos teachers can provide a more rather than less therapeutic environment and one which enables pupils to grow emotionally, to be themselves and to discuss their problems rather than having to resort to other ways of demonstrating that they have difficulties. By developing an ethos of trust, openness and understanding, with a focus on relationships, as well as giving pupils responsibility, teachers can enhance the mental well-being of all pupils.

Early identification

Recognising when a child is suffering from mental health problems is not always easy, but, with the necessary knowledge, understanding and support, teachers can function as the 'front line' of identification, support and referral to other services. As an integral part of their pastoral role teachers should be alert to the signs of mental health difficulties and be aware of the complex range of factors that may be involved. It is important that they know when and how to refer children to mental health services. Research has shown, however, that many teachers have difficulty distinguishing children with these type of problems and that they do not get identified early enough (Daniels *et al.*, 1999). In one study, for example, teachers identified only 40 per cent of the pupils at significant risk (Baxter, 1999). In addition, the responses of teachers in these circumstances can even make things worse for children. It has been suggested that routine screening tests could be adopted to help teachers with this. Baxter (1999: 12) states that:

> Schools, with their captive audience, non-stigmatising context and (almost) total population cover, appear to provide the perfect venue for what would be a cost-effective response to NHS targets for improvement in both adult and child mental health.

There is an urgent need for greater awareness and greater understanding of children's mental health problems amongst teachers and a need for professional development in this area. The Mental Health Foundation (1999) supports this view and highlights a number of components of effective practice in schools for ensuring early intervention for children at risk of developing mental health problems, including:

- early identification and assessment
- work with families as well as children
- interagency collaboration, particularly with health
- training for staff in schools on mental health issues
- a flexible approach, involving consultation with mental health professionals, as well as direct intervention via the educational psychology service.

Intervention with pupils with mental health problems and their families

Children and young people with less severe mental health problems are often not referred to, or are unwilling to approach psychiatric services. Teachers may have no alternative but to deal with these problems as best they can within the school setting. Experience suggests that they feel ill equipped and uneasy about this role and that they lack knowledge and understanding of children's mental health difficulties so they cannot be expected to shoulder this responsibility alone, without support, training and guidance. Increasingly, emphasis is placed on the need for professionals within CAMHS to liaise with other professionals working directly with children and young people. There is also greater recognition of the need for joint services in dealing with children's difficulties. Effective liaison between CAMHS and schools is vital if the model of Tier 1 services referred to earlier is to succeed. This will ensure that children with mental health problems are not left unrecognised with the likelihood of developing more serious problems at a later date. It is hoped that local CAMHS will make themselves more accessible to schools and provide consultation, training and support to teachers in order that they can fulfil their role. There is, in fact, much that CAMHS can do in helping schools to develop innovative strategies for working with all pupils with emotional and behavioural difficulties. To date, however, mental health professionals have been a largely untapped resource within education. It is timely, therefore, to examine the way in which mental health and education services can work collaboratively to address the needs of these most vulnerable, and sometimes most challenging, children.

References

Baxter, J. (1999) Screening for mental health problems in young children: Can we expect teachers to get it right? *Young Minds*, 42, 12–14.

Daniels, H., Visser, J., Cole, T. and de Reybekill, N. (1999) *Emotional and Behavioural Difficulties in Mainstream Schools*. Sudbury: DfEE.

Department of Education and Science (DES) (1989) *Discipline in Schools: Report of the Committee of Enquiry chaired by Lord Elton* (The Elton Report). London: HMSO.

Department for Education (DFE) (1994a) *Pupils with Problems, Circulars 8–13/94*. London: HMSO.

Department for Education (DFE) (1994b) *The Code of Practice on the Identification and Assessment of Special Educational Needs*. London: HMSO.

Department of Health (1995) *A Handbook of Child and Adolescent Mental Health*. London: HMSO.

Fombonne, E. (1998) Increased rates of psychosocial disorders in youth. *European Archives of Psychiatry and Clinical Neuroscience*, 248, 1, 14–21.

Galloway, D., Ball, T., Bloomfield, D. and Seyd, R. (1982) *Schools and Disruptive Pupils*. London: Longman.

Goleman, D. (1996) *Emotional Intelligence*. London: Bloomsbury.

Greenhalgh, P. (1994) *Emotional Growth and Learning*. London: Routledge.

Mental Health Foundation (1999) *The Big Picture: Promoting Children and Young People's Mental Health*. London: Mental Health Foundation.

Mind (1997) *The Bird and the Word: Materials for Mental Health Education in Secondary Schools*. London: Mind.

NHS Health Advisory Service (1995) *Together We Stand: The Commissioning, Role and Management of Child and Adolescent Mental Health Services*. London: HMSO.

Rutter, M. (1991) Pathways from childhood to adult life: The role of schooling. *Pastoral Care in Education*, 9, 3, 3–10.

Rutter, M., Maugham, B., Mortimore, P., Ouston, J. and Smith, A. (1979) *Fifteen Thousand Hours*. London: Open Books.

Weare, K. (2000) *Promoting Mental, Emotional and Social Health*. London: Routledge.

2 Normal and abnormal development

Knowledge of what is normal plays an important part in determining what is abnormal. Therefore, the normal development of children is a fundamental issue in relation to mental health disorders that have been traditionally described in terms of deviations from normal development and behaviour. Whilst the boundary between what is normal and what is abnormal is not distinct, it is important to define as clearly as possible what is normal or age-appropriate behaviour, even though this is necessarily somewhat arbitrary. When considering mental health problems in children and adolescents it is therefore essential to have an understanding of normal child development and the processes involved. Many behaviours are normal at certain ages, but not at others. Also, many mental health problems in childhood and adolescence may be manifestations of disturbed development. Childhood and adolescence are particularly dynamic periods of development involving many changes. These include cognitive, emotional, social, sexual, as well as biological changes. During this period children are transformed from helpless, dependent infants to independent, self-sufficient individuals with their own views. This is, of course, a complex process with much continuity and some discontinuities.

Developmental stages

Many of the different theories of child development suggest that the process takes place in a series of stages. Although it can be helpful to perceive it in this way, it is important to remember that development is a continuous and dynamic process and that transition from one stage to another usually takes place over a period of time. These theories suggest that failure to develop adequately at one stage can seriously affect further development, since each stage lays the foundations for the next. Children's development is a complex and multifaceted process, involving motor and language development, cognitive, emotional and social development, as well as sexual development and the development of moral and ethical behaviour. Failure to develop physically, for example, can have repercussions for children's social and mental well-being since all aspects of children's functioning are interrelated.

Several stage theories of child development are useful in helping to explain normal and abnormal development. The most important of these are the theories of Freud, Piaget and Erikson, which are summarised below.

Freud

Freud was the first theorist to come up with the idea that children's development passes through a series of stages. Unfortunately, his theory was based on the extrapolation of ideas from his work with adult psychiatric patients rather than observations of children, so has, over the years, been seen to be less useful to teachers than other theories. However, Freud's theory is still used by many psychiatrists in their work with children who have mental health problems so it is important for teachers to be aware of it. It is also important because later theorists built on Freud's idea and came up with stages based on their observations of children. The stages of development through which children are considered to pass are outlined briefly below.

The oral stage (0–1 year)

The stage in which children gain greatest satisfaction from oral activity.

The anal stage (1–3 years)

The stage in which children's interest is focused on defecating.

The phallic stage (3–5 years)

The stage in which children's attention is focused on their genitals and the development of sexual identity.

The latency stage (5–12 years)

The stage in which there is a lack of interest in sexuality.

The genital stage(12–18 years plus)

The stage when satisfaction is sought through relationships with the other sex.

Piaget

Piaget's theory is based on extensive observations and research studies with children. It is very well known among educators and is a useful guide to children's cognitive development, although not as useful in considering children's overall psychological development as some other theories. Piaget suggests that there are four stages which children need to pass through in order to achieve an adult level of thinking. These are outlined briefly below.

The sensori-motor stage (0–2 years)

The stage at which children know the world only by looking, grasping or mouthing objects.

The pre-operational stage (2–7 years)

The stage at which children use symbols to help them communicate but these are limited to their immediate experience. Their thinking is based on impressions rather than reality and they have irrational notions of cause and effect.

The concrete operations stage (7–11 years)

The stage at which children have learned to think logically. As long as concepts are in concrete terms they can link cause and effect rationally. However, they are unable to think using abstract concepts.

The formal operations stage (11 years onwards)

By this stage the child has learned to think in both concrete and abstract terms and can solve problems using abstract concepts. However, it is now considered that only around 50 per cent of children will have arrived at this highest level of thinking by the age of leaving formal schooling. It is a level of thinking that is regarded as being well beyond that of primary school children and of many pupils in the secondary school, particularly those with learning difficulties.

Erikson

One of the most useful stage theories of development is that proposed by Erikson (1968), which suggests that children's psychological development progresses by them addressing and resolving specific psychosocial conflicts. Resolution of these conflicts provides a solid foundation for future development whereas inadequate resolution will lead to problems in later development. Erikson's theory covers the entire life span from infancy to old age. It is helpful in pointing out the key issues which children and young people face as they move through life. The conflicts that he identifies are outlined briefly below.

Trust versus mistrust (0–1 year)

The first conflict is concerned with achieving a balance between building up trusting relationships and risking being let down. Consistency of care in the first year of life will build a foundation for the development of trusting relationships with others. Lack of consistency can evoke suspicion and mistrust and lead to difficulties in relating fully to others.

Autonomy versus shame and doubt (2–3 years)

The second conflict children face is concerned with them developing a sense of control over their behaviour and bodily functions. Encountering difficulties with this leads children to doubt their abilities and anticipate failures.

Initiative versus guilt (4–5 years)

At this stage the conflict concerns the development of an increasing sense of personal agency and responsibility. The alternative is to experience increasing feelings of self-doubt and guilt.

Industry versus inferiority (6–12 years)

The fourth conflict, which is the key one during primary schooling, is concerned with children successfully meeting challenges through being industrious as opposed to avoiding challenges, accepting failure and therefore developing an increasing sense of inferiority.

Identity versus role confusion (13–18 years)

The main psychosocial issue for adolescents is the development of a consistent sense of who they are at a time when they are experiencing many changes. Becoming overwhelmed by these changes and the increased expectations of them can lead to failure to develop a consistent sense of personal identity.

Intimacy versus isolation (19–25 years)

The issue to be addressed at this stage is learning to establish an intimate relationship with a partner as opposed to avoiding relationships because of the pain involved in failing in such relationships.

Generativity versus stagnation (26–40 years)

This involves developing a productive existence with achievements in the family and/or employment domains. The alternative is a lack of psychological growth which leads to stagnation.

Ego integrity versus despair (40 years plus)

At this stage the issue is whether one can look back on one's life with a sense of achievement as opposed to feeling that one's life has been futile.

Developmental tasks

A useful way to view the psychosocial conflicts Erikson identified is as challenges or tasks that children have to face in order to develop. This is the approach taken by Havinghurst (1972), who has suggested that there are certain developmental tasks which children must master at each stage of development in order to prepare for later life. Successful mastery of these tasks results in well-adjusted children who are able to cope with the tasks they encounter in later developmental stages, whereas failure to master the tasks results in maladjustment and the inability to complete future tasks successfully. The developmental tasks provide a useful means of assessing children's progress within a number of areas, such as social skills and concept development. As children get older the tasks facing them change, as do their needs – for example, the care and environment required by an infant in order to work on relevant tasks differ markedly from those needed by an adolescent. Failure to make the necessary adjustments within the family can therefore cause difficulties. An analysis of the developmental tasks faced by children at different stages, provided by Havinghurst (1972), is summarised below. He identified the tasks shown below for pre-school-, primary- and secondary-age children.

Developmental tasks of pre-school-age children (up to 6 years)

- Learning to take solid foods.
- Learning to walk.
- Learning to talk.
- Learning to use the toilet for body wastes.
- Learning about sexual differences and behaviour.
- Learning language concepts to describe social and physical reality.
- Developing readiness for reading.
- Learning to distinguish right and wrong.

Developmental tasks of primary-school-age children (around 6–12 years)

- Learning the physical skills necessary for games, for example, throwing, kicking.
- Building self-esteem and a wholesome attitude towards one's body.
- Learning to get along with one's peers.
- Learning appropriate masculine or feminine social roles.
- Developing fundamental skills in reading, writing and arithmetic.
- Developing concepts necessary for everyday living.
- Developing conscience, morality and a core of values.
- Achieving personal independence or autonomy.
- Developing rational attitudes to social groups and institutions.

Developmental tasks of secondary-school-age children (around 12–18 years)

- Achieving new and more mature relations with peers of both sexes.
- Achieving a masculine or feminine social role.
- Accepting one's physique and using the body effectively.
- Achieving emotional independence of parents and other adults.
- Preparing for marriage and family life.
- Preparing for making a living or career.
- Acquiring a set of values, ethics or an ideology as a guide to behaviour.
- Developing socially responsible behaviour.

If, towards the end of the pre-school period, children are experiencing difficulties with any of the tasks of this stage, concerns will be being expressed about their development. For example, children whose walking, talking or learning of language concepts is significantly delayed should be assessed for possible developmental disabilities. Also, children who are still wetting or soiling themselves, particularly during the daytime, will be causing concern as will children who appear to be having difficulty learning socially appropriate behaviour. The list of tasks for the next stage, on the other hand, suggests that primary-school-age children are likely to experience problems at school in areas related to learning difficulties, particularly with the three Rs, as well as issues in personal development, such as independence and self-esteem, and also problems with peer relationships, such as in conflicts with friends and classmates. In contrast, the third list of tasks suggests that secondary-school-age children are likely to experience problems with identity and social relationships, particularly associated with relationships with peers and the opposite sex, as well as with issues related to personal autonomy and preparation for work and family life.

Hierarchy of children's needs

An important perspective on children's development and behaviour is provided by Maslow (1970), who suggested that children have certain basic needs which must be met if they are to reach their potential in all areas of development. If lower-level needs are not met children will be unable to meet higher-order needs and progress towards self-actualisation. Each level of Maslow's hierarchy is described briefly below.

Physiological needs

The lowest level of the hierarchy comprises physiological needs, such as for food and shelter. If children do not get enough to eat they will be unable to concentrate their attention on the various tasks they must address, including their schoolwork. There is also some evidence to suggest that a poor diet is linked with long-term problems, such as hyperactivity and mental illness in adolescence.

Safety needs

This includes physical and psychological safety. Children living in war zones clearly need to focus on their own safety to the extent that attention cannot be given to higher-level needs. However, children can also be afraid for their physical safety in their own homes due to abusing parents, or in their neighbourhoods due to high crime levels. Children in homes where parents are going through a separation or divorce may have their need for psychological safety threatened and therefore may be distracted from addressing the developmental tasks associated with their stages of development.

Love and belonging

The third level is the need for love and belonging, and to feel accepted as part of a group. Children who are withdrawn, isolated or rejected by their peers are therefore unable to move on to address higher-order needs which are critical to the development of sound mental health. They may hide their feelings of rejection or react with antisocial behaviour in order to cover them up.

Self-esteem

This is the need to feel good about oneself. This crucial need is denied to children who are focused too much on earlier needs and threatened when they are subjected to excessive criticism or are ignored by the important people in their lives. The importance of self-esteem in children's development cannot be overemphasised and is discussed in a separate section below.

Self-actualisation

The fifth level of the hierarchy is the fulfilment of one's potential to the maximum extent possible. This is only possible if lower-level needs are being met.

Self-esteem

It is clear from the theories previously discussed that the acquisition of self-worth or self-esteem is one of the most fundamental developmental tasks of childhood. It is therefore not surprising that in children exhibiting signs of behavioural or mental health problems low self-esteem tends to be a common feature.

Self-esteem is the individual's assessment or unconditional appreciation of him- or herself. The term self-esteem is often confused with the self-concept, the sum total of an individual's mental and physical characteristics and his or her evaluation of them (Lawrence, 1987). It has three aspects: thinking (cognitive), feeling (affective) and action (behavioural). Lawrence explains that for teachers it is useful to consider the self-concept as developing in three areas: self-image, ideal self and self-esteem. The self-image is how the individual sees him- or herself whereas the ideal self is what he or she would like to be. Self-esteem is the individual's perception of the discrepancy between the two. How we feel about ourselves is a consequence of how we interpret our experiences and, in many respects, our self-esteem is a cumulative record of how we have been treated and how we treat ourselves throughout life.

Shavelson and Bolus (1982), cited in Lawrence (1987), have proposed a hierarchy of self-esteem which is useful for teachers since it illustrates how the global self-esteem of an individual can be influenced by both academic and non-academic (e.g. social) ability. Children may feel inadequate in some situations more than others. If children who have difficulty learning mathematics, for example, are frequently forced to participate in these activities eventually their overall self-esteem might fall. In addition, if an individual continues to fail in areas of life which are valued by significant others then his or her self-esteem will be affected. It is obvious, therefore, that failure at school can easily lead to low global self-esteem, particularly when children have learning difficulties.

The development of self-esteem

The development of self-esteem depends on parental attitudes, opinions and behaviour, combined with children's experience of mastery of the environment. Over the years children's feelings about their worth and capabilities become increasingly internalised and are less dependent upon the immediate responses of those around them. Self-esteem comes from being loved and wanted, as well as having a sense of belonging. Thus, self-esteem develops from a reference to other groups, such as family and friends. From early childhood onwards children are trying to find their place in groups, through friends, clubs and religious affiliations. As toddlers learn to walk, explore their environment, play, talk and engage in all kinds of social interactions they look to their parents and other adults for their reactions. This is all part of the development of self-esteem. In healthy families parents' reactions are affirming and supportive, even when limits have to be set on children's behaviour. Parents also need to set realistic expectations for their children. Self-esteem therefore initially develops as a result of interpersonal relationships within the family, which gradually give precedence to school influences and those within the larger society. For children of school age, however, self-esteem continues to be affected mainly by the significant people in their lives, usually parents, teachers and peers.

The development of self-esteem takes place throughout childhood, adolescence and adulthood. It is considered to begin in infancy with the development of basic trust and from relationships with empathic others as well as children's emerging capacity to accomplish tasks successfully. If a child is to flourish emotionally and socially parents have to be very attentive to the noises and expressions of babies. It is this sensitivity from familiar figures that gives children the sense of security required for social and emotional competence. A secure attachment is the basis for the capacity to be curious, to learn and to be sympathetic to the concerns of others. In the first year, the development of the sense of oneself as separate from the surroundings is the first step in the development of self-concept and is one of the most important achievements of this period. In the second year of life the infant's ability for self-recognition is usually acquired, with the first categories being age and sex. The realisation of object permanence and intentional behaviour enables the infant to explore and investigate the environment with considerably more confidence. School-age children extend their self-definition to include their likes and dislikes and comparisons with other children. In middle childhood children's social circles widen so that their self-esteem comes to be influenced by a wider range of people. The influence of the attitudes and opinions of others depends upon how highly such people are valued by children.

Important too are children's successes and failures. Children with disabilities may compare themselves unfavourably with others so it may be more difficult for them to maintain a sense of mastery over their environment, which is an important ingredient of self-esteem. By adolescence the self-image has become part of the personality structure, and, though it is still subject to modification, this becomes harder as the years go by. During adolescence there is an extended period of re-evaluation of one's self.

The importance of self-esteem

Those who do not value themselves treat themselves and others badly, although this is usually an unconscious thing. Low self-esteem is often a major factor in abuse, depression, crime, loneliness, low achievement, mental illness and unhappiness. People with high self-esteem are usually more creative, happy and productive. If we accept ourselves unconditionally we can accept praise or criticism of our actions without it affecting our sense of self-worth. This means that we can be more realistic about our achievements and our weaknesses because we are not dependent on the judgement of others. Self-esteem is therefore an important aspect of learning. If we trust ourselves we can risk being wrong and make mistakes.

Both mental health and learning have foundations in self-esteem so creating an environment that fosters high self-esteem can be beneficial for both. Teachers can have a powerful influence on the self-esteem of young people. Children with high self-esteem do better academically, see themselves as in control of their own destiny, have more friends and get along better with their parents. These children also tend to come from families where independent achievements are valued and praised and in which there is a warm and affectionate relationship with parents who set clearly defined and enforced boundaries for behaviour. The impact of families on children's development and behaviour is therefore crucial and is considered next.

The influence of the family on children's development and behaviour

Most of children's development occurs within the family unit. The fact that children are dependent on others means that their relationships with family members have a critical role to play in their development and the context of their family is of major significance in this. Relationships with family members involve aspects of dependency, caring and trust which are critical in children's development. So in order to understand children's development fully it is important to gain a thorough understanding of how families function.

Current models suggest that children's development results from a continual interplay between a changing individual and a changing family and social environment. Families are considered both to affect and be affected by their individual members (Bell, 1968). This suggests that the behaviour of family members is a function of the family system of which they are a part. A change in the family system will inevitably lead to a change in the behaviour of each of the family members. Likewise, a change in an individual's behaviour will cause the family system to change. Also, the functioning of the family system is considered to comprise more than just a summation of the contributions of its individual members. Interactions between family members and the organisational structure of families also play a part in family dynamics (Coopersmith, 1984; Berger, 1984). Intervention at the level of the family system is therefore likely to have more impact than intervention aimed at one of its members. Some writers go even further and claim that treatment of individuals, without taking their families into account, may result in an increase in problems experienced by the family as a whole (Chilman *et al.*, 1988). Therefore, knowledge of how families function is essential in the understanding of children's mental health problems. A useful model for understanding family functioning is provided by the Family Systems Conceptual Framework developed by Turnbull and Turnbull (1986). This framework focuses on four aspects or components of family dynamics: family interactions, family resources, family functions, and the family life cycle. These are discussed briefly below.

Family interactions

This component refers to the relationships that occur within and between the various sub-systems of family members, that is between husband and wife, parent and child and between the children. It also refers to extra-familial interactions, such as those between children and grandparents or those between a father and his work mates. Interactions within and between all these sub-systems will have an impact on children's development and behaviour. Other aspects of family interaction that are crucial to children's development are cohesion, adaptability and communication. The two extremes of cohesion are enmeshment and disengagement. Enmeshed families have weak boundaries between sub-systems and therefore tend to be overprotective of children, whereas disengaged families have rigid sub-system boundaries and exhibit a lack of care for each other and a neglect of children. A healthy family functions somewhere between these two extremes such that children feel cared for but are encouraged to be as independent as possible. Adaptability refers to the family's ability to change in response to events. The more inflexible family members are the more difficulties the family will face in adapting to living with a child with mental health problems. Healthy families are also considered to have open expression of opinions and feelings as opposed to the poor communication and hidden agendas of unhealthy families.

Family resources

This component refers to the various elements of the family, including characteristics of the mental health problem, such as type and severity; characteristics of the family, such as size, cultural background and socio-economic status; and personal characteristics, such as health, ideologies and coping styles. The impact of these factors on children's development and the overall family system is discussed in relation to the microsystem level of the ecological model described later in this chapter.

Family functions

This component refers to the different types of needs for which the family provides, such as economic needs, physical care, recuperation, socialisation, affection, self-definition, educational and vocational needs. All families differ regarding the priorities they attach to the various functions and with respect to which family members are assigned to perform specific roles within the family. However, caring for a child with mental health problems is likely to affect these family functions in certain ways. For example, the family's earning capacity may be reduced because one parent may be unable to work full time owing to the extra demands placed on the family. Also, the family's self-definition, or the way members view themselves and their family, is likely to be changed when a child with a mental health problem is part of the family.

Family life cycle

This component represents the sequence of developmental changes that affect families as they progress through various stages. The family has to change and adapt as children develop. Families are liable to get into difficulties when faced with transition from one phase of development to the next. The challenges facing families nowadays are considerable and one of these is adapting to rearing children as they go through the different stages in their development, which were described earlier. Parents within families, at the same time, traverse their own individual life cycles which are considered to consist of early adulthood, mid-life transition, middle adulthood, late adult transition and late adulthood (Levinson, 1978). Each family member is therefore engaged with developmental tasks associated with each of their children's development and their own individual life cycle stage. In addition, families also go through various developmental or life cycle stages (Carter and McGoldrick, 1980). Consideration of the family's developmental stage is essential when considering children's mental health problems since many of the difficulties that arise can be related to problems in family development as well as individual children's development. A summary of the developmental stages which families pass through, and the associated developmental tasks, is presented in Table 2.1.

The first two stages of the family life cycle are ones in which the adults must address various developmental tasks necessary to prepare them for successful parenting. The next three stages involve the birth of children, their upbringing and their launch into independent adulthood. The final two stages are ones in which parents readjust to family life with children having left the family home. At each stage different developmental tasks need to be addressed.

Table 2.1

Developmental stages of family life	*Examples of developmental tasks at each stage*
1 *Premarital*: courtship period	(a) Becoming independent from parents (b) Appropriate choice of marital partner
2 *Early marriage*: no children	(a) Developing sexual compatibility (b) Balancing autonomy with interdependence
3 *Child-bearing years*: from birth of first child to school entry	(a) Developing nurturing family patterns (b) Adapting to financial reduction
4 *Children in school*: first child from 6 to 18 years of age	(a) Encouraging independence in children (b) Broadening family interests
5 *Reduction in family size*: first to last child leaving home	(a) Support leaving of the children (b) Adapt to family functioning with fewer children
6 *Dyadic independent*: last child leaves home to parental retirement	(a) Develop enjoyment of marital relationship (b) Develop new relationships across generations
7 *Advanced age*: retirement to death of both spouses	(a) Adapt to retirement of spouse (b) Adapt to death of spouse

Source: Adapted from Friesen (1983)

Consideration of the family life cycle, family interactions, functions and resources makes it clear why it is important to see children within the context of their families and to bear in mind what is happening within the family. Many things may happen that interrupt normal family functioning, such as separation or divorce, bereavement and remarriage. All these will have an impact on children's behaviour and development. Although at one time most mental health problems were perceived to be a function of parenting, it is now known that this differs in extent between different problems and is therefore discussed in the individual chapters for specific disorders.

The influence of the social context on children's development and behaviour

Relationships with people outside the family, such as peers and teachers, also help to shape children's behaviour. Children both shape and are shaped by their environment and their psychological make-up is almost always a reflection of these interactions. Children's development and behaviour cannot be understood independently of the social context in which it occurs. The social environment influences the behaviour of children and families and this occurs at several levels. Children's behaviour is strongly influenced by the wider social environment in which they are living, including the extended family, the education system, the services available and community attitudes. This is illustrated by the ecological model of family functioning (Bronfenbrenner, 1979), which is illustrated in Figure 2.1. The model includes four different levels of influence on child development and behaviour: the microsystem; the mesosystem; the exosystem; and the macrosystem.

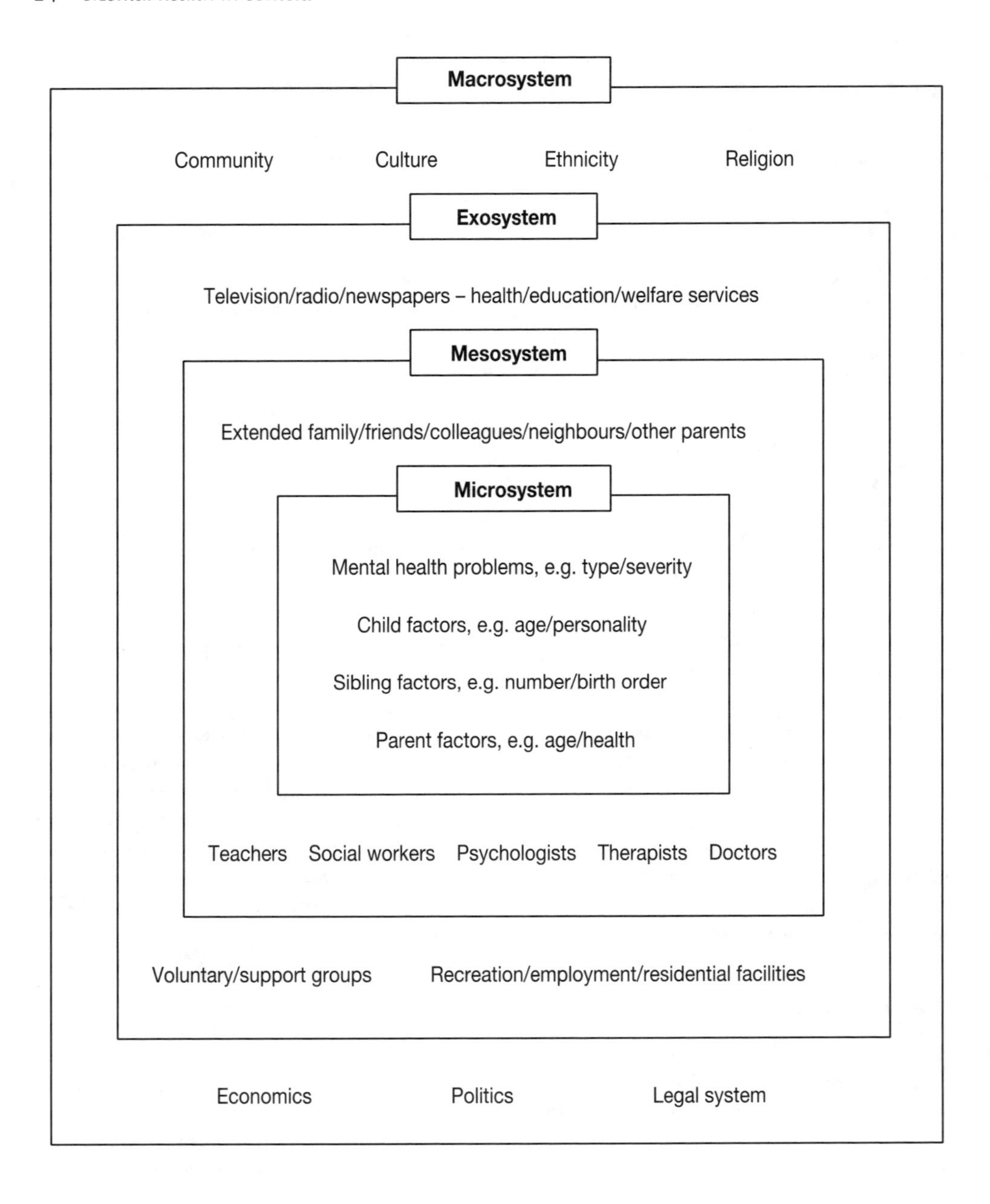

Figure 2.1 Ecological model of child development

The microsystem

The family of a child with a mental health problem or EBD is considered to constitute a microsystem with the child, parents and siblings reciprocally influencing each other. How well this nuclear family functions therefore depends on variables associated with each of its members. First, features of the child's problem itself, such as the type, severity and when it was diagnosed, will have an influence. Uncertainties about the diagnosis, which often occur with problems such as autism, can be more difficult for families to come to terms with than in clear-cut cases. Second, factors associated with children with EBD and their siblings will have an influence on family functioning. Whether the child is the first born, last born, a middle child, an only child or a twin, for example, will have an impact on the family. Third, factors associated with parents themselves, such as their ages, personalities, financial status, employment status, educational levels and the state of their health, and their relationship will have a major influence on family functioning. A healthy marital relationship, for example, will exert a positive influence on the family whereas an unhappy marriage is likely to lead to tension and conflict throughout the family microsystem.

The mesosystem

The family microsystem is influenced by the mesosystem in which it is embedded. The mesosystem comprises the range of settings in which the family actively participates, such as the extended family and the community in which the family lives. The extended family has a key role in determining how well parents cope with having a child with a mental health problem. If the child's grandparents, for example, are understanding and supportive they can have a significant positive influence on family functioning, whereas, if they are in conflict with the child's parents, or have little contact with them, the family misses out on an important source of support. Neighbours, work mates, friends and other parents can also have a positive or negative influence on family functioning. When neighbours are friendly and allow the child into their homes to play with their own children, for example, parents can feel pleased that their family is accepted. In contrast, work mates who talk of their own children's achievements while being too embarrassed to talk about a child with mental health problems turn a possible source of support into one of tension and unhappiness. Typically, some of the parents' friends will find it difficult to adjust to them having a child with EBD and will tend to stay away. The contacts which parents have with professionals, such as social workers, teachers and doctors, can also help to promote healthy family functioning if they are sensitive, understanding, knowledgeable and supportive. When parents find such contacts unhelpful or even offputting this increases stress and leads to reduced feelings of well-being within the family.

The exosystem

The mesosystem is itself influenced by the exosystem that consists of social settings that indirectly affect the family, such as the mass media, the education system and voluntary agencies. The way children with mental health problems are portrayed in the newspapers or on television, for example, will have an impact on the family. When unsympathetic attitudes are perpetuated by the media this does not help families who have such children to integrate into the community. Second, the quality and types of health, education and social welfare services available to parents will have a critical influence on the way that families cope with their child's special needs. Families of children with EBD typically need intensive levels of help in these areas. Third, the availability of support groups which have been established to help the parents of children with mental health problems can be a significant factor in determining how well these families cope.

The macrosystem

Finally, there is the macrosystem which refers to the attitudes, beliefs, values and ideologies inherent in the social institutions of a particular society, which all have an impact on the way the family of a child with a mental health problem will function. First of all, the particular culture in which the family is living will have major effects on the family. If the culture is one which emphasises humanitarian values then there is much more likely to be positive attitudes towards children with special needs than in cultures that emphasise materialism. Also, the specific area in which the family lives will have an impact on many different aspects of family life. For example, it may be easier to cope with a child with EBD in a rural rather than an urban community. The beliefs of the particular ethnic or religious group to which the family belongs will also exert an influence on the way the family reacts to the child's special needs. In addition, different people hold different beliefs about unacceptable behaviour and if the child's behaviour does not fit with the social context, others may consider that behaviour as deviant from normal. Part of the treatment process in some cases may therefore include normalisation of the behaviour in the eyes of significant others. The overall economic situation in the society in which the family lives will affect many aspects of how the family copes with having a child with special needs and political and economic policies will also be influential. The legal system too has a role to play in interpreting the law in individual cases of children with EBD and such rulings are often used to provide guidance for services, thereby affecting large numbers of similar families.

In conclusion, how children with mental health problems function is influenced not only by interactions within the microsystem, but also by interactions with other levels of the entire social system. These all need to be taken into account by teachers when they are working with these children and their families.

Abnormal behaviour

Difficulties arise when considering what is abnormal behaviour in childhood. What adults might perceive as a problem may not be regarded so by children and what parents regard as abnormal might not be seen as such by professionals, and vice versa. In addition, failure to develop may be either a temporary problem or an indication of more serious long-term difficulties. Further, what might be considered abnormal behaviour may be exhibited, at least to some extent, by normal children. It is important that children's stages of development, their ability to adapt to their surroundings and their methods of coping with difficulties are taken into account. Three primary considerations need to be taken into account when identifying abnormal behaviour and mental health disorders. These are:

- evidence of psychological dysfunction or disability;
- evidence of severe distress or impairment;
- evidence of increased risk of further suffering or harm.

Diagnosis of abnormal behaviour

In this chapter various explanations of the normal sequence of and conditions for children's development have been presented. Implicit in much of the discussion is the assumption that deviation from the normal sequence of events leads to abnormal development, which results in children having mental health problems. However, the point was made in Chapter 1 that children's behaviour needs to be seen as spanning a continuum from naughtiness that is within the normal range of behaviour, through emotional or behavioural difficulties, to mental health problems and disorders. The difficulty then is agreeing criteria for deciding whether behaviour is within the normal range or whether it really is abnormal and therefore warrants attention. There is no one agreed system for child and adolescent mental health disorders, but the most widely used guide for making such decisions is what is commonly referred to as DSM-IV. This is the fourth edition of the *Diagnostic and Statistical Manual of Mental Disorders* (American Psychiatric Association, 1994). Within DSM-IV, disorders are grouped together with their own criteria and children who exhibit a sufficient number of symptoms receive the diagnosis. Another system, the ICD-10, the tenth edition of the *International Classification of Diseases* (World Health Organization, 1992), is used more widely in Europe and takes a similar approach.

The classification of mental disorder often seems to have negative connotations, whatever terms are used, but having a classification system creates order and allows broad treatment approaches to be considered for similar cases, as well as providing an agreed system that can be used by different professionals. Being able to classify the problem helps draw on existing research to understand the child and his or her family and to select effective treatment approaches. It should be recognised, however, that many childhood disorders do not fit neatly into categories and there is often an overlap of symptoms between one disorder and another, despite the fact that, over the last few decades, criteria have become more and more refined.

DSM-IV uses what is called multi-axial assessment because rather than put a problem into a single category, it summarises information in five areas or axes in order to provide a more complete picture. These are outlined below.

Axis I: clinical disorders

These include problems such as schizophrenia, school phobia, mood disorders, anxiety disorders, adjustment disorders and identity disorders.

Axis II: personality disorders and cognitive impairment

These include factors which are not the main concern but which may make the problem worse, such as paranoid thoughts or limited intellectual ability.

Axis III: general medical conditions

These include conditions that may influence behaviour, such as a heart condition or a high level of stress.

Axis IV: psychosocial and environmental problems

These include factors that can add to stress and thereby make problems worse, such as bereavement and marriage breakdown.

Axis V: global functioning

This focuses on how children are functioning in their day-to-day lives. It considers psychological, social and vocational domains. It involves an overall rating on a scale from one to a hundred of how an individual is functioning, with one representing persistent danger of serious harm to self or others and a hundred representing superior functioning in a wide range of activities.

For diagnosis, the number and severity of symptoms are vital, as is also the requirement for symptoms to lead to significant impairment in a variety of aspects of the child's life. To some extent, however, the cut-off point is arbitrary and if it is too high there may be some children who need help that do not receive it, whilst if it is too low those that might otherwise be considered normal will be diagnosed with the disorder.

DSM-IV has been criticised for taking the view that mental disorder is inherent within the individual and for not taking into account the contextual factors involved. Such a view can lead to children and families abdicating responsibility for behaviour and to limited treatment interventions. More recently, mental health professionals have taken the view that contextual factors are important and this is reflected in their treatment methods. Despite diagnosis, each individual has a unique personality, background and factors that pertain to their particular situation that need to be taken into account when considering treatment approaches. They will have their own strengths, weaknesses and coping strategies and it is important therefore not to rely solely on diagnosis. The giving of a diagnosis in itself has both positive and negative aspects. On the one hand, the negative effects of labelling at this early stage may not be helpful. Once labelled, children may be perceived and responded to differently by their parents, their peer group, teachers and others. The majority of mental health professionals are aware of these issues and guard against unnecessary and negative labelling, as well as encouraging other professionals to do the same. On the other hand, diagnosis makes it easier for the family to cope as the problem becomes more understandable and acceptable and indirectly this is then likely to have a positive effect on the child. Improved access to services and a more positive attitude from others are additional benefits. The benefits of diagnosis therefore have to be weighed against the negative consequences.

Within the following chapters, which address each of the various types of mental health problems and disorders likely to be encountered by teachers, the DSM-IV criteria are used to define the mental health problems discussed. Where ICD-10 criteria for specific disorders differ significantly from DSM-IV this is noted where relevant.

References

American Psychiatric Association (1994) *Diagnostic and Statistical Manual of Mental Disorders (Fourth edition)*. Washington, DC: American Psychiatric Association.

Bell, R. Q. (1968) A reinterpretation of the direction of effects in studies of socialisation. *Psychological Review*, 75, 2, 81–95.

Berger, N. (1984) Social network interventions for families that have a handicapped child. In Hansen, J. C. (ed.) *Families with Handicapped Members*, 127–137. Rockville, MD: Aspen.

Bronfenbrenner, U. (1979) *The Ecology of Human Development*. Cambridge, MA: Harvard University Press.

Carter, E. and McGoldrick, M. (eds) (1980) *The Family Life Cycle: A Framework for Family Therapy*. New York: Gardner.

Chilman, C. S., Nunnally, E. W. and Cox, F. M. (eds) (1988) *Chronic Illness and Disability*. Newbury Park, CA: Sage.

Coopersmith, E. I. (ed.) (1984) *Family Therapy with Families with Handicapped Children*. Rockville, MD: Aspen.

Erikson, E. (1968) *Identity, Youth and Crisis*. New York: Norton.

Friesen, J. D. (1983) *Marriage and Family Counselling: A Training Handbook*. Victoria: British Columbia Council for the Family.

Havinghurst, R. J. (1972) *Developmental Tasks and Education (Third edition)*. New York: David McKay.

Lawrence, D. (1987) *Enhancing Self-esteem in the Classroom*. London: Paul Chapman.

Levinson, D. J. (1978) *The Seasons of a Man's Life*. New York: Ballantine.

Maslow, A. (1970) *Motivation and Personality (Second edition)*. New York: Harper and Row.

Turnbull, A. P. and Turnbull, H. R. (1986) *Families, Professionals and Exceptionality*. Columbus, OH: Merrill.

World Health Organization (1992) *International Classification of Diseases (Tenth edition)*. Geneva: World Health Organization.

Part II

Recognised mental health disorders

3 Conduct disorder

Steven, a 14-year-old boy, was out of control. Steven's difficulties began shortly after his father left home. At home, he was abusive to his mother and refused to do anything she asked. He teased and tormented his younger sister. He often stayed out late, drank alcohol and had run away from home for short periods. He was frequently in trouble with the neighbours and with the police for vandalism and fighting. At school he was constantly involved in fights, verbally abusive to teachers and disruptive in lessons. He had been excluded on a number of occasions for a limited period because of his behaviour. On one occasion he had threatened a girl with a knife. He had always had problems with his schoolwork and had received some extra support in lessons for his learning difficulties.

Children and adolescents are frequently referred to mental health professionals because their behaviour is inappropriate or out of control. Conduct disorder is one of the most expensive mental health problems, with significant costs being incurred by a number of services, including education, the youth justice services and health. The emotional, social and physical costs to individuals and their families are also high. Antisocial behaviour appears to be a growing problem, requiring urgent attention. Because of their aggressive, disruptive and defiant behaviour, many of these children cause teachers major difficulties, as well as being a major problem for society. Although their behaviour may evoke anger and outrage in others, many children with conduct problems are distressed and in need of help. There is evidence, however, that many teachers do not have the necessary support and training to cope with such pupils, thus increasing the likelihood that they are excluded from school. Such a response only further exacerbates their difficulties, creating a bigger and more long-term problem for society in general. It is important that teachers have a better understanding of these children's problems, develop the skills to address their needs and that they enlist support from other agencies to help alleviate such difficulties.

Diagnosis

Within DSM-IV (American Psychiatric Association, 1994) conduct disorder is defined as a repetitive and persistent pattern of behaviour in which the rights of others or the rules of society are violated. It involves at least three or more of fifteen criteria that fall into the following categories:

- Aggression, including:
  - bullying, threatening or intimidating others;
  - initiating physical fights;
  - using a weapon that can cause serious harm to others;
  - being physically cruel to people;
  - being physically cruel to animals;
  - stealing while confronting a victim;
  - forcing someone into sexual activity.

- Destroying or losing of property, including:
  - deliberately engaging in fire setting with the intention of causing serious damage;
  - deliberately destroying others' property.

- Deceitfulness or theft, including:
  - breaking into someone else's house, building or car;
  - lying to obtain goods or favours or to avoid obligations;
  - stealing items of value without confronting a victim.

- Serious violation of rules, including:
  - running away from home overnight (at least twice);
  - playing truant from school (beginning before the age of 13);
  - staying out all night without parental permission (beginning before the age of 13).

The criteria for conduct disorder in ICD-10 (World Health Organization, 1992) are almost identical. Almost all young people break the rules from time to time and involvement in one or even a few incidents is insufficient for a child to be considered to have a conduct disorder. Diagnosis should only be used where conduct problems occur at school, at home and in the community, thus indicating that the behaviour is not a response to the immediate social context. Conduct problems can be mild, moderate or severe and they can include a diverse range of problems (Loeber *et al.*, 2000). A distinction is also made between childhood onset conduct disorder, that is before the age of 10, and adolescent onset since these are associated with different presenting problems and a different course and outcome.

Differential diagnosis

Over two-thirds of children with conduct disorder also have oppositional defiant disorder (Hinshaw *et al.*, 1993; Loeber *et al.*, 2000). When present alone, this is a less serious disorder, which is less pervasive, where hostility and defiance, such as arguing, blaming others and vindictive behaviour, are the central features. The relationship with conduct disorder is not clear, although cases of conduct disorder are often preceded by oppositional defiant disorder (Webster-Stratton and Herbert, 1994). Conduct disorder can, however, be a precursor to adult antisocial personality disorder in which the individual shows no remorse for his or her activities. For example, there is a minority of school-age children who lack guilt and seem heartless and who have a greater number and variety of problems, although they tend to be more intelligent than other children with conduct disorder. Estimates suggest that a third to over a half of children with conduct disorder also have attention deficit hyperactivity disorder (ADHD) and that there may be a common underlying problem, such as impulsivity, although these disorders are considered distinct (Nottleman and Jensen, 1995). Children with both tend to have more severe problems.

Features

The central feature of conduct disorder is the violation of the rights of others and the disregard for age-appropriate social norms, but it can involve a very diverse range of behaviours. Prominent characteristics are the non-compliance and aggression these children exhibit. Non-compliance can take a variety of forms, such as not doing what is asked, arguing, resistance, or doing the opposite of what is asked. Defiance towards authority figures, such as parents and teachers, is common, as is also the relatively unrestrained aggression and low tolerance these children sometimes exhibit. In young children, for example, temper tantrums are common. Early signs of conduct disorder, often seen initially within the family, include disobedience, lying, stealing and aggression towards others. When the condition worsens this type of behaviour then extends outside the family into the school and the local community. Although these children may project an image of toughness, their self-esteem is low. Symptoms vary with age and with gender. There are two basic types of conduct disorder. Childhood onset, in contrast to adolescent onset, is associated with more serious and persistent antisocial behaviour. Males tend to express themselves in more overt ways, such as fighting and confrontation, whereas females tend to express themselves in more covert ways, such as lying, truancy and running away (American Psychiatric Association, 1994) and suicide attempts are more common in girls with the disorder.

Children with conduct disorder also exhibit impulsiveness, poor peer relations and poor school performance. These children are usually not able to see the effects of their behaviour on others and they often have deficits in social skills. They have little empathy and little concern for the feelings, wishes or well-being of others and have negative relationships with most people. With parents and teachers difficulties tend to revolve around youngsters' defiant behaviour, whilst with peers they centre on aggression and bullying. Peer rejection often leads to lack of self-esteem. These children often lie about their problems, are sophisticated at manipulating others (Sommers-Flanagan and Sommers-Flanagan, 1998) and avoid taking personal responsibility for their actions by blaming others (Kazdin, 1995). In addition, parents often exhibit a sense of helplessness since non-compliance leaves parents, as well as teachers, feeling frustrated and helpless. Parents often have marital, unemployment or psychiatric problems of their own and may have contact with a variety of helping agencies.

Associated problems

Most children and adolescents with conduct disorder have one or more other disorders (Loeber and Keenan, 1994). As well as oppositional defiant disorder and ADHD, depression and anxiety both occur more frequently in children with conduct disorder than in other children. Although this varies with age and gender, about a third to a half have depression, whilst studies on anxiety suggest that it is present in about one-fifth to a half of those with conduct disorder (Harrington, 1995). The presence of anxiety may inhibit aggressive behaviour but understanding of this relationship is limited. Suicidal ideas, suicide attempts and completed suicide are also found at a higher rate than normal in children with conduct disorders, particularly in girls. These children also tend to have lower than average intelligence, academic achievement below the expected level and often have associated learning difficulties. Their non-compliance has direct implications for their learning at school. They have difficulty, for example, in following instructions. This is discussed further in the final section of this chapter. Conduct disorders are also associated with risk-taking behaviour of various kinds, including early sexual activity, drinking, smoking and drug abuse, which can lead to expulsion from school, difficulties with the police, or sexually transmitted diseases etc. (Myers *et al.*, 1993). This means that they often have other health-related problems. The rates of premature death are three to four times higher in boys with conduct disorder. If associated problems are severe children may be unable to live at home or to go to an ordinary mainstream school.

Incidence

Conduct disorder is the most frequently occurring of mental disorders affecting children and adolescents. Its incidence ranges from 6 to 16 per cent in boys and from 2 to 9 per cent in girls (American Psychiatric Association, 1994). However, early, persistent and severe patterns of antisocial conduct only occur in about 5 per cent of children (Hinshaw and Anderson, 1996; Kazdin, 1995). Conduct disorder is more prevalent during adolescence than childhood. The incidence of oppositional defiant disorder has consistently been found to be higher than conduct disorder and ranges from 10 to 22 per cent of children (Nottleman and Jensen, 1995). The number of referrals for children with conduct disorders to all agencies is considered to be increasing.

In childhood, conduct disorder is three or four times more common in boys, although by adolescence this difference decreases (Earls, 1994). In most boys onset occurs before the age of 10, whilst in most girls onset occurs between 13 and 16. There is greater persistence in boys than in girls, although many girls (between 1 and 6 per cent) still display severe conduct problems as young adults. Conduct disorder is universal in that it occurs in every culture and level of society, although different cultures and societies may play different roles in its development and expression. It does, however, tend to be more prevalent in children and adolescents from socially deprived backgrounds.

Causes

There is a diverse range of potential influences on children's behaviour and this is likely to involve a complex interplay of child, family, community and cultural factors (Hester and Kaiser, 1998; Holmes *et al.*, 2001). Numerous factors have been associated with conduct disorder, but it is often unclear whether they increase the risk or are the result of the disorder. Individual child characteristics, parenting practices and family organisation are probably the key factors that influence the likelihood of problems escalating into later life, although genetics and neurobiological factors may play some part, as do also peer relationships and cultural and media influences, in the development of the disorder. These are each outlined below.

Child characteristics

Certain personal characteristics, including a difficult temperament, impulsivity and educational difficulties, place children at risk for long-term conduct problems. Some children have a temperament that makes them harder to bring up than others. Academic and intellectual difficulties often precede conduct disorder, although there is little evidence that school failure is a primary cause. Deficits in language, in problem-solving skills and in how these children process information in social situations may provide a common underlying cause (Hinshaw and Anderson, 1996). Children's characteristics interact with family factors in complex ways.

Family factors

Family difficulties, such as parental conflict, violence, stress and psychological problems, have a strong association with conduct disorder. Typically, these children come from families in which divorce or separation, lack of affection, lack of stable and secure family relationships, and inconsistent management are common. Poor parenting skills, including the reinforcement of negative behaviours and the ignoring of positive ones, promote antisocial behaviour (Patterson *et al*., 1982). Harsh or inconsistent discipline, physical abuse and inadequate supervision have also been noted (Dodge *et al*., 1997). A combination of children's individual characteristics and poor parenting skills is often associated with more persistent and severe problems. Additional stresses on families, such as poor housing, poverty and unemployment, create instability that may further contribute to conduct problems.

Peer relationships

Difficult peer relationships are a risk factor for early-onset conduct disorder and involvement with deviant peers is a powerful predictor of the disorder. In this way, a vicious circle can develop which reinforces negative behaviours. Children with conduct problems are often rejected by non-deviant peers.

Cultural and media influences

Cultural differences in the expression of conduct disorder can be dramatic. One group of children with conduct problems, for example, comes from families who live in communities where delinquent behaviour is accepted and culturally ingrained. These children may live an antisocial life, but they are reasonably well adjusted both socially and emotionally. In addition, a correlation between violence on television and aggressive behaviour has been demonstrated and this can provide a negative model for children to follow.

Genetics

As described above, a number of traits may predispose children to conduct disorder and it has been suggested that half of these may be due to heredity, but the role of genetics needs further study. Temperament and aggression, for example, may be largely inherited. It is thought that a biological backcloth of antisocial behaviour, coupled with an adverse home environment, may interact to produce aggression and conduct disorder.

Neurobiological factors

The need for stimulation in these children may have a neurobiological basis. There are consistent findings that there are neurological deficits in antisocial children compared with others (Moffitt, 1993). Neurobiological factors, such as low arousal and reactivity, however, are thought to play a greater role in early-onset conduct disorder.

Treatment

Children and adolescents with conduct disorder are likely to minimise their problems; therefore, information from others, particularly teachers and parents, is crucial in assessing their difficulties (Kazdin, 1995). The most successful treatments address the pervasive nature of their difficulties and focus on the school, family and community context and children's social skills and academic deficiencies, as well as their behaviour. Conduct problems may occur in response to high rates of family conflict or adverse social situations, so, if interventions are directed at one area alone, other forces are likely to counteract any changes (Dodge, 1993). Treatment not only needs to focus on extreme behaviour, but also on deficits in social skills and learning. Family-focused treatments, such as behavioural parent training, family therapy and multi-systemic therapy, are considered to be the most promising treatments (Brosnan and Carr, 2000; Kazdin, 1997; Kazdin, 2001). Treatment is easier in younger children (Webster-Stratton and Herbert, 1994). Active involvement of parents leads to enhanced positive outcomes and a more long-term effect. It is also important to assess the presence of other disorders since the treatment of other disorders, such as depression, ADHD and substance abuse, may lead to reduction in conduct problems (Sommers-Flanagan and Sommers-Flanagan, 1998). Treatments may include behavioural parent training, family therapy, multi-systemic therapy, cognitive behavioural therapy, medication and, in extreme cases, foster care treatment. These are discussed briefly below.

Behavioural parent training

Behavioural parent training aims to help parents use specific behavioural skills in managing children's behaviour on a day-to-day basis. This is the most widely used and effective treatment, although it may need to be intensive for a more long-term effect (Kazdin, 2001; Serketich and Dumas, 1996). It is generally more effective with younger children. Individual and group programmes are used, as are also manuals of structured courses for parents (Webster-Stratton and Herbert, 1994).

Family therapy

Family therapy focuses on communication, problem solving and negotiation, reducing blaming and negotiation of contingency contracts. This form of treatment may only have a short-term effect; however, reduction of conflict within the family can only be helpful.

Multi-systemic therapy

In multi-systemic therapy the factors maintaining the problem, whether within the home, the child, the family, the school or the peer group, are identified and interventions developed to address them. It is an intensive approach that draws on a range of techniques, such as cognitive skills training and parent training, as well as specialised interventions. Intervention may, for example, involve facilitating communication between parents and the school and arranging appropriate educational placement. In severe cases, multi-systemic therapy is superior to other forms of treatment (Henggeler *et al.*, 1998).

Cognitive behaviour therapy

Cognitive behaviour therapy is an individual form of treatment that enhances children's capacity to deal with conflict and teaches them to identify their thoughts, feelings and behaviours in problem social situations. This type of treatment has been especially successful with older children and those with mild problems from relatively functional families (Kazdin, 1995). However, whilst many children improve, they usually still continue to display conduct problems in excess of their peers.

Medication

A variety of medications have been used to treat conduct disorder, but medication alone is rarely sufficient to reduce aggressive behaviour. It should be used with caution and only alongside other treatments that teach children appropriate behaviour.

Foster care treatment

In severe cases, individuals, particularly adolescents, may be placed temporarily with foster carers who have been trained in behaviour management. This may occur alongside other interventions. Typically, as progress is made, the adolescent spends more and more time within his or her own family and less time with foster carers.

Course and outcome

The course and outcome of conduct disorder are variable. About 7 per cent of children with conduct disorder engage in antisocial behaviour at an early age that continues into adult life. If not resolved in the early years, conduct disorder can therefore become a chronic condition. In contrast, in about 30 per cent of cases it begins in puberty and disappears by early adulthood. The outcome of treatment is better for younger children and, generally, long-term dysfunctional behaviour patterns are more resistant to treatment (Kazdin, 1995). Treatments are more successful with children whose problems are mild and who come from healthy families and communities. Adult outcomes depend on the type and severity of the disorder, as well as the risk and protective factors in the family, child and the community. Conduct problems in childhood have been linked to later criminal behaviour, psychiatric problems, social difficulties, health problems and poor parenting. If left untreated, there is an increased likelihood of antisocial behaviour as adults, but this is not the case with all children. Many factors influence this relationship, such as the age of onset, gender and the presence of other disorders, as well as treatment. Whilst there is a greater likelihood of anxiety and depression in women who had conduct disorder as children, there is a greater likelihood of antisocial personality disorder and substance abuse in men (Offord and Bennett, 1994). Children with both ADHD and conduct disorder are likely to have a poorer outcome.

WHAT CAN TEACHERS DO TO HELP?

Prevention

Conduct disorders in children often create a lot of stress and suffering for everyone involved, which provides a strong argument for an emphasis on prevention, as do also the cost to society and the limited effectiveness of treatment (Offord and Bennett, 1994). Successful prevention includes early identification of children at risk (Holmes *et al.*, 2001), interventions in a range of contexts, particularly in schools, and the arrangement of ongoing support for children and their parents (Hester and Kaiser, 1998). The period from age 1 to 3 is a sensitive period in children's development in determining what is socially acceptable, so, if parents do not confront difficult behaviour at this point, children fail to develop appropriate behaviour and impulse control. Recent efforts have therefore focused on the development of interventions that are effective with very young children.

System-wide prevention programmes in schools and communities have been advocated. Where interventions are directed at parents alone, children show sustained improvements in their behaviour, but there are high rates of relapse and improved behaviour tends not to generalise to school or the peer group. Some programmes, for example, have been directed at high-risk nursery children identified because of their disruptive behaviour and poor relationships at home and school. Programmes focus on academic skills, as well as behaviour and relationships, and include teacher-based classroom intervention. They require close collaboration between parents, teachers and project staff. Preliminary reports suggest that this can lead to improvements in school performance, a decrease in disruptive behaviour, improved peer relations and enhanced parenting attitudes, but the long-term effects have yet to be evaluated (Conduct Problems Prevention Research Group, 1997).

A positive school experience alone has been shown to be a protective factor that may be able to partially compensate for poor family circumstances. Teachers may help, therefore, by ensuring that school is a positive experience for pupils from all backgrounds. They may help by supporting parents who are under stress because of their social circumstances. Parents, for example, may be encouraged to access nursery facilities for younger children or to take up classes to enhance their own academic achievement and their self-esteem. Since learning difficulties are also a risk factor for later development of conduct problems it is important that these are identified early and appropriate intervention given. This can be achieved through an effective screening programme and by all teachers having the knowledge and skills to assess these problems with the help and support of the special educational needs co-ordinator within the school.

Early identification

Young children who show signs of conduct disorder require urgent referral to specialist agencies since the long-term outcome is poor unless they receive early treatment. Once problematic behaviour patterns are entrenched they are more resistant to treatment.

A checklist based on the symptoms given in DSM-IV, for example, may be used to highlight children with difficulties. It is important to get a detailed educational assessment involving measures of school performance, intellectual capacity, language development, reading and arithmetic skills, as well as focusing on unacceptable behaviour. School records can be a valuable source of information in obtaining a complete picture. They may include, for example, information regarding the child's attendance, meetings with parents and the child's interests (e.g. extra-curricular activities undertaken), as well as information about the child's behaviour. The diverse nature of the symptoms of conduct disorder makes it essential to obtain reports from teachers, as well as parents. However, they are often dealing with the child in different contexts and because they have different perspectives, these different sources often do not agree. For example, a teacher, who has high expectations regarding the child's schoolwork, may find him or her defiant and difficult, whereas parents may perceive him or her as helpful and co-operative around the home.

Where aggression and non-compliance are extreme or of great frequency, intensity or duration and where behaviour seems irrational given the circumstances or where there are co-existing problems, increased concern is warranted. Referral for more intensive and specialist treatment may then be required, either through the educational psychologist or through the family doctor. Typically, referral to mental health services often occurs as a result of behaviour problems at school. It is important for teachers to realise, however, that although problems at school may be significant, parents and children may not feel that such a referral is warranted, either because they do not feel there is a problem or because they perceive the problem to be located within the school environment. In these circumstances teachers need to work with parents to develop a supportive programme for children within the school setting and to seek advice from mental health services where available.

Support for children with recognised conduct disorder

As part of the treatment in behavioural training programmes parents are often encouraged to liaise closely with schools so that any strategies may be implemented in both the school and the home environment. It is helpful if teachers can support parents as much as possible with their programme, for example, by allowing children to earn points for their behaviour within the school context. In addition, there are many ways in which teachers can support children with conduct disorders within the school setting. This can include managing behaviour, addressing learning needs, avoiding rejection, encouraging co-operative peer relationships and encouraging them to engage in extra-curricular activities, as well as providing support for parents and ensuring that they get support themselves.

Managing behaviour

Teachers need to conduct an assessment of specific behaviours and to focus on agreeing with parents the main ones to be addressed, thus helping parents to identify the desired outcomes. Antecedents and consequences require close examination. Within the classroom, as far as possible, desired behaviour should be rewarded and inappropriate behaviour either ignored or dealt with through a consistently applied hierarchy of sanctions. In some circumstances, this may involve applying different standards of behaviour to different individuals within a class. Where this is the case it can be helpful to enlist the backing of class members who are mature enough to understand by explaining the reason for this and by explaining that it is only a short-term arrangement to help the individual overcome his or her present difficulties. Teachers should try to focus on the positive attributes of children and to facilitate circumstances in which they can succeed and be liberal with their praise. Strategies should be incorporated into an individual education plan or behaviour support plan, perhaps organised through the special educational needs (SEN) process, that needs to be seen and followed by all teachers and non-teaching staff with whom children come into contact. Herbert (1996) suggests useful techniques for both parents and teachers which include:

- giving commands clearly and slowly;
- making attention and other rewards contingent on appropriate behaviour;
- providing quality time;
- providing fair and clear rules and limits;
- enhancing children's problem-solving skills.

Addressing learning needs

Where children are identified as having conduct disorder problems it is important that a thorough assessment of their learning needs is made and any weaknesses addressed. This can be done through the SEN process by liaison with the SENCO within the school. A formal assessment through the educational psychologist is likely to be warranted. Where learning difficulties are severe children may require special support within the mainstream setting or placement within a special school or unit for children with emotional and behavioural difficulties.

Avoiding rejection

Although children with conduct disorder can be very frustrating to work with, teachers should avoid responses that make them feel rejected since this can only lead to an escalation of their problems. Teachers need to be adept at defusing confrontational situations where they are working with such children for lengthy periods. Training in conflict resolution, alongside behavioural management training, is helpful. Whilst many children with conduct problems are often excluded from school this too can only exacerbate their difficulties. Once not attending school, children may be unsupervised and this further compounds their social problems.

Peer relationships

Teachers should encourage children with conduct disorders to foster friendly relationships with their peers. Providing opportunities for pupils to work co-operatively in small-group settings and focusing on the acquirement of social skills can facilitate this. Where children have become isolated they may be helped to engage with their peers by linking them with others who are particularly sympathetic, although it is important to ensure that the others are not placed in a situation where they are likely to be bullied.

Extra-curricular activities

Since children with conduct disorders often lack self-esteem and have difficulties with peer relationships it can be helpful to find something that children enjoy and can achieve at, such as sports, which can be fostered at school. It is not helpful if children are excluded from activities they enjoy for lengthy periods because of their poor behaviour since it is often these activities that provide them with the only opportunity they have to build their self-esteem. Community-based interventions, such as community centres where children may be exposed to activities involving non-deviant peers and staff experienced at working with children with conduct problems, can be extremely helpful.

Supporting parents

It is important for teachers to understand what it is like to be a parent of a child with conduct disorder and to be able to empathise with them. Teachers have to be able to see it from parents' perspective, as parents are crucial in shaping children's behaviour. These children are often described as tyrants within the home. Their non-compliance gives them a lot of power within the family and it is not unusual for the whole family to be ruled by them. They are exhausting to live with and parents get frustrated that their children do not learn from experience. Children with conduct disorder often show extreme aggression towards their parents. Their behaviour is unpredictable and parents have to live with this day in and day out. On top of this, other children and their parents often spurn them. Parents feel that they are to blame and indeed are often blamed by both lay people and professionals. This means that parents, as well as their children, feel isolated and rejected. This contributes to their feelings of helplessness and a belief that they cannot do anything to alleviate the situation. Because of their despair, they tend to apply strategies inconsistently and without confidence.

It is important therefore that teachers adopt a positive approach and encourage parents to see that they can make a difference. Unless they are constantly encouraged and supported they are likely to give up easily on any strategies suggested. This needs to be an ongoing process and regular reviews need to be set up to support them. It is important to help them focus on children's attributes, which they may often ignore. Working with parents should be a collaborative process involving negotiation and support. Parents should be encouraged to attend individual or group parent training programmes.

Support for teachers

Children with conduct disorders often evoke a range of emotions in those around them, including teachers, particularly where aggressive or violent behaviour may evoke revengeful feelings. These children are likely to cause angry reactions in peers and adults and it can be easy to label them as more negative than they really are. Conversely, others may grossly underestimate pupils' behavioural problems owing to their inexperience or a desire to see the best in them. For these reasons, it is important that teachers, particularly inexperienced teachers, seek the help and support of others within the school and outside agencies when working with these children. Staff support groups may be helpful in both allowing teachers to express their feelings and encouraging the sharing of good practice in the management of these children's behaviour, which can be extremely challenging.

Further reading

Herbert, M. (1996) *Banishing Bad Behaviour: Helping Parents Cope with a Child's Conduct Disorder*. Leicester: The British Psychological Society.

Kazdin, A. E. (1995) *Conduct Disorders in Childhood and Adolescence (Second edition)*. Thousand Oaks, CA: Sage.

Webster-Stratton, C. and Herbert, M. (1994) *Troubled Families – Problem Children: Working with Parents: A Collaborative Process*. Chichester: John Wiley & Sons.

References

American Psychiatric Association (1994) *Diagnostic and Statistical Manual of Mental Disorders (Fourth edition)*. Washington, DC: American Psychiatric Association.

Brosnan, R. and Carr, A. (2000) Adolescent conduct problems. In Carr, A (ed.) *What Works with Children and Adolescents? A Critical Review of Psychological Interventions with Children, Adolescents and their Families*, 131–154. London: Routledge.

Conduct Problems Prevention Research Group (1997) A developmental and clinical model for the prevention of conduct disorder: The FAST track program. *Development and Psychopathology*, 4, 509–527.

Dodge, K. A. (1993) The future of research on the treatment of conduct disorder. *Development and Psychopathology*, 5, 1–2, 311–319.

Dodge, K. A., Lochman, J. E., Harnish, J. D., Bates, J. E. and Pettit, G. S. (1997) Reactive and proactive aggression in school children and psychiatrically impaired chronically assaultive youth. *Journal of Abnormal Psychology*, 106, 37–51.

Earls, F. (1994) Oppositional defiant and conduct disorders. In Rutter, M., Taylor, E. and Hersov, L. (eds) *Child and Adolescent Psychiatry: Modern Approaches (Third edition)*, 308–329. Oxford: Blackwell.

Harrington, R. (1995) *Depressive Disorder in Childhood and Adolescence*. Chichester: John Wiley & Sons.

Henggeler, S. W., Schoenwald, S. K., Borduin, C. M., Rowland, M. D. and Cunningham, P. B. (1998) *Multisystemic Treatment of Antisocial Behaviour in Children and Adolescents*. New York: Guilford Press.

Herbert, M. (1996) *Banishing Bad Behaviour: Helping Parents Cope with a Child's Conduct Disorder*. Leicester: The British Psychological Society.

Hester, P. P. and Kaiser, A. P. (1998) Early intervention for the prevention of conduct disorder: Research issues in early identification, implementation and interpretation of treatment outcome. *Behavioural Disorders*, 24, 1, 57–65.

Hinshaw, S. P. and Anderson, C. A. (1996) Conduct and oppositional defiant disorders. In Mash, E. J. and Barkley, R. A. (eds) *Child Psychopathology*, 113–149. New York: Guilford Press.

Hinshaw, S. P., Lahey, B. B. and Hart, E. J. (1993) Issues of taxonomy and comorbidity in the development of conduct disorder. *Development and Psychopathology*, 5, 31–49.

Holmes, S. E., Slaughter, J. R. and Kashani, J. (2001) Risk factors in childhood that lead to the development of conduct disorder and antisocial personality disorder. *Child Psychiatry and Human Development*, 31, 3, 183–193.

Kazdin, A. E. (1995) *Conduct Disorders in Childhood and Adolescence (Second edition)*. Thousand Oaks, CA: Sage.

Kazdin, A. E. (1997) Psychological treatments for conduct disorder in children. *Journal of Child Psychology and Psychiatry*, 38, 161–178.

Kazdin, A. E. (2001) *Behaviour Modification in Applied Settings*. Belmont, CA: Wadsworth.

Loeber, R. and Keenan, K. (1994) Interaction between conduct disorder and its comorbid conditions: Effects of age and gender. *Clinical Psychology Review*, 14, 497–523.

Loeber, R., Burke, J. D., Lahey, B. B., Winters, A. and Zera, M. (2000) Oppositional defiant and conduct disorder: A review of the past ten years. *Journal of American Academy of Child and Adolescent Psychiatry*, 39, 12, 1468–1484.

Moffitt, T. E. (1993) The neuropsychology of conduct disorder. *Development and Psychopathology*, 5, 1–2, 135–151.

Myers, W. C., Burket, R. C. and Otto, T. A. (1993) Conduct disorder and personality disorder in hospitalised adolescents. *Journal of Clinical Psychiatry*, 150, 578–583.

Nottleman, E. D. and Jensen, P. S. (1995) Comorbidity of disorders in children and adolescents: Developmental perspectives. In Ollendick, T. H. and Prinz, R. J. (eds) *Advances in Clinical Child Psychology*, 17, 109–155. New York: Plenum Press.

Offord, D. R. and Bennett, K. J. (1994) Conduct disorder: Long-term outcomes and intervention effectiveness. *Journal of American Academy of Child and Adolescent Psychiatry*, 33, 8, 1069–1078.

Patterson, G. R., Chamberlain, P. and Reid, J. B. (1982) A comparative evaluation of a parent training programme. *Behaviour Therapy*, 13, 638–650.

Serketich, W. J. and Dumas, J. E. (1996) The effectiveness of behavioural parent training to modify antisocial behaviour in children: A meta-analysis. *Behaviour Therapy*, 27, 171–186.

Sommers-Flanagan, J. and Sommers-Flanagan, R. (1998) Assessment and diagnosis of conduct disorder. *Journal of Counselling and Development*, 76, 2, 189–197.

Webster-Stratton, C. and Herbert, M. (1994) *Troubled Families – Problem Children: Working with Parents: A Collaborative Process*. Chichester: John Wiley & Sons.

World Health Organization (1992) *International Classification of Diseases (Tenth edition)*. Geneva: World Health Organization.

4 Attention deficit hyperactivity disorder

John, a 9-year-old boy and the eldest of three children, was stubborn and argumentative at home. He was reported by his parents to be 'always on the go' and had exhibited difficult behaviour even as a baby. At his primary school, teachers were concerned about his behaviour. He had difficulty waiting his turn, was always disorganised and was extremely restless. In the playground, John was often in trouble. He was not perceived to be the instigator of conflict situations, but he was recognised by some of his peers as a boy whom it was easy to wind up. He was of average ability, but his progress at school was poor and his attainments were a few years behind his chronological age.

Attention deficit hyperactivity disorder (ADHD) is one of the most common and most debilitating disorders amongst school-age children, yet it is probably one of the least well understood. It has received a lot of attention recently, mainly because of the large numbers of children, particularly in the USA, receiving drug treatment for the disorder. Where children have behavioural difficulties and parents are finding it difficult to cope, it is likely that they will turn to teachers for advice and help. ADHD can significantly affect children's progress at school, not only their work, but also their social development and the relationships that they have with teachers and their peers. If not detected early, long-term problems can lead to poor educational achievement and social isolation. For these reasons, it is vital that teachers know about the disorder and are able to offer appropriate support to children in their classes and advice to parents, as well as helping them access other sources of information and guidance.

Diagnosis

Opinions differ about the behaviours which should be used to define ADHD and, whilst some believe there is evidence against it being considered a distinct disorder, others believe that the related elements of hyperactivity, inattention and impulsivity together form one syndrome (Barkley, 1990). The diagnostic criteria for ADHD are therefore divided into three categories. They are given in DSM-IV (American Psychiatric Association, 1994) and include:

– Inattention, where a child:
  - fails to give close attention to details or makes mistakes;
  - has difficulties sustaining attention in tasks or play activities;
  - does not seem to listen when spoken to directly;
  - does not follow through on instructions and fails to finish tasks;
  - has difficulty organising tasks and activities;
  - avoids, dislikes or is reluctant to engage in tasks that require sustained mental effort;
  - loses things necessary for tasks and activities;
  - is distracted by extraneous stimuli;
  - is forgetful in daily activities.

– Hyperactivity, where a child:
  - fidgets with hands or feet or squirms in his or her seat;
  - leaves his or her seat in situations in which remaining seated is expected;
  - runs about or climbs excessively in situations in which it is inappropriate;
  - has difficulty playing or engaging in leisure activities quietly;
  - is always 'on the go';
  - talks excessively.

– Impulsivity, where a child:
  - blurts out answers before the questions have been completed;
  - has difficulty waiting for turns;
  - interrupts or intrudes on others.

For a diagnosis of ADHD at least six of these behaviours have to be demonstrated at a level beyond the normal range. They must be present before the age of 7 and must be evident in more than one setting, that is at home and at school, or in the community. Depending on which category or categories the behaviours of concern predominantly fall within, individuals may be classified as mainly 'inattentive' or 'hyperactive/impulsive' or both. ICD-10 criteria (World Health Organization, 1992), in contrast, focus on hyperactivity rather than inattention (although this view is changing in Europe). More recently there has been an increasing appreciation of the diversity of this group of children.

Differential diagnosis

The main problem with the diagnosis of ADHD is that several different kinds of disorder are often present together and they interact in complex ways. Learning disabilities and emotional and behavioural difficulties, in particular, are common in those with ADHD. Between a quarter and a half of children with ADHD, for example, have a learning difficulty (Barkley, 1990; Kavanagh, 1994) and there are also strong links with speech and language disorders (Shelton and Barkley, 1994). The distinction between ADHD and emotional and behavioural difficulties is a more complex problem. High percentages of children with ADHD also have emotional and behavioural difficulties, such as defiant behaviour, conduct disorder and emotional disorder. It is so common for conduct disorder (see Chapter 3) and ADHD to be intertwined that some have doubted the value of making a distinction (Taylor, 1994; Cooper and Ideus, 1995). Others, such as Hinshaw

(1994), however, believe that ADHD and conduct disorder are separate factors, despite the high correlation between them. The distinction is important because the implications of the two diagnoses are vastly different. It is possible that hyperactivity is a precursor for both, that there is a single cause or that both are associated with chronic failure (Wodrich, 1994). The low self-esteem and the negative cycle of failure children with ADHD experience in all areas of their life may also lead to other disorders.

Features

The symptoms of ADHD can adversely affect children's overall development and can indirectly result in academic failure, low self-esteem, delinquent behaviour, family conflict and social isolation. The features can vary widely, although the major behaviours, as stated earlier, are hyperactivity, inattention and impulsivity. These are discussed in more depth here.

Hyperactivity

Hyperactivity is concerned with excessive movement. It can involve an increase in the rate of normal activities, an increase in purposeless, minor movements that are irrelevant to the task in hand, fidgeting or restlessness. Observations have shown that excessive movement commonly occurs in children with ADHD and that it may be evident even when they are asleep (Taylor *et al.*, 1991). This type of behaviour can be very disruptive and irritating to others and the distinction between what is excessive and what is appropriate in a given situation can be difficult.

Inattention

Inattention can involve attending only briefly to tasks, changing rapidly from one task to another and being distracted by irrelevancies in the environment, as well as concentrating only for brief periods of time. Observations and accounts by parents and teachers show that these type of behaviours are more common in children with ADHD. Whether they are distracted, however, varies considerably with the situation and the task in hand. Such behaviours can have a major adverse effect on children's performance at school and their relationships with teachers, as well as their peers.

Impulsivity

Impulsiveness means acting without reflecting. This might include, for example, thoughtless rule breaking, impetuously acting out of turn and getting into dangerous situations because of recklessness, all of which can be irritating to both peers and adults. Some children, however, can act in these ways for reasons other than thoughtlessness and these behaviours are often seen in children who are defiant or aggressive, as well as those with ADHD (Taylor *et al.*, 1991).

Incidence

The true incidence of ADHD cannot accurately be determined because it cannot be strictly defined or accurately measured (Barkley, 1990). Incidence rates will depend on the definition used, the population studied and the location, as well as the degree of agreement amongst parents, teachers and professionals. The vast apparent differences in the incidence rates of ADHD between the USA and the UK reflect the confusion over diagnosis. Figures in the UK are given as approximately one in a thousand or 0.1 per cent (Rutter *et al.*, 1970) and in the USA as 5 per cent (Miller *et al.*, 1973). ADHD is more common in boys than girls by a ratio of about seven to one. Girls often show attention deficits and impulsivity problems without hyperactivity or conduct disorder problems and because they are easy to manage they may go unrecognised and their needs unmet. Boys, on the other hand, are more likely to show physical hyperactivity and conduct disorder problems. Some British studies estimate that between 1 and 2 per cent of boys in the child population have ADHD (Taylor *et al.*, 1991).

Causes

There is no agreed single cause of ADHD. A wide and complex array of influential factors, which are biological, psychological and social in nature, and which can interact in different ways, are likely to be responsible. The pattern of causes and associations is not the same in all cases (Johnston, 1991). Research findings have been inconsistent mainly because of the frequency of associated disorders. The causes implicated have included genetic factors, brain differences, family and social factors, diet and levels of lead in the bloodstream. These are outlined briefly below.

Genetic factors

ADHD may be principally an inherited condition or there may be a biological predisposition to the disorder. Goodman and Stevenson (1989), for example, estimated that heredity accounted for between 30 to 50 per cent of the disorder, whilst common environmental factors, such as poverty, family lifestyle, pollution or diet, accounted for up to 30 per cent. There is little evidence that ADHD can arise purely out of social or environmental factors, although it may be exacerbated by such factors.

Brain differences

Neurological studies suggest that the irregular metabolism of brain chemicals contributes directly to the behaviour patterns seen in children with ADHD. A deficiency in neurotransmitters in the areas of the brain involved in response inhibition, attention and sensitivity to rewards and punishments may characterise some individuals with the disorder (Zametkin *et al.*, 1990). Less than 5 per cent of children with ADHD have evidence of brain damage caused, for example, by head trauma or brain infection, and more subtle brain injuries, such as birth-related brain injury, have only shown a weak association with ADHD (Barkley, 1990; Wodrich, 1994).

Family and social factors

Family and social influences are not thought to be responsible for the occurrence of ADHD, but they may maintain or exacerbate the disorder (Wodrich, 1994). Hyperactivity, for example, is more common in children from families with marital discord, conflict and hostile parent–child relationships (Taylor, 1994). Parents of ADHD children are more likely to be more negative towards their children than other parents (Cunningham and Barkley, 1979), but this could be a response to the demands of living with a child with challenging behaviour (Barkley, 1990; Taylor, 1994). The development of associated problems, such as conduct disorder, may also be influenced by parenting and social factors.

Diet

A study by Feingold (1975) first introduced the idea that diet may be an influential factor in ADHD and some single case studies have suggested that a change of diet can be beneficial for some individuals. More recent studies, however, have demonstrated little or no effect of a change of diet and Barkley (1990) concluded that there was little evidence to support diet being a causal factor.

Lead

There is presently no basis to assume that lead ingestion is a primary cause of ADHD. Studies so far show a weak association between levels of lead in the bloodstream and ADHD symptoms, but more research is needed in this area (Thomson *et al.*, 1989).

Treatment

Effective treatment must be guided by a thorough assessment, as the complex and varied problems of children with ADHD require separate intervention. It is generally recognised that a single approach is not effective and that treatment plans need to take into account individual needs. Assessment should include observations of children in a variety of settings, including school, and interviews with parents, teachers and children. Early intervention is essential to prevent secondary problems (Lowenthal, 1994). Schooling places particular demands on these children and educational support and classroom management should be an integral part of the treatment plan. These are discussed separately in the final section of this chapter. Collaboration between professionals, especially those within education and health, is necessary and most children with ADHD can be effectively helped when teachers, psychologists and parents work closely together.

Nolan and Carr (2000) concluded that a range of psychological interventions have positive short-term effects on ADHD symptoms. These include child-centred approaches, such as social skills and self-instruction training, family approaches, such as behavioural parent training and family therapy, and school-focused interventions, such as school-based contingency management, as well as combinations of these approaches. Overall, they concluded that multi-component treatment packages, involving child, family and school-based intervention, combined with low-dose stimulant medication were the treatment of choice. They suggest, however, that effective long-term treatment might involve sustained contact with appropriate services, together with more intensive intervention at vulnerable periods, such as a change of school or when entering adolescence. The main treatment measures offered for ADHD are outlined below.

Medication

It has been suggested that medication (stimulants such as Ritalin) can be highly effective in treating ADHD in about 80 per cent of children, although there is no evidence for its long-term effectiveness (Barkley, 1990). There is usually a rapid improvement in overactivity, distractibility and impulsivity. Maximum effectiveness occurs within one to one and a half hours and repeat doses are necessary. Improvements in behaviour, short-term learning, social skills and self-esteem are typically seen within three to six months. Monitoring is important and there may be possible side effects, such as sleep disturbance, irritability and rebound hyperactivity, although these are quite rare. Other treatments are usually required to maximise the chances of long-term improvement.

Behaviour modification

Shaping behaviour through targeting certain behaviours and the use of reward and punishment generally result in improved behaviour, although there is no evidence for generalisation and maintenance of treatment gains with this approach. Barkley (1990) stressed that the problems of ADHD children are so pervasive and so durable that they require individualised, broadly based and long-term intervention and he suggested that a combination of treatment with drugs and behaviour modification is the most effective. Since children with ADHD have difficulty regulating their behaviour, teaching self-control and self-evaluation can be beneficial (Ahonen *et al.*, 1994).

Counselling and psychotherapy

Counselling or psychotherapy is a long-term strategy that can be used to enhance the self-esteem and self-awareness of children with ADHD and equip them with alternative strategies for coping with their difficulties. Family therapy may also be beneficial since it can play a vital role in preventing a negative cycle of behaviour from developing within the family (Dalston, 1995).

Social skills training

Children with ADHD are at a high risk of peer rejection. Social skills training is essential, particularly for those with inattentive symptoms (Erk, 1995). Long-term, multi-faceted programmes are required and parents, teachers and peers need to be involved to create meaningful change (Barkley, 1990).

Parental support

Many parents of children with ADHD have such difficulties in managing that they seek help themselves. Parental involvement is essential and increasing parents' competence has been shown to have a positive effect on children's behaviour (Goldstein and Goldstein, 1990) so programmes used to help children need to be reinforced within the home for maximum effectiveness. Barkley (1990), for example, describes a counselling and training programme for parents, which incorporates education, discussion and training in behaviour modification. The negative reactions of others can result in a vicious cycle of failure and this often determines the way in which the behaviour of a child with ADHD develops (Taylor, 1994). Encouraging acceptance of the child, especially by parents and teachers, is therefore essential (Train, 1996).

Dietary intervention

Although present research indicates that diet has little effect on the symptoms of ADHD, parents often experiment with a change of diet and some professionals still advocate dietary control. Whilst it is probably best not to encourage a change of diet, professionals should support parents who choose to experiment in this way (Taylor, 1994).

Course and outcome

There is general agreement about the fundamental outcomes for children with ADHD: about half grow out of their symptoms and half continue to be disabled to varying extents (Weiss and Hechtman, 1986). There is a reasonable chance of a good outcome, provided that development is not too adversely affected. Hyperactivity tends to diminish with increasing age, but, in adolescence, low self-esteem, poor school performance and poor peer relations often continue and the development of aggressive and antisocial behaviour or delinquency is a major outcome (Barkley *et al.*, 1990). It is thought that children with ADHD are at severe risk of developing conduct disorder as a result of constantly experiencing negative reactions from adults and at the age of 3, hyperactivity is a good predictor of conduct disorder in later childhood (Campbell, 1987). As adults, one-third to one-half may be indistinguishable from other adults, but a higher percentage than the general population engage in antisocial behaviour as a result of their immature personality, aggression or poor family relationships. The severity of symptoms, the presence of conduct disorder, conflict within families, maternal depression and antisocial behaviour of the father are likely to increase the risk of a poor outcome (Barkley *et al.*, 1990). It is difficult, however, to distinguish separate factors that have consequences for later development because of the complex number of variables that may be involved.

WHAT CAN TEACHERS DO TO HELP?

Teachers have an important role to play in the early identification of children with ADHD and encouraging parents to seek appropriate help from other services, as well as supporting children with ADHD in the mainstream school setting.

Early identification

Teachers need to be trained to recognise the behaviours associated with ADHD. Dalston (1995) highlights the signs that teachers need to be alert to in children, such as:

- not being able to sustain attention;
- not waiting their turn;

- demanding instant gratification;
- engaging in fidgeting, kicking, tapping, rocking or fiddling with small objects;
- being unable to follow simple instructions;
- erratic levels of performance;
- frustration;
- poor short-term memory;
- avoidance of eye contact;
- aggressive or argumentative behaviour;
- lack of sensitivity to others;
- rushing about;
- clumsiness;
- a poor sense of safety.

Children with ADHD, but without impulsive behaviour, however, are less easy to detect. They are often labelled as lazy because of their poor concentration and lack of energy and enthusiasm. Unless these children are given help, they are likely to develop associated problems, such as severe loss of self-esteem and lack of motivation. It is vital, therefore, that they are recognised at an early stage.

Once the disorder is identified, parents and children, as well as receiving support from school, should be encouraged to seek a multi-disciplinary assessment and to get expert help from local mental health services. The increasing number of children being diagnosed with the disorder and the importance of getting a holistic picture of children's functioning before an accurate diagnosis can be made have led to the establishment of specialist ADHD multi-disciplinary assessment teams in some local areas. These may involve, for example, an educational psychologist, a clinical psychologist and a psychiatrist. Teachers are more than likely to be asked to contribute towards this assessment procedure. The range of their difficulties means that children with ADHD may receive support from a variety of specialist services, but effective educational intervention is crucial in helping to alleviate their difficulties.

Supporting children with ADHD in the school setting

If some estimates are correct, an average mainstream class is likely to have at least one child with ADHD so it is vital that teachers are able to recognise this and respond appropriately. The demands of schooling are likely to place significant pressures on these children and this may result in a failure to learn and isolation from their peers. Typically, these children are noisy and talkative, disruptive to others in a class, aggressive towards other children, fail to comply with instructions and are unresponsive to discipline. Children with ADHD are often blamed and punished for their behaviour. If teachers react negatively in this way children's behaviour is likely to get worse and this can lead to low self-esteem, poor school performance and even depression. It is important to remember that their behaviour is not deliberate and to avoid dismissing them as naughty. Whilst it is difficult for the teacher faced with a challenging child in a class full of children, if their needs are to be met, it is important to adopt a more positive attitude towards these children. For this, it is essential to ensure that teachers have a full understanding of the disorder. There is then a lot that teachers can do to help children with ADHD, to alleviate their difficulties and to prevent associated problems developing.

Children with ADHD exhibit a wide range of problems in the classroom setting, ranging from being disorganised to being disruptive and, as well as behaviour problems, they often have attendant academic difficulties. In order to determine children's educational needs, a thorough assessment focusing on ability, attainment and behaviour is required.

In some cases, small classes with a well-trained teacher may be required and, for more severe cases, it may be necessary to initiate the formal SEN assessment process and for special educational services or a special educational placement to be provided. However, ADHD itself is not recognised as a special educational need in the UK and this will need to be done on the basis of associated learning or emotional and behavioural difficulties. In these cases, access to appropriate provision may depend on parental choice and the availability of local provision. The needs of many children with ADHD, however, can be met within the normal mainstream classroom if teachers consider how they might be addressed and how their learning might be promoted. This may necessitate adjustment of the curriculum and changes in teaching styles to suit individual children's learning needs, as well as the use of behaviour modification and classroom management techniques, involving parents and liaison with mental health professionals.

Behaviour modification techniques

Teachers need experience and training in behaviour modification and must have appropriate expectations of children with ADHD. They should give as much positive reinforcement and immediate feedback about their behaviour to these children as possible, ignore minor misbehaviour and use sanctions effectively for more serious misdemeanours (Kazdin, 2001). If every incident of poor behaviour is corrected this not only creates a very negative situation for the child, but can also be very time consuming and exhausting for teachers. In some circumstances, it may be appropriate to apply different standards of behaviour to different individuals within a class, but where this is the case it can be helpful to enlist the backing of class members who are mature enough to understand by explaining the reason for this. It is important to make it clear that it is only a short-term arrangement to help the individual overcome his or her immediate difficulties. Children should be encouraged and their self-esteem enhanced by adopting positive practices. For example, teachers should aim to:

- reinforce positively all achievements with rewards that are tangible and appropriate;
- break down tasks into smaller steps that can easily be reinforced;
- praise desired behaviours whilst ignoring inappropriate ones;
- encourage peers to ignore inappropriate behaviour and refrain from negative comments;
- provide opportunities for pupils to share their success with others;
- express reprimands, when required, clearly and calmly and follow them with praise;
- use sanctions, such as time-out and withdrawal of privileges, when necessary;
- monitor children's behaviour without being intrusive;
- encourage children to use self-monitoring and self-report systems.

Classroom management techniques

Hyperactivity is often related to the situation; therefore, in addition to using behaviour modification techniques, teachers can do a lot to improve the classroom environment for these children. It is useful to have the strategies that are most helpful to individual students formalised into an individual education plan, and for these strategies to be adopted by all teachers who have contact with them. Classroom management strategies that help these children include aspects of structure and organisation, communication, providing a distraction-free environment, providing appropriate learning tasks and teaching self-control and problem-solving skills. Specific practices that can be adopted are detailed below.

Structure and organisation

Children with ADHD are by nature disorganised so it is essential for them to have a structured and well-organised routine in their lives. Problems often arise when children have to face an event that has not been planned for in advance. It is helpful if their personal tutor assists them in organising their daily programme. Within the classroom, teachers can help by providing a structured and well-organised routine, defining limits clearly and continually clarifying rules and consequences.

Communication

One of the main difficulties in learning for children with ADHD lies in following instructions as this can prevent them from being able to complete even simple tasks. Methods of communication are therefore important and it can be helpful for teachers to:

- use the child's name and ensure eye contact before communicating;
- give instructions in brief chunks with visual reinforcement;
- ask children to repeat instructions and to write them down in a simple sequence;
- be prepared to repeat instructions frequently.

Providing a distraction-free environment

The physical environment is important. Stress, noise and distraction should be reduced to a minimum. It can be helpful for teachers to:

- sit children at the front of the class and away from windows;
- provide a distraction-free corner or their own work station;
- encourage children to keep everything off the desk that is not needed for the task in hand;
- have a well-organised classroom with minimum movement and low noise level.

Providing appropriate learning tasks

Children with ADHD are more motivated when tasks are interesting and achievable. It can therefore be helpful for teachers to:

- set achievable targets;
- avoid large amounts of desk work and provide opportunities for purposeful movement;

- give alternative activities at intervals to break up concentration time;
- provide interesting learning tasks;
- vary the presentation of tasks, using, for example, computers, colour, etc.;
- recognise that, if the child is on medication, he or she may be more inattentive just before lunch and plan activities accordingly.

Teaching self-control, problem-solving and social skills

Children with ADHD should be given guidance on how to avoid stressful situations and how to cope with their own frustration when things go wrong. It can help to allow children individual time with a member of staff when needed and, within the classroom, to encourage children to use positive thinking techniques and reward them for waiting longer periods of time. Children can be taught to generate several possible solutions to a problem and can be encouraged to engage in co-operative learning.

Parental involvement

Frequent contact with and support for parents can help a great deal. Regular meetings in which parents are given progress reports are useful. Through effective liaison, the same behaviour management strategies can be adopted at home and in school, thus ensuring a consistent approach and making a positive outcome more likely. Discussions with parents might centre, for example, on behaviour modification, positive reinforcement, rewards and sanctions, consistency, expectations and having special time with children each day. If possible, a weekly report to parents on the quality and quantity of work accomplished should be provided and parents encouraged to have as much involvement in the planning of children's education as possible (Hornby, 2000).

Liaison with other professionals

Any educational intervention should be an integral part of the child's overall treatment plan and good communication between mental health services, parents, teachers and children is essential. It can be useful, for example, for the school to hold a regular multi-agency conference to pull together all agencies involved in order to get an overview, share information and discuss strategies. This ensures that agencies are working together rather than in opposition to each other. It is important that, where medication forms part of the treatment plan, issues about expectations and possible side effects are discussed and the responsibility for administration clarified with the mental health team and the family.

Further reading

Barkley, R. A. (1990) *Attention Deficit Hyperactivity Disorder: A Handbook for Diagnosis and Treatment*. New York: Guilford Press.

Cooper, P. and Ideus, K. (1995) Is attention deficit hyperactivity disorder a trojan horse? *Support for Learning*, 10, 1, 29–33.

Hinshaw, S. R. (1994) *Attention Deficit Disorders and Hyperactivity in Children*. Thousand Oaks, CA: Sage.

Wodrich, D. L. (1994) *Attention Deficit Hyperactivity Disorder. What Every Parent Wants to Know*. London: Paul Brooks.

References

Ahonen, T., Luotoniemi, A., Nokelainen, K., Savelius, A. and Tasola, S. (1994) Multimodal intervention in children with attention deficit hyperactivity disorder. *The European Journal of Special Needs Education*, 9, 2, 168–181.

American Psychiatric Association (1994) *Diagnostic and Statistical Manual of Mental Disorders (Fourth edition)*. Washington, DC: American Psychiatric Association.

Barkley, R. A. (1990) *Attention Deficit Hyperactivity Disorder: A Handbook for Diagnosis and Treatment*. New York: Guilford Press.

Barkley, R. A., Fischer, M., Edelbrock, C. S. and Smallish, L. (1990) The adolescent outcome of hyperactive children diagnosed by research criteria: I. An eight-year prospective follow-up study. *Journal of American Academy of Child and Adolescent Psychiatry*, 29, 546–557.

Campbell, S. B. (1987) Parent-referenced problem three-year olds: Developmental changes in symptoms. *Journal of Child Psychology and Psychiatry*, 28, 835–845.

Cooper, P. and Ideus, K. (1995) Is attention deficit hyperactivity disorder a trojan horse? *Support for Learning*, 10, 1, 29–33.

Cunningham, C. E. and Barkley, R. A. (1979) The interactions of hyperactive and normal children with their mothers during free play and structured tasks. *Child Development*, 50, 217–224.

Dalston, S. (1995) Helping Phil keep still. *Association of Teaching and Learning (ATL) Report*, 17, 5, 12–13.

Erk, R. R. (1995) The conundrum of attention deficit disorder. *Journal of Mental Health Counselling*, 17, 2, 131–145.

Feingold, B. F. (1975) Hyperkinesis and learning disabilities linked to artificial food flavours and colours. *American Journal of Nursing*, 75, 797–803.

Goldstein, S. and Goldstein, M. (1990) *Managing Attention Disorders in Children*. New York: John Wiley & Sons.

Goodman, R. and Stevenson, J. (1989) A twin study of hyperactivity: II. The aetiological role of genes, family relationships and peri-natal adversity. *Journal of Child Psychology and Psychiatry*, 30, 691–709.

Hinshaw, S. R. (1994) *Attention Deficit Disorders and Hyperactivity in Children*. Thousand Oaks, CA: Sage.

Hornby, G. (2000) *Improving Parental Involvement*. London: Cassell.

Johnston, R. B. (1991) *Attention Deficits, Learning Disabilities and Ritalin: A Practical Guide*. London: Chapman and Hall.

Kavanagh, J. F. (1994) ADD and its relationship to spoken and written language. *Topics in Language Disorders*, 14, 4, v–viii.

Kazdin, A. E. (2001) *Behaviour Modification in Applied Settings*. Belmont, CA: Wadsworth.

Lowenthal, B. (1994) Attention deficit disorders: characteristics, assessment and interventions. *European Journal of Special Needs*, 9, 1, 80–90.

Miller, R. G., Palkes, H. S. and Stewart, M. A. (1973) Hyperactive children in suburban schools. *Child Psychiatry and Human Development*, 4, 121–127.

Nolan, M. and Carr, A. (2000) Attention deficit hyperactivity disorder. In Carr, A. (ed.) *What Works with Children and Adolescents? A Critical Review of Psychological Interventions with Children, Adolescents and their Families*, 65–101. London: Routledge.

Rutter, M., Graham, P. and Yule, W. (1970) *A Neuropsychiatric Study in Childhood*. London: Heinemann.

Shelton, T. L. and Barkley, R. A. (1994) Critical issues in the assessment of attention deficit disorders in children. *Topics in Language Disorders*, 14, 4, 26–41.

Taylor, E. (1994) Syndromes of attention deficit and overactivity. In Rutter, M., Taylor, E. and Hersov, L. (eds) *Child and Adolescent Psychiatry: Modern Approaches (Third edition)*, 285–307. Oxford: Blackwell.

Taylor, E., Sandberg, S., Thorley, G. and Giles, S. (1991) *The Epidemiology of Childhood Hyperactivity*, Maudsley Monographs No. 33. Oxford: Oxford University Press.

Thomson, G. O. B., Raab, G. M., Hepburn, W. S., Hunter, R., Fulton, M. and Laxen, D. P. H. (1989) Blood lead levels and children's behaviour – results from the Edinburgh lead study. *Journal of Child Psychology and Psychiatry*, 30, 515–528.

Train, A. (1996) ADHD: Towards resolution – a personal view. *Emotional and Behavioural Difficulties*, 1, 2, Summer, 52–60.

Weiss, G. and Hechtman, L. T. (1986) *Hyperactive Children Grown Up*. New York: Guilford Press.

Wodrich, D. L. (1994) *Attention Deficit Hyperactivity Disorder. What Every Parent Wants to Know*. London: Paul Brooks.

World Health Organization (1992) *International Classification of Diseases (Tenth edition)*. Geneva: World Health Organization.

Zametkin, A. J., Nordahl, T. E., Gross, M., King, A. C., Semple, W. E., Rumsey, J., Hamburger, S. and Cohen, R. M. (1990) Cerebral glucose metabolism in adults with hyperactivity of childhood onset. *New England Journal of Medicine*, 323, 1361–1366.

5 Eating disorders

At 14 years old, Emma was pale, sullen and noticeably emaciated. She was emotionally flat and rarely smiled, despite the fact that her parents reported that she had previously had a 'bubbly' personality. She had become increasingly isolated from her peers, although she was a very popular student. Teachers and fellow students were concerned about her dramatic weight loss, but, when confronted, she denied that there was a problem. School staff had expressed concern to her parents on a number of occasions, but they had only recently sought professional help. Emma was described as one of the school's most able students.

Eating disorders are characterised by severe disturbances in eating behaviour. They are serious conditions that can be life threatening so it is essential they are recognised and treated as early as possible. For this reason, it is important that teachers have an awareness of such conditions. In addition, there is a lot that school staff can do to educate children about good eating habits and prevent the development of eating disorders. Anorexia nervosa and bulimia nervosa are the two eating disorders most likely to be encountered by teachers. There is controversy as to whether obesity should be classified as an eating disorder, but it is touched on briefly in this chapter because of its increasing incidence and its relevance to teachers.

Diagnosis

The diagnostic criteria for anorexia nervosa, as given in DSM-IV (American Psychiatric Association, 1994), include:

- the refusal to maintain minimal normal body weight;
- an intense fear of becoming fat or gaining weight;
- a distorted self-perception of body image;
- the absence of at least three menstrual cycles in females.

When considering weight loss, account must be taken of the individual's body build and his or her weight history, as well as age and height. In childhood or early adolescence, the criteria may include a failure to make expected weight gains rather than weight loss. In ICD-10 (World Health Organization, 1992), the criteria are almost the same, although there is less emphasis on body image. The attitude and obsessive thinking that are typical of individuals with anorexia are more significant than the physical symptoms, which, according to Duker and Slade (1988), should not be relied upon alone for diagnosis.

The diagnostic criteria for bulimia nervosa, as given in DSM-IV, include:

- recurrent episodes of binge eating;
- repeated attempts to lose weight;
- self-evaluation that is unduly influenced by body shape and weight.

The ICD-10 criteria (World Health Organization, 1992) for bulimia are largely the same except that there is less emphasis placed on the lack of control over eating during binges.

More recent studies suggest that obesity, on the other hand, is mainly connected with dieting and should not be considered as an eating disorder. It is not included in DSM-IV, but features in ICD-10 as a general medical condition rather than a disorder. It is diagnosed when children are 30 to 80 per cent in excess of their ideal weight.

Differential diagnosis

It is important that anorexia is distinguished from physical illness, depression, obsessive–compulsive disorder and schizophrenia (see the relevant chapters in this handbook). The desire for weight loss and the distorted body image are, however, usually distinctive. When seriously underweight, many individuals with anorexia may show signs of depression as a result of starvation and this requires reassessment once they have gained weight. Obsessive–compulsive behaviour can also be a prominent feature of anorexia and, in some cases, an additional diagnosis of obsessive–compulsive disorder may be appropriate.

The distinction between anorexia and bulimia is crucial because of the different implications for treatment. In bulimia, whilst weight loss may be substantial, it does not fall below a minimum normal weight and the pattern of bingeing and purging (self-induced vomiting or the misuse of laxatives, diuretics or enemas) is distinctive. The medical complications and associated disorders also differ. Whilst anorexia has been linked with mood disorders and obsessive–compulsive disorder, bulimia has been linked more with personality disorders and drug abuse. Individuals with anorexia tend to be superior, aloof and rigid, whereas those with bulimia tend to be guilt ridden and confused. However, many cases are not as clear cut as this might suggest, since some individuals with anorexia have bulimic symptoms and some individuals with bulimia develop anorexia.

Features

Anorexia

The main features of anorexia are:

- fear of becoming fat;
- abnormal eating behaviour;
- the need to maintain control;
- the effects of starvation.

The primary feature of anorexia is the dread of becoming fat. Individuals are convinced that their bodies are too large and they will continue to deny themselves food even when they are extremely emaciated (Steinhaussen, 1994). They pursue their aim of a thin body relentlessly and frequently deny the medical consequences of their behaviour. The self-esteem of individuals with anorexia is highly dependent on their body shape and weight.

Individuals with anorexia exhibit abnormal eating behaviour, typically eat under a thousand calories a day and deny their hunger. When the struggle to maintain this control becomes too much they may resort to rigorous exercise, overeating, self-induced vomiting, use of laxatives and other drugs, although bingeing and vomiting tend to be infrequent in adolescence. Denial is common and they will show much cunning and go to great lengths to dispose of food and avoid eating. The importance of abnormal eating behaviour as a means of maintaining control has been emphasised (e.g. Orbach, 1984). Whilst not eating means maintaining control, eating means feeling out of control. This can greatly affect other aspects of their life, such as their school performance, as individuals can only live up to expectations if they are able to maintain starvation.

The effects of starvation itself are significant since it can cause psychological, physical and biochemical disturbances. Many of the physical signs and symptoms associated with anorexia are due to these effects. The most evident of these is emaciation. Others include sensitivity to temperature change, dry skin, fine downy body hair (called lanugo) on the back, face and arms, a low heart rate, low blood pressure and constipation (Abraham and Llewellyn-Jones, 1987). Menstruation may cease and may not resume for many months or years after a return to normal body weight. Dehydration may develop and vitamin deficiency can be severe. It is not surprising, therefore, that significant general medical conditions, such as cardiovascular problems, impaired renal function, dental problems and osteoporosis, can result. When seriously underweight, many individuals show symptoms of depression, such as mood swings, social withdrawal, irritability, insomnia, and may also engage in self-destructive behaviour. Other associated symptoms, which can have implications for an individual's educational attainment, include poor self-esteem, rigid thinking, lack of initiative and lack of emotional expression.

Anorexia is far less common in boys, but, where it does occur, the main features tend to be unexplained weight loss, profound constipation, obsessional behaviour and rigid daily routines.

Bulimia

The main features of bulimia include:

- an irresistible urge to overeat, followed by self-induced vomiting;
- other forms of purging behaviour;
- a persistent overconcern with body weight and shape;
- emotional instability.

Individuals with bulimia typically exhibit a pattern of bingeing and vomiting. Bingeing is characterised by the rapid consumption of large amounts of food and a sense of lack of control over eating. Although many children and young people may consume large amounts of food in one go, those with bulimia will consume anywhere between 3,000 to 20,000 calories in one go on a regular basis, often several times a day. They tend to delight in the realisation that vomiting enables them to eat as much as they like without gaining weight. Despite this, they are either overweight or of normal weight for their height so there is often nothing in their appearance to suggest that there is a problem. Self-induced vomiting and purging, however, tend to be habit forming and can lead to serious physical complications. Individuals may be secretive about their behaviour. They often have a private place to vomit and do so at specific times. Attempts to stop them are usually met with hostility.

Individuals with bulimia make repeated attempts to lose weight through severely restricting diets, using laxatives or diuretics or by excessive exercise. It is not uncommon, for example, for them to use ten to twenty times the recommended amount of laxatives. This can be dangerous because of the fluid loss and chemical disturbance in the body and physical symptoms often include bloating, nausea, headaches and tiredness (Touyz and Beumont, 1985).

Depression, anxiety and emotional instability are common and these psychological effects can form a vicious circle, leading to a high risk of self-harm and suicide (see Chapter 9). Individuals with bulimia often have low self-esteem, a problem relating to peers and difficulties becoming independent from their parents. Bulimia is rarely seen in males, but, when it is, it may be associated with psychosexual disturbance.

Obesity

Obesity is generally characterised by excess body fat, taking into account the height and weight of the individual, but what is considered normal will also depend on cultural factors. The overriding feature, however, is that individuals eat more and more quickly. They tend to have adverse emotional reactions to diets, which can, for example, lead to irritability, preoccupation, nervousness and depression. Apart from this, they have no particular personal characteristics that are different from others, although they are often believed to be intellectually and personally inferior by parents, peers and even by some professionals.

Incidence

Although estimates vary considerably, anorexia is generally found in less than 1 per cent of the adolescent population, whilst bulimia is found in about 3 to 4 per cent (Mitchell and Carr, 2000). The exact incidence, particularly for bulimia, is unknown and may be underestimated because individuals may not come to the attention of professionals. A recent increase in both has been reported. Onset of anorexia most frequently occurs around the age of 14, with a peak between the ages of 16 and 18, and is typically connected with the transition from childhood to adolescence. It rarely begins before puberty, but there are suggestions that associated mental disturbances may be more severe when it does. Bulimia, in contrast, tends to be connected with the transition from adolescence to young adulthood, with a peak age of onset around 19. The majority of cases of both occur in females. Anorexia, for example, is estimated to be about ten times more likely in females than males (Dally and Gomez, 1990). Both appear to be far more prevalent in Western cultures and industrialised societies, where there is an abundance of food and where thinness is often equated with attractiveness.

The figures for obesity are inconsistent, but there is a general opinion that obesity is widespread. It has been reported that twice as many girls as boys are obese and that there is increasing incidence with age. In one study, for example, whilst 12 per cent of 8- to 11-year-old children were found to be overweight, only 2 to 5 per cent were found to be obese. In the same study, 11 to 17 per cent of teenagers were found to be overweight, but only 2 to 5 per cent were found to be obese (Abraham and Llewellyn-Jones, 1987). Many studies, however, are based on those seeking treatment and this may therefore only represent a small proportion of the true figure (Agras, 1987).

Causes

Eating disorders are probably due to a complex interaction of factors. Many of the same factors are implicated in both anorexia and bulimia, although it is thought unlikely they have a common organic cause. Heredity, brain functions, individual, family, as well as social and cultural factors, may be involved, and precipitating events have also been described. These are outlined below.

Heredity

There is evidence for a genetic basis for eating disorders, although less so in the case of bulimia. It is likely, for example, that there may be a genetic predisposition that is then affected by adverse environmental effects. Whilst a tendency towards obesity may be inherited, in children under 10 there may be a significant environmental component. This being the case, the need for children to learn to control eating behaviour early is vital.

Brain functions

Whilst specific cognitive deficits, such as a distorted body image, can be related to particular brain functions, it is still unclear whether these factors are organic or psychological. Malfunctioning of the hypothalamus has been implicated in anorexia, but more research is needed in this area.

Individual factors

The physical changes and individual challenges that occur in adolescence may cause difficulties that make eating disorders more likely. Some personality traits, such as compliance, perfectionism, and dependence, have been associated with anorexia. In contrast, instability and deficits in interpersonal skills and stress management appear to be common features of individuals with bulimia.

Family factors

There is evidence of conflict, disturbed communication and interaction within families of those with eating disorders. In anorexia, typically, an overprotective mother is driven into an extreme state of anxiety by her daughter's behaviour. In contrast, families of those with bulimia tend to be poorly structured and disorganised, emotionally distant and place little emphasis on independence. Weight problems, physical illness, affective disorders and alcoholism within the family may also play a part. Whilst some families may encourage children to overeat, the exact role of family factors in obesity remains unclear.

Social and cultural factors

The individual's dissatisfaction with his or her body image may be the outcome of social pressure to conform. The emphasis placed on physical attractiveness, thinness and dieting, as well as the pressure to achieve, is associated with an increased risk of eating disorders. Socio-economic factors have been implicated in the case of obesity (Thompson, 1993).

Precipitating events

In the majority of cases onset is triggered by stressful events, such as separation and loss, family disruption, physical illness and even peer rejection and academic failure. Precipitating factors may, however, include being teased by family or friends or preparing for examinations.

Diet and metabolism

Diet and physical inactivity, as well as endocrine and metabolic factors, have been implicated in obesity (Thompson, 1993). It is thought, for example, that obesity might be associated with the body's ability to store energy efficiently. Individuals may underestimate their food intake and therefore eat too much, but they are also often encouraged to do so by their family. This leads to a larger number of fat cells, which is irreversible, and they then have a tendency to store more fat. In adolescence, it is thought that individuals may fail to reduce their food intake after the growth surge, which peaks at 14. Other theories, however, suggest that obesity may be a response to stress or boredom.

Treatment

Eating disorders are serious, life-threatening conditions for which intensive specialist intervention is required. Treatment must be based on a comprehensive and detailed multidisciplinary assessment which addresses the individual's mental and physical state (Steinhaussen, 1994). The individual's motivation for change must also be considered. It is important for treatment to begin as early as possible. As well as the likelihood of medical complications, there are features of anorexia which make treatment particularly difficult. In contrast to those with bulimia, individuals tend to be very poorly motivated and have rigid patterns of thinking that can be difficult to break. Health professionals can find themselves in a difficult position as patients have the right to refuse treatment. A few specialist units and centres for the treatment of eating disorders do exist, but most individuals are likely to be treated as an outpatient in a community setting or in a general adolescent unit. Inpatient treatment is generally recommended when an individual's weight is less than 70 per cent of his or her expected body weight, although other factors may also be taken into account, such as the support available (Steinhaussen, 1994).

Multi-faceted programmes provide the most effective form of treatment for eating disorders. Whilst for anorexia, individual and family therapy and behavioural treatment have been found to be effective, Mitchell and Carr (2000), in an extensive recent review, concluded that family therapy was the treatment of choice. In the same review, both cognitive behaviour therapy and interpersonal therapy were found to be effective for bulimia, but cognitive behavioural intervention was preferred as it led to rapid and sustained improvements in symptoms and adjustment. Typically, treatments offered may include a combination of behavioural treatment, cognitive intervention, individual and family therapy and, in some cases, medication. These are outlined briefly below. The treatment for obesity differs and is discussed separately.

Behavioural treatment

With anorexia, positive reinforcement (e.g. access to recreational facilities) and negative reinforcement (e.g. bed rest) are used to motivate the individual to gain weight according to targets that are set. At the same time as they are presented with food, individuals are encouraged to discuss their feelings. In bulimia, in contrast, the focus is usually on practical measures, like not having food around, avoiding stressful situations and the development of coping strategies, as well as maintenance of weight and reducing inappropriate behaviour.

Cognitive intervention

Cognitive intervention involves identification and examination of the individual's inappropriate thoughts, beliefs and values and replacement with appropriate ones. Cognitive intervention and behavioural treatment are often combined, as in an intervention described by Hollin and Lewis (1988).

Individual therapy

Individual therapy focuses on establishing a trusting relationship with the therapist and exploring feelings, as well as making individuals aware of the effects of starvation or bingeing and purging behaviour on their general condition. With anorexia in particular, individual therapy can be a long and difficult process.

Family therapy

Family therapy usually focuses on family interactions and developing clear lines of communication. Concurrent therapy for parents and adolescents has been shown to lead to sustained weight gain and improvement in the adjustment of individuals with anorexia, particularly where there was a more recent onset (Mitchell and Carr, 2000). The few studies on the use of family therapy for bulimia also suggest positive outcomes.

Medication

Drugs called neuroleptics have been shown to reduce resistance to eating and to increase weight, but the side effects mean that their use is rarely justified. There has also been limited success using appetite stimulants and anti-depressants (Steinhaussen, 1994). Mitchell and Carr (2000), however, concluded that there is little extra benefit in using drugs.

Other forms of treatment

Whilst tube feeding is used very little nowadays, it is still advocated in resistant cases of anorexia. It can, however, have repercussions for the therapist–client relationship

(Steinhaussen, 1994). Other options include surgery, electro-convulsive therapy, hypnosis and dream work. Support might also include group therapy, self-help groups and parent support groups, which are considered to have a positive, but limited, effect.

The treatment of obesity

The treatment of obesity is important since severely obese individuals have a three times greater chance of dying prematurely than others and the benefits of weight reduction include a reduced risk of heart problems, high blood pressure and thrombosis, as well as less tiredness and back pain. The most simple and practical methods for the assessment of obesity are the measurement of skin folds and circumference tests, although other forms of assessment include soft tissue X-ray and the distorting photograph technique.

It is important, however, to recognise that a change in thinking, not just weight, is required for treatment to be effective in the long term. When Thompson (1993) reviewed the traditional forms of treatment, he reported discouraging outcomes. A combination of treatment through a dietician and supportive psychotherapy has so far been shown to be the most effective. A low-carbohydrate, low-fat, high-fibre diet is most frequently adopted because this satisfies the appetite and provides a palatable diet, with a wide choice of foods. Initial weight loss is often dramatic. The individual's motivation and a realistic target weight are the key to successful treatment. Positive reinforcement in the form of material rewards can also help sustain weight loss. The family, as well as the child, needs to change its eating habits in order to maintain any progress made, although care must be taken to avoid blaming individuals and their families. Education about healthy eating habits, the opportunity to share experiences with others and a focus on establishing a more fulfilling social life can also aid treatment. There is some evidence to suggest that those who maintain reduced body weight are those who also incorporate physical activity into their daily routine. Simple practical suggestions, such as using stairs instead of lifts and walking to school, are often useful. Whilst severe obesity can be treated by surgery and jaw wiring, this is not justified in most cases.

Course and outcome

The success of treatment for eating disorders can only be gauged after a prolonged follow-up period, but with early intervention there can be a positive outcome. About half of all patients with anorexia have a good outcome, a quarter a moderate outcome and the remaining quarter a poor outcome. About two-thirds of those with bulimia have a good to moderate outcome and the remaining third have a poor outcome (Mitchell and Carr, 2000). There may be more remissions and relapses with bulimia. A history of substance abuse and a longer duration are associated with a poorer outcome (Keel *et al.*, 1999). In both disorders some individuals recover after a single episode, whilst some suffer periods of relapse. Many maintain their weight and avoid potentially damaging eating behaviour, although they may continue to need counselling through periods of stress as these can lead to relapse. Two-thirds have normal educational careers and gain employment, but only a minority are able to maintain stable relationships. Death can occur in extreme cases of anorexia. The mortality rate is less than 5 per cent and suicide occurs in about 2 per cent of cases.

The outlook is less positive for those who are obese. One in five obese children go on to become obese adults and most regain any weight they have lost. Individuals only succeed if they are motivated to persist with treatment and are prepared to change their lifestyle. Generally, the greater the extent of the obesity the more difficult it is to lose weight permanently. Recovery also depends on age, lifestyle, medical complications and the duration.

WHAT CAN TEACHERS DO TO HELP?

Schools and teachers can do a lot by way of prevention and early identification of eating disorders, as well as providing support for pupils with a history of recognised eating disorders in the mainstream school setting.

Prevention

The increase in eating disorders and the widespread preoccupation with diet and weight among girls in both primary and secondary schools make the issue of prevention especially important for all those who work with children and adolescents, but particularly teachers (Fisher *et al.*, 1995). Both dieting and being overweight can result in a range of physical and psychological problems, yet over half of 15- to 16-year-old girls in a class are likely to be on a diet. The identification of certain risk factors in recent research has led to the belief that preventative programmes in schools could usefully be implemented. Whole-school strategies, for example, might focus on a variety of factors. A number of recent papers (Dixey, 1998) support the need for school-based prevention programmes and a wide range of strategies has been advocated. They have included, for example, a focus on raising pupils' self-esteem, education about healthy eating, as well as intervention with vulnerable pupils.

Raising pupils' self-esteem

Since the appearance of the body and self-esteem are closely related in adolescence, teachers can help by adopting practices that raise pupils' self-esteem. They can encourage children to feel good about themselves and help them to accept themselves as they are. It is important that children are not made to feel that they are failures, especially in circumstances where parents have particularly high expectations. It can sometimes be difficult for teachers, who have been successful themselves, to be sensitive to the problems that establishing a competitive atmosphere in their classroom can create for some vulnerable pupils. This emphasises the importance of providing a wide range of activities so that all individuals can find something they can excel at. The school ethos should promote the belief that individuals are valued for who they are rather than what they can do. This is discussed in more depth in the final chapter of this handbook.

Education about healthy eating

The link between eating habits in the early years and later eating disorders makes it paramount for teachers to encourage children to develop healthy eating habits. This can be incorporated into existing curriculum areas, such as health education programmes or food technology programmes already available in most schools. It is important that all pupils have access to these. Such programmes might explore the cultural and social issues associated with eating and might encourage children to resist cultural and societal pressures, as well as the traditional focus on nutrition and exercise. At the same time, schools can adopt a good role model by providing a nutritious, but interesting, diet within school meals. Other strategies, such as establishing breakfast clubs, can be used to encourage healthy eating habits, whilst opportunities to engage in a range of sporting activities and sensible exercise routines can be encouraged within PE lessons or after-school clubs. The recent introduction of the Government's Healthy Schools Initiative, which focuses on health education in its broadest sense, provides a broad framework for schools to address a wide range of health issues, of which these might form a part. The influence parents have on the healthy and unhealthy eating practices and the attitudes of their children suggests that preventative strategies adopted by schools should also include parents. They could be encouraged, for example, to be involved in healthy eating projects which focus on eating in the home as well as at school.

Discouraging prejudice

Prejudice against children who are different, whether by way of their shape and size or other factors, is learned early. Such prejudice is commonly faced by obese children, but can also be a problem for those who are overly thin. Fatness, for example, has been found to be associated in the minds of children with cheating, dirtiness, laziness, stupidity and a variety of other negative traits (Harris and Smith, 1982). This type of reaction fails to acknowledge and understand the underlying struggle involved. It can exacerbate the difficulties of these children as they may become more isolated and this may lead to depression. It is important therefore that teachers provide good role models and encourage children to accept others as they are.

Intervention with vulnerable pupils

Identification of pupils vulnerable to eating disorders enables them to be monitored and provided with appropriate support. Intervention, for example, might focus on children with low self-esteem, those who have difficulty expressing their feelings, or those who set themselves unrealistically high standards. Support and counselling can, for example, help more vulnerable pupils to cope with the normal stresses of adolescence and lessen the risk of developing eating disorders. This might be achieved through group or individual work, with the support of other professionals, such as the school nurse or the education welfare officer. Where there is concern about an individual's eating habits, but no recognised disorder as such, this should be discussed with parents. Teachers may be able to support the child through some individual work around sensible eating and nutrition, with the school nurse, for example, or, alternatively, by encouraging parents to seek help via their GP.

Early identification

Teachers have a vital role to play in the early identification of eating disorders and referral for appropriate specialist intervention. It is not uncommon for individuals with eating disorders to remain unnoticed for long periods of time, making eventual treatment more difficult. Individuals with anorexia, for example, often use a variety of excuses to avoid eating and try to disguise their weight loss by wearing baggy clothes. There is no specific clinical sign of the presence of bulimia and individuals may hide their bingeing and purging behaviour. For this reason, these individuals often come to light through a concerned friend who informs a teacher. It is vital that teachers take this information seriously and it is important that they know what to look for. There may be particular settings where signs of the weight loss or other physical symptoms characteristic of anorexia are more likely to be spotted, for example in sports or drama lessons. Sensitivity to cold may result in huddling against the radiator or wearing excessive clothing, even when the weather is mild. Slow brain functioning and loss of the ability to think logically and abstractly may be particularly noticeable in some lessons. Coupled with this is progressive academic failure. Teachers should be especially vigilant with pupils who are expected to excel. There may be a noticeable change in personality with a once popular pupil becoming increasingly isolated. In contrast, with bulimia the teacher may notice hoards of food and the effects of vomiting, such as poor teeth and lesions on the hands as a result of putting their fingers down their throat, as well as a variety of excuses to go to the toilet.

Once the disorder is discovered, concerns should be discussed first with other members of staff within the school setting, such as other teachers, the SENCO, the school nurse and the educational psychologist. The pupil is likely to deny the problem so it is important that excuses are not too readily accepted. It is vital to contact parents and encourage them to seek specialist help by referral for a medical assessment through their GP or the schools medical officer, who may then refer on to the relevant mental health services. Parents are likely to be aware that there is a problem, although they may not have confronted it directly. It is important for teachers to take a neutral stance and not to blame the young person or their parents. This sometimes requires great skill as there is a tendency to believe that something physical is wrong or to believe that the young person is just strong willed. When adolescents refuse to get help teachers can support the parents in emphasising that medical advice must be sought.

Support for those with eating disorders

Even when specialist professionals are involved there is a lot that teachers can do to help pupils with eating disorders in school. A pastoral support plan that is regularly reviewed and monitored can be helpful. This might include, for example, contingencies for reducing stress, activities that boost self-esteem and strategies for helping pupils to form new relationships. It is important for an identified member of the school staff to discuss with the doctor or therapist appropriate activities for the young person and to establish an agreement with them and their parents about what they can and cannot do. Given close liaison between school staff and the therapist, teachers can help by making statements that support what the therapist is trying to do. It is important, for example, to avoid saying anything that might encourage the pupil to diet. Cases should be monitored and reviewed regularly. Concerned friends, as well as teachers, can help with monitoring. The school nurse may have a particular role in monitoring and helping children understand the physical consequences of their behaviour. Throughout, communication between children, their parents and school staff is important.

Eating disorders often trigger strong emotions, such as revulsion, anger and frustration, and can be disturbing for others, including the professionals involved. Whilst bulimia may be perceived as over-indulgent and greedy, the determination of individuals to starve themselves in anorexia can be baffling and frustrating. Professionals, like family members, may oscillate between irritation and anxiety which can lead to an inconsistent approach. It is not unusual for professionals to be sometimes at a complete loss as to how to help these individuals. Different interpretations of behaviour can lead to tension between professionals, as well as within the family. Eating disorders therefore have the potential to greatly disturb those who are trying to help and lack of this awareness can make them ineffectual. For these reasons it is vital that teachers get support themselves and have someone with whom they can discuss their own feelings. As well as close contact with the family, teachers should seek support and advice from mental health professionals in the management of such cases.

Further reading

Crisp, A. H. (1980) *Anorexia Nervosa: Let Me Be*. London: Academic Press.

Duker, M. and Slade, R. (1988) *Anorexia Nervosa and Bulimia: How to Help*. Buckingham: Open University Press.

Palmer, R. L. (1982) *Anorexia Nervosa: A Guide to Sufferers and Families*. Harmondsworth: Penguin.

Thompson, S. B. N. (1993) *Eating Disorders: A Guide for Health Professionals*. London: Chapman and Hall.

References

Abraham, A. and Llewellyn-Jones, D. (1987) *Eating Disorders: The Facts*. Oxford: Oxford University Press.

Agras, W. S. (1987) *Eating Disorders: Management of Obesity, Bulimia and Anorexia Nervosa*. Oxford: Pergamon.

American Psychiatric Association (1994) *Diagnostic and Statistical Manual of Mental Disorders (Fourth edition)*. Washington, DC: American Psychiatric Association.

Dally, P. and Gomez, J. (1990) *Anorexia and Obesity*. London: Faber.

Dixey, R. (1998) Healthy eating in schools: Overweight and 'eating disorders': Are they connected? *Educational Review*, 50, 1, 2–35.

Duker, M. and Slade, R. (1988) *Anorexia Nervosa and Bulimia: How to Help*. Buckingham: Open University Press.

Fisher, M., Golden, N. H., Katzman, D. K. and Kreipe, R. E. (1995) Eating disorders in adolescents: A background paper. *Journal of Adolescent Health*, 16, 6, 420–437.

Harris, M. B. and Smith, S. D. (1982) Beliefs about obesity: Effects of age, ethnicity, sex and weight. *Psychological Reports*, 51, 1047–1055.

Hollin, C. and Lewis, V. (1988) Cognitive-behavioural approaches to anorexia and bulimia. In Scott, D. (ed.) *Anorexia and Bulimia Nervosa*, 108–122. London: Croom Helm.

Keel, P. K., Mitchell, J., Miller, K., Davis, T. and Crow, S. (1999) Long-term outcome of bulimia nervosa. *Archives of General Psychiatry*, 56, 63–69.

Mitchell, K. and Carr, A. (2000) Anorexia and bulimia. In Carr, A. (ed.) *What Works with Children and Adolescents? A Critical Review of Psychological Interventions with Children, Adolescents and their Families*, 231–257. London: Routledge.

Orbach, S. (1984) *Fat is a Feminist Issue 2: How to Free Yourself from Feeling Obsessive about Food*. London: Hamlyn.

Steinhaussen, H. (1994) Anorexia and bulimia nervosa. In Rutter, M., Taylor, E. and Hersov, L. (eds) *Child and Adolescent Psychiatry: Modern Approaches (Third edition)*, 425–440. Oxford: Blackwell.

Thompson, S. B. N. (1993) *Eating Disorders: A Guide for Health Professionals*. London: Chapman and Hall.

Touyz, S. W. and Beumont, P. J. V. (1985) *Eating Disorders: Prevalence and Treatment*. Sydney: Williams and Wilkins.

World Health Organization (1992) *International Classification of Diseases (Tenth edition)*. Geneva: World Health Organization.

6 Anxiety disorders

Prior to the Christmas holidays, David, a 12-year-old boy, appeared to be settling in well at secondary school. He was then off school for a period of six weeks with a serious viral infection. When he had recovered from this, he was reluctant to return to school. When pressurised to attend he developed headaches and stomachaches. His mother frequently allowed him to stay at home. His attendance then became erratic. Eventually, any attempts to encourage him to go to school were met with temper tantrums and sometimes a full-blown panic attack when he hyperventilated, began to sweat, trembled, felt dizzy and had difficulty breathing. Seeing him so distressed, his mother refused to pressurise him into going to school and he began to stay at home on most days. Despite offering David a lot of individual support, any attempts the school made to get him to attend failed.

All children experience fear, worry or anxiety as a normal part of growing up, but some children suffer anxiety or fear that is excessive and debilitating. Anxiety-related disorders are some of the most common mental health problems in children and adolescents. Despite this, study of them in children is relatively recent. They often go undiagnosed and untreated and are overlooked because these children, unlike those with some other disorders, generally pose no significant management problem at school. However, if children become anxious and withdrawn and are absent from school for prolonged periods of time they can become increasingly isolated, which can lead to their social, emotional and cognitive development becoming significantly impaired. It is important, therefore, that teachers are aware of the signs and symptoms of anxiety disorders so that they can intervene early.

Nine different types of anxiety disorder are described in DSM-IV (American Psychiatric Association, 1994). Children may be diagnosed with any one of these and some children may be diagnosed with more than one. Obsessive–compulsive disorder and post-traumatic stress disorder are also classed as anxiety disorders, but are distinct enough to warrant separate chapters in this handbook. Anxiety disorders take different forms and include conditions involving fear and panic, as well as anxiety. Fear (or phobia) is an immediate emotional reaction to danger that is characterised by an overwhelming sense of alarm and a strong urge to flee. Panic, in contrast, occurs when the physical symptoms of the alarm reaction of fear take place in the absence of any obvious threat or danger. Anxiety, on the other hand, involves feelings of apprehension and lack of control over future events that may pose a threat. It may therefore be felt even when there is no realistic danger present. Anxiety, fear and panic are discussed separately where relevant throughout this chapter.

Diagnosis

Anxiety

Some children feel anxious when away from their parents or away from home. This is called separation anxiety and it is the most common anxiety disorder in children. It is diagnosed when the intensity of children's anxiety when away from their parents is abnormal for their age and leads to substantial social incapacity, such as the refusal to go to school. The diagnostic criteria for separation anxiety, as given in DSM-IV, include three or more of the following:

- recurrent, excessive distress when separation from parents occurs or is anticipated;
- persistent, excessive worry about losing or harm befalling parents;
- persistent, excessive worry that an event will lead to separation from parents;
- persistent reluctance or refusal to go to school because of fear of separation;
- persistently and excessively fearful or reluctant to be alone or without parents;
- persistent reluctance or refusal to go to sleep without being near parents;
- repeated nightmares involving the theme of separation;
- repeated complaints of physical symptoms when separation from parents occurs or is anticipated.

Other children feel anxious for most of the time for no apparent reason. This is called generalised anxiety. The diagnostic criteria, as given in DSM-IV, include:

- excessive anxiety and worry more days than not about a number of events or activities, such as school performance;
- anxiety or worry associated with three or more of the following: being easily fatigued, difficulty concentrating, irritability, muscle tension or sleep disturbance;
- difficulty controlling the worry.

In both separation anxiety and generalised anxiety symptoms must be present for at least four weeks with onset before age 18 and must cause significant distress or impairment in social, academic or other important areas of functioning.

Phobias

Many children have mild fears, but if fear occurs at an inappropriate age, persists, is irrational or exaggerated, leads to avoidance of objects or situations and causes impairment of normal routines, it is called a phobia. Some children have an extreme and disabling fear of specific things or situations, such as animals, heights or injections, and this is referred to as specific phobia, whilst other children fear being the focus of attention, and this is referred to as social phobia. The individual fears that he or she will act in a way that will be humiliating or embarrassing. The diagnostic criteria for both phobias, as given in DSM-IV, include 'marked and persistent fear that is excessive or unreasonable'. In the case of specific phobia this is 'cued by the presence or anticipation of a specific object or situation'. In the case of social phobia it is cued by 'one or more social or performance situations in which the child is exposed to unfamiliar people or to possible scrutiny by others'. In both cases:

- exposure to the specific stimulus or the feared social situation almost invariably provokes an immediate anxiety response, which, in children, may be expressed by crying, tantrums, freezing, clinging or shrinking from the social situation;
- the individual usually recognises that the fear is excessive or unreasonable, although young children may not;
- the phobic situation is avoided or endured with intense anxiety or distress.

Panic

Panic tends to be a feature of adolescence and is not found in younger children. Whilst panic disorder is relatively rare, panic attacks themselves are quite common. Although a panic attack is not a disorder in itself, diagnostic criteria are provided in DSM-IV. It includes a discrete period of intense fear or discomfort, in which four or more of the following symptoms develop abruptly and reach a peak within ten minutes:

- palpitations, pounding heart or accelerated heart rate;
- sweating;
- trembling or shaking;
- sensations of shortness of breath;
- a feeling of choking;
- chest pain or discomfort;
- nausea or abdominal distress;
- feeling dizzy, unsteady, light-headed, or faint;
- feelings of unreality or being detached from oneself;
- fear of losing control or going crazy;
- fear of dying;
- numbness or tightening sensations;
- chills or hot flushes.

School phobia or school refusal

Some children are referred to as suffering from school phobia or school refusal, but this is not a diagnosis in itself. Whilst use of the term phobia suggests an irrational fear inherent within the child, the term school refusal suggests that these children choose not to go to school. The causes are more complex than either term suggests. Whilst it may be a manifestation of separation anxiety or a specific phobia, there can be many causes. It can, however, create more significant problems for children than other fears and phobias because of the unacceptability of school non-attendance and the fact that it tends to generate massive anxiety in parents and teachers (Blagg, 1987).

Features

Anxiety

Children with separation anxiety worry excessively that they will be separated from their parents or that their parents will come to harm or leave and not return. These children view the world generally as threatening, but the way in which they present can be quite varied. They are typically clingy. Separation from parents, or the threat of it, may result in pleading, tantrums, tears, physical symptoms, sleep problems (including recurrent nightmares) or loss of appetite. These children are often shy, timid, emotionally immature, overdependent on their parents and frequently have difficulty mixing with others. They may also be reluctant to go to school. In adolescence, separation anxiety may manifest itself more in difficulties growing up, taking responsibility and becoming independent from parents. These children's anxiety often disturbs the family and those around them more than it does themselves.

In generalised anxiety disorder, in contrast to other anxiety disorders, the anxiety is widespread and can focus on a variety of everyday, minor events. Periods of worry may be continuous or may only occur a few times a week. These children feel uptight, are unable to relax and they may show physical symptoms, such as muscle tension, headaches or nausea, irritability, lack of energy and sleep problems. Typically, they worry about the future, about past behaviour and about their own competence. They worry about minor everyday occurrences, like what to wear. They seek constant approval from adults, set themselves high standards and worry about meeting others' expectations and when they fail they become highly self-critical. They underestimate their ability to cope with situations and always expect the worst possible outcome. Whilst normal worrying can be set aside to concentrate on other things, these children have difficulty doing this.

Phobias

Children with phobias go to great lengths to avoid the feared object or situation or may face the situation with great effort and try to hide their fear. They may lack the cognitive maturity to recognise that their fear is irrational so their beliefs about the danger of the situation are likely to persist despite the evidence or efforts to reason with them. They often think that something dreadful will happen to them if they are exposed to the situation. They can be preoccupied with these worries to such an extent that this can cause severe distress and disruption to their everyday activities.

Children with social phobia may fear school, public speaking, blushing, crowds or eating and drinking in front of others. They shrink from people they don't know to the extent that this severely interferes with their social development. When in the presence of others they may blush, cling to their parents or try to hide. When encouraged into social situations, they commonly cry, freeze, have a tantrum or withdraw further. For these children speaking up in class and asking questions can produce great anxiety. They are likely to become especially anxious in the presence of authority figures and tend to avoid making eye contact.

Specific phobias are very common in childhood, with different fears peaking at different ages. The most common fear is that of animals, which peaks at the age of 2 to 4, whilst fear of the dark peaks at age 4 to 6, and fear of death or war is common in adolescence. The kinds of specific phobias that can develop in children are limitless, including fear of water, newspapers, mathematics, haircuts and bowel movements.

Panic

Some adolescents experience repetitive, severe panic attacks but have no other symptoms, whilst others begin to experience a progression of distressing symptoms and develop full panic disorder. In these cases they display recurrent unexpected attacks followed by at least one month of persistent worry about having another, constant worry about the consequences of attacks or a significant change in their behaviour that is related to them. They may begin to feel anxious for a considerable part of the time and avoid situations in which they think they might experience an attack.

School phobia or school refusal

School phobia may begin with complaints about school or reluctance to attend, but is characterised by severe difficulty in attending school, often amounting to prolonged absence. It can be accompanied by overt symptoms of anxiety, fear and panic. Typically, it involves severe emotional upset, excessive fearfulness, anxiety, anger, misery or complaints about feeling ill when anticipating going to school. Children may complain of a headache, stomachache or sore throat when about to go to school. They may display irrational behaviours, such as panicking, shaking, pleading, temper tantrums, crying, or refuse to leave the house. Pressure to go to school is often met with physical resistance. Most of these children find it difficult to leave home, but some return home when half-way to school, whilst others, once at school, run home in a state of anxiety (Kearney, 1995). However, they begin to feel better when permitted to stay at home and the absence of difficulties in the school holidays is notable. Many of these children insist that they want to go to school but cannot manage it. In adolescence the disorder is often accompanied by progressive withdrawal from peer activities and social isolation.

It is important to distinguish school phobia from truancy since measures put in place to combat truancy may have the opposite effect on those with school phobia. Typically, in contrast to children who play truant, those with school phobia do so with parents' consent and do not engage in other forms of antisocial behaviour (although this is to some extent an oversimplification). The fact that children's absence may be condoned by parents and therefore authorised by the school can mask the true problem for months or even years, making early intervention difficult and preventing access to the professional help that may be needed.

Associated disorders

Children with anxiety disorders present a complex picture because they often have more than one anxiety disorder (Bernstein and Garfinkel, 1986). About two-thirds of children with social phobia, for example, also have a specific phobia or panic disorder, whilst about 80 to 90 per cent of children with separation anxiety have another disorder, commonly generalised anxiety. School refusal is often associated with separation anxiety, although some children exhibit school refusal as a result of a specific school phobia. The exact nature of the relationship between the different anxiety disorders is unclear. It is thought, for example, that separation anxiety in childhood could be a precursor to panic disorder in later adolescence and adulthood, as about 20 per cent of adults with panic attacks were found to have had separation anxiety or school phobia as children.

These children may also have depression, typically with the anxiety preceding it. About a third of children with separation anxiety also develop a depressive disorder and around a fifth of adolescents with a social phobia have a depressive disorder (Klein, 1994). School phobia has also been associated with low self-esteem, especially in teenagers (Bernstein and Garfinkel, 1986). Evidence of eating and sleep disturbances, as well as school difficulties, is also often present. The association between anxiety and behavioural disorders remains unclear (Klein, 1994). In addition, adolescents may use alcohol or drugs as a means of reducing their anxiety.

Incidence

Significant anxiety disorders are found in 2 per cent of 10- and 11-year-old children, but the incidence of specific disorders varies with age. Mashe and Wolfe (1999) provide the incidence rates and average age of onset for specific anxiety disorders. These are presented in Table 6.1.

Separation anxiety is found more frequently in pre-school and primary school children, at which stage it is also more easily contained and managed. Specific phobias can occur at any age, but seem to peak around the ages of 10 to 13 and tend to decline with age. Social phobia and school phobia tend to develop after puberty and are rare in children under 10 years of age. School phobia peaks between the ages of 5 and 6, between 10 and 11 at the transfer to secondary school and in the early teens (Blagg, 1987). According to Philbrick and Tansey (2000), in the average comprehensive school of about a thousand pupils, one might expect to find two or three pupils at any one time experiencing anxiety that adversely affects their school attendance. School phobia can occur at any time and can have a gradual or sudden onset. Panic attacks are extremely rare in children but very common in adolescents, although panic disorder itself is relatively rare. All anxiety disorders tend to be equally present in boys and girls, although some may be slightly more common in females. Similar fears and anxieties are found in different ethnic groups at similar rates, but the way that they are expressed and their developmental course may differ.

Table 6.1 Incidence and age of onset of specific anxiety disorders in children

Disorder	*Incidence in the general population (%)*	*Average age of onset (years)*
Separation anxiety disorder	6–12	7–8
Generalised anxiety disorder	3–6	10–14
Specific phobia	2–4	7–9
Social phobia	1–3	10–14
School phobia	1–2	10–14
Panic disorder	0.6–4.7 (of adolescents)	15–19
Panic attacks	35–65 (of adolescents)	15–19

Causes

It is likely that a child inherits a predisposition to be anxious or fearful and that other family and environment factors then play a role in its expression. Once anxiety occurs, however, it tends to be self-perpetuating so that it may persist after the original stresses that caused it have disappeared. The factors which have been implicated are outlined below.

Genetics

Some individuals are genetically more prone to anxiety than others and this then manifests itself when certain psychological and social factors are present. Anxiety disorders run in families, although it is uncertain whether this is due to inheritance or the family environment. Children do not necessarily exhibit the same disorders as their parents, so it is more likely that a general disposition for anxiety is passed on and the form that the anxiety takes is likely to be determined by environmental factors.

Family factors

The capacity to deal with stress is an aspect of emotional maturity and if this process of development is slowed or stopped, as with overprotective parents, there is a greater likelihood of anxiety disorders developing. Children with school phobia, for example, tend to come from close-knit families, characterised by poor organisation and discipline and emotional over-involvement. Parents are frequently despairing, they may feel guilty or blame themselves and there may be considerable family conflict.

Individual factors

Individuals with anxiety disorders tend to be sensitive, introverted, dependent and socially and emotionally immature, but of average or above-average intelligence and ability. They have a quiet conformist personality and few friends. They have difficulty coping with everyday stresses.

Social environment

Some children may develop vulnerability due to the stressful environmental conditions associated with low socio-economic status. The wider social environment, such as the school environment, especially in an anxiety-prone child, also plays a part in its expression. Cultural factors also contribute to children's ability to cope with stress.

Life events

Anxiety disorders may be related to adverse life events, including the cumulative impact of a series of relatively minor events or a long series of stresses. In some cases, school phobia, for example, is precipitated by a death in the family. Physical illness in children or their parents may also be contributory.

Brain factors

Anxiety is associated with specific neurobiological processes. The brain system responsible is believed to be overactive in children with anxiety disorders and specific neurotransmitter systems have been implicated. Panic attacks, for example, are thought to be triggered by stimulation of specific areas of the brain that control the release of adrenalin.

The causes of school refusal

The causes of school refusal warrant special mention. Whilst, as stated earlier, the term school phobia suggests an irrational fear, there is always a very real and rational reason for refusal to attend school. Children can, however, suffer for years without the real root causes being investigated. It can be very difficult to separate out deep-seated causal factors from those that are more superficial and precipitate rather than cause the condition. It is important to recognise that it can occur for many different reasons, although it is often precipitated by a specific event, such as change of school or a period at home as a result of illness (Ruprik, 1990). Contributory factors may include the loss of a friend; dislike of school; a change of school; illness; bereavement; bullying; traumatic events within the family; difficulty making friends; fear of failure; fear of being criticised or disciplined by teachers; and unrecognised learning difficulties (Philbrick and Tansey, 2000; Ruprik, 1990). It is important to emphasise that school-related factors may be significant (King *et al.*, 1994) and these are discussed more fully in the final section of this chapter.

School refusal may form part of separation anxiety or a specific phobia and can also form part of depressive disorder. It is often related to separation anxiety and a fear of leaving home, rather than what will happen at school. On the one hand, children may fear something awful will happen to a parent and remain at home to prevent this. On the other, a parent may fear something will happen to the child or they may suffer chronic anxiety themselves and keep the child at home as a companion. The extra attention received at home often acts as a reinforcer. In other cases, it may be an excessive or irrational fear of being socially evaluated or embarrassed and children may refuse to attend school to escape these situations. In many cases it is caused by a combination of school, individual and family factors, thus making it very complex to address.

Treatment

Deciding when anxiety or fear in children is serious enough to warrant treatment is not easy. Sometimes severe disruption to normal routine occurs before parents seek help. Children with anxiety disorders tend to be shy and compliant so their difficulties can go unnoticed. However, many can be helped and early intervention can prevent the development of other problems, such as loss of friends, social and academic failure, low self-esteem and depression.

Although specific treatments vary and it is important that interventions are matched to the individual's symptoms, the main form of treatment is behavioural therapy. This typically involves exposure to the feared situation and direct confrontation of fears and anxieties. Treatments, however, also need to take into account other factors that might be contributing to the problem, such as family dynamics. A combination of approaches is usually the most effective and brief outpatient treatment is preferable (Moore and Carr, 2000). From their review of treatments, Moore and Carr concluded, for example, that a six-session family-based behaviour therapy programme was the treatment of choice for school phobia. On the other hand, for severe anxiety problems a programme of twenty-four sessions of combined individual and family-based cognitive behaviour therapy is the treatment of choice. The main treatments are outlined below.

Behaviour therapy

Behaviour therapy is the main treatment for addressing anxiety disorders and over 70 per cent of children are helped by this type of treatment (Silverman and Kurtines, 1996b). It includes gradual exposure to the feared situation while enhancing strategies for coping. Exposure may be carried out in prolonged and repeated doses called 'flooding' and is typically used in combination with response prevention. This can produce distress and has to be used carefully with children. Another technique used is systematic desensitisation, which involves teaching the child to relax and then exposing her or him to increasing levels of anxiety while he or she remains relaxed. Behavioural analysis can also be used to reveal factors that may unwittingly contribute to the behaviour. Cognitive behavioural therapy, which is also sometimes used, teaches children to understand how their thinking contributes to their anxiety symptoms and how to modify them.

Medication

A variety of medications have been used to treat the symptoms of anxiety in children and adolescents and these are often used in combination with behavioural techniques. Fluoxetine (Prozac), for example, has been shown to be particularly effective for separation anxiety and social phobia (Fairbanks *et al.*, 1997). Findings for the effectiveness of drugs in the treatment of other anxiety disorders, however, have been inconsistent (Popper, 1993). Clinicians often guard against drug use as it can be seen as an easy cure and also suggests that the problem is inherent within the child.

Family interventions

Whilst family factors may not cause anxiety disorders, they are often involved in maintaining the condition since parents have often been manipulated into a helpless, ineffectual role. Family therapy can therefore be an important part of treatment. Some parents, understandably, feel that accommodating the child's wishes is appropriate and caring, but allowing children to avoid fearful situations can be counterproductive. Parents should be encouraged to set clear boundaries, increase parental control and reduce overprotectiveness. Approaches that deal with the family context may have more long-term and lasting effects than those solely focused on the child (Silverman and Kurtines, 1996a).

Course and outcome

The outcome for children with anxiety disorders is usually good and many clear up completely, although this is more likely in milder cases, where children have experienced normal emotional development and where the anxiety is a response to a particular stress. Children who are emotionally immature and overdependent on their parents do less well, as do cases where there appears to be little apparent environmental cause. Almost all children with separation anxiety disorder recover from it, although they may go on to develop other anxiety disorders or another kind of mental disorder. Even students of college age can experience problems of this nature. On the other hand, there is evidence that severe symptoms of generalised anxiety disorder persist, often for years, and may continue into adult life. There is limited information on the long-term outcome of other anxiety disorders, such as social phobia.

For a child with a persistent pattern of school refusal the possible long-term consequences are serious as this may result in both academic difficulties and more entrenched social problems. The success rate with effective treatment is generally 70 per cent or better, but it is considerably higher when the children are younger and problems less entrenched (Blagg, 1987), making it important that teachers seek help early for pupils with these type of problems. In addition, whilst school refusal itself may be treated effectively, more fundamental emotional and social problems may persist.

WHAT CAN TEACHERS DO TO HELP?

There is a lot that schools can do by way of preventative measures to reduce anxiety-provoking situations for pupils within the school environment. Some pupils, however, will be prone to anxiety-related problems and it is important that these pupils are identified early and that they receive early intervention to prevent more intractable problems. Teachers need to recognise that, even when the main cause of the anxiety may lie elsewhere, there may be strategies that they can adopt to help alleviate these children's difficulties.

Prevention

Schools have a vital role to play in reducing children's anxiety (Ruprik, 1990), particularly since anxiety of any form can lead to distractibility and poor concentration that can have a knock-on effect for children's educational progress. Preventative school action should focus on encouraging the attendance of all pupils and making the school a welcoming, safe and secure place. Internal conflict within children, and hence anxiety, is less likely where schools are able to adapt and be flexible to their social and emotional, as well as their educational, needs. Where pupils lack social skills and find it difficult to mix with their peers or to interact with teachers appropriately, for example, this can be a significant factor in the development of anxiety and school refusal. Addressing this deficit can therefore alleviate such problems. Overall, having strategies in place to promote the personal and social development of all pupils, providing them with opportunities to discuss their personal problems with staff with whom they feel comfortable and having an effective pastoral system in place can therefore help alleviate anxiety problems.

Early identification

Early identification and intervention is the key to tackling anxiety problems, because of the vicious circle that can be instigated. There is overwhelming evidence that early intervention results in better outcomes since the treatment of anxiety disorders, school phobia in particular, can be extremely difficult if they have become entrenched. If addressed quickly, however, children often return to school and settle happily in a relatively short time (Ruprik, 1990).

Yet, identification of anxiety problems in children is often delayed. With regard to attendance, the focus in schools now tends to be on addressing unauthorised absence, commensurate with government targets, so anxiety problems may be masked by physical illness and parentally condoned absence. These children can be difficult to identify because they tend to internalise their feelings. On the other hand, they may be treated as truants and a discipline problem, rather than as children with genuine difficulties. For these reasons it is important that teachers have a knowledge of anxiety disorders, are able to spot them early and are trained to handle them sensitively (Blagg and Yule, 1984). Any child who is unhappy in school, whatever the reason, has the potential to develop anxiety problems and teachers should attempt to 'nip the problem in the bud'. They should therefore be alert to signs of extreme or long-term unhappiness in pupils. They should also be aware of pupils who internalise their feelings and those who may not confide in their family for fear of upsetting them, as they will be particularly vulnerable. Where pupils remain unhappy, they should be sensitively probed for reasons and teachers should express their concerns to parents.

Early intervention

Anxiety disorders in children can take many different forms, but school-related factors can often contribute to their development and maintenance and it is now thought that schools could do more to alleviate such problems. In most cases a combination of stresses relating to both home and school are involved though, for some children, anxiety is mainly related to particular aspects of the school situation rather than leaving home or separating from parents. A change of school or an upheaval in school, for example, is cited as one of the most common precipitating factors in school phobia. With any form of anxiety disorder, school-related factors have to be given serious consideration and, even if the root cause is not school related, the school response can be crucial in preventing more deep-seated problems in children who are anxious.

Philbrick and Tansey (2000) suggest a staged approach to pupils showing the first signs of anxiety or reluctance to attend school that can be incorporated into the school-based stages of the Special Educational Needs Code of Practice (DFE, 1994). Anxiety may be due to a variety of problems, but they suggest that good practice should include:

- contacting parents to discuss problems;
- encouraging parents to take an active role in getting their child to school;
- ensuring appropriate class placement;
- investigating concerns about bullying;
- ensuring access to an identified member of staff, who can be approached if the anxiety becomes temporarily overwhelming within school.

Most commonly, these children state that they are afraid of others and do not like being shouted at by teachers, and, on examination, some have educational difficulties that require attention (Blagg, 1987). It is important, therefore, to assess each child's individual situation and consider which interventions would be most helpful. Children whose anxiety is related to difficulties with peer relationships, for example, might benefit from a change of tutor group, whilst those with learning difficulties may benefit from one-to-one support in certain lessons.

As far as possible, when children have only recently stopped attending school or have just started to show the symptoms of anxiety within school, early attention and return to school are advisable. A behavioural approach is often successful if onset is recent and sudden, where parents are motivated and where teachers are supportive and have the flexibility to take account of individual needs (Blagg, 1987; Ruprik, 1990). An action plan, with realistic targets and time scales, which clarifies the tasks to be undertaken and those responsible for implementation, is helpful. This should be formulated in discussion with the child and the family's views taken into account. This can be done through the development of a pastoral support plan (DfEE, 1999), and might include, for example:

- detailed assessment and clarification of the problems;
- a realistic discussion amongst all those involved;
- regular contact with parents;
- planning and target setting with the child to help him or her feel more in control;
- persisting with agreed targets despite setbacks, but with contingency plans;
- alerting all who need to know of the need for vigilance following natural breaks, for example holidays or periods of illness;
- ensuring that all staff are informed about the child's difficulties;
- setting up a regular retreat for the child within school;
- circulating a progress report to raise the profile of the child within the school;
- regular formal and informal follow-up reviews of progress.

Good communication between parents, pupils and the school is central to maintaining the emotional security of any child. Parents should be involved as much as possible as they can help ascertain the root cause and help to establish the best course of action. Lack of understanding by both families and professionals can lead to defensiveness and blaming (Philbrick and Tansey, 2000). On the one hand, parents may see the school as the major cause of their child's distress and, on the other, teachers may be too quick to suggest that factors outside of the school may be responsible. This can lead to a delay in getting the child the most appropriate help. It is important for teachers to recognise the dilemma parents face because, although they may want the child to return to school, they may also find it difficult to cope with the child's distress when they are faced with this situation. Parents need to feel confident that realistic areas of concern will be dealt with, that the child's irrational fears will be handled sensitively and that practical measures will be adopted to ensure that intervention is effective (Blagg, 1987). In many cases, consultation with parents can be sufficient to re-establish the regular school attendance of anxious pupils. More complex cases, however, may require consultation, advice and direct intervention from external agencies.

Intervention with more entrenched cases

The problem of anxiety is usually not solely a school, social or a health problem and, in more difficult cases, successful management may depend on instigating a co-ordinated multi-agency response. If concerns persist or absence becomes more prolonged the pastoral head should seek to gather information from teachers, parents and the child, in order to assess the support that would be most helpful. In addition, a multi-agency assessment of the problem may be required. Where severe problems arise, they are unlikely to be amenable to quick solutions and schools should seek the advice or involvement of other agencies. Further action, for example, might involve seeking advice and support from LEA support services, a formal assessment of learning difficulties or therapeutic support and intervention from mental health services. Where families have been referred to other agencies, for more intensive treatment, the school still has a central role to play since it is essential that contributory school factors, such as bullying, are also considered. Parents of children with anxiety disorders often have difficulty negotiating with professionals and, in such cases, the education welfare officer can be called on by the school to help maintain effective home–school links. In addition, the school may need to consider more flexible approaches to adapt to the child's needs. These might include, for example, placing the child on a part-time timetable and ensuring curriculum continuity by sending work home. However, where this is the case, it is important to stress to the child and the family that this is an interim, short-term measure, rather than a long-term solution to the problem.

In the majority of cases, outpatient treatment and immediate return to school are recommended (Moore and Carr, 2000). However, with severe and chronic cases of anxiety, intensive family and individual work may be needed and, when the family situation appears to be actively maintaining the condition, inpatient treatment may be required. Dealing with the emotional conflicts that may be involved may therefore require medical intervention. In addition, where children have not attended school for some considerable length of time, alternative educational provision for a limited period may be beneficial. This may be provided, for example, within a mental health unit or through attendance at a PRU (Pupil Referral Unit) as a stepping stone to returning to school. It is important to recognise that providing home tuition for any length of time may exacerbate children's difficulties and should therefore not be offered as a long-term solution (Blagg, 1987).

In severe or prolonged cases gradual desensitisation to the anxiety-provoking situation is likely to be required. A child with school phobia returning after a long period off school, for example, can experience high anxiety. If the child is forced to attend he or she may experience a permanent setback. Treatment should progress one day at a time, at the child's pace, with small, achievable targets, but no predetermined milestones and with contingency plans in place. This can take months, but it is essential in such cases, whilst progress is important, to go no faster than the child can cope with. Ruprik (1990) emphasises the importance of remembering the following points:

- it is not the child's fault;
- go at the child's pace;
- keep the family in the picture;
- provide a safe place for the child within school;
- edge the child back into school gradually;
- provide opportunities for flexible and open learning;
- provide education when the child is not at school;
- seek medical help where required.

Further reading

Blagg, N. (1987) *School Phobia and its Treatment*. Beckenham: Croom Helm.

Philbrick, D. and Tansey, K. (2000) *School Refusal: Children who are Anxious and Reluctant to Attend School*. Tamworth: NASEN.

Ruprik, P. (1990) *The Teacher and School Phobia*. Doncaster: Apronstrings Education.

References

American Psychiatric Association (1994) *Diagnostic and Statistical Manual of Mental Disorders (Fourth edition)*. Washington, DC: American Psychiatric Association.

Bernstein, G. A. and Garfinkel, B. D. (1986) School phobia: The overlap of affective and anxiety disorders. *Journal of American Academy of Child Psychiatry*, 25, 235–241.

Blagg, N. (1987) *School Phobia and its Treatment*. Beckenham: Croom Helm.

Blagg, N. and Yule, W. (1984) The behavioural treatment of school refusal: A comparative study. *Behaviour Research and Therapy*, 22, 119–127.

Department for Education (DFE) (1994) *The Code of Practice on the Identification and Assessment of Special Educational Needs*. London: HMSO.

Department for Education and Employment (1999) *Social Inclusion: Pupil Support (Circular 10/99)*. London: DfEE.

Fairbanks, J. M., Pine, D. S., Tancer, N. K., Dummit, E. S., Kentgen, L. M., Martin, J., Asche, B. K. and Klein, R. G. (1997) Open Fluoxetine treatment of mixed anxiety disorders in children and adolescents. *Journal of Child and Adolescent Psychopharmacology*, 7, 17–29.

Kearney, C. A. (1995) School refusal behaviour. In Einsen, A. R., Kearney, C. A. and Schaefer, C. A. (eds) *Clinical Handbook of Anxiety Disorders in Children and Adolescents*, 19–52. Northvale, NJ: Jason Aronson.

King, N. J., Hamilton, D. I. and Ollendick, T. H. (1994) *Children's Phobias: A Behavioural Perspective*. Chichester: John Wiley & Sons.

Klein, R. G. (1994) Anxiety disorders. In Rutter, M., Taylor, E. and Hersov, L. (eds) *Child and Adolescent Psychiatry: Modern Approaches (Third edition)*, 285–307. Oxford: Blackwell.

Mashe, E. J. and Wolfe, D. A. (1999) *Abnormal Child Psychology*. Belmont, CA: Wadsworth.

Moore, M. and Carr, A. (2000) Anxiety disorders. In Carr, A. (ed.) *What Works with Children and Adolescents: A Critical Review of Psychological Interventions with Children, Adolescents and their Families*, 178–202. London: Routledge.

Philbrick, D. and Tansey, K. (2000) *School Refusal: Children who are Anxious and Reluctant to Attend School*. Tamworth: NASEN.

Popper, C. W. (1993) Psychopharmacologic treatment of anxiety disorders in adolescents and children. *Journal of Clinical Psychiatry*, 54, 52–63.

Ruprik, P. (1990) *The Teacher and School Phobia*. Doncaster: Apronstrings Education.

Silverman, W. K. and Kurtines, W. M. (1996a) *Anxiety and Phobic Disorders: A Pragmatic Approach*. New York: Plenum Press.

Silverman, W. K. and Kurtines, W. M. (1996b) Transfer of control: A psychosocial intervention model for internalising disorders in youth. In Hibbs, E. D. and Jensen, P. S. (eds) *Psychosocial Treatments for Child and Adolescent Disorders: Empirically Based Strategies for Clinical Practice*, 63–81. Washington, DC: American Psychological Association.

7 Substance abuse

Peter lived alone with his mother, who was an alcoholic and who was rarely available to help and support him. He initially tried glue sniffing when he was 11 years old with a group of friends. They eventually stopped, but he continued and started to glue sniff on his own. He liked the pleasant sensation and used glue sniffing to avoid difficult situations at home. As he got older, he frequently became intoxicated and rarely went to school. When he did attend he was often in conflict with teachers because the standard of his work had deteriorated. He sniffed more and more often, using increasing amounts of glue and eventually became addicted. His life deteriorated and a negative spiral set in which, without help, he found it impossible to get out of.

Substance abuse is an increasing cause for concern for the public and society as a whole. The government has recently introduced a strategy for dealing with the drug situation in the UK and preventative work with young people forms a key element of this (Parliament. House of Commons, 1998). Whilst substance abuse and dependence are considered mental health disorders themselves, there is also a strong association between substance abuse and other mental health problems, such that one may lead to the other. Substance abuse can have long-term negative effects on a young person's social, mental and physical well-being and can also lead to a cycle of negative effects within generations. It is important therefore that all professionals, including teachers, working directly with young people are able to identify those affected and are able to help them access appropriate treatment. It is vital that teachers are aware of the causes and effects of substance abuse and of what they can do to help.

Definition

The dividing line between drug use and misuse is a blurred one. Different parameters, such as the extent of harm to the individual or society and the extent of drug-related problems, have been used to try to make a distinction, but there is still a lot of debate about this. The term 'drug use' usually refers to experimentation and 'misuse' is typically used to describe use that is harmful (Williams *et al.*, 1996). Two substance use disorders are defined in DSM-IV (American Psychiatric Association, 1994), substance abuse and substance dependence.

The criteria for substance abuse include recurrent substance use:

- resulting in a failure to fulfil major role obligations at school, work or home;
- in situations in which it is physically hazardous;
- resulting in recurrent substance-related legal problems;
- despite persistent or recurrent social or interpersonal problems caused or exacerbated by the effects of the substance.

The criteria for substance dependence include at least three of the following:

- a need for markedly increased amounts of the substance or a markedly diminished effect with the same amount of substance (i.e. tolerance);
- characteristic withdrawal symptoms for the substance or the same substance being taken to prevent withdrawal symptoms;
- taking the substance in larger amounts or over a longer period than was intended;
- a persistent desire or unsuccessful efforts to cut down or control use;
- a great deal of time spent on obtaining, using or recovering from the substance;
- important social, school or recreational activities are abandoned or reduced;
- the substance use is continued despite persistent or recurrent physical or psychological problems that are likely to have been caused or exacerbated by it.

The criteria, however, have been criticised for not taking account of the variety of substance use typical in society and it has been suggested that a continuum of problem severity from social use to abuse and dependence might be more appropriate (Gilvarry, 2000).

Features

Substance abuse

Substance abuse is characterised by recurrent and significant adverse consequences. For adolescents these may include failure to attend school or to perform well at school, social and interpersonal problems, such as verbal or physical fights, getting into trouble with the police in the community and sometimes engaging in physically hazardous activities. Substance abusers may repeatedly be intoxicated or have other substance-related symptoms. They may, for example, be repeatedly absent from school or fail to perform well at school because of recurrent hangovers. They might also be excluded from school for fighting or other forms of antisocial behaviour. Since substance abuse occurs most frequently in individuals who have only recently started taking a substance, it is more common in adolescents than dependency.

Substance dependence

Substance dependence is usually characterised by a strong drive or craving for the substance. A key element, however, is the individual's failure to abstain despite evidence of the problems it is causing. Typically, a great amount of time is spent obtaining, using or recovering from the substance. In some cases, all of the individual's daily activities may revolve around his or her use and important social, school or recreational activities may be abandoned. Youngsters may initially believe that they have control over their drug use but when it becomes habitual there may be strong feelings of being unable to control the frequency of use. Repeated use results in tolerance, withdrawal and compulsive drug-taking behaviour.

Tolerance refers to the need for increased amounts of the substance to achieve intoxication or to achieve the desired effect or a markedly diminished effect with continued use of the same amount of substance. The degree to which tolerance develops varies with different substances. Physically high blood levels coupled with little evidence of intoxication indicate that tolerance is likely. It has, however, to be distinguished from individual variations in responses.

Withdrawal results in cognitive and physical changes when the blood or tissue concentrations of a substance decline in an individual who has maintained prolonged heavy use of a substance, which is then taken to avoid unpleasant withdrawal symptoms. Typically, the substance is taken soon after waking and throughout the day. Withdrawal symptoms vary greatly with different types of substances.

Associated disorders

There is overwhelming evidence for the association of substance use disorders with other mental health problems. With alcohol dependence, for example, it is rare for young people not to have another disorder (Clark *et al.*, 1997). About a third of those with mental health problems have a substance use disorder, which is mainly alcohol related, and up to half of those with a drug problem have another mental health disorder (Regier *et al.*, 1990). Depression and anxiety disorders are common and conduct disorder and ADHD also have a high association with substance use disorders (Wittchen *et al.*, 1998). In the majority of cases it is thought that other disorders usually precede substance abuse. The recent rise in young suicides has also been related to an increase in substance use, with over 50 per cent showing evidence of this.

Incidence

Whilst many young people may experiment with drugs, relatively few develop problems associated with their use. The proportion of those who experiment and become dependent or abuse drugs and which young people are more likely to do so are unknown. Overall, the rate of alcohol and tobacco use is high, and there are high rates of experimentation with other drugs, such as solvents, cannabis and, more recently, hallucinogens, but low rates of heroin and cocaine use, that is less than 1 per cent (Farrell and Taylor, 1994). In one study, for example, almost all 17-year-olds had drunk alcohol, 36 per cent had smoked cigarettes and 42 per cent had used illicit drugs, mainly cannabis (Miller and Plant, 1996). The UK has one of the highest rates of alcohol consumption among young people. The rates of drug use, however, vary with availability and popularity. In the USA and UK drug use has been increasing over the last ten years. There is, for example, evidence of a rise in drug use in the mid-1990s and evidence that a significant number of young people were experimenting earlier with a variety of drugs (Measham *et al.*, 1998). The importance of availability, acceptability and popularity of drugs was also emphasised.

Of all young people that use drugs, however, only a small number will meet the criteria for substance use disorders. Nevertheless, in the general population, there are significant incidence rates for these disorders. In a community sample of 15- to 17-year-old young people, for example, lifetime drug dependence and abuse rates were found to be 3 to 10 per cent, whilst the rate for alcohol dependence or abuse was found to be 5 to 32 per cent (Reinherz *et al.*, 1993). A peak incidence has been reported at 15 to 19 years of age and early initiation found to be associated with the likelihood of dependence (Nelson and Wittchen, 1998).

Effects

The pleasant emotional state or elation that substance use creates, at least initially, motivates the user in many cases. However, it is also often associated with intense negative moods, depression and anxiety, and a vicious circle can develop. There can be detrimental social and financial consequences, as well as adverse physiological effects.

Physiological effects

The physiological effects of drug abuse include intoxication, tolerance, withdrawal and medical complications. During intoxication impairment of concentration, reasoning and judgement are common and, in some cases, long-term use can lead to impaired cognitive functioning, which is also likely to lead to a decline in school performance. A range of associated health problems, such as hepatitis C, which causes liver damage, may bring these young people into contact with health services. They are also at an increased risk, either directly or indirectly, of sexually transmitted diseases and HIV. In addition, all substance use is associated with an increased risk of death. For individuals who inject heroin, for example, the risk of death is thirty times higher than the general population, whilst for those who use other substances there is a smaller increased risk. Particular issues arise with specific drugs, the availability of which will also differ in different parts of the country. A brief account of the effects of some of the drugs commonly available to teenagers is provided below.

Drug	*Effects*
Alcohol	Alcohol is a depressant. Small amounts make people relaxed and talkative, whilst large amounts result in slurred speech, light-headedness, difficulty with co-ordination and even unconsciousness. Heavy consumption is associated with liver, gastrointestinal, neurological and endocrine problems, as well as malnutrition. Associated accidents, such as road traffic accidents, can prove fatal. Death can also occur through an overdose or choking on vomit. Adolescents, whilst unlikely to be dependent, may experience withdrawal symptoms that require medical management.
Tobacco	Smoking increases the blood pressure and pulse rate and lowers the appetite. People find it both relaxing and stimulating, although first-time users often feel sick and dizzy. People become regular users quickly and become dependent. Long-term effects include heart disease, blood clots, lung cancer, strokes, bad circulation and cancer of the throat and mouth. Withdrawal symptoms include headaches, irritability and depression.
Cannabis	Cannabis is the most commonly used illicit drug. The effects vary with the situation, amount used and mood of the user. Effects include

relaxation, an increased sense of well-being, sleepiness, spontaneous laughter, a distorted sense of time and short-term memory loss. It has an immediate effect of impairment of co-ordination and residual effects may last for some days. In the long term it has been associated with bronchitis and cancer. Mild dependence can be experienced and high doses can lead to anxiety and paranoia.

Solvents — Solvent abuse is common in young people, since solvents are cheap and readily available. Solvents include adhesives, typewriter correcting fluids and thinners, butane gas, lighter fuel, fire extinguishers and other aerosols. Glue is usually inhaled from a plastic bag, whilst lighter fuel may be directly sprayed on to the back of the throat, often resulting in breathing problems. Whilst it is usual to get a pleasurable reaction initially and a feeling of light-headedness, lack of co-ordination, confusion and hallucinations may follow. It can make people unconscious or even kill them the first time it is tried. Death may occur through breathing problems or accidental falls. The physical complications associated with solvent abuse are usually reversible, but there is uncertainty about the long-term effects on the brain.

Tranquillisers — Tranquillisers are readily available in many homes and are often taken in association with alcohol use. Their use is characterised by bingeing or the regular taking of large quantities. They calm people down and make them feel drowsy. They are frequently injected and this can lead to physical complications. Dependence, however, tends to be a problem with adults but is unusual among young people.

Heroin-like drugs — There is a wide range of heroin-like drugs. Heroin may be smoked, injected or snorted. It makes people feel drowsy, warm and content. Effects begin quickly and can last several hours. First-time users tend to feel sick and regular use results in higher tolerance. An overdose can be fatal and if injected there is a risk of infection. People can become dependent very quickly and withdrawal symptoms include restlessness, irritability, increased bowel activity, abdominal pain, yawning, sneezing, nausea and vomiting.

LSD or acid — Lysergic acid diethylamide is usually taken in tablet form and has a very powerful effect on how people see and hear things. Heightened perceptions, rapid changes in mood, as well as delusions and hallucinations, are common. The experience can be frightening and disturbing. Heavy use can result in psychotic illness.

Magic mushrooms — Magic mushrooms can make people see and hear things more vividly or even see and hear things that are not there. Users may feel sick or get stomach pains. Hallucinations, distorted perceptions, euphoria and laughter are common, but bad experiences can occur. The biggest risk is eating a poisonous variety by mistake as it can be fatal even in small amounts.

Cocaine — Cocaine is a white powder that is usually snorted, but can be injected. Effects include a sense of euphoria and increased energy, but tiredness or depression may follow. Large doses are dangerous as they can cause a toxic psychosis or even death from heart or respiratory failure.

	Prolonged use can lead to weight loss, paranoia, nasal damage and heart trouble. The sharing of needles can result in HIV or AIDS.
Amphetamines	Amphetamines are stimulants that produce feelings of being alert and increased energy, but can also make people feel more anxious, followed by depression and lethargy. Once addicted, it is very difficult to break the habit. They suppress the need for sleep and food and prolonged use can reduce resistance to illness and lead to physical and psychological damage.
Ecstasy	Ecstasy comes in tablet form. It enhances the emotions and is used to increase energy and feelings of exhilaration, but can also lead to confusion and disorientation. Sudden death has been known, especially if the person is dehydrated and overheated. It is much more dangerous when sold as a mixture with other substances, as is increasingly more common.

Social effects

Poor relationships are common in those who are involved in substance abuse. Conflict within the family is typical and relationships with teachers and peers at school are often poor. This can be the result of a decline in performance or because of associated antisocial behaviour. School drop-out and truancy are common. Youngsters frequently lose contact with friends who do not abuse drugs because of the culture they are drawn into. It can become a solitary occupation, so they become increasingly isolated. Drug-related antisocial behaviour is also likely to bring them into contact with the police. These youngsters require many resources and the overall cost to health, education, youth justice and welfare services is great.

Causes

Anyone can fall into a substance misuse habit. Many factors are associated with misuse and awareness of the complex mixture of influences on young people is essential if the problem is to be tackled effectively. There is little evidence of the relative importance of these factors and different factors are likely to be more relevant at different developmental stages and different stages of misuse. This means that there are no universal causes and individual cases have to be assessed separately. Experimentation may make youngsters want to try it again, or it may make them feel good or help them face a difficulty. They may be unhappy, stressed or lonely, or they may simply become engaged in it through spending increasing amounts of time with others who misuse substances so that it becomes part of their social life. However, whilst experimentation appears to be related to cultural and peer factors and is so widespread that it can be considered a normal part of adolescent risk-taking behaviour, substance abuse tends to occur in young people who are vulnerable. The earlier children start to use substances the greater the risk of developing problems and this is an important factor to consider in prevention. Many factors are thought to increase the risk of substance abuse. They include genetic factors, neurological factors, as well as a wide range of individual, family and environment influences. These are outlined briefly here.

Genetic factors

A tentative link has been established between genetics and drug problems in young people (Rutter *et al.*, 1999). Whilst a genetic influence of around 40 or 50 per cent has been suggested, this is little understood as yet and environmental influences are thought to be more important (Farrell and Taylor, 1994).

Neurological factors

Substance use results in a feeling of elation and is therefore rewarding. It is probable that this is associated with certain areas of the brain that generate an enhanced reward effect (Farrell and Taylor, 1994). Some believe this motivational effect is a major determinant of drug use.

Family factors

A large range of family factors, including poor monitoring and management of behaviour, low parental educational aspirations, family conflict and poor parent–child interactions, have been implicated in substance abuse (Brook *et al.*, 1986). The importance of parental substance abuse and criminality has also been emphasised. Children of alcoholics, for example, have been shown to be at greater risk.

Individual factors

A wide range of individual factors have also been implicated in substance abuse. Children with mental health disorders, such as conduct disorder, are at greater risk of developing substance use disorders. Children with behavioural problems, academic failure and a low commitment to school, as well as those who experience early peer rejection, are at greater risk (Gilvarry, 2000). Affiliations with like-minded peers, and tolerance and acceptance of drug use, are also influential (Williams *et al.*, 1996). In addition, a range of personality factors, such as aggression, a difficult temperament, rebelliousness, impulsiveness, mood disturbances and interpersonal difficulties, may also play a part. On the other hand, individual protective factors include a positive temperament, intellectual ability, a supportive family environment, a caring relationship with at least one adult and an external support system with pro-social values.

Environmental factors

The attitude and tolerance of the local community is a powerful factor, as is also peer pressure, which plays a large part in initial substance use and its maintenance. Other environmental factors, including crime, social deprivation, lack of community support and the availability of drugs, may also be involved (Gilvarry, 2000).

Treatment

Individuals with substance abuse disorder often have complex problems and any treatment offered needs to be based on an adequate assessment of all their needs. This is particularly so where other mental health disorders may be present because of the increased risks associated with these cases, including suicide. This might include, for example, an assessment of physical, social and emotional and mental health functioning, school attainments, peer relationships and parental and family history, as well as the substance use itself. Reports from those with whom the young person has contact, such as teachers, will therefore be necessary.

It is important for a multi-faceted treatment plan to be adopted. Where substance abuse and behavioural difficulties are combined it is important to intervene early to prevent later delinquency, misuse and dependency. Programmes may consist of outpatient, day or inpatient treatment depending on the severity of the problem, the existence of other mental health problems, whether the young person has family and social support and their history of response to treatment. Treatment programmes in the UK, however, have been criticised for being fragmentary. Addiction programmes, for example, may not address other mental health disorders and mental health services are reluctant to be involved in substance use (Williams *et al.*, 1996). Treatment for both needs to be concomitant and a collaborative approach from all the agencies involved should be adopted. There is no universally effective treatment since the young people involved in substance abuse and dependency are a very heterogeneous group, so a multi-systemic approach is likely to be the most effective (Cormack and Carr, 2000). Family intervention, multi-systemic approaches and medication are outlined below.

Family intervention

It is important to engage families in treatment and the superiority of family therapy approaches compared with individual interventions has been reported (Cormack and Carr, 2000). These have focused on boundary setting, improving communication, education, identification of parents' problems and improving family functioning.

Multi-systemic approaches

Multi-systemic approaches that seek to address the multiple determinants of substance abuse, such as family, peer and individual factors, as well as school and community factors, have been described as promising for adolescents with a range of problems (Cormack and Carr, 2000). Where deviant peer group membership is maintaining misuse, for example, alternative peer group activities should be arranged. Where school-based problems are evident, school-focused interventions should be offered. Interventions in the school setting are discussed more fully in the final section of this chapter.

Medication

Whilst several drugs have been used for the rehabilitation of individuals with substance dependence, such as the use of naltrexone for alcohol dependence, their use, especially with adolescents, remains controversial and medication alone is generally considered ineffective (Kaminer, 1994). The severity of associated depression or anxiety may, however, require medication, although the effects are limited to these symptoms. Care must be taken with any medication because of the likelihood of abuse.

Course and outcome

The earlier children start to engage in substance use the more likely they are to develop persistent substance use disorders. An early age of onset is also associated with greater intensity of drug abuse and a worse prognosis in adulthood. The outcome, however, may depend on cumulative use and be substance specific. Negative consequences in early adulthood include poor social functioning, as well as physical and psychological disturbance. Substance abuse has been linked to later delinquency, unemployment, divorce and abortion.

Treatment is better than no treatment, but relapse rates in adolescents are high (up to 85 per cent), mainly in the initial months, and social factors are the most influential in this (Catalano *et al.*, 1991). Drop-out rates are also high (about 40 per cent) and it is felt that more could be done to encourage engagement (Cornwall and Blood, 1998). Generally, the longer the individual is in treatment the more positive the outcome is likely to be. In one study, with inpatient treatment, a third maintained abstinence after six months and a quarter improved (Brown *et al.*, 1990). Regardless of the treatment approach a worse prognosis is likely where substance abuse is severe, where there is a high frequency of use, where there are associated mental health problems and where there are school and legal difficulties (Shoemaker and Sherry, 1991). It is important that attention is focused on young people with more than one disorder because, as well as absorbing a vast amount of services, they have the worst outcome and an increased risk of suicide, attempted suicide and self-harm.

WHAT CAN TEACHERS DO TO HELP?

Schools can be an important focus for prevention of substance use disorders. It is inevitable, in their role as educators, that teachers have a significant role to play in the prevention of substance abuse in children and young people. The way that teachers respond to incidents of substance use can give an important message to other pupils as well as those directly involved. They are also ideally placed to direct young people and parents to sources of appropriate help.

The DFE (1995) provides guidance on drug prevention within schools. Prevention may focus on a number of areas within the school, including:

- school ethos;
- developing a whole-school policy on substance abuse;
- dealing with incidents and suspicions of substance misuse;
- drug education within the curriculum;
- identifying vulnerable children and families.

School ethos

The climate created by teachers and pupils within the school can be important in the message that it conveys to children. It is important that teachers communicate that they will not tolerate the use of drugs on school premises, but at the same time they are sensitive to the needs of pupils in difficulty. Sometimes this can be a difficult balance.

Teachers also need to be vigilant to the possibility that the school may be used as a market for the sale of substances and to alert senior management should they suspect this to be the case. In addition, their responsibility as role models for pupils of an impressionable age must be taken seriously. Their own approach to drugs and their own lifestyle therefore also needs careful consideration.

Developing a whole-school policy on substance abuse

Teachers need to be guided by a whole-school policy on substance abuse of which all those involved with the school, such as teachers, ancillary staff, pupils and parents, are aware so that it is applied consistently. The Standing Conference on Drug Abuse (1999) provides key criteria for the development of an effective drug policy, which include:

- having a trained member of staff to co-ordinate drug education, action and responses;
- involvement of key people, including staff, pupils, parents, carers, school support staff and ground staff;
- obtaining support and advice on policy development, education programmes and management of incidents from external organisations;
- liaison with other local schools and gaining practical support from the LEA.

The Standing Conference on Drug Abuse (1999) also outlines the key components of an effective policy. They recommend that:

- drug education and drug incident management should operate in tandem with a supportive school ethos;
- young people are empowered to make informed choices;
- sanctions used for drug-related incidents are in line with other discipline codes within the school;
- pupils know the drug policy and have a role in its formulation;
- outside support is integrated with the staff role in addressing drug issues;
- policies are systematically monitored, evaluated and reviewed;
- opportunities are provided for parents, staff and pupils to give feedback on the working of the policy.

Dealing with incidents and suspicions of substance misuse

All school staff have a role in responding to incidents of substance misuse and relevant training is essential (Standing Conference on Drug Abuse, 1999). It is important for teachers to bear in mind the possibility of substance abuse when encountering a young person with difficulties. If they suspect drug or solvent abuse it is important that they follow school procedures, as laid out in the school policy, as well as informing parents and directing them towards appropriate help. The DFE (1995) provides a detailed list of signs for teachers to be alert for in groups of children and individuals, as well as objects that might indicate substance misuse. For individuals, these include, for example:

- sudden changes in mood or behaviour;
- irritability or aggression;
- poor attendance;
- decline in school performance;
- lack of interest in physical appearance;
- lack of appetite;
- loss of interest in activities or friends;
- stealing money or goods;
- drowsiness or excessive tiredness;
- the smell of solvents or alcohol.

Within groups, exchange of money in suspicious circumstances, regular absence on certain days and avoiding supervised areas may be an indication, whilst suspicious objects might include, for example, metal tins, syringes and needles, plastic bags, cigarette papers and lighters.

The Standing Conference on Drug Abuse (1999) offers guidance on managing drug-related incidents in schools and, in summary, suggests that:

- management of drug-related incidents should normally be co-ordinated through the school drugs co-ordinator who should be named in the drug policy;
- it is the schools' responsibility to ensure the health, care and well-being of young people in their charge;
- it is not appropriate for schools to take disciplinary action harsher than that which would be imposed by law;
- schools should carefully assess the needs of any young person involved in a drug-related incident;
- it is useful for schools to develop a proactive relationship with their local media;
- schools should develop common responses to drug-related incidents within their local area;
- school staff must call for medical help if they are in any doubt about how to proceed.

All incidents of substance use in school should be taken seriously and teachers, as well as parents and other professionals, need to be prepared to intervene early. It is important to be aware of the distinction between experimentation and drug abuse or dependence when dealing with any incident. Whilst parents should always be informed and the full circumstances surrounding an incident explored, a one-off incident by an otherwise apparently healthy individual is likely to warrant a different response to an incident that reveals more long-term and serious drug abuse or underlying difficulties. In addition, the action taken will depend on the circumstances surrounding the incident. From a safety point of view, young people who are intoxicated should not be allowed to remain on school premises since they may be a danger to themselves and others. Parents should be informed immediately and asked to collect the pupil. They should, however, be allowed to return to school the next day. Where this occurs on more than one occasion it may be helpful to ask parents into school to discuss the problem and for young people to receive more individualised educational programmes focusing on the effects of drugs. Excluded pupils are more vulnerable to further drug misuse and other illegal activity, therefore this sanction should only be used as a last resort (Standing Conference on Drug Abuse, 1999).

Schools need to develop a range of responses to address the variety of possible drug incidents and their underlying causes (Standing Conference on Drug Abuse, 1999). The aim of all interventions should be to promote pupils' understanding and minimise harm. If drug abuse is a regular occurrence there are clearly underlying problems and it may help to provide the young person with access to counselling, for example, by directing them to youth counselling services. This will, however, only be beneficial if the young person is willing to engage in this process and this should not be used as a sanction. Where pupils' difficulties are more serious or widespread, especially if the pupil appears unhappy or depressed, a full assessment of these difficulties may be warranted. This might involve, for example, instigating further assessment within school, as well as by other outside agencies, such as the educational psychologist or the education welfare officer attached to the school, who may be able to provide deeper insight into the pupil's home circumstances. This should be discussed with parents. Young people may require more specialist help, such as access to a specialist centre dealing with addiction or the local mental health services. It is important therefore for teachers to be aware of local services that may be available since the best way to help is often by encouraging pupils and their parents to seek specialist intervention.

Drug education within the curriculum

Information and support should begin in primary school and should involve parents or carers (Standing Conference on Drug Abuse, 1999). There is some evidence that very young children are being introduced to solvent abuse and this supports the need for any programmes to be adopted at an early age. In England and Wales, certain aspects of drug education are statutory requirements as part of the National Curriculum science order (DFE, 1995). This states, for example, that at Key Stage 1 children should be taught about the role of drugs as medicines and that at Key Stage 2 children should be taught about the harmful effects of tobacco, alcohol and other drugs.

Drug education is more effective when integrated into a programme of health education that spans all four key stages (DFE, 1995) and one that actively promotes healthy lifestyles (Standing Conference on Drug Abuse, 1999). This can be provided within science classes or as part of a personal, social and health education (PSHE) programme. This may, for example, form part of the Healthy Schools Scheme recently introduced by the government. A comprehensive programme will present accurate information that is relevant to children's developmental age and, in older age groups, provide opportunities for discussion, decision making and affirmation of feelings, attitudes and values towards drugs. It involves sensitive teaching that is matched to the needs and concerns of the particular pupils within a class (DFE, 1995).

However, overall, the evidence for the effectiveness of educational programmes in schools is limited (White and Pitts, 1998). They frequently involve short interventions and lack the follow-up required for them to be effective. The most effective programmes include both focused and generic approaches, intense intervention with booster sessions and involve interactive strategies (Botvin *et al.*, 1995). However, since children become involved in substance use for a variety of reasons, universal programmes can only have a limited impact. Programmes that involve parents/carers, as well as children, may be more promising. Group work should be undertaken with caution since this can lead to increased drug use in vulnerable children through association with deviant peers. With adolescents, insistence on abstinence as compared with a harm reduction strategy is a contentious issue. Whilst harm reduction should not be the ultimate aim, for some young people a focus on harm reduction, at least in the first instance, may be more realistic (Bukstein *et al.*, 1997).

Identifying vulnerable children and families

Since universal programmes tend to be ineffective at reducing substance abuse and only demonstrate limited, short-term gains, programmes may be more fruitfully targeted at children and families at high risk (Gilvarry, 2000). The most vulnerable groups should be identified for appropriate early intervention. Identification of the causes of substance misuse can help inform the planning of interventions that are consistent and constructive (Standing Conference on Drug Abuse, 1999). The Standing Conference provides examples of risk factors together with possible school actions that might be taken to address them. Children with family problems, behaviour problems and other mental health problems are at particular risk, as are also those who are looked after by the local authority, those who play truant from school and those with parents who have drug problems. Teachers therefore need the training and knowledge to identify early signs of distress so that appropriate help may be given. Vulnerable groups may be targeted through initiatives that focus on social inclusion and disaffection, such as the Sure Start programme, which focuses on very young children in socially disadvantaged areas.

More and more children are born into drug-using families and it is important for teachers to be aware of this and to be able to identify and help these children and their parents in order to break the cycle. Such children are often neglected and unloved because their parents are not able to fulfil a normal parenting role. Teachers are more likely to become aware of drug-dependent parents through their children since parents may be worried that their children may be taken away and can therefore be reluctant to open up to teachers. Children may be embarrassed and lie to cover up. They may become withdrawn. If there are younger children, they may take on a parenting role themselves. Disturbed behaviour in class combined with evidence of neglect could be the result of drug use at home. Children are likely to be significantly affected. They may be reluctant to take other children home and may pretend to be like their peers in order to cover up. This, together with an erratic home situation, is likely to cause considerable tension. Teachers can help support such children by offering a 'listening' ear, but they also need to assess whether the home situation is threatening the well-being of the child. If they are concerned about the child's welfare they should discuss this with social services and, if relevant, initiate child protection procedures. Teachers should not let parents take their child if they are intoxicated, but they should ensure that the child gets home safely. In some cases, it may be necessary to call the social services duty officer and ask him or her to take the child instead. It is helpful if scenarios of this nature have been considered before teachers encounter them, for example in an INSET session devoted to drug use. In addition, boundaries of what is and what is not acceptable should be set out, as far as possible, in the school policy so that teachers have clear guidelines.

Further reading

Department for Education (1995) *Drug Prevention and Schools (Circular 4/95)*. London: DFE.

Gilvarry, E. (2000) Substance abuse in young people. *Journal of Child Psychology and Psychiatry*, 41, 1, 55–80.

Kaminer, Y. (1994) *Understanding and Treating Adolescent Substance Abuse*. New York: Plenum Press.

Standing Conference on Drug Abuse (1999) *Managing and Making Policy for Drug-related Incidents in Schools*. London: Standing Conference on Drug Abuse.

References

American Psychiatric Association (1994) *Diagnostic and Statistical Manual of Mental Disorders (Fourth edition)*. Washington, DC: American Psychiatric Association.

Botvin, G., Baker, E., Dusenbury, L., Botvin, E. and Diaz, T. (1995) Long-term follow-up results of a randomised drug abuse prevention trial in a white middle class population. *Journal of the American Medical Association*, April 12, 273, 1106–1112.

Brook, J. S., Goodman, A. S., Whiteman, M. and Cohen, P. (1986) Some models and mechanisms for explaining the impact of maternal and adolescent characteristics on adolescent stage drug use. *Developmental Psychology*, 22, 460–467.

Brown, S. A., Mott, M. A. and Myers, M. A. (1990) Adolescent alcohol and drug treatment outcome. In Watson, R. R. (ed.) *Drug and Alcohol Abuse Prevention*, 373–403. Totawa, NJ: Humana Press.

Bukstein, O. and the Work Group on Quality Issues (1997) Practice parameters for the assessment and treatment of children and adolescents with substance use disorders. *Journal of American Academy of Child and Adolescent Psychiatry*, 36, (supplement), 140S–156S.

Catalano, R. F., Hawkins, J. D., Wells, E. A., Miller, J. and Brewer, D. (1991) Evaluation of the effectiveness of adolescent drug abuse treatment, assessment of risks of relapse, and promising approaches for relapse prevention. *International Journal of the Addictions*, 25, 1085–1140.

Clark, D., Pollock, N., Bukstein, O., Mezzich, A., Bromberger, J. and Donovan, J. (1997) Gender and comorbid psychopathology in adolescents with alcohol dependence. *Journal of American Academy of Child and Adolescent Psychiatry*, 36, 1195–1203.

Cormack, C. and Carr, A. (2000) Drug abuse. In Carr, A. (ed.) *What Works with Children and Adolescents? A Critical Review of Psychological Interventions with Children, Adolescents and their Families*, 155–177. London: Routledge.

Cornwall, A. and Blood, L. (1998) Inpatient versus day treatment for substance abusing in adolescents. *Journal of Nervous and Mental Diseases*, 186, 580–582.

Department for Education (1995) *Drug Prevention and Schools (Circular 4/95)*. London: DFE.

Farrell, M. and Taylor, E. (1994) Drug and alcohol use and misuse. In Rutter, M., Taylor, E. and Hersov, L. (eds) *Child and Adolescent Psychiatry: Modern Approaches (Third edition)*, 529–545. Oxford: Blackwell.

Gilvarry, E. (2000) Substance abuse in young people. *Journal of Child Psychology and Psychiatry*, 41, 1, 55–80.

Kaminer, Y. (1994) *Understanding and Treating Adolescent Substance Abuse*. New York: Plenum Press.

Measham, F., Parker, H. and Aldridge, J. (1998) The teenage transition: From adolescent recreational drug use to the young adult dance culture in Britain in the mid-1990s. *Journal of Drug Issues*, 28, 9–32.

Miller, P. and Plant, M. (1996) Drinking and smoking and illicit drug use among 15 and 16 year olds in the United Kingdom. *British Medical Journal*, 313, 394–397.

Nelson, C. and Wittchen, H. U. (1998) DSM-IV alcohol disorders in a general population sample of adolescents and young adults. *Addiction*, 93, 1065–1077.

Parliament. House of Commons (1998) *Tackling Drugs to Build a Better Britain: The Government's 10-year Strategy for Tackling Drug Misuse (Cm 3945)*. London: HMSO.

Regier, D. A., Farmer, M., Rae, D. S., Locke, B., Keith, S., Judd, L. and Goodwin, F. (1990) Comorbidity of mental disorders with alcohol and other drug abuse. *Journal of the American Medical Association*, 264, 2511–2518.

Reinherz, H. Z., Giaconia, R. M., Lefkowitz, E. S., Pakis, B. and Frost, A. K. (1993) Prevalence of psychiatric disorders in a community population of older adolescents. *Journal of American Academy of Child and Adolescent Psychiatry*, 32, 369–377.

Rutter, M., Silberg, J., O'Connor, T. and Simonoff, E. (1999) Genetics and child psychiatry: II. Empirical research findings. *Journal of Child Psychology and Psychiatry: Annual Research Review*, 40, 19–56.

Shoemaker, R. H. and Sherry, P. (1991) Post-treatment factors influencing outcome of adolescent substance abuse treatment. *Journal of Adolescent Chemical Dependency*, 2, 89–106.

Standing Conference on Drug Abuse (1999) *Managing and Making Policy for Drug-related Incidents in Schools*. London: Standing Conference on Drug Abuse.

White, D. and Pitts, M. (1998) Educating young people about drugs: A systematic review. *Addiction*, 93, 1475–1487.

Williams, R., Christian, J., Gay, M. and Gilvarry, E. (eds) (1996) *Health Advisory Service: Children and Young People: Substance Misuse Services; The Substance of Young Needs*. London: HMSO.

Wittchen, H. U., Nelson, C. B. and Lachner, G. (1998) Prevalence of mental disorders and psychosocial impairments in adolescents and young adults. *Psychological Medicine*, 28, 109–126.

8 Depression

> At 10 years old Mark was becoming more and more withdrawn and isolated. He felt sad a lot of the time and sometimes felt like harming himself. His teacher described him as a loner who often seemed unhappy. Despite being a good student, he was beginning to have problems concentrating on his work and lacked enthusiasm for activities that he once enjoyed. At home he had trouble sleeping, had little appetite and frequently complained of headaches or stomachaches. The majority of the time he stayed in his room and did nothing. When encouraged to do anything he became moody and irritable.

It is now generally agreed that children can have depression, although it is thought that it may differ to that experienced by adults. This can have implications for many areas of their functioning and their life, but particularly for their involvement in activities at school. The lack of motivation experienced by such children and the pervasiveness of their difficulties can present significant problems. Only with sensitivity to, and understanding of, the nature of this disorder and the underlying feelings involved can teachers encourage children with depression to become re-engaged in school life. If helped effectively, children's self-esteem can be raised and this can also lead to improvements in other areas of their life.

Diagnosis

Most children may be fed up or unhappy some of the time and mood swings are particularly common during adolescence, but these are usually transient states. Some children may also develop some of the symptoms of depression in certain circumstances, for example following a significant loss. Depressive disorder, on the other hand, is more long term and pervasive and children with it tend to be emotionally flat rather than just unhappy or fed up. It is an intense state that significantly impairs the functioning of the individual and isolates him or her from normal life. This type of major depression is the main concern of this chapter, but much of the text also applies to children with depressive symptoms and the strategies discussed in the final section of this chapter may also be used to help these children. Major depression is one of the most under-diagnosed of disorders in children and adolescents. The diagnostic criteria, as given in DSM-IV (American Psychiatric Association, 1994), include:

- depressed mood, but this may include irritability in children;
- loss of interest or pleasure in activities;
- significant weight loss or weight gain;
- disturbed sleep;
- agitation or slowing down;
- fatigue or loss of energy;
- feelings of worthlessness or guilt;
- diminished ability to think or concentrate, or indecisiveness;
- recurrent thoughts of death, suicidal thoughts or actions.

For diagnosis, children must present with a depressed mood or loss of interest in activities nearly every day, together with at least four of the other symptoms. In addition, symptoms must be present for at least two weeks and this must represent a change from previous functioning.

Features

The essential feature of major depression is the change in mood and loss of interest or pleasure in activities, but it also affects children's functioning in a number of other areas (Oster and Montgomery, 1995). The presentation differs with the age and developmental stage of the child (Kazdin, 1990). In infants, for example, depression tends to be associated with eating and sleep disturbances, failure to gain weight, developmental delay and clingy behaviour. School-age children, in contrast, tend to be argumentative and irritable, whilst adolescents often experience feelings of guilt and hopelessness and their mood is more evident. No one pattern fits all children. As well as their mood, children's behaviour, thinking, physical condition and school performance may be affected.

Children with depression experience deep feelings of hopelessness and worthlessness. They rarely smile, often have a frozen stare and they may be tearful or anxious. They have lost interest in their usual activities and even the smallest tasks take a lot of effort. They may make excuses not to be involved in activities or they may appear bored. They feel that they are doomed to failure and see no point in trying. They believe themselves to be inadequate and they worry excessively, particularly about the future. This characteristic attitude often prevents them from seeking the help that they urgently need. Other feelings associated with depression include guilt, shame, over-sensitivity and low self-esteem.

Withdrawal and irritability, however, may be the most evident features. Girls, in particular, are likely to become socially withdrawn, whilst in boys, hyperactivity, restlessness, agitation and aggressive behaviour may be more prominent. This behaviour is often markedly out of character and it is important to recognise that it helps them to avoid painful feelings. They should not be perceived as naughty or bad. They may run away from home or wander aimlessly and there is also a risk of self-harm and suicidal behaviour (see Chapter 9).

In depression, children's thought processes slow down and their reasoning is distorted. They are preoccupied with their own thoughts, which are often extremely self-critical. They have difficulty thinking logically, concentrating, remembering and making decisions. They may also have recurrent thoughts of death or suicidal ideation. Children with depressive disorder often experience disruptions to their sleep and eating patterns, changes in weight, decreased energy, tiredness and fatigue. Complaints of headaches, stomachaches, nausea and other pains are common. Enjoyment is a necessary requirement for learning, growth and play, so the lack of motivation, poor concentration and impaired thinking typical of depression make it inevitable that children's schoolwork will suffer. Their attitude towards school may change completely. In addition, psychosomatic symptoms often lead to poor school attendance and truancy is common.

Associated disorders

Children with depression frequently have other mental health disorders. It occurs most often in conjunction with anxiety disorders, including school refusal, conduct disorder and ADHD, substance-related disorders, eating disorders and learning problems (see the relevant chapters in this handbook). The strongest association is with anxiety disorders, with as many as 75 per cent of children with major depression showing symptoms of anxiety (Merikangas and Angst, 1994). Anxiety tends to precede the depression (Brady and Kendall, 1992) and having both results in a greater impact on the individual's life. Other associated disorders may persist after the period of depression has passed and may warrant their own treatment. Depressive symptoms may also result from medication and some physical illnesses, such as inflammatory bowel disease or endocrine disorders, brain damage and epilepsy.

Incidence

Major depressive disorder is relatively rare in early childhood but becomes more common with increasing age, particularly during adolescence (Harrington, 1995). About 2 per cent of children develop a depressive illness before they reach puberty, although rather more (about 20 per cent) might exhibit depressive symptoms, a small proportion of whom will go on to develop the disorder. On the other hand, between 5 and 10 per cent of adolescents will have a major depressive illness during their teenage years (Fleming and Offord, 1990). Most adults report having their first episode when they were between 15 and 19 years old, but studies of children and adolescents suggest earlier ages of onset of around 11 to 15, most commonly between 14 and 15. Sharp increases occur when children start school and at adolescence owing to the increased pressure on children and young people at these times. In children, boys and girls are equally affected, whilst in adolescents, it is more common in girls by a ratio of two or three to one (Cohen *et al.*, 1993). There is some evidence that the incidence of depressive disorder in children and young adults is rising.

Causes

Depression is usually caused by the effect of stress on an already vulnerable child. Children differ markedly in their response to stress. In some young people, for example, a combination of quite minor factors, such as anticipation of change, loss of friendship and failure to achieve certain goals, can precipitate depression. Once it takes hold depression tends to be self-perpetuating. Common causes include loss of a loved one, a life-threatening illness, child abuse, and bullying or scapegoating. A number of factors have been implicated, including genetics, brain function, cognitive factors, family influences and stress. These are outlined briefly below.

Genetics

It is thought that some adults are more likely to become depressed than others because of their genetic make-up, but whether this applies to children is uncertain. The evidence suggests that, if it starts before puberty or is severe, there is likely to be a genetic component (Strober, 1992).

Brain function

There may be certain areas of the brain that function abnormally during major depression. In children, there are developmental differences in the regulatory mechanisms in the brain and particular stresses may result in lasting changes that alter future responses. This area needs further research.

Cognitive factors

The way a person thinks about themselves, their life and their future and the way they interpret their experiences is thought to play a major role in depression. Children with depression, for example, are less likely to process negative emotions effectively.

Family influences

Family influences have been consistently shown to be influential. Depression is particularly likely to occur when children feel unloved, unwanted or insecure. Physical or emotional neglect is a frequent cause of depression in infants. Negative parent–child interactions and family disruption and discord have also been implicated. A clear link, for example, has been demonstrated with marital discord and divorce (Hetherington *et al.*, 1985).

Stress

Depression in children most often occurs in response to stressful circumstances. Depressive symptoms, for example, have been associated with abuse, bereavement and traumatic disasters. Faced with such adversity, however, some children are very resilient and most young people are unlikely to develop a depressive disorder. Other children are more vulnerable and a series of relatively minor events, such as unexpectedly poor test results or an argument with a friend, may be perceived as total rejection and may lead to depression. Pressure at school, such as learning difficulties, bullying and poor peer relations, can also give rise to depression.

Treatment

Assessing depression in children is difficult because of the typical features associated with the disorder and the difficulty many children have expressing their feelings. If left untreated, however, depression persists so it is important that it is identified as early as possible. If symptoms last more than two weeks then urgent attention is required. Estimation of the suicide risk is an urgent priority and children who have unexplained physical symptoms need careful examination by their GP to ensure that depression is not overlooked. It can be difficult to engage individuals in treatment because of their feelings of worthlessness and they may need to be encouraged. In mild or moderate form, depression may be treated by the GP, but when it is severe, when there are associated disorders, or if other treatments have failed, more specialist help is usually required. Inpatient treatment may be relevant, especially where there is a high risk of suicide, if the individual is no longer eating or drinking or if there is an associated psychotic illness. There are also likely to be associated difficulties, such as poor family and peer relationships and poor academic performance. Addressing these issues can have a major beneficial effect on children's mood. It is important therefore that these are assessed and included in an overall treatment plan (Goodyer *et al.*, 1991), which may therefore include school intervention.

A range of treatments may be offered. Evidence to date suggests that cognitive behaviour therapy is the most effective treatment, although it needs to be continued for some time after remission of symptoms to prevent relapse (Moore and Carr, 2000). Other approaches include individual therapy, family work and medication. It is not uncommon for treatments to be combined. These are outlined below.

Cognitive behavioural therapy

Cognitive behavioural therapy challenges the individual's negative thinking and may be conducted individually or in groups. It has been shown to be a promising technique when used with children (Vostanis and Harrington, 1994). When parents were also involved or received parent training alongside their children gains appeared to be more long term. It may, however, be of most benefit for mild depression and for reducing relapse. Slow and distorted thought processes may prevent some individuals responding to this approach, which may then have to be combined with drug treatment.

Medication

There is no real evidence for the effectiveness of anti-depressants when used with children (Ambrosini *et al.*, 1993), although they do tend to be used with adolescents. It is recommended that their use is best restricted to those with severe depression, who do not respond to other forms of treatment. Side effects relating to cardiovascular function are possible. Another group of drugs, serotonin re-uptake inhibitors (e.g. Prozac), have been shown to be effective with adolescents (Kutcher, 1997), although not formally approved for use with children. Side effects of nausea and vomiting are common so they should be used with caution. All these drugs can be dangerous if taken in an overdose and should therefore not be used for those with suicidal tendencies.

Individual therapy

Individual therapy focuses on helping children to express their feelings and to understand and come to terms with stressful events. There is some limited evidence that interpersonal therapy can alleviate adolescent depression, particularly when it is less severe, and that social skills training, which aims to alleviate depression by improving peer relationships, can help with depression in childhood (Harrington, 1995). Psychotherapy, drama therapy and play therapy may also be beneficial.

Family therapy

It is important that parents gain insight into their child's problems and feelings. Family therapy, which focuses on modifying patterns of interaction and belief systems within the family, may be required to break the pattern of scapegoating in the family, which may be a causative or reinforcing factor. Although often advocated, there has been no systematic evaluation of family treatment for childhood depression.

Course and outcome

Onset of depression may be gradual or sudden. The average duration in adolescence is from seven to nine months, with severe cases lasting about a year. The long-term outcome for depression in childhood or adolescence is not favourable. Although rates of recovery are high, so are the rates of relapse. The risk of a repeat episode is about 60 per cent (Harrington *et al.*, 1990). Where the depression is a result of stresses that can be removed children generally do well and about 90 per cent of children recover from their first episode within one and a half to two years and functioning returns to normal. In 20 to 30 per cent of cases, some symptoms may remain for longer causing some distress, whilst in 5 to 10 per cent of cases, the full disorder may remain for two or more years. Depressive disorder is a recurrent condition with a cumulative chance of recurrence. A significant proportion of youngsters develop a chronic pattern that persists into young adulthood (Keller, 1994). The earlier the age of onset the more serious the condition is likely to be and the greater the likelihood of recurrence and long-term social, emotional and economic consequences that can be a burden for the family. Where there are associated disorders there also tends to be a poorer outcome. On the other hand, a high self-esteem, good coping skills, satisfactory school achievement, outside interests and positive relationships with family and friends make recurrence less likely (Merikangas and Angst, 1994).

WHAT CAN TEACHERS DO TO HELP?

Teachers have an important role to play in prevention, early identification and in supporting children with depression in school. There is a danger, because these children are often withdrawn and present no management problems for teachers, that they do not get the help and support that they need.

Prevention

Children under stress and at risk of depression need a close relationship with a sensitive adult, who can provide them with a sense of security and the feeling that someone cares. This is particularly the case in situations where parents are unavailable to their children, whatever the reason. The accessibility and availability of teachers to their pupils is therefore important in the prevention of depression and needs to be ensured through a structured and effective pastoral care system. Teachers should spend time with children who are unhappy or sad and talk to their parents to try to establish the underlying cause. Strategies can then be employed within the school to prevent additional stresses on those who are vulnerable. Options might include, for example, providing counselling or group work, a quiet room or a trusted adult for children to go to when they feel stressed, or being excused from certain activities for a limited period. These strategies could be incorporated into a pastoral support programme for individuals. For adolescents, membership of the peer group is vital in helping them cope with the transition to adulthood. As such, an isolated individual, often described as a loner, who has to cope with the additional stress of a sense of loss or failure may be particularly vulnerable and may be at a high risk of depression and suicidal tendencies. Teachers should be alert to these signs, and, as well as offering a supportive relationship, might also enlist the help of peers and other agencies to support vulnerable individuals.

Children who are depressed tend to come from families under stress, so anything that teachers can do to support parents, as well as children, can be helpful. Teachers should work closely with parents to develop effective preventative measures. After-school activities, holiday schemes, as well as access to nursery and playgroup provision for younger children, may be appropriate. Teachers can also initiate links with other agencies, such as health visitors, education welfare officers or social workers, that can support the family in different ways. Where teachers have developed informal relationships with local mental health professionals these can be used for informal consultation to help make decisions about when referral might be appropriate.

Early identification

Teachers can help by knowing what to look for and raising concerns when they feel that children appear to be troubled. Cause for concern is warranted where there is a noticeable, sometimes dramatic, change in mood, behaviour or functioning that is out of character and where this follows stressful events. Where poor school attendance is due to physical illness that appears to have no apparent physical cause teachers should also be concerned. Many of the symptoms of depression, such as poor concentration, lethargy, tiredness, lack of energy and limited motivation, will be evident in lessons and may be revealed through a formal school assessment. Other signs include poor appetite, difficulty making decisions, poor peer relationships, poor learning and frequent negative statements (Long, 1999). All sources of information, from teachers, parents and the children themselves, should be used to provide the best overall picture of children's functioning over a period of time. Parents may not understand what their child is going through and tend to underestimate the extent of their difficulties. Knowing when to intervene can be difficult, but where symptoms are evident over a prolonged period, affect all areas of the child's life and are linked with stressful events, it is important that action is taken.

By having an awareness of the symptoms of depression teachers can alert the appropriate services and get children the help that they need. Depression is potentially life threatening so the young person's safety must be paramount. Suicidal thoughts and attempts (see Chapter 9) should always be taken seriously and individuals concerned always referred for a mental health assessment. More serious signs of depression, for example, include marked changes in personality, lack of interest in personal appearance, verbal threats of suicide and preoccupation with death (Long, 1999). If children's problems are severe or school support has not helped, they and their parents should be encouraged to seek expert professional help. In the first instance, this might involve a visit to their GP, but ultimately they should seek the help of a psychologist or psychiatrist. If in doubt, teachers should discuss their concerns with others, such as the SENCO, school doctor, school nurse and educational psychologist, or through consultation with local mental health services (Long, 1999). The family may deny the problem and may need to be seen a number of times before responding to treatment.

Support in school

Most children who become depressed respond to positive care and support. If the child and the parents agree, it can be helpful for teachers to consult the mental health professionals involved in the case as to how best to help. Whilst it is important to tell children that they have an important role to play in helping themselves, there is a lot that teachers can do in school to help to strengthen their self-esteem and prevent further problems. Strategies might include, for example:

- a daily programme of planned activities;
- encouraging positive thinking;
- recording achievements, thoughts and feelings;
- giving children responsibility;
- using listening skills.

A daily programme of activities

By changing what they do, the way that children with depression think and feel can be altered. Involvement in activity can give them a sense of purpose and make them want to do more. Teachers are in a good position to encourage this. A daily programme of activities, agreed with parents and children and incorporated into a pastoral support plan, is a good way of raising self-esteem. Activities should be based on children's interests, skills and abilities and should include some that are challenging, but not too difficult, and others that are likely to be satisfying and enjoyable despite being easier. It is helpful to start the day with a task the children are able to accomplish and get a sense of achievement from. Tasks should be broken down into small steps. They should not include activities children feel unable to do and work should not be allowed to build up as this may make matters worse. Having failed, they are likely to become more depressed. Children should be encouraged to take each task in turn and only to move on once the first is complete. As many distractions as possible should be eliminated and it may be helpful to prompt them about what they are supposed to be doing and when. Breaks and lunchtimes should be planned so that children do not have to try and fill long periods of time. Where children have difficulty relating to their peer group, social skills training may be appropriate. The teacher can help by planning their programme with them at the end of each day and encouraging them to engage in new activities and to mix with their peer group. It is important to recognise that friends may need help to find new ways of interacting with them.

Encouraging positive thinking

The way individuals think affects how they feel. For children with depression, this is an important area to work on as negative thinking can act as a barrier to learning, as well as affecting other areas of functioning. Children with depression therefore have to be told that they have done well. Teachers should use praise liberally to encourage children to focus on what they have achieved, rather than what they have not achieved. These can be ordinary everyday things, rather than anything special. Depressed children, for example, often think that they will fail at anything they do and teachers can help by challenging these negative thoughts. This requires care as a poor mark or a negative comment by a teacher can reinforce their view. Children with depression can be encouraged to engage in positive rather than negative self-talk. It can help to encourage them to write down any negative thoughts and replace them with positive ones. When children feel that a task is too difficult, for example, teachers can help by encouraging them to reflect on things they have achieved in the past. In this way, they can help children to be aware of their negative thoughts and to counteract them, as this is a skill that can be practised and learnt. Teachers should have realistic expectations of children and make it clear to them that they do not expect perfect work. At the same time, they can also encourage children and their families to have realistic expectations.

Recording achievements, thoughts and feelings

Teachers should involve children in reviewing their progress and, in particular, in recording their achievements. They can be encouraged to set aside time each evening to note what they have done during the day. Alongside each task they have achieved they can record their thoughts and how this made them feel at the time. This could be done as part of their homework. A diary of this nature can be an integral part of children's schoolwork, as well as giving them a concrete picture of what they have achieved and how they felt to reflect on at times when they feel depressed. In their minds, these children frequently focus on their negative points, whereas recording of this kind can show them that they have achieved something positive. This can be helpful as it not only challenges their beliefs, but also helps them to find out more about themselves.

Giving children responsibility

It may be easy for teachers to take responsibility for children with depression, in the belief that this is being helpful, but they should be given important tasks to do and be involved in making decisions as much as possible. This might include, for example, giving children simple responsibilities, such as being book monitor or watering the plants. Parents, who may find this even more difficult, should also be encouraged to allow their children to make decisions and to take responsibility for themselves and their behaviour. In the long term, children need to be able to manage the depression themselves.

Using listening skills

Depression in children may in part be caused by rejection and, so, it is particularly important that they feel that someone cares about them. For this reason, a willingness to offer support and showing care and concern are the best ways of helping. Offering children individual attention, perhaps at a set time each day, giving them full attention and listening to them are helpful in this respect. The establishment of a consistent relationship with a caring adult can be a vital factor in preventing more long-term difficulties. Where teachers themselves feel unable to fulfil this role, it may be possible for other school support staff, such as the adult mentors available in some schools, to befriend children and adopt this role. For example, listening skills may be used to help them explore their feelings, which may prevent negative feelings from building up. It is important to stress that this is not a substitute for individual therapy or counselling, but it can provide children with a safety net to avert problems in school and can alert teachers to potential stresses before they become too overwhelming.

At the same time, these children can be clingy and teachers or other support staff may need to take care not to become over-involved, not to make promises they are unable to keep and to be realistic in what they can do to help. Teachers need to establish their own boundaries and make them clear to children. Depression can be difficult to understand. It is easy to feel impatient with individuals and to expect them to help themselves, but they often feel lonely and afraid and do not know how to do this. It is not simply a question of cheering up, and telling them to do so will just confirm that no one understands what they are going through. In addition, children with depression often have deep-seated negative feelings and sometimes project their feelings of helplessness on to others, making those who are trying to help feel rejected. This can be disturbing. Those offering support need to protect themselves from taking this rejection personally and being overwhelmed by negative feelings, as this can render them less than helpful to these students. For these reasons, teachers attempting to engage with these children should have an opportunity to share their own feelings and should seek support from mental health professionals so that they are able to offer the most effective form of help.

Further reading

Barker, P. J. (1992) *Severe Depression: A Practitioner's Guide*. London: Chapman and Hall.

Hammen, C. (1997) *Depression*. Hove: Psychological Press.

Harrington, R. (1995) *Depressive Disorder in Childhood and Adolescence*. Chichester: John Wiley & Sons.

Long, R. (1999) *Understanding and Supporting Depressed Children and Young People*. Tamworth: NASEN.

McRae, M. (1986) *A State of Depression*. Basingstoke: Macmillan Education.

References

Ambrosini, P. J., Bianchi, M. D., Rabinovich, H. and Elia, J. (1993) Anti-depressant treatments in children and adolescents. I. Affective disorders. *Journal of American Academy of Child and Adolescent Psychiatry*, 32, 1–6.

American Psychiatric Association (1994) *Diagnostic and Statistical Manual of Mental Disorders (Fourth edition)*. Washington, DC: American Psychiatric Association.

Brady, E. U. and Kendall, P. C. (1992) Comorbidity of anxiety and depression in children and adolescents. *Psychological Bulletin*, 111, 244–255.

Cohen, P., Cohen, J., Kasen, S., Velez, C., Hartmark, C., Johnson, J., Rojas, M., Brook, J. and Streuning, E. (1993) An epidemiological study of disorders in late childhood and adolescence. 1. Age and gender specific prevalence. *Journal of Child Psychology and Psychiatry*, 34, 851–867.

Fleming, J. and Offord, D. (1990) Epidemiology of childhood depressive disorders: A critical review. *Journal of American Academy of Child and Adolescent Psychiatry*, 29, 571–580.

Goodyer, I. M., Germany, E., Gowrusankur, J. and Altham, P. (1991) Social influences on the course of anxious and depressive disorders in school-age children. *British Journal of Psychiatry*, 158, 676–684.

Harrington, R. (1995) *Depressive Disorder in Childhood and Adolescence*. Chichester: John Wiley & Sons.

Harrington, R. C., Fudge, H., Rutter, M., Pickles, A. and Hill, J. (1990) Adult outcomes of childhood and adolescent depression. I. Psychiatric status. *Archives of General Psychiatry*, 47, 465–473.

Hetherington, E. M., Cox, M. and Cox, R. (1985) Long-term effects of divorce and remarriage on the adjustment of children. *Journal of American Academy of Child and Adolescent Psychiatry*, 24, 518–530.

Kazdin, A. E. (1990) Childhood depression. *Journal of Child Psychology and Psychiatry*, 31, 121–160.

Keller, M. B. (1994) Depression: A long-term illness. *British Journal of Psychiatry*, 165 (supplement 26), 9–15.

Kutcher, S. (1997) The pharmacotherapy of adolescent depression. *Journal of Child Psychology and Psychiatry*, 38, 755–767.

Long, R. (1999) *Understanding and Supporting Depressed Children and Young People*. Tamworth: NASEN.

Merikangas, K. R. and Angst, J. (1994) The challenge of depressive disorders in adolescence. In Rutter, M. (ed.) *Psychosocial Disturbances in Young People: Challenges for Prevention*. Cambridge: Cambridge University Press.

Moore, M. and Carr, A. (2000) Depression and grief. In Carr, A. (ed.) *What Works with Children and Adolescents? A Critical Review of Psychological Interventions with Children, Adolescents and their Families*, 203–232. London: Routledge.

Oster, G. D. and Montgomery, S. S. (1995) *Helping your Depressed Teenager: A Guide for Parents and Caregivers*. New York: John Wiley & Sons.

Strober, M. (1992) Relevance of early age of onset in genetic studies of bipolar affective disorder. *Journal of American Academy of Child and Adolescent Psychiatry*, 31, 606–610.

Vostanis, P. and Harrington, R. (1994) Cognitive-behavioural treatment of depressive disorder in child psychiatric patients: Rationale and description of treatment package. *European Journal of Child and Adolescent Psychiatry*, 3, 111–123.

9 Suicidal behaviour and deliberate self-harm

Vicky was a girl of 15 with a long history of severe sexual abuse by her father. She received ongoing psychotherapy from the mental health services to help her deal with this. She was bright and conscientious and had a flair for art, which her school encouraged. There were, however, many times when she found it difficult to cope with her feelings. On these occasions she often cut her arms superficially. Her teachers found this behaviour difficult to deal with in a mainstream school setting. On two occasions she took an overdose of paracetamol. It took many years of therapy before she was able to replace these methods of coping with more appropriate strategies.

Suicidal behaviour and deliberate self-harm in children and especially adolescents are of increasing concern, as there is evidence of their increase over the last few decades. They are also thought to be occurring at younger ages. Although it was once thought that children were incapable of suicidal thoughts and ideas because of their lack of understanding of the finality of death, this has been shown not to be the case. Even children as young as 3 have been known to talk about wanting to kill themselves. Suicide and self-harm, especially in young people, are emotive issues and they can raise intense feelings in those involved, including professionals, as well as family and friends. This makes it a particularly difficult issue to deal with. It is important that teachers, who may find themselves in the position of having to deal with such situations, are aware of the issues and are given support from relevant health professionals.

Definition

Suicidal behaviour can take a range of different forms as suicidal motivation varies considerably. The term 'deliberate self-harm' is generally used to cover all acts of self-harm, self-injury and attempted suicide. Those who engage in deliberate self-harm are usually ambivalent about whether they want to die or have not thought through the consequences of their behaviour (Vaughan, 1985). Individuals, however, can die through misjudgement, particularly where paracetamol is used because it can cause death in relatively small overdoses through damage to the liver. The most common form of self-injury is cutting, but it can also include bruising, scraping, burning and other self-inflicted wounds. Superficial cutting may be inflicted in order to gain immediate relief from 'overwhelming mental tension', whilst attempted suicide can be a way of trying to get others to act or take control, a way of getting temporary relief from social problems, or it may be a way of abdicating responsibility (Vaughan, 1985). Despite these different motivations, there is, however, a strong association between attempted suicide, deliberate self-harm and subsequent suicide which means that all incidents of self-harm must be treated seriously.

The distinction between young people who intentionally try to kill themselves or succeed in committing suicide and those who deliberately harm themselves, but do not necessarily want to die, is an important one. Whilst there is some overlap between these groups, there are often different factors involved and these have to be understood if individuals are to get the help that they need (Vaughan, 1985). The degree of intent in children, however, is often difficult to assess since children may find this difficult to express and parents may be unaware of children's thoughts. For these reasons, any form of self-harm in children should be treated as potentially suicidal behaviour (Pfeffer, 1986). Pfeffer suggests a continuum ranging from suicidal ideas, suicidal threats and mild attempts that are not life threatening to serious attempts that may lead to death.

Features

The majority of suicide attempts in adolescents are not premeditated. In one study, for example, up to 70 per cent reported that they acted on impulse, with half having thought about it for less than fifteen minutes beforehand and only 10 to 15 per cent having thought about it for more than a day (Piacentini *et al.*, 1991, cited in Shaffer and Piacentini, 1994). Most deny persistent intent and are glad that they recovered. Many teenage girls under stress take minor overdoses or cut their wrists without having a wish to die. Some, however, can miscalculate and, as a result, this can be fatal. In practice, it is often hard to establish serious intent and in all cases it is essential for a mental health assessment to be conducted and treatment offered. Suicidal children do, however, tend to have an intense preoccupation with death and this could be considered a warning cue to the possibility of suicidal tendencies (Pfeffer, 1986).

Whilst there is some overlap between those who attempt suicide and those who complete it, since previous attempts have been made in about a third of cases of completed suicide (Shaffer and Piacentini, 1994), there are also differences, however. About half of all children who completed suicide had discussed or threatened suicide within twenty-four hours of their death. The main features of those who succeed in committing suicide include:

- previous suicide threats or behaviour;
- a higher level of suicidal intent;
- a lower rate of affective disorders;
- availability of highly lethal means;
- models of successful or attempted suicide within their environment, whether within their own family, through a friend, within the neighbourhood or within the media.

The most common method of attempting suicide is by self-poisoning and the most common form of overdose in the UK is with paracetamol (Hawton and Fagg, 1992). The fact that irreversible liver damage can occur with twenty-five or more tablets, makes this a considerable cause for concern. According to Carlson (1990), in the UK, overdoses, carbon monoxide poisoning and the use of firearms were commonly used by girls. More violent methods tend to be used by males, for whom shooting, hanging and carbon monoxide poisoning were the most common. This is, at least in part, determined by availability. In the USA, for example, a large majority of teenage boys commit suicide by shooting themselves since guns are often readily available.

Associated disorders

Over 90 per cent of children who have attempted suicide have been diagnosed with other mental health disorders and approximately two-thirds of children who commit suicide meet the criteria for a disorder, whilst the remaining third also exhibited symptoms. Affective disorders, conduct disorder and substance abuse all put adolescents at an increased risk. Depression is common, but it is important to remember that a substantial number of children who attempt suicide are not depressed and not all children with depression harm themselves. In conjunction with this, Brent (1987) identified two subgroups of children – one group of depressed, hopeless youngsters with high suicide intent who made premeditated lethal attempts and another group of youngsters with adjustment or behavioural disturbance who made impulsive attempts of varying lethality.

Incidence

Completed suicide is very rare under the age of 12, after which it becomes progressively more common, increasing markedly in the late teens and continuing to rise until the early twenties (Shaffer, 1974). It is thought that the sharp increase in adolescence may be linked to increases in affective disorder and alcohol abuse at this age. In 1989, the suicide rate in the UK for children aged 5 to 15 was around 0.8 per 100,000 and for young people aged 15 to 19 years it was 7.6 per 100,000 (Shaffer and Piacentini, 1994). In North America and Europe suicide is more common in males than females of all ages, except the very young. Teenage suicides, particularly in males, have increased in Europe and the USA over the last forty years. There is particular concern about the increase in the rates of suicide in males aged 15 to 24, which is thought to be linked to increases in substance and alcohol abuse. Rates also vary within regions and cultures: for example, in the USA, suicide is a lot less common among blacks than whites. It is thought that this might be due to subtle variations in attitudes.

Although completed suicide is relatively rare in children under 12 years of age, suicidal ideas, threats and attempts are relatively common (around 1 per cent). In children under 12, boys demonstrate suicidal behaviour more frequently than girls. Suicidal thoughts and behaviour, however, are much more common during adolescence. As many as 10 to 20 per cent of adolescents demonstrate relatively serious suicidal ideas, but only a small, but significant, minority act on them (Center for Disease Control, 1991). In teenagers, whilst girls are more likely to demonstrate suicidal behaviour, adolescent boys present with more serious forms. Children from every type of social background may be vulnerable.

In the UK, approximately 19,000 young people a year are referred to hospital for incidents of deliberate self-harm, mainly involving drug overdoses or self-injury (Hawton and Fagg, 1992). In Western Europe over the last forty years there has been a huge increase in the number of young people who deliberately harm themselves, but this has recently started to stabilise. Girls outnumber boys by a ratio of three or four to one in incidents of deliberate self-harm, many of which involve drug overdoses. Self-injury is also thought to be twice as prevalent amongst girls as boys, but many of these incidents may not be recorded. Many women who injure themselves report that they started to do so during childhood or adolescence.

Causes

Suicidal behaviour of any form is complex and is usually the result of a combination of children's previous life experiences, immediate environmental stresses and their present mental state. Whilst suicide mainly affects predisposed individuals, such as those with major depression, the decision is often impulsive. In most cases there is an identifiable precipitant in the few days before the event. Three different groups of individuals may be distinguished. First, some young people have shown no previous signs of suicidal behaviour, but may be under stress with exams or relationship difficulties, or may have recently experienced bereavement. Given appropriate support, these youngsters are unlikely to repeat the attempt. Second, other young people have shown signs of emotional or behavioural problems beforehand and need specialist help. Third, some young people have had serious and complex problems for some time, have had a history of attempts and are at a greater risk of repeated suicidal behaviour.

Precipitants

Whilst there have usually been previous difficulties, suicidal behaviour frequently provides escape from an immediate crisis and extreme fear, unhappiness, hopelessness or rage usually precedes the event. Relationship difficulties, with family or friends, are the most commonly reported precipitant of adolescent suicide attempts. In males, unemployment and drug and alcohol problems are also common (Hawton and Fagg, 1992). An upset, such as an argument with parents or breaking up with a friend, often acts as the last straw. Other common precipitants include incidences of humiliation, the threat of separation from a boyfriend and seeing a film involving suicide. Other less common precipitants include school problems, an abusive environment and bereavement. Many of these youngsters do not know how to get help and have no relatives or friends to support them. In about a third of cases there is no external precipitant, but these individuals generally have acute depression.

Risk factors

The specific factors that have been found to increase the risk of suicidal behaviour in children include certain personal characteristics, family factors, stressful events, social and biological factors. In addition, the means to commit suicide has to be readily available, although, in cases where suicide is premeditated, the intent and the presence of depression and substance abuse are likely to be the overriding factors. The main factors are outlined below.

Personal characteristics

All forms of mental health problems carry an increased risk of suicide. Children with depressive disorder are at a particularly high risk and it is also common in children with conduct disorder and/or substance abuse. Alcohol consumption also seriously adds to the possibility of long-term damage associated with an overdose. People with chronic physical illness are also at a greater risk, probably due to depression. Certain cognitive deficits have been found in children who demonstrate suicidal behaviour, including, for example, the way they think about themselves and make judgements about situations. Children who deliberately harm themselves often also have school-related problems. Their academic attainment is often poor and they commonly have problems relating to teachers and peers.

Family factors

Children from families with a high rate of mental disorder and those who have a relative or friend who has harmed or killed themselves are at greater risk. Whilst this may involve a genetic component, it is thought that imitation may also play a role. Lack of supportive relationships within the family also place children at increased risk (Taylor and Stansfield, 1984). Instability, parent–child conflict and marital conflict, are common. Conflicts often arise from unresolved issues about what is or is not age appropriate and this can act as a trigger for suicidal behaviour in vulnerable youngsters.

Stressful events

These children have frequently experienced major traumatic events, including bereavement, parental separation and physical or sexual abuse. Some school-related events can also cause children additional stress, for example examinations, bullying or exclusion.

Social factors

Social isolation and lack of support place children at increased risk. Children out of school at a time when they are particularly vulnerable, for example, may be at increased risk because of the lack of support available to them. The wider cultural environment may also be influential. There is some evidence, for example, that suicidal behaviour is facilitated by exposure to news or stories about suicide.

Biological factors

The rate of suicide is greater in adults when they have low levels of serotonin in the cerebrospinal fluid and this may be the case for children as well. This work is in its early stages, but it may eventually provide evidence for a neurological basis for depression and suicidal behaviour in some individuals.

Treatment

It is essential that all children who have attempted suicide or deliberately harmed themselves have a mental health assessment and this should take place as soon as possible. It is important to establish whether their behaviour constitutes a serious suicide attempt, requiring immediate supervision, as well as long-term treatment. It is considered more serious, for example, when it is carried out in isolation in circumstances that make discovery unlikely, where preparations for death have been made and a suicide note left. In the first instance, most children and adolescents who attempt suicide will be seen in the casualty department of their local hospital. Immediate medical considerations take precedence, but a mental health assessment is usually initiated simultaneously.

Most individuals are offered outpatient treatment while inpatient treatment is usually reserved for those at increased risk. This includes those with persistent suicidal ideas or a history of recurrent attempts, those with depressive or psychotic symptoms or alcohol abuse, those who have no one who can ensure their safety and those with poor communication within the family. As well as formal treatment methods, providing support for individuals within their normal environment is also vital and it is here that school personnel can play an important role (discussed in the final section of this chapter). Adult studies suggest that therapeutic intervention of any type has a positive effect in reducing further attempts and that no one treatment is superior. Whilst the core treatment is individual psychotherapy, family therapy, cognitive therapy, medication and group therapy may also be offered.

Individual psychotherapy

The development of a trusting relationship with the therapist allows individuals to express their feelings and conflicts. Cognitive problem-solving techniques may be used to enhance their ability to cope in other ways. Throughout all phases of treatment, children's suicidal tendencies are carefully monitored. If, however, the underlying problems have not been addressed, there may be repeated attempts.

Family therapy

Family work is an important aspect of treatment for all suicidal children. Family therapy focuses on reducing family conflict and stress, which is essential for the child to be able to cope. Parents are helped to respond more appropriately to their children and to understand their own conflicts.

Group therapy

The main aim of group therapy is to develop peer interactions and to reduce children's sense of loneliness and isolation, as well as enhancing children's support systems and developing their understanding of themselves and others. Caution, however, has been suggested in using group therapy with suicidal children as, unless it is skilfully handled, it can reinforce suicidal ideation (Shaffer and Piacentini, 1994).

Medication

Medication may be appropriate for the treatment of injuries and physical illness, as well as in the treatment of underlying mental disorders, such as depression. Certain medication will not be appropriate, however, for example, where there is further risk of overdose.

Additional support

Typically, additional support involves identifying a group of people who can be available to children in their normal environment on a daily basis. This may include school personnel, as well as family and peers, who can carry out certain tasks to help support children emotionally, thus decreasing the risk of suicidal behaviour. It is important that these people have direct access to mental health support and can be advised on appropriate intervention.

Course and outcome

A high proportion (about 50 per cent) of adolescents who attempt suicide experience continued disturbance and make further attempts, whilst up to about 10 per cent may subsequently kill themselves (Shaffer and Piacentini, 1994). The factors which predict repeated attempts include being male, having more than one previous episode, family psychopathology, poor social adjustment, the presence of mental health disorder and depressive symptoms. In addition to repeated attempts, suicidal behaviour in young people has also been linked to being unmarried or divorced in adult life, criminal behaviour and future alcohol problems. Generally, however, if the individual was well adjusted prior to the suicidal behaviour there tends to be a good outcome.

WHAT CAN TEACHERS DO TO HELP?

Teachers have an important role to play in educating children about stress and strategies for coping with it, as well as in the early identification of children at risk of suicide or deliberate self-harm and helping them to access appropriate help. In addition, it is important that teachers have thought through how to deal with suicidal children and the incidents of deliberate self-harm which they may encounter in the school setting.

Prevention

Suicide prevention strategies in schools may be focused on a variety of areas. These may include:

- educational programmes;
- helping children cope with stress;
- providing a supportive environment and an effective pastoral system;
- early identification and referral of pupils at risk;
- limiting access to methods.

Educational programmes

Young people rarely get the opportunity to discuss the issue of suicide and this can lead to ignorance of the facts. Educational programmes can be used to raise awareness of the problem and to provide staff and students with information about mental health resources. Through such programmes they can also be encouraged to view suicidal thoughts and self-harm as a response to stress, rather than a sign of mental disorder (Shaffer and Piacentini, 1994). Alternative strategies for coping with stress can then be discussed. Such a programme could form part of a comprehensive personal and social education (PSE) curriculum. There is no evidence, however, that educational programmes modify attitudes about suicide or encourage more students to seek help. In addition, because of the sensitive and potentially dangerous nature of the topic, schools should seek advice and support from mental health professionals in helping them to develop and implement a suitable programme and should always consult with parents beforehand.

Helping children cope with stress

In their daily interactions with pupils, teachers can help raise awareness about the nature of stress and how to deal with it effectively. Pupils can be taught appropriate ways of coping, thus minimising the risk of suicidal behaviour in some young people. Children and parents can also be educated about where they can go to get help with feelings of hopelessness and suicidal impulses, whether this is through local counselling or support services or crisis services. Crisis services are provided by telephone hotlines. These may be general services, such as the Samaritans, for anyone in need of support, or for individuals with more specific problems, as in Rape Crisis. These are usually staffed by specially trained adults who will listen to young people and inform them how to access appropriate local services. There is a need to develop services and procedures and to raise awareness and acceptability of using hotlines, particularly among boys. Teachers may have a role to play in this, by ensuring that such services are advertised and that children at risk are aware of their availability. It is helpful if a directory of local and national services is readily available within the school for teachers to access when appropriate.

A supportive environment and an effective pastoral system

A supportive school environment and an effective pastoral system can play a vital role in helping children deal with personal problems. Teachers need to be alert to potential problems and be able to notice when a child is upset, withdrawn or irritable and to help him or her address these difficulties. Where teachers are willing to listen to pupils' personal problems this can help prevent difficulties becoming major crises to which children might respond in less appropriate ways. Thus, providing all pupils with individual personal time with a trusted adult when they need it can be a successful preventative measure. In addition, more intensive support from a member of staff trained in counselling may be helpful. An effective pastoral system can therefore be crucial in supporting children, especially those who are vulnerable and lack support outside of the school. The importance of valuing all pupils should be stressed and a policy of non-rejection can be a helpful strategy. Exclusion from school, for example, can leave some vulnerable pupils without their only means of stability and support, so, in these circumstances, alternative strategies should be sought.

Early identification and referral of children at risk

Improvements in the identification and treatment of mental disorders, particularly depression and schizophrenia (see relevant chapters in this handbook), play a significant part in suicide prevention. Depression especially tends to go undiagnosed in children and adolescents, yet these children are at a high risk of suicide and deliberate self-harm. Teachers need to be alert to the signs that children are in considerable distress or that they may be depressed. Once identified they can be referred for more specialist help through their GP or local mental health services. Recognition of specific disorders is discussed in the relevant chapters of this handbook.

Limiting access to methods

For health and safety reasons teachers should always take care with medicines, poisonous chemicals and sharp instruments. Potentially dangerous materials should be locked away and this should form part of a health and safety policy within the school of which all teachers and support staff are aware. Given that suicide attempts are often impulsive acts, it is obvious that limiting access to methods of carrying it out can prevent suicide. If students appear to be in considerable distress, particularly where they have been known to make previous attempts to harm themselves, teachers should be extremely vigilant. This may be particularly relevant for teachers of children with emotional and behavioural difficulties, who are likely to be at increased risk.

Dealing with suicidal children and incidents of deliberate self-harm

It is important that school personnel are able to recognise and work with suicidal children, but, understandably, they may be frightened or worried about having to deal with a crisis situation. They may lack the required insight and training and, for this reason, it is vital that they are aware of their own limitations and are able to recognise when they need the support of other professionals.

Faced with such an incident, medical attention is likely to be the first priority. Where relevant, first aid should be administered, children should be taken to the casualty department of the local hospital and parents should be informed. Once admitted to hospital there is probably little for the teacher to do except to give those responsible for medical treatment all the relevant information and to support the parents, who may feel guilty and ashamed. An assessment of the degree of both immediate and future risk is automatically obtained from the mental health services before the youngster is allowed to leave the hospital and follow-up treatment organised.

However, it is important not to forget that other children who witnessed the event or friends of the victim may need additional individual support. Studies have shown that the peers of those who attempt or commit suicide may be greatly affected and carry an increased risk of psychiatric disturbance and suicidal behaviour (Ho *et al.*, 2000). Intervention with those in the victim's school or community might help other children understand the death, minimise scapegoating and reduce the likelihood of imitation. Individual time with a member of staff trained in counselling may be the most helpful option, although some children may be more seriously affected and require specialist help. There may be practical things the teacher can do at this stage that will help facilitate the individual's return to the school, such as sensitively informing peers. The individual is likely to feel ashamed and this can make it difficult to return to school. It is vital that the teacher conveys acceptance and concern for the plight of the individual. If the pupil is off for a prolonged period, it is important that the school is kept informed and that teachers are able to demonstrate their continued concern by keeping in contact when children are in hospital, since this encourages an expectation of return to normal life.

Assessment of risk

Teachers may find themselves confronted with a potentially suicidal young person without knowing how to assess the risk involved. The threat of suicide can be very intimidating and can place a terrible burden of responsibility on an inexperienced teacher. Under such anxiety-provoking circumstances, an assessment framework is helpful (Pfeffer, 1986). The first step when a risk is suspected is to gather all the relevant information together. The teacher may already know the young person well, but should also check their records as these can give important clues as to how the young person normally copes with stress. The following aspects, as outlined by Pfeffer, should be considered:

- previous suicide attempts – this is the most useful predictor of future behaviour and detail should be sought about previous attempts and how serious they were;
- behaviour – antisocial and aggressive behaviour make self-harm and suicide more likely and drug or alcohol abuse further increases the risk;
- home circumstances – whilst an unstable family background contributes to increased risk, those in care, with no current family at all, are at an even greater risk;
- mental and physical illness – evidence of mental disorder may be apparent and physical illness should not be overlooked as those who attempt suicide frequently feel that their health is poor, also serious illness often precedes an attempt;
- current problems – these may include loss of any kind, such as a person or even loss of status, as well as social isolation and loneliness, which can have a severe effect on children and young people, even when children have alienated themselves from others by their own behaviour.

When information is not readily available, an attempt should be made to find out as much as possible from the individual by sensitively steering the conversation to the relevant areas. Having gained some understanding of the individual's background and current emotional state, the teacher should be able to decide whether a degree of risk is present. This then needs to be raised with the young person as they are in the best position to judge the degree of risk and how long and under what circumstances they can be trusted to control their behaviour. They should be asked to comply with a statement that they would not harm themselves and, if unable to do so without qualification, an element of risk is present.

Teachers are obliged to take whatever steps seem necessary to prevent a vulnerable child from taking his or her life. Where there is a certain or imminent risk, teachers should initiate child protection procedures and contact social services (see Chapter 18 on child abuse for a more detailed discussion). Potential dangers should be removed and the individual should be accompanied at all times until it is possible to conduct a mental health assessment. A clear plan of action is beneficial, as the individual may be feeling confused and helpless. Even when there is felt to be no risk of suicide or further self-harm, this type of behaviour indicates the need for help so teachers should ensure that an appropriate referral is made.

Where there is a possible or slight risk, there may be no need for urgent action but it is important to take precautions against increasing the risk. It is helpful, for example, to find out if there are any other agencies or professionals involved with the individual, and to gain permission for contact. Medical and psychiatric personnel are not always easily accessible to teachers, although informal networks may already exist and should be used as a form of support in such circumstances. A designated mental health co-ordinator in the school can be helpful in these circumstances. Teachers should be encouraged to form active relationships with mental health professionals to provide them with support when working with suicidal children. An effective collaborative relationship can be important in helping them to become aware of their own limitations and to assess their own capabilities in their work with suicidal children. Maintaining such a link can be most valuable in enabling them to provide the optimum support for the children in their charge. Liaison with mental health professionals is discussed further in the final chapter of this handbook.

Children should be encouraged to express their feelings. It is important to listen well and to acknowledge the difficulties they are experiencing. Following this, personal problems may be discussed and ways of tackling them addressed. Although referral to another agency, such as social services or mental health services, may be required to sort out the main problem, the quality of relationship with the teacher can help prevent further distress developing in the school situation. By sharing their negative feelings it is likely that the risk will be reduced. It is important, but sometimes difficult, to avoid making glib reassurances, since this will only convince them that no one understands them. Behaviour is often a response to overwhelming problems so dealing with these should be broken down into small, achievable, realistic and manageable goals. Children who deliberately harm themselves often have school-related problems. Their academic attainment is often poor, typically below average, and they commonly have problems relating to teachers and peers. If the problems are in part school related some simple goals should be set to address them. No matter what plans of action are decided, the teacher should always ask to see the child again shortly after the event. This demonstrates that the pupil matters, that the teacher cares and that the child's further existence is important. Even when young people are difficult to relate to because they are anxious, ashamed or mistrustful, being there at a time of crisis can be very important to them. For this reason, it is crucial to try to maintain some form of regular contact with them, as this may be the only way they get the support they need to prevent further suicidal behaviour.

Communication with parents

In all cases where children threaten or attempt suicide or self-harm, even when they have told teachers in confidence, parents should be informed as soon as possible since the child may be at risk. A helpful approach is to encourage children as far as possible to tell parents themselves. However, where abuse within the family is indicated it may be relevant to contact social services prior to informing parents. Parents will generally be relieved that there is someone else to share their burden with them so teachers should maintain close liaison with them. However, parents may have become frustrated with youngsters who have continually created tension by self-harming behaviour and they may be less than sympathetic. On the other hand, some children may have tried to hide their behaviour from their family so this knowledge may come as a shock. Parents are likely to feel ashamed and embarrassed. The most helpful approach is for teachers to try to put them at their ease and to help them deal with this by being non-judgemental.

Referral of children who are a suicide risk to mental health services

Everyone who has taken an overdose needs an urgent medical assessment by a doctor as soon as possible, since even small amounts of some medication can be fatal. All young people who self-harm should have a specialist mental health assessment before leaving the hospital and this is usually undertaken by a child and adolescent psychiatrist. One of their most important functions is for teachers to be able to recognise potentially suicidal children and refer them as promptly as possible to appropriate mental health services for comprehensive assessment and treatment of mental health disorders and suicidal risk. Their direct everyday contact with children places them in a unique position and schools may constitute the most important referral source to mental health services for evaluation and treatment. Recognition of children at risk often requires pooling of information from a variety of sources and about a variety of aspects of the child's behaviour so as to gather a complete picture. As such, it often necessitates good communication within the school between teachers, the SENCO and the headteacher, as well as others who have contact with the child, such as the educational psychologist or the education welfare officer, where relevant. In this role, too, teachers have to work closely with parents in order to get them the most appropriate help and to assist them in obtaining treatment for their child. This can be difficult because parents can be reluctant since they may feel guilty or that they are to blame. In these circumstances, teachers need to stress the importance of intervening early and that treatment can help.

Ongoing support for those with suicidal tendencies

It is important that supports are provided within the school setting as this can be an area of stress and conflict for children. Children with a history of suicide attempts or self-harm should be encouraged to inform teachers and others within school when they feel vulnerable as this can prevent problems escalating and can prevent suicidal behaviour. Educational programmes aimed at teaching children to recognise the signs of impending suicidal behaviour can also be helpful in preventing it.

Teachers need to provide a support system within school that allows children to speak about their distressing feelings and suicidal tendencies and encourages them to talk about their worries. They can help by listening and helping children to find their own solutions to problems (Hornby, 1994). This should be done by someone with whom the child feels comfortable and someone who they trust, preferably chosen by the child, who needs to be available whenever the child feels distressed. This work should not take the place of individual psychotherapy or counselling, which it is not the teacher's role to provide. It should be focused on dealing with specific conflict situations within school and providing a supportive relationship until the child can see the therapist. Even so, this can be challenging work and should not be taken on lightly. It can be difficult for professionals to cope with children who harm themselves. It can be emotionally draining work and they too need support both from within school and from health professionals. The teachers involved should have direct access to support from a mental health professional and should be aware of their own limitations and prepared to acknowledge when they have reached the limit of their competence. In addition, the necessary procedures need to be in place for the child to remove him- or herself from the classroom and a potentially threatening situation with the minimum of fuss. The child should be praised for recognising a potentially difficult situation and for adopting an appropriate coping strategy in such circumstances.

Teachers should liaise with parents and encourage them to seek help if there are family problems that are affecting them or the child. It is difficult for parents to cope with children who are harming themselves and they are usually grateful for all the support they can get. They often feel angry, frightened or guilty and, when incidents occur, it is hard for them to know the best course of action. It is beneficial for teachers to maintain regular contact with parents and to take on a supportive role.

Further reading

Burningham, S. (1994) *Young People under Stress: A Parent's Guide*. London: Virago.

Hawton, K. and Catalan, J. (1987) *Attempted Suicide: A Practical Guide to its Nature and Management*. Oxford: Oxford University Press.

Pfeffer, C. R. (1986) *The Suicidal Child*. New York: Guilford.

Vaughan, P. J. (1985) *Suicide Prevention: A Working Guide to Recognition and Prevention*. Birmingham: PEPAR Publications.

References

Brent, D. (1987) Correlates of medical lethality of suicide attempts in children and adolescents. *Journal of American Academy of Child and Adolescent Psychiatry*, 26, 87–91.

Carlson, G. A. (1990) Suicidal behaviour and psychopathology in children and adolescents. *Current Opinion in Psychiatry*, 3, 449–452.

Center for Disease Control (1991) Attempted suicide among high school students – United States, 1990. *Morbidity and Mortality Weekly Report*, 40, 633–635.

Hawton, K. and Fagg, J. (1992) Deliberate self-poisoning and self-injury in adolescents: A study of characteristics and trends in Oxford, 1976–1990. *British Journal of Psychiatry*, 161, 816–823.

Ho, T., Leung, P. W., Hung, S., Lee, C. and Tang, C. (2000) The mental health of the peers of suicide completers and attempters. *Journal of Child Psychology and Psychiatry*, 41, 3, 301–308.

Hornby, G. (1994) *Counselling in Child Disability*. London: Chapman and Hall.

Pfeffer, C. R. (1986) *The Suicidal Child*. New York: Guilford.

Shaffer, D. (1974) Suicide in childhood and early adolescence. *Journal of Child Psychology and Psychiatry*, 15, 275–291.

Shaffer, D. and Piacentini, J. (1994) Suicide and attempted suicide. In Rutter, M., Taylor, E. and Hersov, L. (eds) *Child and Adolescent Psychiatry: Modern Approaches (Third edition)*, 407–424. Oxford: Blackwell.

Taylor, E. A. and Stansfield, S. A. (1984) Children who poison themselves: I. Clinical comparison with psychotic controls. *British Journal of Psychiatry*, 145, 127–132.

Vaughan, P. J. (1985) *Suicide Prevention: A Working Guide to Recognition and Prevention*. Birmingham: PEPAR Publications.

10 Soiling and wetting

Samantha, a 13-year-old girl, was still soiling and wetting during the day and at night-time. At home, her parents constantly cleaned up after her. At school, she soiled or wet herself on average about three times a day, sometimes remaining in her soiled clothes for long periods. Peers avoided her since she constantly smelt of urine and faeces. She appeared emotionally and socially immature, was frequently moody and often sulked when she did not get her own way. She made up stories, often told on others to get them into trouble and frequently distracted others from their work. When challenged, she always denied her behaviour. She was of average ability but her lack of motivation meant that her attainment was poor for her age. As she got older, despite a lot of support, it was becoming increasingly difficult to maintain her in her mainstream school.

Wetting (enuresis) and soiling (encopresis) are classified as mental health disorders, despite the fact that a better understanding has led to a view that they may be a result of physical difficulties, as well as indicative of underlying emotional problems. Although children are often referred to mental health clinics with the problem of wetting, it is generally agreed that this is better perceived as a developmental problem and that it is less likely to be related to emotional difficulties than soiling. Soiling and wetting may exist alone, together, or as part of other disorders. In a significant minority of children, the problems of soiling and wetting continue beyond what is considered the normal age. This can lead to distressing and persistent difficulties that can affect many aspects of their lives. In school, this can lead to practical problems, social difficulties and, because of associated difficulties, can impinge on children's educational progress. It is important that teachers have an understanding of the factors involved so that they can handle such problems discreetly and sensitively, as such children are frequently very embarrassed about their difficulties. There are practical ways in which teachers can help to make the school environment less stressful for these children.

Diagnosis

The diagnostic criteria for soiling (encopresis), as given in DSM-IV (American Psychiatric Association, 1994), include:

- the repeated passage of faeces in inappropriate places, for example in clothing or on the floor;
- at least one such event a month for at least three months;
- a chronological age of at least 4 years (or an equivalent developmental level).

Although the criteria specify a chronological age of at least 4, the age at which children normally acquire bowel control varies in different cultures and with different parental expectations. It is generally accepted within a British culture that this is attained by the age of 3 or 4, barring occasional accidents. Soiling may be classed as primary, where children have never established faecal continence, or secondary, where children have had an established period of continence before it began.

The diagnostic criteria of wetting (enuresis), as given in DSM-IV, include:

- the repeated voiding of urine into the bed or clothes (involuntarily or intentionally);
- occurrence at least twice a week for at least three consecutive months or significant distress or impairment of functioning when it occurs less frequently;
- a chronological age of at least 5 years (or an equivalent developmental level).

The age at which children gain control over their bladder varies widely and differs according to different cultures. In most children it is achieved by the age of 3, but in a small proportion wetting can continue for some considerable time. In DSM-IV a distinction is made between nocturnal only (wetting the bed) and diurnal only (daytime wetting) and a combination of both. Nocturnal enuresis, the most common type, typically occurs during the first one-third of the night, whereas diurnal enuresis most commonly occurs in the early afternoon on school days. As with soiling, wetting may be classed as primary, where children have never acquired normal bladder control, or secondary, where they have had control for at least six months and then lost it again.

Differential diagnosis

For diagnosis, soiling and wetting must not be due to the physiological effects of a substance (e.g. laxatives or diuretics) or the result of a general medical condition (e.g. diabetes, spina bifida or a seizure disorder). Soiling and wetting can be features of other disorders, such as conduct disorder, adjustment difficulties and learning disabilities, but in these cases they are usually considered secondary. There is thought to be an association between wetting and soiling, but the relationship at present remains unclear.

Features

Soiling

Different types of soiling behaviour have been described and the features are often closely related to causal factors. Several important distinctions need to be made (Murphy and Carr, 2000), including whether:

- soiling occurs during the day, at night or at any time;
- the child has never been toilet trained or has been free from soiling for a period;
- soiling is intentional or unintentional;

- it occurs with or without constipation and overflow incontinence;
- both soiling and wetting are present;
- soiling is a single problem or a sign of wider adjustment problems.

Soiling can occur with or without constipation and overflow incontinence. When present, this can result in the passage of the large amount of faeces being painful, thus encouraging further retention and a vicious circle can be set up. As the rectum becomes more distended there may be a lessening of the signals that indicate the need for defecation. Eventually liquid or semi-liquid faeces may leak round the blockage resulting in what is called 'overflow'. Stools are abnormal in appearance and consistency.

Alternatively, stools may be of normal consistency and appearance. Where soiling is due to failure to gain bowel control, for example, stools are normal in consistency and appearance but are randomly deposited in clothes, often both at home and at school. Usually, the child has never established continence. Where there is adequate bowel control and stools are normal, breakdown of control may occur in circumstances of psychological stress and such a secondary problem usually occurs between the ages of 5 and 8. In other, usually more severe, circumstances of psychological stress, there may be no loss of control, but the child may deliberately deposit stools in inappropriate and unlikely places, such as in baths, on furniture and smeared on walls, as well as in clothing. Soiling in these cases often may not occur at school, even though it may be a frequent occurrence at home and the pattern of soiling appears to cause marked distress to the family. Children and adolescents exhibiting this type of behaviour, called 'provocative soiling' by Goodman and Scott (1997), frequently deny their soiling behaviour. It is often indicative of severe and multiple underlying social and emotional problems. There may be difficulties in relationships within the family and other evidence of mental health disorder, including antisocial behaviour and conduct disorder (see Chapter 3).

Wetting

The essential feature of enuresis is the inappropriate passing of urine, often while asleep at night, resulting in a wet bed, or during the day, resulting in wet clothes. In most cases, this is involuntary, but occasionally it may be intentional. Most commonly, it is primary and the only symptom is passing urine whilst asleep. This may sometimes be accompanied by an increased frequency of urination during the day. In a smaller number of cases there is both nocturnal and diurnal enuresis. As with soiling, the features are closely related to the cause of the problem. Urinary infection is most common in those who wet frequently and during the day, and in girls. There is some evidence that wetting itself may cause infection and a vicious circle may develop with infection enhancing the risk of incontinence and vice versa. There is an association between structural abnormalities, incomplete bladder control and low responsiveness to cues that signal that the bladder is full amongst those who wet during the day. There is also a highly significant association between soiling and wetting, especially when the former is linked with constipation (Von Gontard, 1998).

Associated difficulties

At least one in five children who soil show significant psychological problems. Soiling can affect many aspects of children's development and can lead to a number of associated difficulties, which may have damaging consequences. Children who soil tend to present as unhappy, tearful, miserable and sometimes distressed individuals. They often do not feel physically well. Headaches and stomachaches, eating problems and poor height and weight are common. They often have poor relationships with their family and their peers and they may have associated behavioural difficulties, including temper tantrums. This can be children's way of coping with their difficulties, although in the long term, this type of behaviour can be more debilitating for the children than the soiling itself. Soiling places a lot of stress on families and parenting can be difficult and frustrating. In fact, 10 per cent of children who soil are on the child protection register (Buchanan, 1992). These children often experience isolation from their peers at a time that is crucial for their social and emotional development. Schooling problems are also common and these are discussed in more detail in the final section of this chapter.

Mental health problems are two to six times more common in children with enuresis than in the general population, but psychiatric disturbance is present in only a minority and over half of children with enuresis are emotionally normal. A variety of disorders, however, particularly conduct and emotional disorders, can complicate the condition. Such problems are more likely in those who wet during the day, those with secondary enuresis and those with other developmental problems, as well as girls. It is thought that this association may have more to do with how wetting is handled by the children, their families and others (Shaffer, 1994). Wetting can cause major stress in families and can become a major embarrassment to children and adolescents. Parents often have mixed feelings of concern and irritation. They may think that wetting occurs out of laziness or might be done on purpose, or that they are to blame. Lack of understanding may make them respond with anger, punishment, rejection or humiliation. This can lead to feelings of anxiety or guilt and it can cause great unhappiness and distress for these children. The amount of impairment depends on the limitations placed on their social activities, the effect on their self-esteem and the degree of isolation by peers and rejection by parents or carers. Unless adequate hygiene measures are taken, children are likely to develop rashes, soreness and a persistent smell that is a social handicap. Inevitably, wetting during the day has wider and more serious consequences because of its impact on others.

Incidence

Soiling occurs in about 2 per cent of children between 3 and 5 years of age and is three times more common in boys than girls (Hersov, 1994). In 10- to 12-year-old children the rate is about 1.3 per cent for boys and 0.3 per cent for girls. It decreases in frequency with age, until by age 16, it is almost zero.

At age 5 about 7 per cent of boys and 3 per cent of girls wet their bed, but by age 10 these figures are 3 per cent and 2 per cent respectively. At 18 years of age only 1 per cent of males and fewer than 1 per cent of females do so (Shaffer, 1994). Involuntary wetting during the day is far less common and, in contrast, is also found more frequently in girls than boys. It is uncommon after the age of 9. Only about 3 per cent of 6-year-old children, for example, have diurnal enuresis. Approximately 80 per cent of children with enuresis have primary enuresis, whilst secondary enuresis is less common, with onset most often between the ages of 5 and 7, and it is rare after 11. There are higher prevalence rates amongst the less educated and large, broken and impoverished families, as well as amongst children living in institutions.

Causes

In many cases of soiling and/or wetting there is unlikely to be a single causal factor and the exact cause may never be clear. Both may be a result of poor toilet training or stress, but there may also be a physical cause. Children cannot easily be divided into those with an emotional and those with a physical basis for their difficulties, as was once thought (Buchanan, 1992). It is probably only in a small minority of cases that such behaviour is intentional. Soiling and wetting have been associated with a range of factors, including physical causes, poor toilet training and stress, as well as developmental and neurological disorders. These are outlined below.

Physical causes

Children can become constipated for a variety of reasons, but, once established, it is self-perpetuating and can play a significant role in maintaining soiling behaviour. Bowel movements may be suppressed to avoid accidents, to avoid painful defecation, because of anxiety about going to the toilet in a particular place, because of a battle over toilet training or due to stressful toilet training, and this can lead to constipation. Primary enuresis may be due to inadequate physical development of the necessary muscles or other developmental problems, whilst primary daytime wetting can be an indication of physical abnormality of the urinary tract. Production of urine may be abnormally large and this may make it difficult for the child to learn bladder control (Shaffer, 1994). Children who continue to wet the bed may have a deficiency of anti-diuretic hormone in their sleep and produce more urine than their bladders can hold. If they fail to wake up when they need to urinate, they wet the bed.

Heredity

Enuresis and constipation tend to run in families. About two-thirds of children who soil, for example, also have constipation and almost a quarter of their families have a history of constipation (Buchanan, 1992). A hereditary disposition is therefore likely and when this is combined with family stress or inconsistent toilet training may make it more likely that a child develops a soiling or wetting disorder.

Delayed or poor toilet training

Some children have never learned to control their bladder or their bowel movements. In such cases, this may reflect inconsistent or neglectful toilet training. Primary enuresis, for example, is more often associated with poor toilet training and parenting in socially disadvantaged circumstances than with developmental problems. Starting toilet training after twenty months is associated with a higher rate of wetting.

Stress

Many families are able to identify stresses in the children's environment that they feel are responsible for the soiling or wetting problem, for example, the birth of a sibling, admission to hospital, starting school or separation from parents. A clear relationship between secondary, but not primary, enuresis and stressful life events or upset has been established. It has been suggested too that soiling may be indicative of sexual abuse since children who soil often exhibit similar symptoms to those who have been sexually abused. In these cases, however, it is vital to examine the whole picture and caution is warranted since the relationship between sexual abuse and soiling remains unclear and a lot of damage can be done through misdiagnosis.

Emotional disturbance

Emotional problems are more likely to result from, rather than cause, soiling or wetting behaviour. It is wrong, for example, to assume that all children who soil are emotionally disturbed. Isolation by peers and anger and rejection by parents or carers, for example, can have a marked impact on children's emotional development. A relationship between constipation and depression, however, has long been recognised. Whether it is a causal factor or a result of the soiling remains unclear. A vicious circle is formed and children need help to get themselves out of a pattern that can lead to long-term detrimental effects.

Developmental and neurological disorders

Soiling and wetting can be related to developmental and neurological problems. Soiling, for example, is more common in children of low birth weight and those who soil are significantly more likely to have stomachaches, vision problems or speech disorders. Some children may have minor abnormalities, such as disturbances in motor or adaptive functions of the colon or mechanism of defecation, which have left them vulnerable to a later soiling problem. Children with spina bifida and cerebral palsy often have neurological deficits which have major effects on both bladder and bowel control.

Individual characteristics

It is possible that there may be certain personality types that are more vulnerable to soiling or wetting problems. There may be certain children, for example, that are less able to deal with constipation and the pain of defecation. Children who soil are more likely to isolate themselves and to show excessive dependency, and their parents often describe them as worried.

Treatment

With careful treatment, the majority of children with soiling or wetting disorders respond well in a relatively short time (Buchanan, 1992). However, despite the fact that children are often greatly distressed by their symptoms, few parents seek treatment and when they do, doctors frequently provide inadequate or no treatment. There is a tendency to believe that the children will grow out of these conditions. The social and personal problems associated with soiling and wetting, however, mean that it is important that treatment is received early to prevent additional problems developing. A variety of factors, physical and emotional, may be responsible for soiling and wetting behaviour and treatment needs to address each of these. It is important to eliminate physical causes by a thorough physical examination, but even where a likely emotional cause has been identified, physical as well as behavioural interventions are usually required. In the minority of cases, where there are associated emotional and behavioural problems, these may need to be assessed and treated in their own right.

With soiling, behavioural intervention combined with laxative treatment has been found to be the most effective form of treatment (Thapar *et al.*, 1992). Most children improve significantly within the first two weeks and over 75 per cent maintain these improvements. Behavioural methods, particularly the use of the urine alarm, have also proved to be the most effective form of treatment for wetting, although these may be combined with medication, in the form of a nasal spray which increases the amount of anti-diuretic hormone at night (Murphy and Carr, 2000). Some cases, however, may be particularly resistant to treatment. When soiling is deliberate, for example, families often need help from a range of sources. Effective treatment provides practical relief for the family, as well as emotional and social benefits for children. Whatever the approach, support and reassurance for the child and the family are important. In can be helpful to explain these conditions as developmental problems. Behavioural intervention, physical treatment and psychotherapy are discussed below.

Behavioural intervention

Behavioural intervention involves establishing toilet routines through the use of rewards. It is important to set realistic targets, keep careful records and use a variety of appropriate rewards, such as star charts, and not to reward children for just being clean or dry as this can encourage retention. Children can also be taught how to respond to their body's signals, to establish regular habits, and never to delay going to the toilet. It can, however, be difficult to engage the family and to ensure that such a programme is correctly administered. Explaining the physical nature of the problem can help defuse the anger of parents, siblings and others and help them to be more understanding. For soiling, behavioural intervention is usually combined with laxative treatment, discussed below.

For wetting, the enuresis alarm is the most successful technique for a long-lasting cure. It consists of a small pad in the child's pyjamas or underpants connected to an alarm that is carried in a pocket or on a wristband. When the alarm goes off the child is expected to get up, go to the toilet and clear up any mess. It is easy to sabotage so children's co-operation is important. Parents are central for success and are encouraged to use rewards and praise and to take care that they do not unwittingly reward wetting. Success rates of around 80 per cent within two months have been reported, although roughly a third may have a significant relapse in the six months to a year after treatment stops. It is equally effective in those who wet during the night and during the day and with secondary and primary enuresis. Despite its success rate, however, parents often abandon treatment prematurely. The outcome is less positive where there is a high degree of family stress, associated mental health disorders, when children also wet by day and when the children lack motivation.

Habit training may be a more acceptable treatment for children who wet during the day and this focuses on identifying the time of day when wetting is most likely to occur and providing reinforcement for anticipating needing the toilet during this period. For those who wet the bed, parents are instructed to have the child drink lots of fluid and then delay urination for longer periods in an effort to strengthen bladder control. This is combined with hourly waking for trips to the toilet and a clean-up routine, together with positive reinforcement on dry nights. However, an alarm is also often needed to establish initial continence. A combination of dry bed training and the alarm results in a success rate of about 75 per cent, with a 21 per cent relapse rate after a year (Whelan and Houts, 1990). In less severe cases simple incentives such as, earning stars or tokens, are often enough to make the child respond to night-time bladder fullness.

Physical treatment

For soiling, treatment typically involves the use of laxatives and increasing the intake of dietary fibre. Where there is constipation with overflow, the bowel needs to be unblocked and a normal toilet routine established. In a few cases, lubricants and enemas may also be required. The aim is to maximise completeness of rectal emptying and to enhance the sensations related to defecation and continence, as well as facilitating the timing of defecation. Following this, behavioural methods are used to establish a healthy toilet routine. It has been shown that, in some cases, once the constipation is treated effectively, emotional and behavioural problems also decrease (Buchanan, 1992).

For wetting, the synthetic anti-diuretic hormone desmopressin, though inappropriate for the under 5s, can be given before bedtime, either as a tablet or nasal spray. It eliminates or reduces bed wetting in 70 per cent of cases within a few days, but in most cases, children relapse as soon as it is stopped. Behavioural treatment is therefore required to maintain improvements. Medication should be continued until the child has been dry for at least one month and then gradually reduced. In combination with an alarm it gives a higher and more long-term cure rate. This is particularly the case in cases of severe wetting or where there are associated behavioural and family problems. Side effects reported have included nasal pain and congestion, conjunctivitis, as well as headaches, nausea, abdominal pain. Some anti-depressants have also been shown to be successful for night-time wetting, but relapse again is common. There can be dangerous side effects and their use has been questioned on an ethical basis.

Psychotherapy

Soiling has been considered a symptom of underlying anger or conflict and psychotherapy advocated. Studies, however, are few and inconclusive, although some have indicated success where this form of support has been offered to parents or both parents and children (Thapar *et al.*, 1992). The success of a behavioural programme, however, requires structure and stability within the family and, for this reason, it has been suggested that family therapy may be needed before effective toilet training can begin. Cognitive therapy can help children see themselves more positively and challenge their irrational thoughts. Where soiling or wetting is due to stress, psychotherapy may help establish coping mechanisms and where it is due to toilet phobia it is important that children's anxieties are explored.

Course and outcome

Whatever the type of soiling, persistence into adulthood is unusual and the great majority of cases are resolved by the mid-teens (Goodman and Scott, 1997). As a general rule, the longer children have been soiling the longer they will take to get clean. Even when they have been clean for a six-month period, children will need advice on how to manage the condition and how to respond to relapses. A chronic course is more likely where there are associated problems, whether they are behavioural, developmental, academic, family or social, and where children and families are less open to change.

Although most children with enuresis grow out of it in time, treatment is important to prevent the development of associated difficulties, particularly emotional and social problems. After the age of 5, the rate of spontaneous remission is low, between 5 and 10 per cent per year. Most become continent by adolescence, but in about 1 per cent of cases it continues into adulthood. The best predictor of a positive outcome is the motivation to succeed and adherence to the treatment programme (Murphy and Carr, 2000). The prognosis is worse for secondary enuresis, where there are associated emotional disorders, where there is family disorganisation and parent interactions with the child are intrusive or coercive (Kelly, 1996), and where relatives have had similar problems (Barclay and Houts, 1995).

WHAT CAN TEACHERS DO TO HELP?

Whilst soiling and wetting in children and adolescents tend to occur more frequently at home than they do in school, they can lead to a variety of associated schooling problems that can have serious, long-term detrimental consequences. Teachers can help in prevention, early identification and by supporting children with recognised problems in the school setting.

Prevention

Children may be reluctant to use school toilets for a variety of reasons. This can lead to retention and serious physical problems, such as constipation. It is important, for this reason, that the toilets in school are readily accessible and maintained in a reasonable condition. Teachers should also be vigilant for signs of the misuse of toilet areas, for example for smoking and bullying, as these can discourage others from using them. Whilst children should be encouraged to adopt a healthy toilet routine and to go to the toilet at breaks and lunchtimes rather than in lessons, it is not helpful, particularly with younger children, to refuse to allow them to go to the toilet, whatever the circumstances. Teachers can also help prevent children developing soiling or wetting problems as a result of stress by providing appropriate support for vulnerable children in school. An effective pastoral system in which teachers are available to listen to pupils when they are experiencing difficulties and to help them address their problems can alleviate stress for some pupils. This might mean, for example, providing support in lessons, liaison with parents, providing counselling, or accessing external agencies that can support families in different ways depending on the cause of the stress.

Early identification

Problems of soiling and wetting are likely to be more evident at home than at school and parents may be reluctant to discuss them with teachers because of embarrassment or because they feel that the problem reflects badly on them. Where teachers suspect that a problem exists, they should discuss it with children and their families in a sensitive manner and not blame the parents or the child. It is important to establish when, where and how often soiling or wetting occurs, to discuss likely causes and to decide an appropriate course of action for dealing with the problem in school. Where children wet only at school, for example, they may be reluctant to use the school toilets or to excuse themselves from lessons. In these cases a suggestion to teachers that they tactfully encourage children to use the toilet may be all that is required. Where the problem is not so easy to solve, parents should be encouraged to take children to their family doctor in the first instance for a physical investigation. If a physical investigation has already been conducted, then parents should return to their doctor or a referral should be made for possible psychological intervention, either through the local mental health services or through the educational psychologist.

Support for children in school

When supporting children with recognised difficulties with soiling or wetting teachers may help by providing assistance with practical management, by addressing associated school-based problems, such as attendance problems, difficult behaviour and poor peer relationships, and by providing advice and support for parents.

Practical management

Where children have problems with soiling or wetting at school, they should be given a pass that allows them to go to the toilet whenever they need to without being questioned. It is important to recognise that not being allowed to go to the toilet can have disastrous consequences for these children. Retention can create significant physical problems and an accident can create enormous embarrassment for them and, in some circumstances, may lead to more long-term problems with school attendance. Where accidents do occur, these should be handled discreetly and children should be allowed to go to the toilet and deal with it themselves. It can help to have an agreed signal that indicates to teachers that an accident has occurred, thus avoiding focusing on the child and adverse responses from other pupils. Where pupils are following a habit-training or alarm programme this should be discussed with parents and strategies agreed that are, as far as possible, consistent so that parents feel supported. Children should be encouraged to take a survival pack, including, for example, clean clothes, plastic bags and a flannel, to school and to clean up after themselves as this form of practical help takes the pressure off them and their parents. Helpful strategies can be incorporated into a pastoral support programme, of which all teachers with whom children come into contact are aware.

Addressing associated problems

Children who soil or wet frequently have other health-related problems, such as headaches or stomachaches, which are likely to result in time off school. Where this is the case, it is important that children are encouraged to return to school as soon as possible as they may be reluctant to attend school because of their attendant difficulties and this can easily develop into a more long-term problem. While they are off school they should be provided with the support required to maintain their schoolwork, as getting behind can create additional stress for them.

Children who soil or wet may also exhibit difficult behaviour. In cases where it appears that soiling and wetting are deliberate and an integral part of antisocial or defiant behaviour this is a more challenging problem to deal with and has to be seen within a wider context (see Chapter 3). This is often an indication of more widespread and severe problems so behavioural difficulties may need to be treated separately. They may be severe enough to warrant attendance at a special school as these children may find it very difficult to cope in a normal school environment. Referral to the educational psychologist may therefore be an appropriate strategy. However, others may develop antisocial behaviour as a way of dealing with the negative peer reactions that they often experience, since it is far easier for them to reject others than be rejected themselves. Unless this is understood and sensitively handled it can lead to exclusion from school and further rejection and isolation from their peer group.

Children with these types of problems frequently have difficulties in forming relationships with their peers. Teasing, name calling and social stigmatisation are common peer reactions to children who wet or soil themselves. When witnessed, teachers should take this seriously and discourage it without focusing too much attention on individuals, since it can lead to long-term social and emotional difficulties for these children. Friendships should be encouraged, perhaps by linking children with a particularly supportive member of the class.

Advice and support for parents

Teachers may be the first port of call for parents with children who have problems with soiling or wetting at home and they are in a good position to advise parents on dealing with this type of problem. Suggesting referral to the family doctor to determine in the first instance if there are any physical problems, for example, can be helpful. Teachers can also help parents set up a programme of incentives for children using star charts. In addition, they can provide a link for parents, through the school nurse, to health professionals who can provide enuresis alarm equipment and further guidance. Where children are already on a programme of treatment, parents should be encouraged to maintain this and apply it consistently. Teachers can do this by emphasising the benefits to be gained for parents, as well as their children.

Further reading

Buchanan, A. (1992) *Children Who Soil: Assessment and Treatment*. Chichester: John Wiley & Sons.

Herbert, M. (1996) *Toilet Training, Bedwetting and Soiling*. Leicester: British Psychological Society.

Hersov, L. (1994) Faecal soiling. In Rutter, M., Taylor, E. and Hersov, L. (eds) *Child and Adolescent Psychiatry: Modern Approaches (Third edition)*, 520–528. Oxford: Blackwell.

Shaffer, D. (1994) Enuresis. In Rutter, M., Taylor, E. and Hersov, L. (eds) *Child and Adolescent Psychiatry: Modern Approaches (Third edition)*, 505–519. Oxford: Blackwell.

References

American Psychiatric Association (1994) *Diagnostic and Statistical Manual of Mental Disorders (Fourth edition)*. Washington, DC: American Psychiatric Association.

Barclay, D. and Houts, A. (1995) Childhood enuresis. In Schaefer, C. (ed.) *Clinical Handbook of Sleep Disorders in Children*, 223–252. Northvale, NJ: Jason Aronson.

Buchanan, A. (1992) *Children Who Soil: Assessment and Treatment*. Chichester: John Wiley & Sons.

Goodman, R. and Scott, S. (1997) *Child Psychiatry*. Oxford: Blackwell Science.

Hersov, L. (1994) Faecal soiling. In Rutter, M., Taylor, E. and Hersov, L. (eds) *Child and Adolescent Psychiatry: Modern Approaches (Third edition)*, 520–528. Oxford: Blackwell.

Kelly, C. (1996) Chronic constipation and soiling in children: A review of the psychological and family literature. *Child Psychology and Psychiatry Review*, 1, 59–66.

Murphy, E. and Carr, A. (2000) Enuresis and encopresis. In Carr, A. (ed.) *What Works with Children and Adolescents? A Critical Review of Psychological Interventions with Children, Adolescents and their Families*, 49–64. London: Routledge.

Shaffer, D. (1994) Enuresis. In Rutter, M., Taylor, E. and Hersov, L. (eds) *Child and Adolescent Psychiatry: Modern Approaches (Third edition)*, 505–519. Oxford: Blackwell.

Thapar, A., Davies, G., Jones, T. and Rivett, M. (1992) Treatment of childhood encopresis – a review. *Child: Care, Health and Development*, 18, 343–353.

Von Gontard, A. (1998) Annotation: Day and night wetting in children – a pediatric and child psychiatric perspective. *Journal of Child Psychology and Psychiatry*, 39, 4, 439–451.

Whelan, J. P. and Houts, A. C. (1990) Effects of a waking schedule on primary enuretic children treated with full spectrum home training. *Health Psychology*, 9, 164–176.

11 Obsessive–compulsive disorder

> As a 14-year-old boy, Colin's thoughts centred on fear of dirt and contamination. He would wash his hands many times a day, often for over half an hour at a time. Any attempts to stop him were met with resistance. His hands were red and inflamed. He constantly feared dirt and germs and eventually he could think of little else. He went out of his way to avoid touching books and other items that might be contaminated. He often became upset and was embarrassed by his symptoms. His behaviour affected his relationships at school and severely disrupted his work, despite the fact that he was considered an above-average student for his age.

Obsessive–compulsive disorder (OCD) is often grouped with other anxiety-related disorders because anxiety and discomfort are a central component. It is, however, distinguished as a separate disorder in DSM-IV (American Psychiatric Association, 1994) and ICD-10 (World Health Organization, 1992). Although the evidence for considering OCD as a separate disorder is extremely limited, the distinctive features of obsessions and compulsions separate it from other anxiety disorders (discussed in Chapter 6 of this handbook) and for that reason, we have chosen to devote a separate chapter to it here. OCD often goes unrecognised in children and adolescents and this means that they do not get the treatment that could alleviate much of their suffering. Teachers are in an ideal position to observe children's behaviour and it is important that they have an awareness of the features of the disorder so that appropriate help can be sought. At the same time, with understanding, there is a lot that teachers can do to help alleviate the difficulties of these children in the school setting.

Diagnosis

The diagnostic criteria for OCD, which are divided into obsessions and compulsions, are given in DSM-IV as:

- Obsessions that are:
  - recurrent and persistent thoughts that are intrusive, inappropriate and cause marked distress or anxiety;
  - not excessive worries about real-life problems;

- resisted by the individual;
- recognised as a product of the individual's own mind.

– Compulsions that are:
  - repetitive behaviours or mental acts that the individual feels compelled to perform in response to an obsession or according to rules that must be applied rigidly;
  - aimed at preventing or reducing distress or a dreaded event or situation.

OCD usually involves having both obsessions and compulsions, although individuals may have only one or the other. Minor obsessions and compulsions are common in childhood and most children go through a phase of insisting on certain kinds of order and routine because this makes them feel secure. Behaviours, such as avoiding cracks in the pavement, and feeding and bedtime rituals are quite common, especially in younger children. The term OCD does not apply to these children. It also does not apply to individuals who occasionally have morbid thoughts, for example about dying. The symptoms of OCD are far more severe and persistent and for OCD to be diagnosed they must be time consuming (take up at least one hour per day) and cause distress and disruption to the daily lives of the child and his or her family. The number and frequency of, and resistance to, the obsessions and compulsions are therefore important in distinguishing the disorder. Individuals with OCD can be secretive so the disorder may go unrecognised for many years. This means that individuals do not get appropriate treatment until the disorder is well established, yet early intervention can help avoid much suffering and the likelihood of developing associated difficulties. In addition, the diagnosis of OCD can be hindered by its relationship with other mental health problems and medical disorders, discussed next.

Differential diagnosis

Overlap with a range of other mental health disorders can make the diagnosis of OCD difficult, although most are relatively easy to distinguish in practice. They include depression, other anxiety-related disorders, Gilles de la Tourette syndrome, schizophrenia, eating disorders, an obsessional personality and brain damage (see other relevant chapters in this handbook).

A large proportion of individuals (between 20 and 66 per cent) suffer both depression and OCD and in these cases, the symptoms of depression need to be treated first. In contrast to OCD, the focus in depression is usually on something central to the individual's life, such as a bereavement (Toates, 1990). OCD is also commonly associated with other anxiety disorders, although in these the anxiety is generally directed at distinct objects or places and there is no accompanying ritualistic behaviour. Gilles de la Tourette syndrome is characterised by multiple tics that may be combined with complex patterns of behaviour and it has been reported to be the most problematic disorder to distinguish from OCD (Walter and Carter, 1997). The distinction is important because the treatment methods are very different. OCD can also appear superficially the same as schizophrenia, but individuals with OCD can be distinguished as, in contrast to those with schizophrenia, they are able to recognise that their thoughts are their own. A small proportion of females with OCD have a past history of anorexia nervosa. The two disorders may co-exist and symptoms may become intertwined. It is also important to make a distinction between individuals with OCD and an obsessional personality, although such individuals may be more prone to the development of OCD (De Silva and Rachman, 1992; Toates, 1990). Brain damage caused by injury or neurological disease can result in symptoms of obsessive and compulsive behaviour, but these tend to have a mechanical quality and there are generally other signs of brain damage, such as deficits in memory and learning ability. There is no evidence of any brain damage in the majority of individuals with OCD, although children with autism and severe learning difficulties can develop some elements of the disorder.

Features

Obsessions and compulsions often occur together and are closely related, but this is not always the case. Most children with OCD have multiple obsessions and compulsions. Some, however, may experience one or the other, although obsessions alone tend to be quite rare since they are almost always accompanied by compulsions (Last and Strauss, 1989). Whilst symptoms tend to come and go over time, they can become a major life activity, causing severe distress and leading to serious social disability, with individuals becoming house bound. OCD can create enormous stress within families as it can take over their whole lives.

Obsessions

Obsessions take the form of unwelcome, unexpected thoughts that are beyond the control of the individual, who tries to resist or suppress them. Individuals are able to recognise, however, that they are a product of their own mind. The most common types of obsession concern thoughts about contamination, imagining having harmed oneself or others, repeated doubts and the need to have things in a particular order to prevent a dreadful event taking place. Obsessions are time consuming and distracting and may take the place of other, more productive or worthwhile forms of behaviour. They frequently, for example, result in poor performance on tasks that require concentration, such as reading. In addition, many individuals avoid items that provoke obsessions to such an extent that this can seriously restrict their general functioning.

Compulsions

Compulsions are acts performed over and over again, often according to certain 'rules'. The performance of compulsions, the purpose of which is to prevent or reduce anxiety or distress or to prevent a dreaded event, is aimed at making the obsessions go away. Compulsions are excessive and not connected in any realistic way with the event they are designed to prevent. Individuals are compelled to undertake this behaviour no matter how foolish they seem or how much trouble it may cause. Typical compulsive behaviours include hand washing, ordering and checking or mental acts, such as counting or repeating words silently. For example, individuals with obsessions about being contaminated may reduce their distress by washing their hands until their skin is raw and inflamed. Those with obsessional thoughts may relieve their anxiety by counting over and over again. Rituals can become quite complex and, in some cases, individuals perform rigid acts according to elaborate rules for no apparent reason. One boy, for example, had to switch the lights on and off three times and then touch each corner of the door before he could leave a room.

Personality characteristics

As well as obsessions and compulsions, those with OCD also have characteristic personality traits (Weiner, 1982). Weiner described these children as on the threshold of panic all the time. They were cautious and reflective, had difficulty making decisions, and had an excessive need for certainty. They were meticulous and imposed orderliness in their lives. Homework, for example, had to be copied out three or four times, but as a necessity rather than a joy. They appeared stiff and uncomfortable and their behaviour was cautious, constrained and rigid. To others they appeared unemotional, but their intense emotions were kept to themselves and their feelings were often intellectualised and minimised.

Incidence

The overlap of OCD with other disorders and the fact that many sufferers are secretive and do not seek help make estimates of the incidence difficult. Estimates in children and adolescents have been around 2 per cent, whilst estimates in the general population have varied from as low as 0.05 to 3 per cent (Bebbington, 1990). In adults, equal numbers of males and females have the disorder, but in children and adolescents there tends to be more boys than girls with the disorder, by between two or three to one. It has also been suggested that, in boys, OCD starts earlier and tends to be more severe. OCD usually begins in adolescence or early adulthood, although it can start at any time from pre-school age to adulthood, and in most cases onset is gradual. In boys, onset generally occurs between 6 and 15 and in females between 20 and 29 years of age. Most adults with the disorder report having had a variety of neurotic symptoms in childhood, although it often goes undetected at this stage (De Silva and Rachman, 1992). As with adults, washing is the most common type of compulsion found in children, whilst checking and ordering are also particularly frequent.

Causes

There is no single proven cause of OCD, but a number of factors have been implicated, including heredity, brain structure and function, hormones and parental influence, and precipitating factors have also been highlighted. These factors are outlined below.

Heredity

Twin studies and the rate of the disorder in biological relatives both suggest that there is a genetic component to OCD. It is thought that a genetic tendency to be emotionally oversensitive can predispose individuals to the disorder (De Silva and Rachman, 1992; Toates, 1990).

Brain structure and function

Recent research has suggested that OCD involves problems in communication between the front part of the brain (the orbital cortex) and the deeper structures (the basal ganglia) (Wise and Rapoport, 1989). It is thought that insufficient levels of the chemical messenger serotonin are involved. It is unlikely, however, that this accounts for the whole picture, as, even with high doses of such drugs, individuals never become completely symptom free.

Hormones

It is now thought that hormones may be a causal, rather than a secondary, factor. OCD can be worse during puberty and, in females, symptoms are often associated with the menstrual cycle. Hormone therapy has been shown to be effective in some cases, but more study is required in this area.

Parental influence

Whilst there is a tendency for those with OCD to be timid and overdependent and to come from a home environment which is excessively controlled and lacking in expressed emotion, many also come from normal backgrounds (Weiner, 1982). Rather than OCD being a result of poor parenting, it is thought likely that individuals imitate the coping strategies exhibited by their parents. OCD is found across cultures in essentially the same form so there are no particular cultural influences (De Silva and Rachman, 1992).

Precipitating factors

In some cases the onset of OCD has been associated with significant life events, stress and trauma, but in 30 to 50 per cent of cases no precipitating factors are evident (Toates, 1990). The development of OCD has also been linked to underlying feelings of anxiety and anger and it is thought that it can be a way of dealing with and controlling such feelings (Weiner, 1982).

Treatment

A variety of treatment methods for OCD have been described. In a recent review by Moore and Carr (2000) the preferred treatment was found to be a combination of medication (clomipramine) and cognitive behaviour therapy, which included psychoeducation, symptom mapping and monitoring, anxiety management training, exposure and response prevention, as well as parent training. Inpatient treatment is very rarely necessary. Treatments have, however, included behavioural therapy, psychotherapy, support groups and family work, as well as cognitive therapy and medication. These are outlined below.

Behavioural therapy

Behavioural therapy is the main form of treatment for adults with OCD and a few studies have suggested that it is also effective for children (Wolff and Rapoport, 1988). A combination of exposure to the stimulus for compulsion and response prevention is the most effective form of treatment. Symptoms, their time duration and their triggers are noted in detail and then the therapist and the child work out a plan for gradually increasing exposure to the triggering stimulus (e.g. dirty hands) without carrying out the response (e.g. hand washing). This results in a gradual reduction in anxiety. An assistant may be asked to provide children with reassurance or to ensure that they carry out the exposure.

Cognitive therapy

Cognitive therapy is aimed at reducing inappropriate thought processes and replacing them with appropriate ones. Whilst such techniques may be helpful, alone they have been shown to be less effective than behavioural treatment. When combined with exposure and response prevention they can make treatment more effective.

Medication

Studies have demonstrated the effectiveness of treatment with serotonin re-uptake blockers for OCD in children, as well as adults (Goodman, 1990). Symptoms were found to improve in 75 per cent of cases, generally within three weeks. Medication, however, is best combined with behavioural and cognitive treatment to get more complete results and to prevent relapse. Side effects that include nervousness, restlessness, tremor, sweating, flushing, nausea and insomnia have been reported. Where there is associated depression or anxiety this can greatly affect the outcome of treatment and medication may be more helpful in these cases.

Support groups

Support groups for individuals and families dealing with OCD have been a recent advance (Rapoport *et al.*, 1994). It has been reported that many individuals have opened up and responded to the chance to share their concerns. Contact with other sufferers can be important in reducing isolation (Lenane, 1989).

Family work

As family factors, such as marital stress, overprotection and family dynamics, can interfere with the effectiveness of treatment, the involvement of the family in treatment is also an important consideration (Rapoport *et al.*, 1994). It is important to remain neutral and not to blame the family.

Course and outcome

In the majority of individuals, the course of the disorder may fluctuate, with periods of stress and fatigue often exacerbating the condition. As with many mental health disorders, if caught earlier there is more chance of a good outcome. Mild cases too are more likely to have a positive outcome, but OCD can be one of the most disabling mental health disorders and, if left untreated, it can lead to complete social isolation and loss of employment in adulthood (Marks, 1987). Few studies have followed the course of the disorder in children, but those that have (e.g. Zeitlin, 1987) suggest that in between 50 and 75 per cent of cases symptoms persist into adulthood and a significant number of early onset cases become intractable cases in adults.

WHAT CAN TEACHERS DO TO HELP?

OCD is classified as an anxiety disorder and anything that teachers can do to reduce anxiety-provoking situations for children in the school setting could be considered helpful in terms of preventing the development of this disorder. Strategies are discussed in Chapter 6, which is focused on anxiety disorders, and Chapter 21 on promoting mental health in schools. Teachers can also help by being alert to the signs of OCD in children and adolescents and by providing intervention and support for children with OCD within school.

Early identification

Early identification of OCD is important because it has implications for the success of treatment, yet OCD often goes unrecognised at this stage. Children generally do not request help themselves and early identification can be difficult because the disorder involves largely cognitive features that are not visible to the observer and because of the overlap with a range of other disorders. Children are also more likely to engage in rituals at home rather than at school in front of their peers or teachers. Teachers may, however, notice a gradual decline in schoolwork due to children's lack of concentration and preoccupation. An awareness of the features of the disorder and close liaison with parents where there are concerns can highlight the difficulties and facilitate access to appropriate treatment. It is important that, where there is concern, children and parents seek professional help and that a detailed mental health assessment is undertaken. Teachers can help by recommending an early referral to local mental health services and by encouraging parents and their children to engage in a programme of treatment.

Supporting children with OCD in the school setting

Children with OCD can lead a very difficult life and the environment within school can be particularly stressful for them. Toates (1990), when writing about his own experience of the disorder, for example, described school life as 'a mixture of pain and pleasure'. Children with OCD are prone to stress-related problems, such as headaches and upset stomach, and frequently do not feel well physically. This may be due to the general stress of having the disorder, poor nutrition or lack of sleep. Children with OCD are often intelligent, but find it difficult to apply themselves to learning so often lack progress in certain areas. They are frequently loners and non-conformists and this can make it difficult for them to fit in with their peer group. With awareness and understanding, however, teachers can make the situation less stressful for them. In consultation with parents, strategies might include:

- providing information about OCD for children and parents;
- reducing anxiety-provoking situations, such as avoiding the playground;
- providing a positive environment in the classroom;
- fostering friendships with peers;

- setting reasonable limits for behaviour;
- addressing learning needs (perhaps through individual education plans);
- being alert to signs of relapse.

Providing information about OCD for children and parents

The symptoms of OCD can be confusing and frustrating. Faced with an OCD sufferer in their class, teachers need to learn about the disorder and help children to learn about the disorder by ensuring that they have access to information. Teachers can help children to understand that treatment can be helpful and that this is an essential step towards accessing appropriate help. However, if a child denies that there is a problem or refuses treatment this may be very frustrating and, in this situation, all that the teacher can do is alert parents and continue to offer information and support.

Reducing anxiety-provoking situations

Reducing anxiety-provoking situations within school can be beneficial. This should be discussed with parents and reasonable measures taken, whilst not restricting too much of what the child is able to do. It may, for example, be helpful for the child to remain with a friend in the classroom at playtimes. Mornings and evenings can be particularly difficult for children with OCD. In the mornings they often feel that they must do their rituals right for the rest of the day to go well. At the same time, they fear being late and want to get to school on time. Consequently, they feel pressurised, stressed and irritable. In the evenings they may feel compelled to finish all their rituals before they go to bed, but at the same time they know they must get their homework done, as well as needing sufficient sleep. This means that some children stay up late and are then exhausted the following day. Thus, a vicious circle is easily developed. OCD symptoms often take up a great deal of children's time and energy, making it difficult for them to complete the tasks expected of children of their developmental age, such as homework. It is important that the teacher is aware of these difficulties and that allowances are made. Children's self-esteem can be negatively affected because their OCD symptoms constantly lead them into embarrassing situations. Failure to complete their homework, for example, can create intense embarrassment for these children and teachers should therefore handle such situations with discretion rather than with confrontation, which can only create further embarrassment for them.

Providing a positive environment

A supportive atmosphere at school can help improve the outcome of treatment, whilst negative comments or criticism can often make the symptoms of OCD worse. Teachers' involvement may be perceived as interference by the child, in which case it is important for teachers to be as kind and as patient as possible. Abstinence from ritualistic behaviour should be praised and rituals, if evident in school, should not be inadvertently reinforced by offering the child undue attention at this point. Interruptions to ritualistic behaviour may be met with hostility and resentment, and support and encouragement are essential. Generally, telling children to stop their behaviour usually does not help and can make them feel worse, since they are not able to comply with this request. Instead, it is important to take a positive approach and praise any attempts to resist compulsive behaviour and focus attention on the positive aspects of the child's work. Children with OCD can appear to be defiant, particularly as they dislike having to undertake these behaviours themselves, but it is vital that teachers do not perceive or treat these children as naughty. It is important to restore lost self-esteem and confidence so opportunities for praise should be capitalised upon. At the same time, all problems should not be attributed to the OCD and, when faced with each situation, other factors that might play a part should be considered.

Fostering friendships with peers

Children with OCD worry that they will be ridiculed or fear that they are going mad because they are aware that their thinking is different from their friends and family. They frequently feel that they are 'bizarre' or 'out of control' and as such, they find it difficult to mix with their peer group and make friends. Reassurance that they are not 'crazy' can be helpful. They usually try very hard to conceal their rituals from their peers and this alone can make peer relationships stressful. The amount of time they spend preoccupied with obsessions and compulsions also means that they have less time for mixing and forming relationships. Peers often react negatively to ritualistic behaviour and find it strange and difficult to cope with. Others may be intrigued to witness ritualistic behaviour. Children with OCD frequently get teased and ridiculed. When the disorder is severe, relationships can therefore become impossible. It is important to protect children from negative reactions. Anything teachers can do to help children feel accepted within their peer group and improve their chances of making friends can be beneficial. This may include, for example, attaching them to a particularly sympathetic member of the group.

Setting reasonable limits for behaviour

It is important to work closely with parents to gain a greater understanding of what the disorder means for the child and to set consistent limits. It is important that children or adolescents know what is expected of them. Children with OCD often have occasions when they may be extremely angry with their parents, usually because they will not comply with the child's unreasonable demands. Even when parents set reasonable limits, children with OCD can become excessively angry or anxious and this may manifest itself in the school situation. They should be encouraged to deal with their anger in appropriate rather than inappropriate ways. Such anger, for example, does not justify physical or verbal abuse, which should not be tolerated. The boundaries must be made clear and they should be treated like others in this respect. If outbursts occur to the extent that they become intolerable within the school situation, further professional help should be sought.

Addressing learning needs

On top of the factors already described, which can make the school situation a stressful environment, children with OCD may have difficulty being receptive to learning. They can be tense, preoccupied and anxious all of the time. OCD symptoms often take up a great deal of their time and energy, making it difficult for them to complete the tasks expected of them at their developmental age. Preoccupation with obsessions can make concentration for lengthy periods on a particular task very difficult and they may not be able to tolerate frustration resulting from tasks they perceive to be too difficult to achieve.

This is exacerbated by the fact that they are often reluctant to communicate their feelings. Teachers can help by giving instructions for a task one at a time and making instructions available in a variety of forms, both written and verbal. As children with OCD tend to be those who have difficulty expressing their thoughts and feelings, they may also have particular problems with creative work where this is required. They may lack the necessary language to achieve this and should be encouraged to use a variety of mediums, such as music, art, or drama, to try and express themselves.

Being alert to signs of relapse

Once recovered, individuals should be treated normally, but teachers need to be continually alert to the signs of a relapse, since others are more likely to notice this before the individuals themselves. It is best in this situation to point out the symptoms early and suggest to the child and to the parents that a return visit to the professional who treated the child may be required, as well as discussing and instigating strategies in school that may be helpful

Further reading

De Silva, P. and Rachman, S. (1992) *Obsessive-Compulsive Disorder: The Facts*. Oxford: Open University Press.

Toates, F. (1990) *Obsessive-Compulsive Disorder: What is it? – How to deal with it*. London: Harper Collins.

References

American Psychiatric Association (1994) *Diagnostic and Statistical Manual of Mental Disorders (Fourth edition)*. Washington, DC: American Psychiatric Association.

Bebbington, P. (1990) The prevalence of obsessive-compulsive disorder in the community. In Montgomery, S. A., Goodman, W. K. and Goeting, N. (eds) *Obsessive-Compulsive Disorder: Current Approaches*, 7–18. Gosport: Duphar Laboratories.

De Silva, P. and Rachman, S. (1992) *Obsessive-Compulsive Disorder: The Facts*. Oxford: Open University Press.

Goodman, W. K. (1990) Fluvoxamine in the treatment of obsessive-compulsive disorder. In Montgomery, S. A., Goodman, W. K. and Goeting, N. (eds) *Obsessive-Compulsive Disorder: Current Approaches*, 64–73. Gosport: Duphar Laboratories.

Last, C. G. and Strauss, C. C. (1989) Obsessive-compulsive disorder in childhood. *Journal of Anxiety Disorders*, 3, 295–302.

Lenane, M. (1989) Support groups. In Rapoport, J. (ed.) *Obsessive-Compulsive Disorder in Children and Adolescents*. Washington, DC: American Psychiatric Press.

Marks, I. M. (1987) *Fears, Phobias and Rituals: Panic, Anxiety and their Disorders*. Oxford: Open University Press.

Moore, M. and Carr, A. (2000) Anxiety disorders. In Carr, A. (ed.) *What Works with Children and Adolescents? A Critical Review of Psychological Interventions with Children, Adolescents and their Families*, 178–202. London: Routledge.

Rapoport, J. L., Swedo, S. and Leonard, H. (1994) Obsessive-compulsive disorder. In Rutter, M., Taylor, E. and Hersov, L. (eds) *Child and Adolescent Psychiatry: Modern Approaches (Third edition)*, 441–454. Oxford: Blackwell.

Toates, F. (1990) *Obsessive-Compulsive Disorder: What is it? – How to deal with it*. London: Harper Collins.

Walter, A. L. and Carter, A. S. (1997) Gilles de la Tourette's syndrome in childhood: A guide for school professionals. *School Psychology Review*, 26, 1, 28–46.
Weiner, I. B. (1982) *Child and Adolescent Psychopathology*. New York: John Wiley & Sons.
Wise, S. and Rapoport, J. L. (1989) Obsessive-compulsive disorder: Is it a basal ganglia dysfunction? In Rapoport, J. L. (ed.) *Obsessive-Compulsive Disorder in Children and Adolescents*, 327–347. Washington, DC: American Psychiatric Press.
Wolff, R. A. and Rapoport, J. L. (1988) Behavioural treatment of childhood compulsive disorder. *Behaviour Modification*, 12, 252–266.
World Health Organization (1992) *International Classification of Diseases (Tenth edition)*. Geneva: World Health Organization.
Zeitlin, H. (1987) *The Natural History of Psychiatric Disorder in Childhood*, Institute of Psychiatry Monograph No. 29. Oxford: Oxford University Press.

12 Schizophrenia

At 13 years old Susan presented as a neglected, forlorn and helpless young girl. Her teachers described her as 'odd'. She often appeared preoccupied and had lost interest in her schoolwork and her friends. Her behaviour was unpredictable – she could be pleasant and co-operative or loud and defiant for no apparent reason. When challenged about her behaviour, she walked out of lessons and sometimes left school and went home. She had become increasingly isolated from her peers and spent more and more time out of lessons, claiming that she felt unable to cope with the work. Her schoolwork became more and more disrupted and her life more chaotic. Her behaviour created problems in lessons and her schoolwork often remained incomplete. However, work that was completed was neatly presented and well written for an average girl of her age. She frequently became agitated and paced up and down the classroom in a frantic state. In conversation, it became difficult to follow her train of thought. She frequently thought that others were talking about her. Her teachers became increasingly concerned for her welfare.

Schizophrenia is a serious mental illness that usually affects young people in late adolescence or early adulthood. It is a psychotic disorder, which means that it is characterised by major abnormalities of thinking, beliefs and perception, a lack of insight and a loss of contact with reality. Research into schizophrenia in childhood and adolescence is sparse and information is mainly gained from studies of adults. It is difficult to know, therefore, to what extent these findings can be applied to individuals who are still developing mentally and emotionally. A lot of psychotic disorders go unrecognised and untreated for a considerable length of time, with consequent implications for individuals and their families. Schizophrenia is a severely disabling disorder, both mentally and socially, that has a profound effect on daily functioning and, as such, it has long-term implications for social and mental well-being. It is therefore important that it is diagnosed early and that teachers are aware of the signs of the disorder in young people so that they can direct parents to appropriate assessment and treatment services.

Diagnosis

The diagnostic criteria for schizophrenia, as given in DSM-IV (American Psychiatric Association, 1994), include:

- delusions;
- hallucinations;
- disorganised speech;
- grossly disorganised or catatonic behaviour;
- negative symptoms, such as being emotionally flat.

Symptoms must have lasted for at least six months and individuals failed to achieve the expected level of interpersonal, academic or occupational achievement. The ICD-10 (World Health Organization, 1992) diagnostic criteria are similar but symptoms require only one month's duration and, in contrast to DSM-IV, ICD-10 does not specify the number of symptoms required, making it more likely that cases are diagnosed. Two types of schizophrenia are distinguished in children and adolescents, depending on the age of onset. 'Very early-onset' schizophrenia occurs before the age of 13 and 'early-onset' schizophrenia occurs before the age of 17 or 18. A universally accepted definition of schizophrenia is not available and Werry and Taylor (1994) conclude that neither set of diagnostic criteria is entirely satisfactory. The diagnosis of schizophrenia in children and adolescents is serious, with major implications for children's lives. It should therefore only be made following a thorough assessment and where symptoms are multiple, pervasive, persistent and the effect on functioning is substantial (Werry and Taylor, 1994). Mental health professionals generally tend to be unwilling to label young people with such a diagnosis. A definite diagnosis cannot always be made during the first episode and can only be done by following the course of the disorder and the recurrence of symptoms. In adolescence, for example, a young person may have brief episodes and then go on to develop schizophrenia at a later date. These sorts of cases require close monitoring.

Differential diagnosis

In most cases, the diagnosis of schizophrenia presents little difficulty, but a wide variety of general medical conditions can include psychotic symptoms so these need to be excluded through physical tests and examinations. It is important for a neurological assessment to be undertaken to exclude conditions like epilepsy. It is also important to eliminate the possibility of drug-induced states. Mood swings are common during certain phases of schizophrenia and other affective disorders must also be excluded. Pervasive developmental disorders, such as autism, and obsessive–compulsive disorders need to be considered, although the distinction of schizophrenia from autism is now well established.

Features

The features of schizophrenia often develop gradually and can have a devastating effect, not only on the child, but on his or her family and those around him or her. Episodes often begin abruptly with a feeling that something awful is about to happen (Seeman *et al.*, 1982). Individuals become anxious and excessively self-conscious, so much so that they are unable to concentrate on what others are saying and doing and do not notice what is going on around them. Many individuals feel worthless, despicable and even evil at this stage, and they are likely to become clinically depressed. The impact on children's functioning should not be underestimated. Three main types of symptoms, abnormal perceptions, delusional thinking and thought disorder, characterise schizophrenia. There are, however, also other negative symptoms, such as cognitive and social impairment, and additional physical symptoms that can have a profound effect on an individual's life.

Abnormal perceptions

Hallucinations are the most consistently reported symptom in early-onset schizophrenia. Hallucinations are perceptions that occur in the absence of any, or sufficient, stimuli and are, therefore, not observed by anyone else. They can also occur in non-psychotic states in children, but this is uncommon. Care must be taken with children, however, as they may have difficulty accurately describing hallucinations, which can be confused with imagery. The hallucinations are usually auditory (Werry, 1992), but can be visual, tactile or olfactory (Andreasen, 1987). They tend to be command or persecutory in nature and children may hear voices that are outside of their control talking to them directly or in the third person (Werry, 1992). This can be frustrating, tiring and disturbing for the individual (Seeman *et al.*, 1982). It is important to note that these voices are actually heard, rather than imagined, and that they can become so real and compelling that children's attention can be totally consumed by them at the expense of other things going on around them. The voices may provide a commentary on children's actions, they may be perceived as belonging to a significant person in their life or they may shout insults or instructions to the individual, often urging self-harm or harm to others.

Delusional thinking

Delusions are rigid, false beliefs that are inappropriate to the person, their culture, peer group or developmental level and do not respond to reasonable explanations to the contrary. They are often bizarre and unbelievable. The frequency with which delusions are found in children with schizophrenia varies greatly (Werry, 1992). Most are of a paranoid form, especially in older children, and they often focus on those who are significant in the child's life. Children with schizophrenia may believe that those around them are hostile and threatening and that everything that is happening refers to them in some way. This can have a devastating effect on the individual's family (Seeman *et al.*, 1982). Delusional beliefs tend also to reflect the daily activities of children and their concerns. Themes such as monsters, ghosts and animals, for example, are common (Russell, 1994).

Thought disorder

The frequency of thought disorder in children with schizophrenia varies from 40 to 80 per cent (Werry, 1992). This results in difficulty expressing thoughts, incoherence, illogical thinking and in switching from one idea to another in a random fashion. This makes it difficult for others to follow their conversation. Attention may focus unduly on one subject for no apparent reason. Intrusive thoughts often focus on subjects important to their heart; for example, a child who loves animals may have thoughts of harming them (Seeman *et al.*, 1982). In addition to unwanted thoughts, the mind may also become blank suddenly for no apparent reason. These experiences can be very frightening and it may seem to children as if they have been 'taken over'.

Negative symptoms

The symptoms described above are called positive symptoms because they add to the individual's experience. The negative symptoms associated with schizophrenia, such as lack of emotion, lack of motivation, stereotyped behaviour and difficulty in socialising (Andreasen, 1987), have not been studied much in children, but they can have a devastating effect on the individual. They can result in withdrawal into oneself and may eventually lead to a change of personality (Seeman *et al.*, 1982). These symptoms may be the first to develop, but often persist and can be a major source of long-term disability. Lack of emotion and inappropriate feelings are common in early-onset schizophrenia and this makes children seem remote and difficult to get to know (Werry, 1992). Depressive symptoms are also frequent and individuals often lack interest in themselves and neglect their hygiene and their appearance (Asarnow *et al.*, 1994). Disorganisation is another aspect of negative symptoms. This may be particularly relevant for early-onset schizophrenia because of the effect that this may have on development (Werry and Taylor, 1994).

Physical symptoms

Physical symptoms can include severe agitation, slowness of movement and strange postures and mannerisms. Motor disorder may consist of inappropriate facial grimacing and connotations or unpredictable or violent behaviour. However, these tend to be rare in early-onset schizophrenia (Werry, 1992). Other common features include lack of eye contact, an eating disorder component and constant thirst (Seeman *et al.*, 1982).

Incidence

Schizophrenia is usually diagnosed in late adolescence or young adulthood, between the ages of 15 and 35, but onset can take place in early childhood. It affects one in a hundred people in the adult population (Clark and Lewis, 1998) and in 80 per cent of victims onset occurs between the ages of 16 and 25 (World Health Organization, 1992). The exact incidence is very difficult to estimate as accurate information is not available and studies use different criteria for diagnosis. It appears to be very rare before middle childhood and, even in adolescence, the incidence is probably less than three in every 10,000 young people (Hoare, 1993). There is an increasing incidence with increasing age. However, up to 5 per cent of adults may have experienced their first episode before the age of 15 (Asarnow and Asarnow, 1994). Schizophrenia affects more males than females, by a ratio of two to one (Russell, 1994). It appears with the same incidence and with similar clinical features in different cultures, although the manifestation of the illness may be influenced by different cultural aspects (Seeman *et al.*, 1982).

Causes

The causes of schizophrenia are considered to be multi-factorial and complex (Werry and Taylor, 1994). Although it is thought that biological factors play a major role, the course of the disorder may be influenced by psychological and social factors and these are outlined below.

Genetic factors

There is strong evidence for a genetic component to schizophrenia, probably of the order of 70 per cent (Kendler *et al.*, 1996). It is widely accepted that a predisposition to schizophrenia is inherited (Seeman *et al.*, 1982). There is some limited evidence that the genetic risk to relatives is even higher with early-onset schizophrenia (Werry, 1992). It is likely that multiple genes are involved (Werry and Taylor, 1994).

Brain damage at or around birth

Early damage to the brain, through birth complications and viral infection, for example, can contribute to schizophrenia (Werry and Taylor, 1994). Recent research indicates that something may occur during pregnancy or around birth. Factors implicated include hypoxia, low birth weight and exposure of the mother to viral infection. These may be the key initiating events amidst a complex array of risk factors.

Brain abnormalities

Brain imaging studies suggest that brain abnormalities occur in some adults with schizophrenia (Leff, 1996) and evidence of malfunctioning of the neurotransmitter receptors in the brain is now being found in children as well. Although there is still no general agreement about the nature of the abnormality, it is believed that it occurs very early, even before birth, and that schizophrenia is, therefore, a neurodevelopmental disorder (Murray and Lewis, 1987). This is reinforced by the fact that children with schizophrenia have a higher incidence of developmental abnormalities than normal children. Those who develop the disorder in later life often show slight delays in motor, cognitive and social development, such as speech or language delay, lower intelligence and decreased attention span.

Environmental factors

Environmental factors are now thought to account for less than 20 per cent of the disorder. Previous ideas that bad parenting practices were responsible have been completely discredited. Some clinicians believe that family interactions play a causal role, although research evidence for this tends to be lacking and it is now thought that such factors precipitate rather than cause the disorder.

Precipitating factors

Precipitating factors, such as social adversity, major life events and the influence of close personal relationships, can affect the course of schizophrenia (Werry and Taylor, 1994). Stress frequently contributes to the initial appearance and subsequent recurrence of schizophrenia in adults and this is probably an important factor in children as well (Seeman *et al.*, 1982). With teenagers, for example, contact with a highly emotionally involved parent can precipitate a relapse. Other identified triggers include family upheaval, hormonal changes, viral infections and the use of drugs (Seeman *et al.*, 1982).

Treatment

Despite the need to be cautious, it is important that the diagnosis of schizophrenia is made early because of the devastating effect that the disorder can have on relationships, the possibility of chronic illness and the likelihood of irreversible damage. Lack of a diagnosis may result in parents being blamed and families withdrawing to avoid embarrassment and criticism. It is important that they are given information and support otherwise the individual's support network may break down, with potentially adverse effects.

Schizophrenia is treatable, but not curable. A thorough assessment and early intervention is crucial in achieving effective treatment and a favourable outcome (Birchwood *et al.*, 1997; Howe, 1995). Treatment, however, can be difficult because those with schizophrenia often refuse treatment and the Mental Health Act may need to be applied, the implications of which are discussed more fully in the final part of this handbook. Understanding, acceptance of the condition and reassurance are also important ingredients of treatment (Seeman *et al.*, 1982), as is also the development of a trusting relationship with the family. In children and adolescents the close integration of medical, social and educational intervention is required. This may include, for example, access to inpatient, day patient and community care, paediatric services, educational facilitates and respite, rehabilitative and welfare services. It is important that families also get constructive practical help. Treatment may involve medication, electro-convulsive therapy, individual therapy, various forms of family support and group therapy. These are outlined briefly below.

Medication

Anti-psychotic drugs, which reduce the transmission of the brain chemical dopamine, are usually the central component of treatment, but they are not a comprehensive treatment alone (Barrowclough and Tarrier, 1997). They reduce hallucinations, delusions and illogical thought processes and have been shown to have a beneficial effect in children (Spencer and Campbell, 1994). However, the right level of medication can take up to two years to achieve and children may experience uncomfortable side effects, such as weight gain, muscle stiffness, dry mouth, tremor, restlessness and bouts of excessive tiredness. Some of the newer anti-psychotic drugs may eliminate some of the unpleasant side effects (Thomas and Lewis, 1998). Medication can be used to rescue an individual from breakdown and to prevent further relapse if taken regularly at a level which enables the individual to function effectively (Seeman *et al.*, 1982). Difficulties may arise, however, because sufferers may refuse their medication.

Electro-convulsive therapy

Although the use of electro-convulsive therapy is controversial, it has been shown to be helpful for some patients with schizophrenia, especially those who respond poorly to drugs. Studies do suggest long-term benefits, but there appears to be little consensus regarding its role in treatment and it is unlikely that it would be considered in the early stages of the illness or with children or adolescents.

Individual therapy

In adults, individual therapy, including social skills training, counselling, cognitive behavioural therapy and vocational rehabilitation, has been shown to be effective (Clark and Lewis, 1998; Seeman *et al.*, 1982). The gaining of insight is often a turning point in a proper recovery. Individuals require a long-term, trusting one-to-one relationship with someone who is able to provide reassurance, as well as opportunities to test reality.

Family support

It is essential for professionals to work in close collaboration with the family. Parents can play an important role in ensuring that children take their medication and in helping them to cope better with their difficulties. There is clear evidence that family support reduces subsequent relapse and promotes better social functioning (Dixon and Lehman, 1995). Interventions may include psycho-educational and behavioural approaches, practical support and formal family therapy. Education about the illness is considered essential for an effective long-term treatment (Clark and Lewis, 1998). A focus on family communication patterns in family therapy may also be beneficial (Asarnow *et al.*, 1994). Support groups for both the patient and the family may be helpful (Werry and Taylor, 1994).

Group therapy

Group therapy can be useful in order to reduce the individual's social isolation and this might be particularly relevant for children and adolescents as it can counteract apathy and withdrawal. A variety of activities, such as sports and music, should be introduced to try to remotivate the individual so that he or she is able to re-engage actively with society (Seeman *et al.*, 1982).

Course and outcome

The lifestyles of individuals with schizophrenia can range from potentially normal and independent to severely disabled and dependent on services. Although all remain at risk of further breakdown and potential damage, the course of the disorder can be greatly affected by using appropriate strategies to avoid further relapses. Some individuals may have no more than one episode, although they may need to take medication indefinitely to avoid relapse. Some may have intermittent breakdowns, whilst others become chronically ill. About 10 per cent will need ongoing intensive care because of the severity of their illness. Suicides occur in between 10 and 13 per cent of victims.

Only a small minority of children and adolescents will recover without further episodes (Asarnow, 1994; Werry, 1992) and early-onset schizophrenia is an extremely disabling and chronic condition (Clark and Lewis, 1998). This emphasises the need for rehabilitation and vocational measures as an essential part of treatment. The chances of a good prognosis may improve with a normal developmental history, no previous personality problems, above-average intelligence, an acute, stress-related onset rather than an insidious onset, and good home circumstances and relationships. A single acute attack in a previously normal child or adolescent may go no further. But, when symptoms develop gradually and there is a previous history of developmental and personality abnormalities, there is likely to be a poorer outcome, the possibility of prolonged dependency and the need for long-term psychiatric care.

WHAT CAN TEACHERS DO TO HELP?

Teachers have a role in early identification and referral, providing information for assessment and maintaining contact with children during periods of inpatient assessment and treatment, as well as supporting young people with schizophrenia in the school setting.

Early identification and referral

It is important for teachers to be aware of the signs and symptoms that can lead to serious mental illness, such as schizophrenia. These children may show signs of early developmental delay, such as language delay and clumsiness (Watkins *et al.*, 1988). Onset is likely to be gradual and deterioration in social and cognitive skills may be the first sign that something is wrong (Clark and Lewis, 1998). Teachers may notice such changes, but they are rarely linked to schizophrenia (Yung *et al.*, 1996). Children may be wrongfully considered lazy or as having a less severe psychological problem. It can be many months before it is recognised that they have a serious mental illness. Many victims show few early symptoms and onset can be sudden, in which case teachers should not reproach themselves for not having recognised the signs earlier.

Mental illness should be considered when children or adolescents exhibit 'odd' or unexplained behaviour, resulting in a marked change in character or personality. Whilst it is important not to raise children's and parents' anxieties unnecessarily, it may be helpful for teachers to contact the local child and adolescent mental health service on an informal basis to discuss their concerns. Informal consultation of this nature may help clarify whether their level of concern is appropriate and help them to decide on the most appropriate course of action. If there continues to be cause for concern, it should be discussed with parents, and the family encouraged to contact their GP for children to have a full medical examination.

Teachers' role in the assessment period

It is likely that children will spend a period of time in an inpatient unit for more detailed assessment and for the correct treatment to be established. Teachers can provide valuable information for the assessment. This should be as specific as possible, detailing changes in behaviour, strategies adopted and their outcomes. Other areas of particular relevance include levels of attention and concentration, evidence of thought disorder, academic achievement, and the individual's relationships with staff and other children. The educational needs of children or adolescents suffering from schizophrenia may require special consideration and a formal SEN assessment might therefore be required. Specialised educational resources, such as a special day or residential unit, either on a temporary or a long-term basis, may be needed for children to cope following an acute episode, especially where they are severely impaired and where family difficulties are more intractable (Werry and Taylor, 1994). Education is vital since, in the long term, the likelihood of employment is a key factor in a successful outcome. The more normal their environment the better and the ultimate aim should be for them to return to their mainstream school.

During periods of inpatient assessment and treatment it is helpful if teachers maintain ongoing contact with mental health professionals, children and their families and are kept informed of children's progress. Once treatment has been established, it is important to remember that, whilst initially many areas of life may be disrupted, everyday functioning need not be affected. Individuals are usually able to carry on life as before, provided that treatment is continued. An important part of a teacher's role can be to reinforce the fact that there is still a future for the individual. This interest can be conveyed by making regular contact, showing an interest in what they are doing whilst they are away from school and keeping them updated on what is happening at school. Regular visits may be appreciated so they enable children to maintain a link with the outside world and with at least some sense of normality. At this stage, it is inevitable that there will be times when teachers feel helpless and unsure of what to do, in which case the mental health team should be approached for support and guidance.

Support for children within the school setting

Plans for reintegration will naturally raise anxieties for teachers, as well as children. Being well informed, having an opportunity to discuss concerns and feeling well supported can help to allay teachers' fears. They need to know who to contact for guidance and they need to know that there is a back-up plan if things do not go smoothly, at least in the early stages. A meeting, attended by all those involved, usually the child, the parents, the teacher and the key nurse from the mental health team, to develop a reintegration plan, with clear aims, time scales and responsibilities that are realistic and clearly set out, can be very useful. The plan may need to be reviewed and adapted a number of times and the school may need to be very flexible in order to accommodate children's needs throughout this period. Return to school is likely to raise a number of areas of concern for children and teachers so it is important that these are addressed beforehand. Teachers can be helpful and supportive by:

- establishing a daily routine;
- having clear expectations;
- managing behaviour;
- enhancing relationships;
- enhancing motivation;
- being alert to signs of relapse;
- supporting parents.

Establishing a daily routine

Setting up a daily routine can be helpful as these children have difficulty coping with constantly changing demands and once a routine has become established management is likely to become easier. Too much excitement is unhelpful so they should be encouraged to have periods of stimulation and periods of rest. A positive start to the day and a healthy lifestyle are also beneficial.

Having clear expectations

These children may find the idea of returning to school threatening and frightening. They may lack confidence but should be gradually encouraged to take more responsibility. It is important that individuals are clear about what is expected of them, in terms of both their behaviour and their work. Allowances may have to be made for a temporary period, but there is also a danger that children begin to enjoy preferential treatment and as a result have no investment in recovery. A balance, therefore, has to be achieved. It is helpful to make clear, both to the individual and to other pupils, that, when fully recovered, expectations will be raised. There can be a lot of stresses in the school environment and it is important to keep these to a minimum. Handing work in or completing a task in a certain time, for example, may prove difficult.

Managing behaviour

It is important that individuals are perceived as 'seriously ill' rather than 'difficult' and treated as such. The more comfortable children feel the more likely they are to behave well. Strategies for addressing inappropriate behaviour should be discussed. It may be helpful, for example, for children to leave the classroom, without fear of reprisal, when they feel uncomfortable and having a consistent member of staff to whom they can go when they are having difficulties can provide an invaluable form of support. Any need for supervision should be discussed with the child, the family and the mental health team during the planning stages.

Uncertainty and inconsistency may provoke anger so it is important to be clear, explicit and as predictable as possible and, as far as possible, teachers should remain calm. If confrontation does arise, dealing with the matter privately may help calm the individual down and defuse the situation. The opportunity for teachers to express their own feelings, share concerns and discuss strategies in a non-threatening environment, perhaps through regular staff support meetings, can prove invaluable.

Enhancing relationships

The social pressure can be enormously stressful for these children so it may be helpful to arrange times for them to work in a small-group setting. Contacting old friends for the first time can present problems and, whilst this should be encouraged, children should not be forced into situations in which they do not feel happy. It may be helpful to allow the individual time with a particularly sympathetic friend at certain times during the school day. The competitive atmosphere in school can be another source of stress so it is important teachers show that they value individuals for themselves and their personal qualities.

Enhancing motivation

In the initial stages, children may lack enthusiasm and have difficulty facing the day. Allowances may need to be made for absences and poor punctuality, at least to start with. It is important for teachers to contact home when individuals do not turn up, as knowing they are missed and realising that their schoolwork is important in this way may resolve the problem. It is helpful to set work at the beginning of the day that they find most enjoyable. Praise can also be an invaluable tool in stimulating motivation. As they begin to relax more their interest will return.

Setting easily achievable targets

There will be periods where children lack concentration or attention and may appear slow at completing tasks. This should not be allowed to become an area of conflict. It may be due to the medication they have been prescribed or their preoccupations. Small, easily achievable targets may help to restore confidence. It may be helpful to begin by not expecting speed and not giving time constraints. Instructions for tasks should be short and simple to prevent confusion and avoid conflict.

Teachers' prime concern should be children's educational competence and this should be based on a detailed assessment. When there are clear signs of continuing illness, the teacher must decide on areas of priority for behaviour and work. Routine, predictable and non-stressful tasks are important for the individual to master first and it is perhaps easiest, in the earlier stages, to expect children to do things that they enjoy. It is important to keep in mind throughout this period that these children are recovering from serious illness. It is vital that all those involved in working with such children, especially in secondary school, are aware of their limitations. A consistent approach is needed if conflict is to be avoided. It is helpful if this is discussed with children and families in a supportive way and that the information that is shared with other teachers is only that which is essential to facilitate educational progress. This may best be achieved through use of the Special Educational Needs Code of Practice (DFE, 1994) and the provision of an individual education plan that could be developed in conjunction with the mental health team, children and their parents. A pastoral support programme, as recommended for pupils with emotional and behavioural difficulties, may also be used to inform planning at this stage (DfEE, 1999).

Being alert to signs of relapse

Whilst the responsibility for medical care remains with the mental health team, the teacher should be alert to signs and symptoms that can be suggestive of relapse. Each individual has their own set of early warning signs, which may include lack of concentration, preoccupation, irritability, mood swings, self-consciousness, difficulties in thinking, social withdrawal, suspicion of others and sleeplessness. It is very important for them to be able to recognise this and for those around them to be alert to these signs, so that relapse can be anticipated and planned for. Control can often be re-established by removing the trigger (often overstimulation) and increasing medication. The individual has to learn to achieve a balance between over- and understimulation. When symptoms begin to develop, lowering expectations and slowing the programme of activities can reduce the pressure. Promptly administered, this can prevent severe breakdown so a normal programme can continue when the crisis has passed. For chronic sufferers respite and befriending can help. If there are concerns at any stage, the initial step should be to discuss this with the child and the parents. Teachers may wish to tell the therapist about children's behaviour, but the most helpful approach is for the teacher to be able to discuss this in front of children and their parents. A joint meeting with the therapist and the family may be a better option. The individuals' appointments with the therapist are a vital safeguard to their mental health and should be respected.

Supporting parents

Families often need help with everyday practical difficulties and moral support to prevent family breakdown. In the few cases where drugs do not relieve paranoid symptoms, or where there is a lack of co-operation from children or adolescents, unpredictable and violent behaviour may put others at risk. This may make it necessary for the child to be removed from the family household for a short period, during which family support is vital. Violence, however, is usually the result of untreated or neglected symptoms and this can be prevented if all those involved watch for warning signs of breakdown or relapse. It is important for professionals to recognise the difficulties that families may encounter when trying to cope with this illness and the support that they may require. They often feel blamed and de-skilled, so sensitive treatment at times of trauma is essential to prevent them giving up altogether.

Further reading

Howe, G. (1995) *Working with Schizophrenia: A Needs Based Approach*. London: Jessica Kingsley.

Seeman, M. V., Littmann, S. K., Plummer, E., Thornton, J. F. and Jeffries, J. J. (1982) *Living and Working with Schizophrenia*. Milton Keynes: The Open University Press.

Werry, J. S. and Taylor, E. (1994) Schizophrenia and allied disorders. In Rutter, M., Taylor, E. and Hersov, L. (eds) *Child and Adolescent Psychiatry: Modern Approaches (Third edition)*, 594–615. Oxford: Blackwell.

References

American Psychiatric Association (1994) *Diagnostic and Statistical Manual of Mental Disorders (Fourth Edition)*. Washington, DC: American Psychiatric Association.

Andreasen, N. C. (1987) The diagnosis of schizophrenia. *Schizophrenia Bulletin*, 13, 25–34.

Asarnow, J. R. (1994) Annotation: Childhood-onset schizophrenia. *Journal of Child Psychology and Psychiatry*, 35, 1345–1371.

Asarnow, J. R., Thompson, M., Hamilton, E. B., Goldstein, M. J. and Guthrie, D. (1994) Family expressed emotion, childhood-onset depression, and childhood-onset schizophrenia spectrum disorders: Is expressed emotion a non-specific correlate of child psychopathology or a specific risk factor for depression? *Journal of Abnormal Child Psychology*, 22, 129–146.

Asarnow, R. F. and Asarnow, J. R. (1994) Childhood-onset schizophrenia: Editor's introduction. *Schizophrenia Bulletin*, 20, 591–597.

Barrowclough, C. and Tarrier, N. (1997) *Families of Schizophrenic Patients: Cognitive Behavioural Intervention*. Cheltenham: Stanley Thornes.

Birchwood, M., McGorry, P. and Jackson, H. (1997) Early intervention in schizophrenia. *British Journal of Psychiatry*, 170, 2–5.

Clark, A. F. and Lewis, S. W. (1998) Practitioner review: Treatment of schizophrenia in childhood and adolescence. *Journal of Child Psychology and Psychiatry*, 39, 8, 1071–1081.

Department for Education (DFE) (1994) *The Code of Practice on the Identification and Assessment of Special Educational Needs*. London: HMSO.

Department for Education and Employment (1999) *Social Inclusion: Pupil Support (Circular 10/99)*. London: DfEE.

Dixon, L. B. and Lehman, A. F. (1995) Family interventions for schizophrenia. *Schizophrenia Bulletin*, 21, 631–643.

Hoare, P. (1993) *Essential Child Psychiatry*, Edinburgh: Churchill Livingstone.

Howe, G. (1995) *Working with Schizophrenia: A Needs Based Approach*. London: Jessica Kingsley.

Kendler, K. S., MacLean, C. J., O'Neill, F. A., Burke, J., Murphy, B., Duke, F., Shinkwin, R., Easter, S. M., Webb, B. T., Zhang, J., Walsh, D. and Straub, R. E. (1996) Evidence for a schizophrenia vulnerability locus on chromosome 8p in the Irish Study of High-density Schizophrenia Families. *American Journal of Psychiatry*, 153, 1534–1540.

Leff, J. (1996) Schizophrenia: Aetiology, prognosis and course. In R. Jenkins and V. Field (eds) *The Primary Care of Schizophrenia*, 5–15. Norwich: HMSO.

Murray, R. M. and Lewis, S. W. (1987) Is schizophrenia a neurodevelopmental disorder? *British Medical Journal*, 295, 681–682.

Russell, A. T. (1994) The clinical presentation of childhood-onset schizophrenia. *Schizophrenia Bulletin*, 20, 631–646.

Seeman, M. V., Littmann, S. K., Plummer, E., Thornton, J. F. and Jeffries, J. J. (1982) *Living and Working with Schizophrenia*. Milton Keynes: The Open University Press.

Spencer, E. K. and Campbell, M. (1994) Children with schizophrenia: Diagnosis, phenomenology and pharmacotherapy. *Schizophrenia Bulletin*, 20, 713–725.

Thomas, C. S. and Lewis, S. (1998) Which atypical anti-psychotic? *British Journal of Psychiatry*, 172, 106–109.

Watkins, J. M., Asarnow, R. F. and Tanguay, P. (1988) Symptom development in childhood onset schizophrenia. *Journal of Child Psychology and Psychiatry*, 29, 865–878.

Werry, J. S. (1992) Child and adolescent (early onset) schizophrenia: A review in light of DSM-III-R. *Journal of Autism and Developmental Disorders*, 22, 601–624.

Werry, J. S. and Taylor, E. (1994) Schizophrenia and allied disorders. In Rutter, M., Taylor, E. and Hersov, L. (eds) *Child and Adolescent Psychiatry: Modern Approaches (Third edition)*, 594–615. Oxford: Blackwell.

World Health Organization (1992) *The ICD-10 Classification of Mental and Behavioural Disorders: Clinical Descriptions and Diagnostic Guidelines*. Geneva: World Health Organization.

Yung, A. R., McGorry, P. D., McFarlane, C. A., Jackson, H. J., Patton, G. C. and Rakkar, A. (1996) Monitoring and care of young people at incipient risk of psychosis. *Schizophrenia Bulletin*, 22, 283–303.

13 Autism

> Simon attended a mainstream school until he was 13 years old, although he spent the majority of his time in the SEN department where he received individual help. Although his teachers recognised that his behaviour was unusual, they were uncertain what was wrong with him. He had a fascination for trains and would repeat sentences and questions to do with trains constantly and with total disregard for the context of the conversation. In interactions he always appeared distant, never maintained eye contact and appeared to disregard the feelings of others. He frequently made thoughtless comments that offended others, both teachers and pupils. He had always had great difficulty socialising with his peers, but as he grew older they became less tolerant of his 'odd' behaviour and he became more and more isolated. Teachers were concerned that he may be bullied. As an adolescent, too, his increasingly sexualised behaviour, which was particularly difficult to cope with in the school setting, became a serious cause for concern.

Over the years autism has been considered a mental illness, an emotional disturbance, a personality disorder, a communication disorder, a mental handicap, a developmental disability and, more recently, an information processing problem (Williams, 1996). Currently, autism continues to be classified as a pervasive developmental disorder, a term which refers to children and adults who have severe lifelong difficulties in social and communication skills beyond those accounted for by general developmental delay. More and more children are being diagnosed with an autistic spectrum disorder. It is important that teachers are aware of the features of the disorder and have an understanding of its implications for learning, as well as being able to identify the disorder in its early stages so that appropriate help may be given.

Diagnosis

DSM-IV (American Psychiatric Association, 1994) specifies three areas of deficit for a diagnosis of autism:

- Impairment in social interaction, as manifested by at least two of the following:
  - marked impairment in the use of multiple non-verbal behaviours, for example eye contact;

  - failure to develop peer relationships appropriate to developmental level;
  - lack of social or emotional reciprocity;
  - lack of spontaneous seeking to share enjoyment, interests or achievements with others.

- Impairments in communication, as manifested by at least one of the following:
  - delay in or total lack of the development of spoken language;
  - impairment in the ability to initiate or sustain a conversation with others;
  - stereotyped or repetitive use of language or idiosyncratic language;
  - lack of varied, spontaneous make-believe play or social imitative play appropriate to developmental level.

- Restricted, repetitive and stereotyped patterns of behaviour, interests and activities, as manifested by at least one of the following:
  - apparently inflexible adherence to specific, non-functional routines or rituals;
  - stereotyped and repetitive motor mannerisms;
  - persistent preoccupation with parts or objects;
  - preoccupation with one or more stereotyped and restricted patterns of interest that is abnormal either in intensity or focus.

The recognition of some type of abnormality before the age of 36 months is required for diagnosis. Different degrees of autistic features are now recognised and autistic children vary widely in both the manifestation of and the level of severity of the disorder. In many cases no diagnosis of autism is made, since a child's development may not be sufficiently delayed, or there may be a failure to recognise the child's social impairments.

Asperger's syndrome is another pervasive developmental disorder that warrants special mention here because in many ways it is very similar to autism. There is ongoing debate about whether or not it is a variant of autism or whether it refers to higher functioning individuals with autism. Children with Asperger's syndrome display the same type of social impairments and restricted and stereotyped interests as children with autism but not their general delays in language and cognitive development. Other distinctions between the two disorders are discussed in relevant sections throughout this chapter.

Differential diagnosis

Many autistic children exhibit a range of non-specific problems that are found in many other psychiatric conditions, as well as in normal children. Diagnosis is based on a pattern of deficits, but if the features in one area predominate it can easily be confused with other disorders, so a full and detailed picture is vital. Health visitors and GPs, for example, can misdiagnose slow development or deafness instead (Humphreys and Ramm, 1987). It is the pervasiveness, severity and persistence of many of the features that make it distinct. There is some overlap between autism and a number of other childhood disorders, including:

- learning disability;
- childhood schizophrenia;
- developmental language disorders;
- attention disorders;
- social deprivation.

The majority of autistic children have learning disabilities, as impaired cognitive ability is a feature shared by both disorders. Approximately 60 per cent of autistic children have measured IQs below 50, 20 per cent between 50 and 70, and 20 per cent of 70 or above (Ritvo and Freeman, 1978). However, appropriate social behaviour, the motivation to communicate and a different pattern of intellectual impairment differentiate children with learning disabilities from those with autism. Children with schizophrenia have higher IQ and language levels, as well as delusions and hallucinations that are particularly characteristic. In contrast to those with autism, children with language disorders are usually attentive and responsive to others, have a more normal intelligence and do not exhibit stereotyped behaviours. Autism can co-exist with ADHD, and this is especially the case with Asperger's syndrome, but again children with pure ADHD do not show signs of the severe social impairment and communication difficulties of autistic children. Children who have experienced severe neglect may show language delay, abnormal social behaviour, exhibit odd habits or stereotyped behaviours but do not exhibit the peculiar language and communication difficulties and avoidance of social contact of autistic children.

Features

The main features that are characteristic of autism fall into the categories of:

- social deficits;
- communication difficulties;
- restricted and stereotyped behaviours and interests.

Social deficits

It is the profound and pervasive impairment in social behaviour typical of autism that is the most handicapping feature. In the pre-school years these children have minimal involvement with their parents, lack interest in other children, have unusual eye contact and a limited range of facial expressions. Difficulties in reciprocal social interaction and the inability to form relationships are most characteristic. They appear to lack empathy and may say or do socially inappropriate things. They often relate to people as objects and can form strong attachments to inanimate objects. They usually avoid play situations with peers and will engage in solitary activity. This preference for being alone continues to be evident as they grow older (Schreibman, 1988). Most autistic children, however, do not show deficits in all of these areas and many of them exhibit behaviours for brief periods or in particular situations that may seem surprisingly social (Lord and Rutter, 1994). Children with Asperger's syndrome tend to be more proactive in their social relationships (Howlin, 1998).

Communication difficulties

Although autism is characterised by delayed language acquisition it is the deviant quality of communication that is most specific to autistic children. Approximately 50 per cent never develop functional speech and those who speak characteristically display language that is qualitatively different from that of normal children and children with other language disorders (Ricks and Wing, 1975). Children with Asperger's syndrome, in contrast, lack early language delay. Autistic children do not engage in reciprocal conversation. Their questions are usually only connected with their preoccupations. Speech is repetitious or more of a monologue than a form of social communication. Their comprehension may be severely impaired and they may repeat certain sounds, words or phrases over and over again. Typically, children refer to themselves as 'you' or by name. Abnormalities of pitch, stress, rhythm and intonation, as well as the making up of words, are also common.

Restricted and repetitive interests and behaviours

Whilst younger and less able children tend to collect or manipulate objects, older children may become fascinated with particular topics. Children may become preoccupied with a specific part of a toy or unusual objects. Even when interests are age appropriate they can become so intense and overwhelming that they effectively prevent the child taking part in other activities (Howlin, 1998). Older, more able children often develop complex routines with objects that they act out over and over again. They sometimes engage in compulsive rituals, the intensity of which can be very strong. As they mature they may become upset if daily routines are not followed to the letter or if trivial aspects of the environment are changed to the extent that family life may be severely disrupted (Aarons and Gittens, 1992). Stereotyped behaviours, which interfere with the acquisition of more normal behaviour, may include rhythmic body rocking, jumping, head bobbing and arm or hand flapping. Some children, especially the least able, injure themselves deliberately, commonly, for example, by banging their head or biting their hands and fingers.

Cognitive functioning

Although the majority of autistic children have learning disabilities and impaired cognitive ability, a minority of autistic individuals have unusual cognitive skills, such as exceptional ability in drawing or mathematical calculations, in addition to the typical pattern of deficits, and are referred to as autistic savants (Rimland, 1964). Children with Asperger's syndrome generally, however, have a higher level of cognitive functioning than those with autism.

Incidence

Incidence rates for autism tend to be unreliable owing to inconsistency of diagnosis. The core syndrome affects about 2.5 children in 10,000, with boys outnumbering girls by about three or four to one (Humphreys and Ramm, 1987). Estimates for Asperger's syndrome, in contrast, are considerably higher, with figures varying between three and seven per 1,000 and with the majority being male (Ehlers and Gillberg, 1993).

Causes

Autism is a complex disorder that may not be due to a single cause. It may be that a variety of influences affect neurological development at an early stage (Humphreys and Ramm, 1987). The factors that have been implicated are outlined below.

Social environment

Systematic research has failed to support any more than a minor role for the social environment in the development of autism (Lord and Rutter, 1994). The belief that faulty parenting or family factors are involved has now been discredited, although raised anxiety levels within the family may reduce children's ability to cope (Aarons and Gittens, 1992).

Cognitive deficits

It is thought that a fundamental cognitive deficit to do with the way that information is processed prevents those with autism being able to predict the behaviour of other people (Happe, 1994). Hypotheses about the possible neurobiological basis of deficits in information processing and attention have been formulated, but basic deficits have yet to be established (Bailey *et al.*, 1996).

Genetic factors

Bailey *et al.* (1996) concluded that a strong genetic component exists, that a pattern of interacting genes results in the overall clinical picture and that autism might include genetically distinct sub-varieties. Over the years autism has been associated with a number of genetic disorders.

Pregnancy and birth factors

Factors associated with pregnancy and birth have been implicated. There is generally a high incidence of pre-natal problems in children with autism compared with their siblings and normal children (Nelson, 1991). Recent research has also indicated that certain viruses may be implicated in the cause of autism (Aarons and Gittens, 1992).

Brain damage and dysfunction

All of the available evidence supports the conclusion that autism is caused by abnormal brain development that begins before birth but which may not demonstrate its effects in behaviour until the end of infancy, when the child should be beginning to develop meaningful language (Trevarthen *et al.*, 1996). In nearly every case of autism, evidence of abnormality in the brain can be found (Gillberg, 1988).

Treatment

Autism requires a rigorous multi-disciplinary assessment process involving a combination of reports from parents and teachers, observation and standardised assessment (Lord and Rutter, 1994). A wide range of treatments has been advocated, but there is no substantiated proof of effectiveness for any of them. Individual needs must be assessed and each underlying problem specifically addressed (Williams, 1996). Williams notes that many treatments show a lack of understanding of the underlying problems associated with autism either by addressing the symptoms or by focusing on helping the individual cope with a problem rather than dealing with it. There is little information on which programmes are best for which children, since all generally claim they are effective for all autistic children. It is important to acknowledge the individual nature and the variety and pervasiveness of children's problems and to recognise the need to employ a range of techniques depending on the individual's pattern of skills and abilities. Different forms of treatment are outlined below.

Medication

There has been much interest in the drug treatment of autistic children over the last two decades, but, despite this, no specific treatment has been substantiated and many have potentially negative side effects (Schreibman, 1988). Careful use of medication may have a place in the treatment of some individuals when it is combined with other forms of intervention (Lord and Rutter, 1994).

Therapies

A wide range of therapies (e.g. speech, occupational, physical, music and psychotherapy) are available and their appropriateness depends on the individual deficits and needs of the child. Most autistic children benefit from some focused training in communication and some from help with motor and social skills (Williams, 1989). Psychotherapy with autistic children is generally ineffective (Rutter and Bartak, 1973), although some argue that it can give the therapist insight into the child's confusions and fears and can increase the child's awareness and capacity to regulate feelings (Trevarthen *et al.*, 1996).

Behavioural treatment

Successful application of behavioural treatment has had a major impact on the management of difficult behaviours, the acquisition of self-help skills and the educational treatment of autistic children (Schreibman, 1988), but limits of likely outcomes and of the maintenance and generalisation of changes are now recognised (Lord, 1984). However, intensive behavioural treatment beginning at a very young age, such as that pioneered by Lovaas (1987), may lead to major gains for many children (McEachin *et al.*, 1993). Those receiving intervention between the ages of 2 and 4, for example, make better progress than those that receive similar help at a later stage.

Education

There has been extensive research directed at the development of effective education for these children. Lord and Rutter (1994: 584) state that: 'Education has been by far the most powerful source of improvement for autistic children and adolescents in the last fifty years'. Important developments include the design of appropriate curricula, the provision of specialist teachers, research into the design of classrooms and the transition of autistic children to less restrictive environments (Schreibman, 1988). Educational aspects are discussed more fully in the final section of this chapter.

Family support

Family support may take a variety of forms, including the teaching of management techniques, emotional support, practical help (e.g. respite services) and providing information regarding local and national resources (e.g. support groups). It is important to remember that different families may require different kinds of support and that they vary in their ability to cope (Lord and Rutter, 1994).

Course and outcome

Autism is a lifelong condition and, whilst good services, such as education, family support and behavioural intervention, can make a real difference in social outcome, they do not remove the basic deficits. All autistic children are different, but the likelihood of complete independence is limited (Lord and Rutter, 1994). Those with Asperger's syndrome, however, have a better outcome in terms of later independence and social functioning. It is the child's language ability, cognitive level, overall level of behavioural disturbance and adaptive functioning that determine the prognosis (Venter *et al.*, 1992). In addition, the earlier the treatment the greater the benefits.

Individuals with a severe developmental delay will require supervised living and working situations throughout their life. Some may be able to function in local authority residential homes in a group setting with supervision and support. More able autistic individuals may be able to attend courses for children with special needs at further education college or residential courses that promote independence. However, even the most able often fail to survive in the world of work because of their social impairment. They need help finding and keeping jobs, coping with responsibilities and social demands. Overall results, however, do indicate that there have been improvements in the levels of functioning attained by people with autism owing to better treatment and better education (Howlin, 1998). More are living independently, more are in jobs and fewer spend their lives in institutional care.

WHAT CAN TEACHERS DO TO HELP?

Given the incidence of children within the full range of autistic spectrum disorders, it is likely that teachers will encounter several of these children throughout their careers (Howlin, 1998). It is therefore crucial that teachers are alert to the early signs of autism as many children with mild forms of the disorder will be taught within mainstream schools. Teachers also need to know what approaches they can adopt to maximise the educational potential of such children.

Recognising the early signs of disorders on the autistic spectrum

It is vital that teachers are able to recognise the early signs of autism since a delay in diagnosis can only exacerbate children's difficulties. This is especially important for pupils who have not been given a diagnosis, who have managed to cope up to secondary level in mainstream schools and who may have received little individual help (Howlin, 1998). Real improvements are only likely to occur if their underlying difficulties are recognised.

Whilst a diagnosis of autism will have a major impact on any family, many problems can be minimised with appropriate management strategies. Early intervention, therefore, can prevent later problems and lead to a more positive outlook.

There is no single identifiable factor that raises parents' suspicions, but many parents of children later diagnosed with autism have serious concerns about their child's development in their first year. These are usually to do with communication, play or social interaction. Language development is often the first cause for concern, although parents of those who later develop Asperger's syndrome tend to worry about their child's social and behavioural development as much as their communication difficulties (Howlin and Moore, 1997). Screening by family doctors and health visitors can lead to identification of those most at risk. Once identified, children should be referred for a multi-disciplinary assessment.

Educational provision

It is important to remember that all autistic children are different, that they vary in their academic ability and their behaviour. Some will need to attend specialised autistic provision, such as specialist schools, units or classes, whereas others will benefit from the academic stimulation that a mainstream school provides (Howlin, 1998). However, few LEAs provide specialist facilities for autistic children and these are insufficient to meet the needs of all those within the autistic spectrum. Some may therefore be taught in schools for children with severe or moderate learning difficulties, EBD schools or schools or units for children with language disorders, as well as in mainstream provision. The advantages and disadvantages of the different settings will depend on the child's academic ability and behaviour. This can present a difficult dilemma for parents. For the majority of high-functioning children with autism the chances of living a full and independent life can depend on whether they obtain qualifications at school. Whilst parents may realise that a mainstream school may have difficulty catering for their child's needs, they may also be aware that denying the child access to the normal curriculum may limit his or her chances of progress in later life.

Early placement in a playgroup or nursery is recommended as this provides social experiences at the same time as allowing children's difficulties to be clarified (Aarons and Gittens, 1992). The first few years of schooling can prove to be a nightmare for children and families. As children grow older their behaviour often becomes more difficult, and this can cause problems at primary school. For some children early education in specialist provision may be required initially, especially if there are marked behavioural problems, but once these are under control, transfer to a mainstream school may be possible (Schreibman, 1988). Their educational needs can fluctuate widely over time so it is important that children are regularly monitored and assessed and their placement reviewed. Autistic children often find coping with change difficult and periods of transition, such as the move from primary to secondary school or the move from school to college or work, are likely to prove particularly difficult so it may be necessary to provide extra support at these times.

Secondary school can pose more challenging problems for these children. The impersonal environment, the large numbers of pupils and constant changes of teachers frequently exacerbate their difficulties. In adolescence, they tend to have no friends, may be bullied and are often set up by other children. They may constantly be in trouble with teachers for their lack of organisation, lateness and their erratic approach to their work. These difficulties can lead to anxiety and a reluctance to go to school. It is vital that teachers of autistic children are given training and information. Without this, they may be unable or unwilling to provide these children with the special help that they need and this can lead to several changes of school.

Addressing areas of deficit

Successful education of children with autism is a particular challenge because of their wide-ranging areas of difficulty, but significant gains can and do occur when appropriate methods are used. The uneven profile of their difficulties can prove extremely disconcerting for teachers and this can lead some teachers to believe that these children are lazy or disobedient, rather than experiencing genuine difficulties (Howlin, 1998). The first step in teaching these children is recognition that they may require a different approach and a willingness to adapt teaching methods. Many different approaches to teaching children with autism have been advocated. It is important to remember that it is the underlying social impairment and communication difficulties that result in poor behaviour so targeting these areas of deficit is vital (Howlin, 1998). Goals should include fostering social and communicative development, enhancing problem solving and decreasing the behaviours that interfere with learning.

Social deficits

Mixing with peers can be very beneficial in the socialisation of children with autism, especially young children (Lord, 1984). Interactions need to be carefully structured and reinforced by teachers otherwise the motivation of peers tends to wane (Howlin, 1998). The chances of peer rejection rise with age. Older children often get themselves into trouble because they will do what peers ask of them in their desperation to make friends. Some fundamental guidelines for children can be helpful, including, for example, not commenting on people's physical characteristics and never doing things that are known to be naughty no matter how many children tell you to do it (Howlin, 1998). More specific strategies for addressing social behaviour, adapted from Attwood (1998), for example, might include:

- teaching children how to play and share with others;
- encouraging a friend to play with a child at home;
- encouraging children to join clubs and societies;
- teaching children to observe others for cues about what to do in social situations;
- encouraging them to think about how a person will feel before they respond;
- helping them to understand and express their emotions;
- teaching children to understand the perspective of others through role play;
- encouraging co-operative and competitive games;
- modelling how to relate to an autistic child for other children;
- encouraging friendships with peers;
- using a teacher's aide to raise children's social awareness;
- providing social skills groups for adolescents.

Language deficits

Specific strategies can be employed for improving children's language skills, thereby enhancing their ability to communicate with others. These might include, for example, as adapted from Attwood (1998):

- teaching children appropriate opening comments for conversations;
- teaching them to seek help when they are confused;
- encouraging them to have the confidence to admit they do not understand;
- teaching them the cues of when to reply, interrupt or change a topic;
- modelling sympathetic comments for them;
- using speech and drama techniques to facilitate conversation;
- teaching them to think about how their comments may be misinterpreted;
- explaining metaphors and figures of speech;
- teaching them how to modify stress, rhythm and pitch to emphasise key words;
- encouraging them to think rather than say their thoughts when near others;
- reducing anxiety-provoking situations that may inhibit speech.

Managing behaviour

Attention can maintain problem behaviours. Techniques such as time-out, extinction or differential reinforcement can serve an important role in managing behaviour, but it is also important for teachers to understand why children with autism behave as they do and to recognise their underlying social and communication problems. A particular problem for staff in mainstream schools is the apparent rudeness of these children. This can be personal and therefore difficult to deal with. Knowing that this is to do with their inability to understand the impact of their behaviour on others can help. It may not be productive to offer detailed explanations of why certain behaviours are not acceptable – it may be preferable to set simple rules and insist that they are kept.

Unstructured time, such as lunch breaks, can be stressful for these individuals and problem behaviours tend to occur during these times. It is therefore helpful to structure the whole of the day, including breaks and lunchtimes. It may be necessary for children to be allowed to remain in a classroom or the library at break times or during group games sessions, which they may also find particularly challenging. Allowing pupils to avoid activities that are beyond their levels of competence can reduce stress and possible conflict areas. They may have difficulty in certain lessons and teachers should be aware of this and modify expectations accordingly. Whilst children may require some pressure to complete tasks, if this becomes excessive it is likely to manifest itself in their behaviour, such as temper tantrums, aggression or self-injury, which should always be considered an indicator of stress and attempts made to avoid this.

Constructive application of interests and routines should be used to improve motivation or as means of social contact. Interests can provide a healthy means of relaxation and enjoyment. Controlled access can therefore be helpful. It is helpful to impose some routines as these make life more predictable for the individual and reduce stress. To avoid domination by the individual's stereotyped behavioural routines a balance is required and it is important sometimes to insist on compromise. Anything that can be done to reduce levels of anxiety and minimise the impact of change will be helpful in reducing this type of behaviour and prevent it becoming an obstacle to learning.

Motor clumsiness

Motor co-ordination, where there are difficulties, can be improved by including appropriate exercises and games within the curriculum, such as catching and throwing exercises and the use of adventure playground equipment, for example. Handwriting, which may be a problem for some children, can be addressed using remedial exercises and through learning to use a keyboard for some pieces of work. Children should be encouraged to slow down the pace of rapid movements. They may be referred to a relevant medical specialist for help with other problems, such as tics, or may receive remedial programmes from an occupational therapist.

Enhancing learning

Successful learning for children with autism depends on having a well-structured, individualised programme. Numerous studies have stressed the need for structure in teaching children with autism and this can have a positive impact on their behaviour, as well as their learning ability (Howlin, 1998). Tasks should be broken down into simple steps and the requirements made clear by indicating how much is to be completed or when the task is to be finished. It helps, for example, for children to have a personalised timetable indicating the amount of work to be completed by the end of each lesson. Practical tasks requiring direct interaction from the child can be beneficial. Instructions should be given clearly and where possible non-verbally as well as verbally. Children with autism may not be able to reflect on the learning experience in a way that makes it meaningful (Powell and Jordan, 1997). Teachers need therefore to build in time during the lesson to reflect with these childen on what they have learnt and how it relates to past and future learning. Good classroom management techniques are important. It is helpful, for example, if children have their own work station and are situated away from other distractions in the classroom. Some children with autism have sensory sensitivity. It is helpful to know if this is the case so that their particular sensitivities, such as certain sounds or intense levels of light, can be avoided.

Home–school liaison

Children's progress is likely to be compromised unless parents and teachers work closely together and respect each other's views and practices (Howlin, 1998). Limited generalisation of effects may occur if there is no consistency of approach between home and school. Parents will need considerable support to guide them through the complex process of educational assessment. Sometimes the judgement of parents may conflict with that of professionals and they will need to be fully aware of their legal rights and can be directed to support groups and special advice, if needed, that can offer them informed and practical help. Ideally, there should be ongoing liaison and negotiation between home and school.

It is important to involve parents in any programme of intervention, particularly in the early stages of learning (Trevarthen *et al.*, 1996). Regular feedback meetings or reports on progress to parents can be helpful. Homework can be a major problem requiring close liaison between home and school. Information from parents can be invaluable in helping teachers to address pupils' needs. The importance of giving parents faith in themselves and in their own ability to help their child cannot be underestimated (Howlin, 1998). Many programmes offer parents clear guidelines on what they can do to help their child, but in addition they need to be given time, support and encouragement.

Support from other professionals

Teachers are under considerable pressure and it can help enormously to have the support of colleagues and other professionals, particularly those with expertise in dealing with autistic children. All school staff need to agree to follow the approach adopted since inconsistency can seriously jeopardise the effectiveness of any intervention. It is therefore important that all staff who teach the child have an opportunity to get together to discuss the case, share strategies and resources and that an individual education plan is developed that all teachers are aware of. Specialist autistic teachers in the LEA can be called upon for support and advice. They may have resources that mainstream teachers can access easily. The educational psychologist and the local mental health service may also be able to offer support and advice.

Further reading

Aarons, M. and Gittens, T. (1992) *The Handbook of Autism: A Guide for Parents and Professionals*. London: Routledge.

Attwood, T. (1998) *Asperger's Syndrome: A Guide for Parents and Professionals*. London: Jessica Kingsley.

Howlin, P. (1998) *Children with Autism and Asperger Syndrome: A Guide for Practitioners and Carers*. Chichester: John Wiley & Sons.

Maurice, C. (ed.) (1996) *Behavioural Intervention for Young Children with Autism: A Manual for Parents and Professionals*. Austin, TX: Pro-Ed.

Powell, S. and Jordan, R. (1997) *Autism and Learning: A Guide to Good Practice*. London: David Fulton.

References

Aarons, M. and Gittens, T. (1992) *The Handbook of Autism: A Guide for Parents and Professionals*. London: Routledge.

American Psychiatric Association (1994) *Diagnostic and Statistical Manual of Mental Disorders (Fourth edition)*. Washington, DC: American Psychiatric Association.

Attwood, T. (1998) *Asperger's Syndrome: A Guide for Parents and Professionals*. London: Jessica Kingsley.

Bailey, A., Phillips, W. and Rutter, M. (1996) Autism: Towards an integration of clinical, genetic, neuropsychological, and neurobiological perspectives. *Journal of Child Psychology and Psychiatry*, 37, 1, 89–126.

Ehlers, S. and Gillberg, C. (1993) The epidemiology of Asperger's syndrome: A total population study. *Journal of Child Psychology and Psychiatry*, 34, 1327–1350.

Gillberg, C. L. (1988) The neurobiology of infantile autism. *Journal of Child Psychology and Psychiatry*, 29, 257–266.

Happe, F. (1994) Annotation: Current psychological theories of autism: The 'theory of mind' account and rival theories. *Journal of Child Psychology and Psychiatry*, 35, 2, 215–229.

Howlin, P. (1998) *Children with Autism and Asperger Syndrome: A Guide for Practitioners and Carers*. Chichester: John Wiley & Sons.

Howlin, P. and Moore, A. (1997) Diagnosis in autism: A survey of over 1200 patients. *Autism: The International Journal of Research and Practice*, 1, 135–162.

Humphreys, A. and Ramm, S. (1987) Autism: the isolating syndrome. *Special Children*, October, 14, 16–19.

Lord, C. (1984) The development of peer relations in children with autism. In Morrison, F. J., Lord, C. and Keating, D. P. (eds) *Applied Developmental Psychology*, 1, 165–229. New York: Academic Press.

Lord, C. and Rutter, M. (1994) Autism and pervasive developmental disorders. In Rutter, M., Taylor, E. and Hersov, L. (eds) *Child and Adolescent Psychiatry: Modern Approaches*, 569–593. Oxford: Blackwell Scientific.

Lovaas, O. I. (1987) Behavioural treatment and normal educational and intellectual functioning in young autistic children. *Journal of Consulting and Clinical Psychology*, 55, 3–9.

McEachin, S. J., Smith, T. and Lovaas, I. O. (1993) Long-term outcome for children who receive early intensive behavioural treatment. *American Journal of Mental Retardation*, 97, 4, 359–391.

Nelson, K. (1991) Prenatal and perinatal factors in the etiology of autism. *Pediatrics*, 87, 761–766.

Powell, S. and Jordan, R. (1997) Rationale for the approach. In Powell, S. and Jordan, R. (eds) *Autism and Learning: A Guide to Good Practice*, 1–14. London: David Fulton.

Ricks, D. M. and Wing, L. (1975) Language, communication and the use of symbols in normal and autistic children. *Journal of Autism and Childhood Schizophrenia*, 5, 191–222.

Rimland, B. (1964) *Infantile Autism*. New York: Appleton-Century-Crofts.

Ritvo, E. R. and Freeman, B. J. (1978) National Society for Autistic Children definition of the syndrome of autism. *Journal of Autism and Childhood Schizophrenia*, 8, 162–167.

Rutter, M. and Bartak, L. (1973) Special educational treatment of autistic children: A comparative study. II. Follow-up findings and implications for services. *Journal of Child Psychology and Psychiatry*, 14, 241–270.

Schreibman, L. (1988) *Autism*. Newbury Park, CA: Sage.

Trevarthen, C., Aitken, K., Papoudi, D. and Robarts, J. (1996) *Children with Autism: Diagnosis and Interventions to Meet their Needs*. London: Jessica Kingsley.

Venter, A., Lord, C. and Schopler, E. (1992) A follow-up study of high functioning autistic children. *Journal of Child Psychology and Psychiatry*, 33, 489–507.

Williams, D. (1996) *Autism: An Inside-Out Approach*. London: Jessica Kingsley.

Williams, T. (1989) A social skills group for autistic children. *Journal of Autism and Developmental Disorders*, 19, 143–156.

14 Special educational needs

Ricky was 16 years of age and in a special class for pupils with moderate learning difficulties. He had suffered brain damage at birth and was blind in one eye. He was a well-behaved young man who would quickly engage adults in a friendly conversation. He could read adult books accurately with appropriate expression but understood hardly anything of what he had read. He was a close friend of two other boys who had been in the same special class as him in primary school. Ricky lived at home with his mother as his father had died a few years earlier. He attended school regularly and participated willingly in all activities except physical education, which he did not like. The class spent one day per week on work experience at various jobs in local businesses and factories. It was on one of these days when Ricky's supervisor called the school to say that he was just sitting staring into space. When he was collected from work he was unable to communicate or function normally and was taken home. His family doctor referred him to the psychiatric ward of the local hospital where he was diagnosed as being 'vulnerable to occasional psychotic episodes'. In time it was clear that these episodes occurred when Ricky felt overwhelmed by stress. When he left school he was unable to cope with a job in open employment, like his two friends, and was placed in a sheltered workshop where the demands on him were less and he could be supervised more closely.

Definition

This chapter is concerned with children with special educational needs (SEN) who need additional help at school but who are also at increased risk of developing mental health problems. The term SEN encompasses children with a wide range of difficulties including dyslexia, visual impairment, hearing impairment, learning difficulties, physical disabilities and communication difficulties. It also includes children with autism and Asperger's syndrome as well as those with emotional and behavioural difficulties, such as ADHD, which are discussed in other chapters.

Each of the above groups of children exhibit higher levels of mental health problems than the general population. For example, deaf children are three times more likely to show psychiatric disturbance than hearing children (Hindley, 1993); blind children are vulnerable to adjustment and personality disorders (Warren, 1994); children with spina bifida or cerebral palsy often exhibit inattention and hyperactivity (Wills, 1993); children with dyslexia are around three times more likely to exhibit behaviour problems than other children (Mash and Wolfe, 1999); and children with severe learning difficulties exhibit three to four times more behaviour problems than children with IQs in the normal range (Dykens, 2000).

It is therefore important that teachers have knowledge of the different types of SEN, be aware of the increased likelihood of mental health problems with this group and learn strategies for preventing and ameliorating such problems.

Features

The mental health problems experienced by children with SEN include all those exhibited by children without disabilities that are discussed in other chapters. Difficulties which occur more frequently with these children include: conduct disorders; ADHD; depression and suicide; soiling and wetting; obsessive–compulsive disorders; and schizophrenia. There are also other difficulties with a high prevalence in children with SEN which are quite rare in the general population, such as stereotypical and self-injurious behaviour (Singh, 1997).

The criteria used for identifying the above difficulties in this population are the same DSM-IV (American Psychiatric Association, 1994) and ICD-10 (World Health Organization, 1992) criteria used in the general population and discussed in the other chapters. However, it is suggested that, in using these criteria, the overall development of children with SEN needs to be taken into account. For example, when considering whether an 8-year-old child with severe learning difficulties, who has a mental age of 4, also has ADHD, normal expectations for a 4-year-old child must be used as a guideline.

Incidence

The incidence of children with SEN in schools in the UK is generally estimated to be around 20 per cent, with approximately 3 per cent of these having statements of SEN. Prevalence rates vary widely between the different types of SEN, with moderate learning difficulties, hearing impairment and emotional and behavioural difficulties being the largest groups, whilst physical disabilities and visual impairment are the smallest groups (Stakes and Hornby, 2000).

The incidence of mental health problems also varies between the different types of SEN. For example, a significant proportion of children with EBD are considered to have mental health problems, while around half of children with severe learning difficulties show evidence of having mental health problems (Cormack *et al.*, 2000).

The incidence of specific mental health difficulties also varies within each type of SEN. For example, in children with learning difficulties rates of schizophrenia range from 1 to 9 per cent compared with 0.5 to 1 per cent in the general population, and rates of ADHD range from 7 to 15 per cent compared with 3 to 5 per cent in the general population. Rates of substance abuse and anxiety disorders, however, are lower in children with learning difficulties than in the general population (Dykens and Hodapp, 2001).

Causes

SEN are caused by a variety of factors. For example, genetic causation is the explanation for SEN such as Down's syndrome and muscular dystrophy. Some SEN are caused by difficulties within the pregnancy, as in deafness caused by the effects of maternal rubella on the developing foetus. Others are due to problems in the birth process, such as children with cerebral palsy whose brains have been deprived of oxygen. Yet others are due to the effects of childhood diseases, such as measles or meningitis, which can cause blindness, deafness or learning difficulties. Finally, some SEN, in particular emotional and behavioural difficulties, are considered to be at least partly caused by family, school and societal factors. These causes of SEN are discussed in detail in many texts on SEN, for example Hallahan and Kauffman (1991).

The development of mental health problems in children with SEN may be due to the same causal factors as in the general population or to additional risk factors related to their SEN. These risk factors are considered to fall within four broad domains: psychological; familial; social; and biological (Dykens, 2000; Dykens and Hodapp, 2001). These are discussed below.

Psychological factors

Various psychological factors are associated with increased risk of mental health problems in children with SEN. First, the specific impairment or disability will make some aspect of functioning more difficult. For example, impaired communication found in children who are deaf or who have language difficulties often leads to social skill deficits and peer relationship problems. Also, cognitive impairment in children with learning difficulties results in reduced problem-solving skills and difficulties in coping with the demands of everyday life. These difficulties may lead to anxiety, depression or aberrant behaviour.

Second, difficulties in developing a realistic self-concept and an adequate level of self-esteem are common in children with SEN. With many of these children, particularly those with learning difficulties, this is due to repeated experiences of failure in their learning histories. This is associated with feelings of uncertainty and even 'learned helplessness', which in turn can lead to anxiety, depression and other problems.

Third, children with SEN are prone to developing personality styles that are associated with increased likelihood of mental health problems. Examples of these are an 'outer directed orientation' in which children become dependent on others for solutions to their problems and the development of social styles in which they are too friendly or too wary of others. The adoption of such personality styles can lead to dependency, withdrawal, depression, impulsivity and helplessness.

Familial factors

Stress within the family of a child with SEN can also lead to mental health problems. It is now recognised that stress levels in such families are higher than in the general population, especially for mothers. Levels of stress in the family are influenced by various factors including the child's SEN, particularly the presence of health or behaviour problems. Stress is also mediated by parental coping styles and the adequacy of support for the family. It has also been found that marital discord or parental health problems increase the likelihood of these children developing mental health problems (Dykens, 2000).

Biological factors

Children with SEN often have associated disorders that can add to their adjustment problems. For example, a high proportion of children with severe learning difficulties have epilepsy which itself has been associated with mental health problems. Around 60 per cent of children with cerebral palsy and 30 per cent of those with visual impairment also have severe learning difficulties and 17 per cent of those with severe learning difficulties are deaf (Dykens, 2000). Further, certain genetic syndromes are associated with specific types of mental health problems. For example, children with Fragile X syndrome are prone to problems with relationships and activity levels, whilst those with Prader–Willi syndrome are prone to obsessive–compulsive behaviour, and those with Down's syndrome are prone to stubbornness and withdrawal. More information on specific syndromes can be found in Gilbert (1996).

Social factors

Children with SEN are at increased risk of both physical and sexual abuse and of exploitation by others in many aspects of life. They are also at risk of experiencing social stigma because of their disability or impairment. This has important implications for employment opportunities, self-esteem and the development of adjustment problems. It can lead to withdrawal and depression.

Children with SEN are also at increased risk of ostracism and rejection by their peers. For example, children with learning difficulties are often teased and bullied by their non-disabled peers. These peer relationship difficulties can lead to depression and suicidal tendencies.

Treatment

The treatment of mental health problems in children with SEN generally takes one of three forms: medication, behaviour therapy or counselling. These are outlined below.

Medication

As with the general population, prescribed drugs are widely used to treat the mental health problems exhibited by children with SEN. For example, it has been estimated that up to 20 per cent of children with severe learning difficulties living in the community are prescribed drugs to treat their disturbed behaviour and psychiatric disorders (Dosen, 1993). Disorders treated with drugs in this population include schizophrenia, depression, ADHD and various forms of anxiety (Aman and Singh, 1988). Responsiveness to medication in most children with SEN is similar to that of other children with the same problem except in those with severe learning difficulties where there is increased risk of atypical reactions or various side effects. However, in most cases medication alone does not successfully treat many types of disorder and other forms of intervention, such as behaviour therapy, need to be used along with the medication (Moss and Lee, 2000).

Behaviour therapy

The same behavioural analysis and modification techniques which are widely used to treat emotional and behavioural difficulties in the general population are also used with children who have SEN (Kazdin, 2001). For example, rewards and time-out are used to treat conduct problems and cognitive behaviour therapy is used to treat depression. Other behavioural techniques, discussed in the relevant chapters, are used to treat anxiety, phobias, psychosomatic behaviour, schizophrenia, obsessive–compulsive disorder, and sexually deviant behaviour (Gilbert *et al.*, 1998). Intervention is aimed not only at reducing undesirable behaviour but also at developing social skills which can replace the problematic behaviour and promote overall personal development (Dosen, 1993). Also, specific behavioural strategies are used with children with severe learning difficulties who develop problematic behaviours common to this group, such as self-injury, pica (ingesting inedible items) and rumination (repeated regurgitation of food) (Singh, 1997).

Counselling

Individual, group and family counselling are all used to deal with the mental health problems experienced by children with SEN. Counselling methods used may need to be adapted to suit children with different types of SEN; for example, more play techniques, games and simplified language are needed in order to counsel children with learning difficulties. Thompson and Rudolph (2000) suggest that, in addition to addressing specific mental health problems, the goals of counselling interventions with children with SEN should include: helping children to understand and adjust to their SEN; facilitating personal, social, recreational and independent living skills; enhancing self-esteem; collaborating with other agencies; contributing to educational planning; and counselling parents and other family members to help them understand and adjust to the child's strengths and limitations.

Course and outcome

It is only in the last fifteen years that attention has turned to the mental health problems of children with special needs so there is a scarcity of research evidence regarding the effectiveness of treatment and the long-term outcomes for these children as they become adults. Research that has been conducted has been done with children who have learning difficulties (Dykens and Hodapp, 2001; Moss and Lee, 2000). In an early paper Corbett (1985) suggested that the level of behaviour problems found in younger children tends to remain the same in adolescence, whereas the level of emotional problems, such as anxiety and fearfulness, decreases as children get older. However, Kiernan and Kiernan (1994) found that the proportion of children with severe learning difficulties who had challenging behaviour increased with age. Clearly, there is a need for research on the effectiveness of treatment for mental health problems and the long-term outcomes of such intervention for children with the various types of special needs.

WHAT CAN TEACHERS DO TO HELP?

There are many things that teachers can do to reduce the likelihood of children with SEN developing mental health problems. First, teachers can find out exactly what children's difficulties and needs are by talking with parents, previous teachers and any specialists who are involved with them. Second, teachers can make a point of focusing on children's strengths as well as weaknesses since maintaining their confidence and increasing their self-esteem are important, both in optimising their learning and promoting their mental health. Third, teachers can use buddy systems, peer tutoring and co-operative learning methods within their classes in order to develop children's social skills and optimise academic achievement. Fourth, teachers can give lots of praise and encouragement to children with SEN and maintain high yet realistic expectations of what they can achieve. Fifth, teachers can work in partnership with parents, for example, involving parents in reinforcing learning or behavioural programmes at home. Sixth, teachers can work closely with SEN specialists in planning learning experiences and behaviour change programmes. For example, teachers should ensure that they participate in individualised educational planning meetings at school.

The key to preventing and ameliorating the mental health problems associated with children with SEN in schools is for teachers to identify children with SEN as early as possible and then develop appropriate programmes for them. A brief overview of information on the identification of SEN and strategies for teaching children with the different types of SEN follows. It is only possible to provide limited information here and more information can be found in texts on teaching children with SEN (e.g. Hallahan and Kauffman, 1991; Stakes and Hornby, 2000).

Learning difficulties

Children with moderate learning difficulties have below-average intellectual ability with IQ scores of around 50 to 75 points. They are typically not identified until the early years of primary schooling. The trend is towards educating more and more of these children in ordinary schools but some remain in special schools or units. Children with severe learning difficulties have well below-average intellectual ability with IQ scores of below 50 points. They have difficulties in coping with most aspects of life. They are typically identified during their pre-school years. Most of them are educated in special schools or units in mainstream schools but an increasing number of them are attending mainstream schools, particularly in the early years of primary schooling.

Identification

Children with learning difficulties have:

- a short attention span;
- difficulty understanding instructions;
- difficulties learning reading, writing and number skills;
- delayed speech and language skills;
- poor fine and gross co-ordination skills;
- behaviour that is immature and prefer to be with adults or younger children.

Teaching strategies

- Start from what the child knows and go at the pace of the child.
- Break tasks down into small steps, teaching one step at a time.
- Ensure tasks are within the child's capacity in order to ensure success.
- Use semantic or concept mapping to build on the child's existing knowledge.
- Include lots of repetition and reinforcement to facilitate learning.
- Focus on oral language skills and social skills, such as following directions.
- Use practical activities: games, simulations, role plays and field trips.
- Use concrete materials and hands-on experiences, such as counting using money.
- Provide a range of resource materials: visual aids, such as charts/artefacts.
- Provide access to computers for drill, skill building and word processing.
- Decide on priorities: what the child must, should or could learn.
- Set achievable targets and review progress towards these regularly.

Specific learning difficulty (dyslexia)

Dyslexic children have specific learning difficulties in the areas of spelling, writing, reading and/or mathematics but can function well in other aspects of the curriculum. The vast majority of children with specific learning difficulties are educated in mainstream classrooms.

Identification

Children with specific learning difficulty have:

- a discrepancy between their oral language skills and written work;
- difficulties with auditory or visual processing skills;
- short-term memory or sequencing problems;
- problems with concentration, organisation or left–right orientation.

Teaching strategies

- Sit the child towards the front of the class and minimise copying from the board.
- Emphasise oral/practical approaches, for example semantic mapping.
- Select material to match the child's reading level and interests.
- Break tasks into small steps and allow adequate time for completion.
- Select and highlight most important spelling errors, not all of them.
- Get the child to use 'look, cover, write, check' to learn spellings.
- Use audio-visual aids, such as video/audio recorder or language master.
- Get the child to use a word processor with spell-checker as much as possible.
- Teach study skills, for example Survey, Question, Read, Recite, Review.
- Facilitate phonological awareness, for example, through rhymes and listening exercises.

Hearing impairment

There are two types of hearing impairment, conductive and sensori-neural. The majority of hearing-impaired children have conductive losses, are mildly or moderately deaf and cope in mainstream classes with a little extra help. Children with sensori-neural deafness tend to have severe or profound losses and may need to attend special units or schools for deaf children.

Identification

Children with hearing impairment:

- find listening difficult;
- are slow in learning to talk;
- have unclear speech;
- feel insecure and confused in class;
- do not hear clearly in a noisy classroom;
- can be withdrawn and often wait for cues from other children.

Teaching strategies

- Use visual clues to reinforce what is being said.
- Emphasise important instructions or key words.
- Prepare children for the introduction of a new topic.
- Write new vocabulary on the blackboard.
- Give homework instructions when the class is quiet.
- Allow a friend to check that the instructions and information are understood.
- Rephrase as well as repeat phrases and words not understood.
- In oral lessons make sure the pace of the discussion is not too fast.
- When other children answer questions repeat their answers.
- Make sure children can see the teacher's face when they need to listen.
- Don't walk about the room when giving instructions.
- Keep classroom noise as low as possible.
- Avoid giving notes to the class orally.
- Adapt outdoor activities to ensure full participation and safety.

Visual impairment

The vast majority of children with visual difficulties have what is termed partial sight or low vision and most are found in mainstream classes or special units within mainstream schools. There is a wide range of levels of visual difficulty and also several differing forms of visual impairment each with different implications for the child's education. A small proportion of this group are totally blind and they are mostly educated in special schools or units within ordinary schools.

Identification

Children with visual impairment:

- can be clumsy;
- have poor hand–eye co-ordination;
- may hold their heads in unusual ways;
- may frown, make faces or squint more often than normal;
- often complain of headaches or dizziness;
- have poorly formed handwriting;
- may have difficulty in seeing the blackboard;
- become tired more quickly than other children.

Teaching strategies

- Encourage the child to use visual aids prescribed, for example, glasses, magnifiers.
- Seat the child appropriately in classroom, for example, in the middle, towards the front.
- Make sure lighting is suitable; eliminate glare from the child's desk and the blackboard.
- Use worksheets with correct print size, enlarged if necessary.
- Ensure good contrast on any visual materials used – black and white is best.
- Supplement visual information with verbal explanation.
- Use concrete materials and hands-on experiences wherever possible.
- Allow more time to complete tasks and breaks in order to combat fatigue.

Physical disabilities

Types of physical disabilities found in mainstream schools include: cerebral palsy; muscular dystrophy; spina bifida; polio; arthritis; limb deformities; epilepsy; heart defects; asthma; cystic fibrosis.

Identification

Children with physical disabilities have:

- an unusual gait or difficulty with hopping, skipping, running or jumping;
- a poor sitting or standing posture/poor eye–hand, or foot, co-ordination;
- clumsiness/jerky movements/tremors/seizures/black-outs;
- bone or joint deformities/painful, stiff or swollen joints;
- difficulty breathing, or can tire easily.

Teaching strategies

- Have contingency plans in place for emergencies.
- Ensure the child has all the physical aids he or she needs.
- Ensure physical access, for example ramps into buildings, handles in toilets.
- Make sure the child is able to sit comfortably, in a good position to see.
- Adapt activities so the child can participate in physical education.

- Provide maximum access to information and communication technology.
- Allow more time to complete tasks and rest periods to prevent fatigue.
- Be understanding about time off needed for therapy or hospitalisation.
- Send home classwork when children are off school.

Communication difficulties

Communication difficulties often co-exist with other disabilities, especially hearing impairment, cerebral palsy and moderate to profound levels of learning difficulties. Thus, the majority of children with more severe degrees of speech and language difficulties are found in special schools or units in mainstream schools. However, mild to moderate levels of such difficulties are common in mainstream classes.

Identification

Children with communication difficulties have:

- articulation problems (e.g. substituting r for w in speech);
- fluency problems (e.g. stammer or stutter);
- voice disorders (e.g. hoarseness or high-pitched voice);
- delayed speech or language (e.g. in children with severe learning difficulties);
- disordered receptive or expressive language (e.g. in dyspraxic and autistic children).

Teaching strategies

- Listen to children carefully to determine speech/language difficulties.
- Be a good model of appropriate speech and language.
- Seat child with others who are good speech models.
- Use rhymes etc. to encourage clear articulation.
- Use role playing, debates, puppets, etc., to develop oral language skills.
- Use audio-visual aids such as video/audio recorder or language master.
- Use language children can understand; simplify complex statements.
- Use non-verbal clues (e.g. gestures, body language, visual aids).
- Define, highlight and reinforce new vocabulary used.
- Be patient with stutterers; give them time to express themselves.
- Accept the verbal contributions of all students.
- Refer on those with complex problems to a speech-language therapist.

Further guidance

Further guidance about the needs of children with various types of SEN is available from:

- the school's SENCO;
- educational psychologists;
- LEA advisers or education officers for SEN;
- teachers in special school or special units;
- associations for the deaf or visually impaired children, dyslexia, children with learning difficulties (e.g. RNIB, RNID, MENCAP).

Further reading

Brearley, G. (1997) *Counselling Children with Special Needs*. Oxford: Blackwell.

Hallahan, D. P. and Kauffman, J. M. (1991) *Exceptional Children: Introduction to Special Education (Fifth edition)*. Boston: Allyn and Bacon.

Singh, N. N. (ed.) (1997) *Prevention and Treatment of Severe Behaviour Problems: Models and Methods in Developmental Disabilities*. Pacific Grove, CA: Brooks/Cole.

Stakes, R. and Hornby, G. (2000) *Meeting Special Needs in Mainstream Schools (Second edition)*. London: David Fulton.

References

Aman, M. G. and Singh, N. N. (1988) *Psychopharmacology of the Developmental Disabilities*. New York: Springer-Verlag.

American Psychiatric Association (1994) *Diagnostic and Statistical Manual of Mental Disorders (Fourth edition)*. Washington, DC: American Psychiatric Association.

Corbett, J. (1985) Mental retardation, psychiatric aspects. In Rutter, M. and Hersov, L. (eds) *Child and Adolescent Psychiatry: Modern Approaches (Second edition)*. Oxford: Blackwell.

Cormack, K. F. M., Brown, A. C. and Hastings, R. P. (2000) Behavioural and emotional difficulties in students attending schools for children and adolescents with severe intellectual disability. *Journal of Intellectual Disability Research*, 44, 2, 124–129.

Dosen, A. (1993) Diagnosis and treatment of psychiatric and behavioural disorders in mentally retarded individuals: The state of the art. *Journal of Intellectual Disability Research*, 37, (supplement 1), 1–7.

Dykens, E. M. (2000) Annotation: Psychopathology in children with intellectual disability. *Journal of Child Psychology and Psychiatry*, 41, 4, 407–417.

Dykens, E. M. and Hodapp, R. M. (2001) Research in mental retardation: Toward an etiologic approach. *Journal of Child Psychology and Psychiatry*, 42, 1, 49–71.

Gilbert, P. (1996) *The A–Z Reference Book of Syndromes and Inherited Disorders (Second edition)*. London: Chapman and Hall.

Gilbert, T., Todd, M. and Jackson, N. (1998) People with learning disabilities who also have mental health problems: Practice issues and directions for learning disability nursing. *Journal of Advanced Nursing*, 27, 1151–1157.

Hallahan, D. P. and Kauffman, J. M. (1991) *Exceptional Children: Introduction to Special Education (Fifth edition)*. Boston: Allyn and Bacon.

Hindley, P. A. (1993) Psychiatric aspects of hearing impairments. *Journal of Child Psychology and Psychiatry*, 38, 101–117.

Kazdin, A. E. (2001) *Behaviour Modification in Applied Settings*. Belmont, CA: Wadsworth.

Kiernan, C. and Kiernan, D. (1994) Challenging behaviour in schools for pupils with severe learning difficulties. *Mental Handicap Research*, 7, 177–201.

Mash, E. J. and Wolfe, D. A. (1999) *Abnormal Child Psychology*. Belmont, CA: Brooks/Cole.

Moss, S. and Lee, P. (2000) Mental health. In Thompson, J. and Pickering, S. (eds) *Health Needs of People with Learning Disability*. London: Harcourt Brace.

Singh, N. N. (ed.) (1997) *Prevention and Treatment of Severe Behaviour Problems: Models and Methods in Developmental Disabilities*. Pacific Grove, CA: Brooks/Cole.

Stakes, R. and Hornby, G. (2000) *Meeting Special Needs in Mainstream Schools (Second edition)*. London: David Fulton.

Thompson, C. L. and Rudolph, L. B. (2000) *Counseling Children (Fifth edition)*. Pacific Grove, CA: Brooks/Cole.

Warren, D. H. (1994) *Blindness and Children: An Individual Differences Approach*. Cambridge: Cambridge University Press.

Wills, K. E. (1993) Neuropsychological functioning in children with spina bifida and/or hydrocephalus. *Journal of Child Clinical Psychology*, 22, 247–267.

World Health Organization (1992) *International Classification of Diseases (Tenth edition)*. Geneva: World Health Organization.

Part III

Psychological reactions to adverse situations

15 Bullying

Carol was referred for psychiatric treatment when she was 13 years of age, having taken an overdose of paracetamol. Six months previously she had been involved in a major incident of bullying in which a group of girls severely attacked her on her way home from school. She had been refusing to go to school for a number of months. Despite a number of changes of school and numerous attempts to support her reintegration, she continued to have problems with school attendance. She was also involved in further incidents of self-harm and attempted suicide.

Being bullied can seriously affect children's mental health, particularly as there is a tendency for those who are bullied to suffer in silence and to internalise the problem. As well as lacking confidence, having poor self-esteem and being isolated and lonely, they may develop insecurity and anxiety arising from continually feeling under threat. Some may experience sleep problems, eating disorders, phobias, depression, suicidal thoughts or even post-traumatic stress. Problems of this kind can persist long after the bullying ceases and create long-term damage that can last into adulthood. Children may also develop physical illness as a result of the trauma and stress they suffer. The cost, in terms of the pupils who drop out of school, develop significant problems or attempt to kill themselves, can be considerable. There is a growing awareness of the problem. Anti-bullying policies in schools are now statutory and many schools make a real effort to address the problem. Despite this, bullying continues to cause many children a lot of suffering. Children have a right to a distress-free school environment. It is important that teachers are aware of the distress that bullying can cause and its possible long-term consequences. It is vital that they take the issue seriously and adopt strategies to address the problem in their school.

Definition

Bullying is aggressive behaviour that intentionally hurts or harms another person. It is repeated and involves a power imbalance, such that it is difficult for the victim to defend him- or herself. It is important to realise that not all forms of aggressive behaviour towards others constitute bullying. Children who get involved in fights, for example, are not necessarily bullies, since those involved may share equal status.

Bullying can include any of the following: hitting or punching; kicking, tripping someone up; taking or spoiling someone else's things; name calling and teasing; nasty looks or threats; racist remarks; spreading nasty rumours or stories about another child; not letting someone join in; and isolating, or not talking to, someone. Some forms of bullying are therefore more obvious, whilst others are more subtle. Bullying behaviour may be seen as lying on a continuum, with things like name calling at one end and assault and extortion at the other, although it is important to note that the former can be just as painful for the victim (Tattum and Lane, 1989).

Features

Bullying is a complex phenomenon, but it has some essential features (Besag, 1989), including that:

- it involves a conscious desire to hurt someone and put them under stress;
- it may be physical, verbal or psychological in nature;
- it may be conducted by an individual or a group of individuals;
- the victim is repeatedly singled out for hurtful treatment;
- it may cause distress or fear through the threat of future incidents;
- it is directed against an individual who is unable to defend him- or herself.

It is now generally accepted that there is bullying in almost all schools, but it can be difficult to recognise because of the secrecy which often exists. For this reason, it is important to conduct research, usually through anonymous questionnaires, to find out the extent of bullying in the school before trying to tackle the problem. Teachers need to be adept at identifying children who have been or are being bullied. It may not become apparent until it is evident that there is something seriously wrong, for example when a child refuses to go to school. In general, any of the following signs and symptoms may be an indication of bullying, but caution must be adopted since they may also be an indication of other difficulties. As well as signs of physical injury, pupils who are being bullied, for example, may:

- be unwilling to go to school;
- change their route to school every day;
- start producing poor schoolwork;
- have personal items destroyed or missing;
- ask for money or begin stealing;
- start acting out or hitting other children;
- cry themselves to sleep, wet the bed or have nightmares;
- stop eating;
- develop stomachaches and headaches;
- become withdrawn;
- attempt suicide.

They may give improbable explanations for some of the above or refuse to say what is wrong. It is important to understand the psychological characteristics of those involved in bullying in order to be able to recognise it when it occurs and to intervene effectively (O'Moore and Hillery, 1991). All those involved in bullying, both victims and bullies, tend to be disadvantaged, have poorer school attainment, poorer concentration, below-average personal hygiene and more problems at home than those not involved. However, the characteristics of victims and bullies present a complex picture. Some children, for example, are both bullies and victims, whilst sub-groups of both bullies and victims have also been identified (Wolke *et al.*, 2000).

Bullies

Bullies, in addition to being aggressive towards peers, are often aggressive towards teachers, parents and siblings as well. They have little empathy with their victims. The majority of 'pure' bullies are thought to be healthy individuals who enjoy school, have highly developed social skills and are often the most confident children, rather than being insecure or unpopular pupils, as was once thought, although this remains controversial. As many as over 30 per cent may exhibit conduct disorder (see Chapter 3) or may be at increased risk of persistent conduct problems (Wolke *et al.*, 2000). In contrast, there is also a small distinctive group of bullies, labelled 'anxious bullies', who lack confidence and have few likeable qualities (Stephenson and Smith, 1989). This minority conforms to the more traditional view of the bullies as insecure or unpopular pupils.

Victims

Any child can become a victim of bullying. Some children experience one-off incidents, whilst a number appear to be constant victims. Bullying often focuses on children who are passive and lacking in self-confidence. In the main, they tend to be anxious, insecure, cautious, sensitive, quiet and often serious, with a negative view of themselves. Physical appearance is now thought to be less of a significant factor, although there may be individual exceptions (Tattum and Lane, 1989). Victims themselves are usually confused about why they are picked on (Macleod and Morris, 1996). Certain groups of children are more vulnerable to bullying. Children with a disability or SEN, for example, have been found to be two or three times more likely to be bullied than mainstream pupils, but they are also more likely to bully others (Smith, 1999). Pupils of ethnic groups report similar levels of bullying, although they were rarely bullied by those of the same ethnic group.

In contrast to the typical victim there appears to be a small group of victims that provoke bullying, who are more assertive and confident than other victims (Stephenson and Smith, 1989). These children have more in common with bullies. Whilst many victims never tell teachers of their distress, 'provocative victims' have a tendency to complain frequently to their teachers, even though the bullying appears to be self-provoked. This can create significant management difficulties for teachers, since it is important for all incidents to be followed up, and they often spend considerable amounts of time and effort investigating such incidents.

Bully–victims

Whilst it has always been acknowledged that some children are both bullies and victims, a recent piece of research suggests that many bullies are also victims (Wolke *et al.*, 2000). Children who are both bullies and victims tend to be the most anxious and the most unpopular. They are generally more emotionally unstable, are easily provoked and frequently provoke others.

Incidence

It is now widely accepted that bullying probably occurs in almost all schools and that it is more widespread than most parents and teachers think. Research has consistently shown that teachers greatly underestimate the amount of bullying that goes on in their schools (Tattum and Herbert, 1997; O'Moore and Hillery, 1991). Most children get involved in bullying at some time during their school career, as a perpetrator, a victim or an onlooker. Only a small number of children, however, become regular bullies. Estimates of the incidence of bullying are varied. Surveys suggest that over 25 per cent of primary pupils and about 10 per cent of secondary pupils suffer incidents of bullying 'sometimes or more frequently', whilst 10 per cent and 3 per cent respectively suffer incidents once a week or more frequently (e.g. Whitney and Smith, 1993). About a third of girls and a quarter of boys are at some time frightened of going to school because of bullying (DFE, 1994). There is much evidence for a decline in bullying as children get older (Smith, 1999). However, the majority of children do not tell teachers, perhaps because they have no confidence in teachers' ability to help (Besag, 1989), so the true extent of the problem is difficult to gauge. There is no doubt that bullying is one of children's major concerns and the proportions of children involved are relatively high.

Name calling and teasing are the most common forms of bullying. Whilst boys use their physical strength more, girls are more likely to rely on excluding someone from a group or spreading hurtful rumours (Elliott, 1991). The majority of bullying in primary schools occurs in the playground, whilst in secondary schools the incidence of bullying in the playground is only slightly higher than in the classrooms and in the corridors, suggesting that it may be witnessed by teachers (Macleod and Morris, 1996; Smith, 1999).

Causes/influences

Bullying is a complex problem with a range of different influences. It depends on the psychology of the bully, the response of the victim, the support of others, as well as the context in which it occurs (Smith, 1999). Influences include variables at individual, family, school and community level (Smith and Thompson, 1991). These are outlined briefly below.

Individual factors

There are different motivations for bullying. It may simply be a thoughtless act or something to do when bored. Some children may see nothing wrong with it, because they do not understand or care how much it hurts others or because they think that the individual deserves it. For others, it may be a sign that they are troubled or anxious, unhappy at home or have been bullied themselves. Equally, characteristics of the victim, such as temperament, shyness, lack of social skills or lack of friends, may make him or her susceptible to bullying.

Family factors

Bullying is a form of socially learned behaviour and family factors, such as cold child rearing, high levels of discord and violence, lack of rules and poor monitoring of behaviour, are also influential (Besag, 1989). Parents may have indicated that using strength and humiliating others are acceptable ways to behave. Victims, on the other hand, typically come from supportive, loving and sensitive families. When exposed to aggressive behaviour or treated unfairly, they find it very difficult to cope. Some victims come from overprotective or enmeshed families where children have not developed the social skills or coping strategies to deal with such incidents (Smith, 2000).

School factors

There is no doubt that bullying cannot be considered in isolation and consideration needs to be given to the context in which it occurs (Besag, 1989). The incidence of bullying varies considerably between schools and it is likely that the school ethos is an important influential factor. This is discussed in more depth in the final section of this chapter.

Community factors

Wider neighbourhood, community and social factors can also be influential. Attitudes to violence, social class differentiation, socio-economic stress on families, and violence and harassment generally are also thought to play a part.

Protective factors

For some children the strength of their internal resources and the support of their peers can make all the difference in enabling them to protect themselves and in developing strategies to deal with bullying successfully. Others, in contrast, are powerless to defend themselves against even the slightest incident (Macleod and Morris, 1996). Very few children, however, can stand up to constant scapegoating, intimidation or violent assault. In practice it is often difficult to identify who is at risk and who is resilient.

Effects

Bullying can have serious consequences for victims and perpetrators. It can sometimes be difficult for adults to understand the distress that bullying can cause to vulnerable children, but even persistent name calling can make children very unhappy. The effects, however, are often difficult to gauge as individuals react very differently to similar situations, which therefore have to be judged on their own merits (Macleod and Morris, 1996).

The effects of bullying can be wide-ranging. It can impact on children's schoolwork, their attendance, as well as their psychological and physical well-being (Sharp, 1995). It can lead to unresolved anger and resentment (Tattum and Herbert, 1997). Left untreated such reactions can evolve into depression, physical illness and even suicide. Bullying can create a sense of isolation and provoke extreme anxiety in some children. Ongoing, persistent problems can lead to more serious mental health problems, such as school refusal, depression and suicide (Wolke *et al.*, 2000). Bullied children are significantly more likely to report sleep difficulties, bed wetting, feeling sad, headaches and stomachaches (Williams *et al.*, 1996). Bullying may result in lack of self-confidence, difficulty making friends and withdrawal. For this reason it is important that teachers can spot incidents of bullying early so that more deep-seated psychological problems are prevented. For a small percentage of victims it can have a seriously debilitating effect, ruining their chances of academic and social achievement. Bullying is also one of the major reasons that children run away from home. A relentless campaign of victimisation can lead some children to such despair that they believe that suicide is the only way out. Few victims seek help and boys are far less likely to seek help than girls.

The effects of bullying are likely to be greater where children are also experiencing other stressful events at the same time, such as parental divorce or bereavement (Branwhite, 1994). It is important, therefore, that teachers communicate with parents and are aware of pupils' circumstances. Children's experiences are also likely to affect the well-being of their family in addition to themselves.

The aggressive behaviour of bullies, if unchallenged, can lead to violence and crime in adult life. Bullying behaviour in the early teenage years, for example, has been shown to lead to juvenile delinquency and family abuse (Farrington, 1993) and, in one study, 60 per cent of 12-year-old boys who were bullies at school were convicted of a criminal offence by the age of 24 (Olweus, 1993). Evidence strongly suggests that bullying is part of a more general pattern of antisocial behaviour, with long-term consequences for society.

Bullying incidents also affect those who witness them and observe the distress of others. Bystanders are likely to be aware of how quickly the attacker can change the focus of their attention. This may lead less aggressive pupils to be easily drawn in by group pressure and it may also instil fear in others. In this way, bullying can affect the atmosphere of a whole class, or even a whole school.

Treatment/intervention

Treatment of the individual can only provide a partial answer to the problem of bullying. To be truly effective in tackling bullying it is crucial that children are encouraged to tell adults when there is a problem. Following this, teachers and others must be prepared to affirm that bullying is unacceptable, that children have a right to a safe environment and to provide them with appropriate support. There is much that teachers can do to prevent bullying and to help victims and bullies. This is the subject of the final section of this chapter. Detection can help the bully, as well as the victim.

There may be a substantial number of children involved in bullying who need treatment over and above what teachers can provide. Children with emotional difficulties resulting from bullying, for example, may need counselling or psychotherapy, to help them express their feelings, reduce the emotional impact and to regain their self-confidence. Assertiveness and social skills training may also be beneficial. Bullies may also benefit from treatment but often reject any form of help that is offered. Whilst realistic and firm guidelines may help them control their behaviour, helping them to achieve success in other ways can make a difference and some may benefit from counselling. They may be frightened and ashamed of their behaviour and through counselling they can begin to like themselves and to stop hating others. Successful intervention, however, will depend on addressing the underlying cause of the behaviour. Where it appears to be a result of more deep-seated and underlying emotional problems individuals should be encouraged to seek specialist help.

WHAT CAN TEACHERS DO TO HELP?

First, teachers can help by recognising that bullying is a problem, since it is still often tolerated and ignored by teachers. Signs of children's distress and anxiety may not be apparent at school so their fears may be dismissed as attention seeking and teachers may feel that parents are being overprotective (Young, 1998). Bullying may sometimes be dismissed as horseplay and considered to be part of the normal process of growing up, so teachers do not intervene (Glover *et al.*, 2000).

Enquiries about bullying have now become part of the OFSTED inspection process and successful legal actions have been taken against schools in which pupils were persistently bullied. This makes it more imperative that schools address the problem. Bullying is everyone's responsibility and research shows that if everyone involved with the school takes a firm stand against bullying it is likely to be far less common. Parents, non-teaching staff, such as school nurses and lunchtime supervisors, governors and even the wider community, as well as teachers and pupils should be involved (Tattum and Herbert, 1997).

The DFE anti-bullying project resulted in reductions in different types of bullying behaviour and, as a result of this, every school was given an anti-bullying pack (DFE, 1994). Some schools, however, do far better than others with regard to tackling bullying. To be effective a multi-faceted, multi-level, whole-school approach is needed. Variables at individual, class, school, family and community level affect bullying and they all need to be addressed and regularly reviewed (Tattum and Lane, 1989). In addition, short-, medium- and long-term strategies are required (Tattum, 1993). There is no single solution, but whole-school intervention has been shown to result in a significant reduction in bullying (Thompson and Arora, 1991). There is a need to implement a range of strategies with some focused on prevention and others focused on the effective management of bullying incidents.

Prevention

Prevention programmes are designed to send a message that bullying will not be tolerated in the school setting. Attention needs to focus on creating a supportive culture and a safe and secure learning environment for all pupils since the ethos of the school is crucial in managing bullying. Strategies for creating a positive school ethos are discussed more fully in Chapter 21. Good prevention programmes have a number of components, which may include the development of a whole-school anti-bullying policy, gathering information about bullying within the school, ensuring adequate supervision of pupils during breaks and lunchtimes, classroom rules against bullying, school conferences, raising awareness of bullying issues through inclusion in the school curriculum and peer support schemes. Some of these are now discussed.

Anti-bullying policies

Since September 1999 all schools have been legally required to have an anti-bullying policy so all teachers and parents should be aware of the procedures in place to deal with bullying in their school (Jenner and Greetham, 1995). The relationship between bullying and discipline is important and the anti-bullying policy should form part of an overall behaviour policy (DFE, 1994). It needs to include clear rules that are backed by an appropriate hierarchy of sanctions, as well as systems to support victims. Most children and adolescents do not approve of bullying, but in the absence of clear guidance and procedures they usually tolerate it because they see it as part of normal peer interaction. Bullying needs to be dealt with in a firm but supportive manner, thus exposing pupils to good role models. It is important to be aware of systems that may inadvertently maintain bullying and to encourage friendliness, promote co-operation and amicable resolution of conflicts.

Policies are only effective if they are revisited on a regular basis and backed by continuous training for staff and pupils. Bullying presents a challenge for teachers, but they have a central role to play and to fulfil this they need training and guidance. All teaching staff and non-teaching staff should be alert to the signs of bullying and act promptly and firmly. Teachers need to be taught about the psychology of bullying, the skills to identify it, the techniques to maintain control within the classroom and an understanding of group dynamics may also be helpful (Macleod and Morris, 1996). Following training, opportunities should be made available for teachers to practise in real situations, supported by more senior members of staff. In addition to training, teachers need to examine their own attitudes to aggressive behaviour and to provide good role models (Tattum, 1993). The majority of children depend on adults to respond to bullying incidents and their decision to tell a teacher may depend on this (Tattum and Lane, 1989). Some teachers may think that doing something about bullying is likely to create more difficulties or that if it is ignored it is likely to go away. But, if a child's behaviour is having a detrimental affect on another, it should be taken seriously. It can be difficult to know when to intervene and to establish facts, especially from younger children, since friendships can chop and change easily at this stage. Children and adults have different concepts of bullying, but the majority of children do want adult intervention and, as an authority figure, the teacher can do a lot to influence the situation and promote group cohesion.

Supervision

Studies suggest that most bullying takes place during school hours at times when children are less closely supervised and in relatively large groups. Specific times and places, such as the playground, dinner queues, in the classroom and travelling to and from school, have been highlighted (Tattum and Lane, 1989). Vigilance is essential and it is important for teachers to be visible in corridors and in the playground. Information can be gathered to help identify places where bullying is likely to occur. Mid-day supervisors should be trained to keep an eye open for potential conflict between pupils and to deal with bullying incidents. Play areas can be made more constructive and all staff made sensitive to the social interactions of pupils in order to prevent children from becoming isolated. Supervision is particularly required where patterns of behaviour expected in school conflict with those of the wider community.

The curriculum

Curriculum approaches can be used to harness the feelings of the majority of the peer group against bullying and should be seen as a vehicle for changing pupils' attitudes, values, beliefs and behaviour (Smith and Shu, 2000; Tattum, 1993). Teachers must talk about the possibility of bullying with pupils when they first arrive. Strategies to cope with bullying and self-protection techniques should form part of the normal school curriculum (Besag, 1989). Children need to know that some situations might be impossible to deal with alone. Peer group pressure can be used to discourage bullying. The attitudes of others affect the way pupils behave and it has been found that what children think of bullies and victims is a powerful determinant of what happens in practice (Tattum, 1993). Pupils are generally supportive of victims and it is important to challenge onlookers to decide whether they disapprove or choose to condone bullying behaviour.

Conflict resolution techniques can be used to teach students alternatives to violence when resolving their interpersonal problems (Peterson and Skiba, 2000). These programmes rely on ongoing discussion and instruction to change the perceptions, attitudes and skills of students. They may cover a variety of topics, including the prevalence of conflict, expressing feelings, managing anger, appreciating diversity and coping with stress. They should form part of a broader programme and need to be evaluated by individual schools. A number of such programmes have documented positive changes in pupils' attitudes and behaviour, but they need commitment and have to be consistently applied. In addition, there is a need to consider teaching approaches across the curriculum as boredom may be a factor in encouraging bullying by some individuals (Tattum and Lane, 1989).

Peer support schemes

More recently considerable interest has developed in peer support, befriending and mediation as approaches to bullying (Smith, 2000). Such programmes have been found to reduce, eliminate and prevent bullying problems, as well as improve the overall school climate (Peterson and Skiba, 2000). Some pupils who have been bullied may prefer to talk to another pupil rather than their teachers or parents. Peer counselling can provide pupils with the opportunity to talk about their experiences, help them understand these and how to combat the situation. Staff support for peer counsellors, however, is vital as victims may share difficult feelings, such as suicidal impulses, which they will find difficult to deal with. In peer mediation student mediators are taught to help resolve conflict among their peers. They are taught the skills to help keep minor conflicts from escalating into more serious incidents (Bodine and Crawford, 1998). Pupils are guided to move from blaming each other to devising solutions acceptable to both parties. A well-conducted programme, which is adequately planned and in which students are well trained, can change the way students approach conflict. Other knock-on benefits include an improved school climate generally, fewer fights and exclusions, increased self-esteem and improved academic performance of mediators (Johnson and Johnson, 1996).

Effective management of bullying incidents

The way that incidents of bullying are dealt with is crucial as this gives an important message to other pupils, as well as those directly involved. It is important to intervene in all incidents, including verbal bullying, and a prompt, appropriate response is required. It is important to assemble the facts, discuss and agree the options, report back and follow up. It takes courage for children to tell adults they are being bullied. They may need a lot of reassurance and it is important to involve them in making plans for tackling the problem.

An appropriate response will depend on the nature, intensity, duration and number of incidents, as well as the intention and motivation of the bully. According to Tattum and Lane (1989), it might include, for example:

- listening to the victim's account;
- reassuring him or her that action will be taken;
- indicating to the bully that his or her behaviour is unacceptable;
- giving the bully a constructive task to do;
- increasing levels of supervision;
- enlisting the co-operation of parents;
- establishing class support for the victim;
- organising additional support for the victim or the bully.

Those offering help need to be aware that victims may experience feelings of shock, anxiety and acute anger, and as a result can be highly emotional. In particular cases, exclusion of the bully or even involvement of the police may be necessary as a last resort. Accurate records should be kept of all incidents of bullying and all school staff should report any concerns about bullying to an appropriate member of the pastoral staff. Where incidents are more serious, statements should be taken from the pupils, witnesses involved, parents contacted and details kept on pupils' files.

The most effective approach, particularly with younger children, can be to focus on the whole group rather than the bully and the victim so a support group approach to bullying in schools has been advocated (e.g. Young, 1998). Essentially, following an interview with the victim, a peer support group is set up. These children are asked for their suggestions as to how they may help address the problem and then charged with the responsibility for putting these strategies into practice. Some time later a review with the victim and then the group is held. The value of this approach is that no one can be seen to be unfairly punished, school staff are seen to take action along DfEE guidelines, other children are involved in a positive way and, in the majority of cases, it has been proved to be effective.

Long-term support for victims and bullies

Once the immediate incident has been dealt with, more long-term support may then be required for both bullies and victims. Bullies need to learn that it is wrong and unfair to bully others. The process of intervention, however, should be educational rather than punitive. Interventions might include, for example, trying to get them to appreciate how the victim feels, using group pressure and teaching techniques, such as conflict resolution and problem solving. They can also involve improving self-confidence, making sure that the bully's learning needs are met, as well as behaviour modification programmes (Tattum and Lane, 1989). However, Arora (1991) concluded that school efforts are often better targeted at supporting victims rather than trying to change the behaviour of bullies, which is frequently ingrained.

Victims can be helped by strategies that focus on improving their confidence and self-esteem, improving their friendships and social skills, as well as assertiveness training. Teachers should actively encourage mixing through structured activities, giving responsibility and using a befriending system (Besag, 1989). However, the extent of these children's difficulties may be considerable and they may require input from psychologists or mental health workers (Branwhite, 1994). They can develop more long-term mental health problems and, where teachers suspect or are aware of severe cases of bullying, they need to be alert to signs of more serious problems developing. Strategies put in place to help victims and bullies can be incorporated into a pastoral support plan, of which all teachers that have contact with the child are aware (DfEE, 1999).

Parental involvement

Parental involvement in all aspects of bullying is helpful. Parents are often unsure what to do when faced with this problem. They need to be informed of the school's attitude and approach to dealing with bullying. Teachers have a key role to play in working with parents to manage their children's behaviour. A focus on parenting skills, for example, may be relevant to tackling the issue for some children who persistently bully others. In addition, bullying is likely to have a greater impact when children are already suffering distressing life events (Branwhite, 1994). Open lines of communication between parents and teachers are therefore important in raising teachers' awareness of children's circumstances.

Involvement of other agencies or services

Schools cannot be expected to solve the problem of bullying alone. It is often a widespread and persistent problem and they need to enlist the help of other agencies within the local community. It is important to consider how best to involve outside agencies in helping the school. They may, for example, be brought in to talk to children. There are also a number of services, such as behaviour support services, that can offer advice and help in developing policies and how to set up effective anti-bullying programmes. LEA support services may offer specific approaches and interventions for helping with bullying through staff training or work with individuals. The role of the educational psychologist can be paramount in helping those who bully others (Tattum and Lane, 1989), whilst the school's education welfare officer may be able to offer group work and support for children finding it difficult to attend school. They also sometimes do work on self-esteem with vulnerable pupils at the transition period, which can be helpful in preventing children becoming victims of bullying. Clear channels of referral from teachers to other agencies and services for those needing more specialised help are also important. A wide range of people can therefore be helpful in different ways.

Further reading

Besag, V. E. (1989) *Bullies and Victims in Schools*. Milton Keynes: The Open University Press.

Department for Education (DFE) (1994) *Bullying: Don't Suffer in Silence: An Anti-bullying Pack for Schools*. London: HMSO.

Elliott, M. (ed.) (1991) *Bullying: A Practical Guide to Coping for Schools*. Harlow: Longman.

Sharp, S. and Smith, P. K. (1994) *Tackling Bullying in Your School*. London: Routledge.

Smith, P. K. and Thompson, D. (1991) *Practical Approaches to Bullying*. London: David Fulton.

References

Arora, C. M. J. (1991) The use of victim support groups. In Smith, P. K. and Thompson, D. (eds) *Practical Approaches to Bullying*, 37–47. London: David Fulton.

Besag, V. E. (1989) *Bullies and Victims in Schools*. Milton Keynes: The Open University Press.

Bodine, R. J. and Crawford, D. K. (1998) *The Handbook of Conflict Resolution Education: A Guide to Building Quality Programmes in Schools*. San Francisco: Jossey-Bass.

Branwhite, T. (1994) Bullying and student distress: Beneath the tip of the iceberg. *Educational Psychology*, 14, 1, 59–71.

Department for Education (DFE) (1994) *Bullying: Don't Suffer in Silence: An Anti-bullying Pack for Schools*. London: HMSO.

Department for Education and Employment (1999) *Social Inclusion: Pupil Support (Circular 10/99)*. London: DfEE.

Elliott, M. (1991) Bullies, victims, signs, solutions. In Elliott, M. (ed.) *Bullying: A Practical Guide to Coping for Schools*, 9–14. Harlow: Longman.

Farrington, D. P. (1993) Understanding and preventing bullying. In Tonry, M. and Morris, N. (eds) *Crime and Justice: An Annual Review of Research*, 17. Chicago: University of Chicago Press.

Glover, D., Gough, G. and Johnson, M., with Cartwright, N. (2000) Bullying in 25 secondary schools: Incidence, impact and intervention. *Educational Research*, 42, 2, 141–156.

Jenner, S. and Greetham, C. (1995) Forming a whole-school anti-bullying policy. *Pastoral Care in Education*, 13, 3, 6–13.

Johnson, D. W. and Johnson, R. T. (1996) Conflict resolution and peer mediation programmes in elementary and secondary schools: A review of the research. *Review of Educational Research*, 66, 459–506.

Macleod, M. and Morris, S. (1996) *Why me? Children Talking to Childline about Bullying*. London: Childline.

Olweus, D. (1993) *Bullying at School: What We Know and What We Can Do*. Oxford: Blackwell.

O'Moore, A. M. and Hillery, B. (1991) What do teachers need to know? In Elliott, M. (ed.) *Bullying: A Practical Guide to Coping for Schools*, 56–69. Harlow: Longman.

Peterson, R. L. and Skiba, R. (2000) Creating school climates that prevent school violence. *Preventing School Failure*, 44, 3, 122–129.

Sharp, S. (1995) How much does bullying really hurt? The effects of bullying on the personal well being and educational progress of secondary-aged students. *Educational and Child Psychology*, 12, 81–88.

Smith, P. K. (1999) England and Wales. In Smith, P. K., Morital, Y., Junger-Tas, J., Olweus, D., Catalano, R. and Slee, P. (eds) *The Nature of School Bullying: A Cross-National Perspective*, 68–90. London: Routledge.

Smith, P. K. (2000) Bullying and harassment in schools and the rights of children. *Children and Society*, 14, 294–303.

Smith, P. K. and Shu, S. (2000) What good schools can do about bullying: Findings from a survey in English schools after a decade of research and action. *Childhood*, 7, 193–212.

Smith, P. K. and Thompson, D. A. (eds) (1991) *Practical Approaches to Bullying*. London: David Fulton.

Stephenson, P. and Smith, D. (1989) Bullying in the junior school. In Tattum, D. and Lane, D. A. (eds) *Bullying in Schools*. Stoke-on-Trent: Trentham Books.

Tattum, D. (1993) *Understanding and Managing Bullying*. Oxford: Heinemann.

Tattum, D. and Herbert, G. (eds) (1997) *Bullying: Home, School and Community*. London: David Fulton.

Tattum, D. and Lane, D. A. (1989) *Bullying in Schools*. Stoke-on-Trent: Trentham Books.

Thompson, D. and Arora, T. (1991) Why do children bully? An evaluation of the long-term effectiveness of a whole-school policy to minimise bullying. *Pastoral Care in Education*, 9, 8–12.

Whitney, I. and Smith, P. K. (1993) A survey and the extent of bully/victim problems in junior/middle and secondary schools. *Educational Research*, 35, 3–25.

Williams, K., Chambers, M., Logan, S. and Robinson, D. (1996) Association of common health symptoms with bullying in primary school children. *British Medical Journal*, 313, 17–19.

Wolke, D., Woods, S., Bloomfield, L. and Karstadt, L. (2000) The association between direct and relational bullying and behaviour problems among primary school children. *Journal of Child Psychology and Psychiatry*, 41, 8, 989–1002.

Young, S. (1998) The support group approach to bullying in schools. *Educational Psychology in Practice*, 14, 1, 32–39.

16 Parental separation and divorce

Jane was 12 years old when she was referred to an educational psychologist because she had been caught stealing both at school and at home. In the first interview it became clear that her stealing was a cry for help. She lived with her father and stepmother, who, when the psychologist visited the home, was openly antagonistic towards her stepdaughter. It also emerged that she was being prevented from seeing her natural mother with whom she still had a strong bond. The psychologist saw Jane for a few sessions of supportive counselling during which time no further stealing occurred. However, it was not possible to change Jane's stepmother's attitude towards her and a few months later Jane called to see the psychologist to explain that she had decided to live with an aunt in a different part of the country.

Teachers are likely to encounter many children within their classes whose parents have divorced or separated. It is important that they understand the effect this can have on children, the possible associated difficulties that this may give rise to and how they can help support such children.

Definition

This chapter is concerned with children who develop mental health problems following the separation or divorce of their parents. Studies have consistently shown that, although not all children in this situation develop such problems, they are more likely to do so than children from stable families (Hodges, 1991). Because of the increased occurrence of divorce in Western societies it is now common for teachers to discover that many of the children in their classes have experienced the divorce of their parents.

A further complication in these children's lives is that most parents who divorce eventually remarry creating stepfamilies of which their children automatically become members. In stepfamilies, children who may still be adjusting to the divorce now have to adjust to another adult in the family who in some ways takes the place of their absent parent and is therefore a natural target for their negative feelings. In cases where the new adult has children from a previous relationship who join the family, life gets even more complicated and there is further potential for children to develop mental health problems (Visher and Visher, 1979).

Features

The adjustment difficulties experienced by children whose parents have separated or divorced vary greatly from child to child. However, there is a tendency for boys to exhibit conduct or other overt behavioural problems whereas girls tend to experience more difficulties in relationships with parents, other family members, teachers and friends (O'Halloran and Carr, 2000). Specifically, the types of behaviour that are associated with parental separation and divorce include:

- restlessness;
- day dreaming;
- withdrawal;
- concentration problems;
- aggressiveness;
- acting out behaviour;
- lying and stealing;
- depression;
- regression to an earlier stage of development;
- loss of self-esteem;
- oversensitivity to criticism;
- peer relationship difficulties;
- deterioration in academic achievement;
- delinquency.

Children who experience the separation or divorce of their parents are therefore at increased risk of developing emotional and behavioural difficulties (Hodges, 1991). The likelihood that such difficulties will result depends partly on the extent to which their needs are met within the school. In order for teachers to provide for the special needs of these children they need to know about the family difficulties which they are likely to experience and about the reactions to parental separation common to children of different ages. These aspects are discussed later in the chapter. First, it is important to establish just how many children are likely to experience mental health problems following the separation or divorce of their parents.

Incidence

Parental separation and divorce are no longer unusual occurrences that affect only a small minority of families. Figures from the 1991 census show that, in the UK, around one in three marriages end in divorce. Cox and Desforges (1987) suggested that, before they reach the age of 16, one in five children would experience the divorce of their parents, while an unknown number would be affected by parental separation. However, a survey of 836 Year 7 pupils from six comprehensive schools in the north of England found that 25 per cent, or one in four pupils, had already experienced the separation or divorce of their parents (Branwhite, 1994). It has been estimated that around two-thirds of these children will exhibit noticeable changes in behaviour at school and approximately a quarter will develop long-term adjustment difficulties (O'Halloran and Carr, 2000).

Causes/influences

Family disruption is often a serious problem in the first year or two after a separation. There are changes in living arrangements with one or both parents having to move house. The additional costs of running two homes instead of one generally leads to both parents being financially worse off with all the extra stresses this brings. Splitting up also typically disrupts the parents' social lives with the couple's friends now divided between the two parents or drifting away from both. Parental roles also change drastically with custodial parents now attempting to fulfil the roles of two parents within the family home and non-custodial parents adjusting to occasional and typically diminishing contact with their children. These changes lead to deterioration in physical and mental health for most parents in the two years following separation. Common complaints are anxiety and depression, mood swings, identity problems, vulnerability to colds and flu and exacerbation of pre-existing medical conditions (O'Halloran and Carr, 2000).

Given all these changes, parents tend to be so involved with their own feelings and problems in adjusting to their new situation that they overlook the needs of their children. Discipline in the home can be inconsistent as parents oscillate between being authoritarian and easy going depending on their own mood swings. As a consequence of these factors parents may not notice the pain which children are experiencing. So at the very time when children need most support their parents are least able to provide it because they are overwhelmed by their own problems.

Another potential difficulty for children is the style of co-parenting that their parents adopt. Three distinct co-parenting styles have been identified in families affected by separation or divorce: co-operative, parallel and conflictual (Hetherington, 1989). Ideally, co-operative co-parenting is adopted, in which an agreed set of rules and routines is used to manage children's behaviour in both custodial and non-custodial homes. Unfortunately this occurs in only a minority of cases. Much more common is parallel co-parenting in which each parent has their own set of rules for the children and no attempt is made to integrate them. This is confusing for children and can lead to them experiencing adjustment and behavioural problems. However, the most damaging of the three styles is conflictual co-parenting in which parents do not talk directly with each other but channel communication through their children who are forced into the role of go-between. This almost always results in long-term adjustment problems for the children involved.

Studies of families where there has been a divorce, conducted in the USA (Morgan, 1985), have shown that at least one member of each family has exhibited disruptive behaviour or serious distress. In most cases the most seriously affected family members are the children. However, it must not be forgotten that parental divorce has an impact on all members of the extended family, including grandparents, who face the possibility of being denied access to their grandchildren (Myers and Perrin, 1993). This can also happen with aunts and uncles and has the effect of reducing children's extended family support network at the very time when they need it most.

Risk/protective factors

Boys are more likely than girls to experience adjustment problems following a divorce. Vulnerable children are also at increased risk (O'Halloran and Carr, 2000). Children are regarded as vulnerable if they have a history of serious illness or injury, or if they have pre-existing learning or behavioural difficulties. They are also more vulnerable to adjustment problems if relationships between either parent and the child have been difficult before separation or if there has been inconsistent, harsh or lax discipline in the home. Chronic family problems, such as severe marital discord, domestic violence or parental adjustment difficulties, also place children at increased risk, as do stressful situations such as bereavements or physical or sexual abuse occurring within the family. Adjustment difficulties are also more likely if children have negative beliefs, such as that they caused the separation or have the ability to get their parents back together again or are likely to be abandoned by the custodial parent. Also, long-term adjustment problems are much more likely following separation if there is continuing conflict between the parents, especially if children are actively involved in this by one or both parents.

In contrast, children are less likely to develop adjustment problems where there is a history of good previous psychological adjustment and where parents have provided a stable and nurturing family life. Specific protective factors are high self-esteem and realistic beliefs about the divorce, as well as good problem-solving and social skills. Other protective factors are minimal conflict between parents following separation and good adjustment to the changes by both parents. A track record of coping well with previous stressors and life transitions is also crucial, as is the availability of social support for children and their parents.

Effects of separation and divorce on children

A variety of factors contribute to a child's ability to cope with parental separation (Morgan, 1985). These are outlined below.

Age of the child

In general, the older children are at the time of divorce the less detrimental effects there will be. However, there are marked differences in the ways children of different ages react to parental separation. Pre-school children have difficulty fully understanding the situation and tend to react in one of two ways. They either attempt to deny the reality of the separation by pretending that nothing has changed or become very upset and regress to more immature behaviour with perhaps loss of independence in dressing, feeding or toileting. Pre-school children often fear the loss of the other parent when one has left the family home, so they may cling more closely to the remaining parent or get very upset at routine separations (Cox and Desforges, 1987).

Children of primary school age tend to find it particularly difficult to adjust to parental separation since they understand enough about the situation to make denial a less useful option than with younger children, but at the same time they have not developed the coping strategies which older children typically use (Morgan, 1985). Common problems at this age are therefore associated with feelings of guilt or anxiety which children may experience. They may feel guilty, believing that in some way they have caused the separation, or they may become anxious about the possibility of the other parent leaving them. Many younger primary-school-age children experience feelings of intense sadness or depression which they find very difficult to understand. They can be highly emotional with aggressive behaviour alternating wildly with episodes of crying (Hodges, 1991).

Children of secondary school age tend to experience either anger or depression. Their academic work may be seriously affected or they may participate in delinquent acts (Morgan, 1985). They often experience embarrassment about the family break-up and try to keep it a secret from their friends. They are much less likely than younger children to use denial or to regress in their behaviour. They have the ability to express their opinions and feelings, including their anger towards the parent they blame for the separation. Conflicts between both the parents and their teenage children may be intensified by the divorce.

Gender of the child

Boys are generally considered to have more problems than girls in adjusting to divorce because typically it is the father who leaves the family home, depriving boys of a male figure with whom to identify.

Maturity of the child

How well children cope will depend on their emotional maturity and whether there are any other complicating issues in the child's life. For example, adopted children whose parents are divorcing tend to have greater difficulties coping with the situation than other children.

Financial situation of the parents

Often when one parent leaves the family home both parents face financial hardship. This may mean that custodial parents find it difficult to spare money for children to go on school trips or that non-custodial parents may not be able to afford to come to see children, or to take them out, as often as they would like.

Degree of discord before the divorce

For families in which there has been considerable conflict, hostility and instability, separation and subsequent divorce of the parents may be accompanied by feelings of relief in the children. Divorce may be easier for children in this situation to accept than those in families where parents have kept their disagreements away from the children.

Extent of conflict after the divorce

When both parents co-operate in maintaining relationships with their children following separation it is much easier for children to adjust to the situation than when there is continual animosity between the parents. The most difficult situation for children to cope with is the one in which parents try to sour or break off the relationships between their children and the other parent. This situation almost inevitably leads to children experiencing emotional or behavioural difficulties.

Child's relationship with each parent

When a child is particularly close to the parent who moves out of the family home the separation will be much more difficult for the child to adjust to than when the child is closer to the parent who remains in the home.

Child's relationship with siblings

Children who have siblings typically find it easier to cope with divorce than only children do, since parental separation usually leads to siblings developing closer relationships with each other.

Child's own ability to cope with stress

Children will cope with the stress associated with parental separation in their own idiosyncratic ways. Exactly how they react will be influenced by their past experiences of coping with traumatic events.

Availability of emotional support

A major factor in determining how well children will cope with the divorce of their parents is the availability of people to talk to about their concerns and feelings. As suggested above, they may receive some support from their siblings but other family members are likely to be too concerned with their own feelings to be able to help. This emphasises the importance of children gaining support from people outside the family. Teachers are therefore key sources of support since they typically know children better than any adult outside their families and can be confidential and objective in providing help.

Treatment/intervention

Treatment for children who have experienced the separation of their parents needs to help them resolve the specific psychological tasks involved in coming to terms with divorce. Six key tasks have been identified by Wallerstein (1983):

- acknowledging the reality of the marriage breakdown;
- disengaging from parental disputes and distress and resuming normal activities;
- adapting to the losses and potential losses involved: intact family, family home, family friends and extended family members, the non-custodial parent;
- resolving anger and self-blame;
- accepting the permanence of the divorce and letting go of the fantasy of a reunited family;
- achieving realistic hope regarding their own future relationships.

A variety of types of intervention have been found to be effective in helping children and adolescents resolve these psychological tasks and learn to cope with the consequences of parental separation and divorce. The major forms of these are described below.

Group counselling

One type of intervention is group counselling programmes which may be conducted in schools or community settings. Hodges (1991) considers that group approaches are often the most helpful for children affected by divorce because of the benefits gained from the group process itself. Children discover that their fears and feelings are shared by others, which helps them to come to terms with these. They also get ideas from other children about possible solutions to some of the problems they are experiencing. In addition, the group format encourages children to help and support each other and this process enhances their self-esteem as well as their confidence about being able to cope with their own situation. Hodges describes several group programmes that involve a wide range of intervention strategies and activities including personal sharing, feeling games, sentence completions, role playing, writing, drawing, videos, puppetry and bibliotherapy.

O'Halloran and Carr (2000) reviewed nine studies which evaluated group programmes for children affected by divorce which were conducted in schools or outpatient settings. They found that programmes typically involved from six to twenty-four group sessions and were led by professionals skilled in counselling, sometimes with teachers as co-leaders. Programme content usually consisted of supportive psycho-education plus training in problem-solving, social and stress management skills. The supportive psycho-education component involved providing children with a safe place to express their feelings and beliefs related to their parents' separation, as well as providing information about the experience of coming to terms with the divorce. Almost all the programmes were found to be effective in helping children cope with divorce. It was also found that the effectiveness of such programmes was enhanced when parents received counselling which focused on meeting their children's needs and improving parent–child relationships.

Individual counselling

Another type of intervention is individual counselling sessions with children whose parents have separated. McConnell and Sim (2000) report on an evaluation of a counselling service set up specifically for such children. Children received between three and twenty-one weekly counselling sessions forty-five minutes long using a combination of play therapy and emotionally focused counselling. A key feature of successful cases was found to be the involvement of the custodial parent in the counselling. Since a high proportion of cases in which parents were not involved were considered to be unsuccessful the authors question the value of providing such counselling when parents are not involved. In their conclusion they support Hodges's (1991) contention that individual counselling of children from divorced families should only be conducted in combination with counselling provided for one or both parents.

Family therapy

Hodges (1991) suggests that family therapy is often the treatment of choice for children finding it difficult to cope with divorce. This is because family therapy attempts to involve everyone involved in the situation and is aimed at bringing about changes in the entire family. This is likely to have a more helpful and lasting impact than interventions aimed at children or parents alone. Hodges outlines four different types of family therapy – psychoanalytic, strategic, structural and behavioural – and describes specific strategies which are used with families dealing with divorce. He suggests that family therapy should be avoided when custody is an issue, where there is a history of violence in the family or when one parent is unavailable owing to abandonment or imprisonment. He discusses the use of family therapy with single-parent families and suggests that it is a particularly useful approach for intervention with stepfamilies.

Life can be even more complicated and stressful for children who become part of stepfamilies when either or both of their parents remarry. Further psychological tasks are added to those they already face as a result of the divorce. Visher and Visher (1979) suggest that these tasks include:

- coping with intensified feelings of loss related to their original family and absent parent;
- dealing with divided loyalties between biological parents and stepparents;
- coping with unrealistic expectations, such as being able instantly to love a stepparent;
- adjusting to membership of two families with different rules and routines;
- coping with feelings of uncertainty about where they really belong;
- establishing relationships with the other stepchildren;
- adjusting to additional children born into their new families.

Papernow (1984) has proposed that stepfamilies need to pass through a series of stages in order to achieve a satisfactory family life. Family therapy for stepfamilies should therefore be focused on helping them to work through these stages. The stages are as follows:

1. Fantasy stage – the dream of the family where everyone loves everyone else.
2. Assimilation stage – the gradual realisation that the family is not perfect.
3. Awareness stage – different family structure and associated feelings become clear.
4. Mobilisation stage – conflict emerges as family structure begins to change.
5. Action stage – consensus is reached on family structure and operation.
6. Contact stage – formation of more intense stepfamily relationships.
7. Resolution stage – family rules and routines are established and closer relationships are formed.

WHAT CAN TEACHERS DO TO HELP?

Teachers are in an excellent position to help children cope with the effects of divorce and to provide guidance to parents in separated families and stepfamilies. First, teachers are knowledgeable about child development and are skilled in the observation and analysis of children's behaviour. They are therefore able to identify changes in children's behaviour which are indicative of their difficulties in adjusting to parental separation or divorce. Second, teachers are in regular contact with children and have the opportunity to develop sufficient rapport for children to feel comfortable enough to open up and talk about the things that are bothering them. Third, when teachers develop effective two-way communication with parents they are in an ideal position to provide guidance to parents and to collaborate with them in dealing with children's difficulties (Hornby, 2000). Many children whose parents have separated or divorced report that they would have liked someone at the school to encourage them to talk about their feelings and reactions to their situation and to suggest relevant books for them to read (Morgan, 1985). A range of specific strategies which teachers can employ to help children cope with the separation of their parents has been suggested by Cox and Desforges (1987). These are discussed below.

Developing a school policy

Teachers need to acquaint themselves with the school policy for dealing with pupils attending school who are experiencing or have experienced the separation or divorce of their parents. They need to know what is expected of teachers and of parents in the event of a separation. A school's expectations of parents in this situation should be written in the handbook which parents receive when their child enters the school. The statement needs to say that the school should be informed about any disruptions in home circumstances, including parental separation, which may affect a child's behaviour or progress at school.

Organising support at school

For children who are experiencing disruption and unhappiness at home the school can provide a haven of calm and security which itself is very therapeutic. In addition, having a well-organised system of pastoral care is very important so that pupils have the opportunity to develop a good rapport with their class teacher, form tutor, head of year or head of house. Teachers acting in their pastoral capacity can thereby provide children with extra attention and support in order to help them cope with their parents' separation. Other members of the school staff, such as teacher aides and lunchtime assistants, can also provide such help since pupils with difficulties often form a rapport with them.

Teachers can also ensure that the PSE curriculum used in the school includes sessions on coping with parental separation and divorce. Alternatively, the topic can be made the subject of class discussions held during form tutor periods, using a developmental group counselling strategy such as that proposed by Allan and Nairne (1984). This takes whole-class groups through a five-stage process as follows:

1. introduce the topic;
2. explore relevant thoughts and feelings;
3. develop a better understanding of the situation;
4. decide on appropriate action;
5. clarify what has been learned.

Providing counselling and guidance

Teachers are in an excellent position to provide supportive counselling both to parents who have separated and to their children. Pupils are more likely to open up and talk about their problems with teachers or other school staff with whom they have developed a good rapport than with outside specialists, such as educational psychologists or education welfare officers. The same applies to parents. They are much more likely to talk about their concerns with their child's teacher than to a professional counsellor.

In order to provide supportive counselling to pupils and parents, teachers need to develop effective listening skills and basic counselling skills. Hornby (2000) presents a model of counselling which is suitable for dealing with the vast majority of problems likely to be of concern to parents and children. However, the model emphasises the importance of knowing when to refer on parents or pupils for more specialist help. For example, while teachers may be happy to counsel parents about difficulties their children are having it would be more appropriate to refer parents who want to discuss their own relationship problems to a specialist agency, such as Relate.

However, a form of intervention that can be particularly helpful in the hands of teachers is that of providing guidance to parents of children involved in a divorce. Thompson and Rudolph (2000) consider that useful suggestions which teachers can pass on to parents are:

- talk with your children about the divorce emphasising that they are not at fault;
- observe and listen to your children in order to identify any fears or misunderstandings;
- avoid blaming or criticising the other parent;
- avoid using children as go-betweens – deal directly with your ex-spouse;
- develop a support network of friends, family members and others for you and your children;
- arrange regular visits for the absent parent to assure children they are loved by both parents;
- talk with children about the future so they know what to expect;
- avoid asking children to take on responsibilities beyond those expected for their age.

Involving both parents

When teachers continue to involve both parents following a separation or divorce it sends an important message to the children and their parents. This message is that children need both parents to be interested in their education and welfare despite the fact that they are now living apart. It is therefore important for teachers to send letters of invitation and copies of school reports to each of the parents. Divorced parents should be given the opportunity to decide whether they will attend parents' evenings together or separately. If they are able to attend together then the school can provide a neutral setting for parents to discuss their children's education. If necessary, teachers can represent the child's point of view, mediating in any conflict between parents. In addition to providing appropriately for these children's special needs at school, teachers can be of invaluable assistance to their parents.

Providing practical help

Teachers can provide help to divorced parents whose children live with them on a number of practical matters. First, since many families experience financial difficulties following a separation or divorce, teachers can check whether children are eligible for free school meals. Receiving free school meals not only eases the financial burden on parents but also communicates to other members of staff that parents may find it difficult to provide money for school trips and the like. Second, at times of family disruption children may not be able to find a calm place to do their homework so the provision of a homework centre at the school can be a tremendous help. Third, practical considerations, such as providing a safe place for pupils to leave bags packed ready for weekend access visits, can make life easier for children and also reinforce the acceptability of their situation.

Keeping records

It is helpful for teachers to keep records of the family circumstances of the pupils for whom they are responsible. Teachers need to have the names and addresses of both natural parents and any stepparents. They need to record when the separations and divorces have occurred and to have a record of the custody and access arrangements for each child whose parents have divorced. For example, is custody shared or does the child live mainly with one parent and see the other only at weekends? Teachers also need to record any legal restrictions placed on contacts between children and one or other of their parents. In addition, it is useful to keep a record of the problems which children have experienced at school since the separation. These records need to be continually updated and can eventually be made available to subsequent teachers.

Providing relevant reading material

Teachers can help children adjust to their new situation by ensuring they have access to books which deal with separation and divorce, such as that by Mitchell (1982). Teachers can also suggest books to parents that will help them to gain a better understanding of their children's needs following a separation, such as that by Burgoyne (1984).

Further reading

Cox, K. M. and Desforges, M. (1987) *Divorce and the School*. London: Methuen.
Hodges, W. F. (1991) *Interventions for Children of Divorce (Second edition)*. New York: John Wiley & Sons.
Hornby, G. (2000) *Improving Parental Involvement*. London: Cassell.
Visher, E. B. and Visher, J. S. (1979) *Stepfamilies: A Guide to Working with Stepparents and Stepchildren*. New York: Brunner/Mazel.

References

Allan, J. and Nairne, J. (1984) *Class Discussions for Teachers and Counsellors in the Elementary School*. Toronto: University of Toronto Press.
Branwhite, T. (1994) Bullying and student distress: Beneath the tip of the iceberg. *Educational Psychology*, 14, 1, 59–71.
Burgoyne, J. (1984) *Breaking Even: Divorce, Your Children and You*. Harmondsworth: Penguin.
Cox, K. M. and Desforges, M. (1987) *Divorce and the School*. London: Methuen.
Hetherington, M. (1989) Coping with family transitions: Winners, losers and survivors. *Child Development*, 60, 1–14.
Hodges, W. F. (1991) *Interventions for Children of Divorce (Second Edition)*. New York: John Wiley & Sons.
Hornby, G. (2000) *Improving Parental Involvement*. London: Cassell.
McConnell, R. A. and Sim, A. J. (2000) Evaluating an innovative counselling service for children of divorce. *British Journal of Guidance and Counselling*, 28, 1, 75–86.
Mitchell, A. (1982) *When Parents Split Up: Divorce Explained to Young People*. Edinburgh: MacDonald.
Morgan, S. R. (1985) *Children in Crisis: A Team Approach in the Schools*. London: Taylor and Francis.
Myers, J. E. and Perrin, N. (1993) Grandparents affected by parental divorce: A population at risk? *Journal of Counseling and Development*, 72, 1, 62–66.
O'Halloran, M. and Carr, A. (2000) Parental separation and divorce. In Carr, A. (ed.) *What Works with Children and Adolescents? A Critical Review of Psychological Interventions with Children, Adolescents and their Families*, 280–299. London: Routledge.
Papernow, P. L. (1984) The stepfamily cycle: An experiential model of stepfamily development. *Family Relations*, 33, 355–363.
Thompson, C. L. and Rudolph, L. B. (2000) *Counselling Children (Fifth Edition)*. Belmont, CA: Brooks/Cole.
Visher, E. B. and Visher, J. S. (1979) *Stepfamilies: A Guide to Working with Stepparents and Stepchildren*. New York: Brunner/Mazel.
Wallerstein, J. (1983) Children of divorce: The psychological tasks of the child. *American Journal of Orthopsychiatry*, 53, 230–243.

17 Bereavement

Wayne, who was 14 years of age, had been suspended from school for being disruptive and for using abusive language to a teacher. This kind of behaviour was uncharacteristic of Wayne so the school asked its educational psychologist to interview him and report to the governors on whether he should be reinstated or excluded. In the course of the interview it emerged that Wayne's grandfather, to whom he had been very close, had recently died. Wayne was clearly very upset and confused about this and had not been given an opportunity to talk to anyone about it. When this information was passed on to the school governors they agreed to take him back and assigned a teacher Wayne knew well for him to talk to. His parents also said they would ensure that they gave Wayne opportunities to talk about the loss of his grandfather. Apparently, his uncharacteristic disruptive behaviour at school had been a cry for help.

The case of Wayne presented above is unfortunately fairly typical of the way in which schools and parents handle children's emotional problems resulting from their reaction to a bereavement. Teachers react to the children's behavioural difficulties with disciplinary measures. Parents are not sure what to say or do, so they do nothing! It is important that teachers are able to offer support to children who have been bereaved and to their parents.

Definition

This chapter is concerned with children who develop mental health problems following bereavement. Death is a topic that is generally paid insufficient attention to by parents and teachers, mainly because most people know very little about children's reactions to death or how to help them cope with bereavement. The chapter therefore considers the effects on children of bereavement and provides guidelines for teachers and schools on how to provide appropriately for children's needs following the death of a family member, friend or other significant person.

The fact that children coping with bereavement tend to develop emotional and behavioural difficulties was first highlighted by Rutter (1966) who found that twice as many children who had lost a parent by death attended the Maudsley Hospital psychiatric clinic than would be expected from death rates in the general population. He also found that about 14 per cent of children attending a child guidance clinic had been bereaved of a close relative in the recent past. Rutter observed a variety of problems in children who had been bereaved, including antisocial behaviour, depression and various phobias.

Features

The adjustment difficulties experienced by children who have experienced a bereavement may include the following (Morgan, 1985):

- regression to an earlier stage of development;
- hostile reactions to the deceased;
- hostile reactions to others;
- eating disorders;
- bed wetting;
- sleep disturbances;
- other psychosomatic disorders;
- attempting to replace the deceased;
- adopting the mannerisms of the deceased;
- aggressive behaviour;
- discipline problems;
- learning difficulties;
- denial;
- withdrawal;
- guilt;
- anxiety;
- panic.

Incidence

Experiencing the death of someone close to them is a common occurrence among school children. A survey of 836 Year 7 students from six comprehensive schools in the north of England found that 61 per cent of them had experienced the death of a relative (Branwhite, 1994). Some children will lose a parent through death while others will experience the death of a sibling or another close family member such as a grandparent. Others will have to cope with the loss of a close friend or someone they know less well such as a classmate or teacher. It is reported that between 3 and 5 per cent of children under 18 years of age lose a parent by death and that one year after their parent's death around one in five of these children still exhibit clinically significant adjustment problems (Moore and Carr, 2000).

Causes/influences

When a death occurs it affects all members of the family. Parents may be struggling to cope with their own emotional adjustment and therefore may be unable to provide their children with the help they need. Parents also may not be aware of their children's understanding of death or of the likely effects of such traumatic events on children. Most importantly, parents may not know what can be done to help children to cope.

In addition, adults often try to shield children from the realities of death. They want to protect children from having to experience painful feelings and therefore contrive to keep children out of conversations about death and away from situations, such as funerals, where others may be grieving. Unfortunately, when adults do not talk to children about death and do not let them participate in funerals they tend to become confused and distressed (Charkow, 1998).

To make matters worse, children are often aware that their parents are upset following the death and tend to put on a brave face to avoid burdening parents further. Because of this, and parents' preoccupation with their own pain, children's needs are often overlooked. The result of this is that many children have problems coming to terms with their loss. This is why it is so important that teachers know how to help these children and are able to provide appropriate guidance to their parents.

Risk/protective factors

The way in which children react to someone's death will be influenced by several factors (Morgan, 1985), discussed below.

The age of the child

One important factor is the age of the child. Very young children and pre-adolescents may be the most vulnerable – very young children because they are still dealing with the issue of separation from their parents and pre-adolescents because it is an important time for the development of sexual identity. Also, children's understanding of death progresses from a complete lack of awareness through several phases of increased comprehension until an adult view is attained. From birth to approximately 2 years of age children are considered to have no concept of death as such. They may experience grief due to separation from people they have developed close relationships with but have no realisation of the finality of death.

Children aged 3 to 5 tend to view death as being similar to sleep. They do not see it as a permanent state, nor do they understand that all living things must eventually die. Between the ages of 5 and 9 children come to realise the finality of death but still are not aware that it is universal. This usually happens from about 9 years of age when children may become upset at the idea of death in general and in particular about the possibility of their parents dying. From 9 to 12 years children become aware of the finality, inevitability and universality of death and because of this often experience some anxiety associated with such thoughts. Teenagers tend to become defiant of death, almost daring death to occur by playing games such as 'chicken', in which they run across the road in front of cars.

Relationship with the deceased

A second important factor in children's reactions to a death is their relationship with the person who has died. For young children the loss of the mother may have a bigger impact on them, particularly in traditional families where mothers spend considerably more time with the children than fathers. However, for boys who have reached school age the death of their father may be more significant because of the loss of a male figure to identify with and to help in disciplining them. For example, it has been found that higher rates of delinquency are recorded for boys who have lost their fathers than those whose mothers have died (Morgan, 1985). Also, when children are particularly close to one or other parent, as often happens, the loss of this parent will be more traumatic for them. In contrast, when children have a particularly strained relationship with one parent, the death of this parent can be accompanied by an improvement in their mental health.

Circumstances of death

Sudden, accidental, suicidal and violent deaths are usually the most difficult to come to terms with since the bereaved were not able to 'say goodbye' to the deceased (Charkow, 1998). Also, when a person dies from a terminal illness it is possible to partly prepare for the death and experience anticipatory grief. Deaths due to suicide or murder are the hardest for children to come to terms with because of the additional difficulty of finding some meaning in why the death occurred.

Children's personality

A fourth factor is the child's personality. Children who are able to express emotions easily will pass through the grief process with fewer problems than those who keep their feelings to themselves. Also, extroverted children with lots of friends and interests will generally cope better with bereavement than timid or introverted children.

Previous experience of death

A fifth factor in determining children's reactions to bereavement is their previous experience of death and the extent to which previous losses in their lives have been resolved. Children who have previously experienced the death of a distant relative or family pet will be better prepared for the death of someone close to them than children who have had no previous bereavements. However, children who are still coping with the death of a close family member, such as a grandparent, may be particularly badly affected by another significant loss such as a school friend.

Gender

Dyregrov (1991) points out that, although there is little research on this issue, there is some evidence that boys often have greater difficulty in coping with bereavement than girls. He considers this may be due to boys having more difficulty talking about death and showing their feelings, as well as his finding that more girls than boys had a good friend who they could talk with and gain support from.

Social support

Finally, the availability of social support is another important influence on the way children cope with bereavement. Children need to understand what has happened and express their grief so it is very important for them to have available caring and empathic adults with whom they can talk as and when they need to. The absence of such support will make it much more difficult for them to come to terms with the death (Charkow, 1998).

Effects of bereavement on children

Webb (1993) considers that children's grief is different from that of adults because of the following factors:

- children's understanding of death is limited by their age and level of cognitive development;
- children have limited ability to verbalise their feelings;
- children have limited capacity to tolerate emotional pain;
- children are sensitive about bereavement making them different from their peers.

However, Webb (1993) agrees that, like adults, children do pass through a process of grieving. This is discussed below.

The grief process

Some writers consider that children go through similar stages of grief to adults, while other writers think that children's grieving is different, as suggested by the three-phase model proposed by Morgan (1985). The first phase is one of 'protest', when the child refuses to accept that the person is dead and, for some children, involves angry attempts to get them back. In the second phase children experience hurt, despair and disorganisation as they begin to accept the fact that the person has really gone. The third phase is one in which hope develops as children begin to reorganise their lives without the deceased.

Most models of the grieving process for children (e.g. Kubler-Ross, 1969; Worden, 1996) suggest that it can be viewed as a continuum of reactions through which they must pass in order to come to terms with their loss – for example, shock, denial, anger, sadness, detachment, reorganisation and adaptation (Hornby, 1994). The initial reaction of children when they first find out about the death is typically one of shock and confusion which can last from a few hours to a few days. This is typically followed by denial or disbelief of the reality of the situation in which children find it difficult to believe that the traumatic event has occurred. As a temporary coping strategy denial is useful in providing time to adjust to the situation. It is only when denial is prolonged and intense that it is problematic.

Following denial, children typically experience anger associated with the loss. They may search for a reason for the loss having occurred or for someone to blame. Alternatively, underlying the anger may be feelings of guilt about somehow being responsible for the death. Sadness may follow anger and is a reaction which, more than any other, is reported to pervade the whole grieving process. Some children spend a lot of time crying while others cut themselves off from contact with friends. It is important to realise that sadness and even temporary depression are a normal part of the grieving process.

Following sadness children tend to experience a feeling of detachment, when they feel empty and nothing seems to matter. Life goes on from day to day but it has lost its meaning. Reorganisation follows detachment and is characterised by realism about the situation and hope for the future. Children begin to focus less on the negative aspects of the loss and can find something positive about the situation. Finally, children reach a point when they have come to terms with the situation and exhibit an emotional acceptance of or adaptation to the loss. They are fully aware of the significance of the loss but are determined to get on with life as best they can.

However, in reality, the grieving process is not as clear cut as simply moving from stage to stage would suggest. Although one reaction may be uppermost at a particular time, the other reactions will also be present to some extent. For example, children who seem to be mainly reacting with aggression and anger will also be feeling sad as well. In contrast, children who appear to be withdrawn and detached will also be experiencing anger and sadness. The grieving process is considered to be a normal healthy reaction to the experience of bereavement (Kubler-Ross, 1969). Most adults will take at least two years to come to terms with the loss and this is probably also a reasonable guideline for children.

It is important to realise that passage through the grieving process can be accelerated or retarded by what people do and by what others around them say. Children who refuse to face up to the loss and do not allow themselves to experience the feelings triggered by the grieving process will take longer to come to terms with the situation. It is important to do the 'grief work' associated with a loss in order to adjust to it (Worden, 1996).

Relationship to the bereaved

Parent

The death of a parent is generally thought to be the most traumatic event that can happen to a child. Morgan (1985) suggests that, when a parent dies, a child is faced with three major tasks. First, the child must come to terms with the reality of the death itself. Second, the child must adapt to the changes in the family that will result from the loss of a parent. Third, the child must learn to cope with the permanent absence of one parent.

Although guilt is probably an inevitable reaction to death for all ages it can be particularly devastating to a child. Young children may believe that bad things happen because they have been naughty, so they may blame themselves for their parent's death. Children may react by regressing to an earlier stage of development or may attempt to deny the reality of the death by carrying on as normal and apparently being unaffected by it. But then children are likely also to experience physical symptoms such as loss of appetite or sleep problems.

Children sometimes exhibit hostile reactions to their dead parent and other people apparently because they feel the deceased has unjustly deserted them. Alternatively they may idealise the deceased as a means of avoiding the negative feelings they may have. Identifying with parents who have died by perhaps taking on some of their interests is seen as a constructive reaction, whereas trying to take their place, perhaps even developing some of the symptoms that appeared during the illness, is considered to be potentially harmful and should be discouraged.

There are some common signs, which teachers should look out for at school, that are indicative of children struggling to cope with the loss of a parent (Morgan, 1985). These include unsociability, despondence, forgetfulness, inattention and a 'couldn't care less' attitude.

Sibling

It is widely acknowledged that the death of a child is a profound loss since it runs against the natural order of events and therefore challenges people's fundamental assumptions about the universe. The death of a sibling can leave children feeling vulnerable and afraid for their safety and that of other family members. Parental grief is typically intense, debilitating and long lasting. Since very few parents avail themselves of counselling most of them are likely to be struggling to cope with their own grief for months or even years. They therefore may be unable to provide sufficient help to their remaining children in coping with their reactions to the bereavement for possibly a substantial period of time. Morgan (1985) suggests that, when their own grief prevents parents from maintaining healthy parental relationships, surviving children are placed at risk of developing psychological problems. For example, younger children can react to the death of an older sibling by regressing to babyish behaviour in an attempt to prevent themselves growing to an age when death could occur. Alternatively, older children may become preoccupied with their own futures, anxious about whether they too will soon die.

Aware of their parents' grief, some children attempt to take the place of their dead sibling, perhaps by acting like them, even when this behaviour is not appropriate for their age. Children can experience considerable guilt, either about things done to, or not done for, dead siblings when they were alive, or about enjoying the feeling of having parents to themselves. If not recognised and dealt with during childhood these guilt feelings can lead to depression which can carry on into adult life and in extreme cases become a precursor to suicide (Morgan, 1985). Another possible problem occurs when parents displace their anger and other intense emotions onto the surviving children who may sense their parents' hostility and feel that they are being punished for the death of their sibling.

Other significant people

It is often overlooked that the death of other family members, such as grandparents, cousins, aunts or uncles, can have a significant impact on children. This is especially so when there has been a particularly close relationship with the deceased. Also, the death of friends, classmates or teachers can be quite traumatic for children.

Incidents that involve the death of several school children, usually due to accidents, tend to have a high profile because they are widely reported in the media. They actually happen quite infrequently but their impact when they do occur can be devastating to the families involved and to the children's school friends. The impact is of course greatest on those children who survived the accident who commonly experience such reactions as depression, sleep disturbances, bed wetting, stomach problems, concentration difficulties and fear of hospitals, being hurt or of dying (Morgan, 1985). In severe cases, this can result in post-traumatic stress disorder, discussed separately in Chapter 19.

Unfortunately, the typical parental approach to children who have been affected by such an incident is to try to get them to forget the experience as quickly as possible. Parents not only avoid talking about it but also try to prevent children from discussing it with other people. Their reason for doing this appears to be a fear that children will become even more upset if they talk about it, whereas by not discussing it openly parents are adding to their children's trauma by indirectly suggesting that it is too frightening to deal with. In fact, parents are generally unaware that their unwillingness to discuss such things openly may have more to do with their anxiety about coping with their own reactions than about protecting their children.

Grief in children

Worden (1996) suggests that there are several key points which people working with children who have been bereaved need to be aware of:

- experiencing the death of someone close is traumatic for children but need not lead to serious difficulties if appropriate help is given;
- how children mourn is determined by their levels of both cognitive and emotional development;
- children aged 5 to 7 are a particularly vulnerable group since their cognitive development is such that they are beginning to understand the finality of death but they do not have the personal and social skills to be able to cope with the situation;
- mourning a childhood loss can be re-triggered at various points during adult life such as when the child gets married or reaches the same age as the parent who died;
- it is important for teachers and other professionals who work with children who have been bereaved to develop preventive approaches rather than waiting for problems to occur. In order to do this, teachers need to understand the tasks involved in the process of mourning and to be familiar with the principles of grief counselling.

Treatment/intervention

Interventions to help bereaved children must address the four tasks of mourning (Worden, 1996). These are to:

- accept the reality of the loss;
- experience and work through the pain of grief;
- adjust to an environment in which the deceased in missing;
- find ways of remembering the deceased while investing energy in other relationships.

Treatment for bereaved children can take the form of individual counselling sessions, bereavement groups or family therapy.

Individual counselling

Individual counselling with bereaved children needs to involve techniques which are appropriate for the developmental level of the child. For younger children some form of play is used so that they project their feelings and concerns onto the play materials (Webb, 1993). This can involve doll play, drawing, puppetry, drama or story telling. For older children different forms of artistic expression, such as drawing, painting or sculpting, may be used (Allan, 1988). Alternatively, some form of writing, such as writing a letter to the deceased or writing a poem or a journal which focuses on feelings, can be used (Allan and Bertoia, 1992).

Bereavement groups

Getting bereaved pupils together in small groups of four to eight children can be very useful. The usual format involves around six sessions of up to an hour held at weekly intervals. Such groups are usually led by a teacher, counsellor or psychologist who has experience of grief counselling. In bereavement groups children can express their feelings and learn that others have similar reactions (Dyregrov, 1991). They can share ways of coping with their experiences and talk about different ways of handling difficult situations. Techniques which can be used in such groups include: having children bring in mementoes of the deceased; reading stories about death and dying; and having a box into which children can anonymously put questions to be discussed.

Family therapy

Working with the bereaved child's family can be very helpful in making sure that parents as well as children get help in coming to terms with the loss. Webb (1993) identifies two family tasks which need to be addressed. These are: shared acknowledgement of the reality of the death and of the experience of loss; and the reorganisation of the family system in order to reinvest energy in other relationships and pursuits. As with bereavement groups the typical format involves around six sessions of around an hour held at weekly intervals in the family home. Sessions typically discuss a range of topics including events surrounding the death, appropriate expression of grief and communication within the family.

Grief counselling

According to Worden (1996), there are ten major principles and procedures of grief counselling. The application of these principles to children who have suffered bereavement is discussed below.

Helping the child actualise the loss

The first task of grieving is to accept fully that the loss has occurred – that the person is dead and will not return. This can be facilitated by encouraging children to talk about the person who has died and how the death happened. Family members and friends typically discourage children from talking about such things either to spare their own pain or in the wrongly held belief that it is not helpful to dwell on the loss. However, like adults, children may need to talk about the death over and over again to someone who has the patience to listen.

Helping children to identify and express feelings

Helping children to become aware of and express their feelings about their loss is the most important task of grief counselling. According to Worden (1996), the most problematic feelings experienced by people who have been bereaved are anger, guilt, sadness, anxiety and helplessness. It is difficult for adults, let alone children, to realise that they feel anger towards the deceased. So this anger is generally projected onto other members of the family or doctors or other children or even teachers. Sometimes the anger is turned inward and experienced as depression or guilt. Older children may feel guilty about how they behaved towards the deceased. Younger children may feel guilty because they believe that they were in some way responsible for the death.

Sadness is a natural reaction to a major loss but the expression of sadness is often problematic. This is because it is best expressed through crying, which in some societies is discouraged since it is regarded as a sign of weakness. The anxiety experienced by bereaved children is partly related to their feelings of helplessness, of not being able to cope without the deceased parent or sibling. The anxiety also stems from children's increased awareness of the vulnerability of other family members and themselves to death.

Helping the child to live life without the deceased

As well as coping with their grief, bereaved children also need to be able to deal with the practical difficulties that result from their loss. A child who has lost a parent or an older sibling, for example, will probably be expected to take on more responsibility around the home. A child who has lost a close friend will need to seek out other friendships.

Helping the child to reinvest emotional energy

Children need to be helped to find ways of maintaining the memory of the person who has died whilst at the same time reinvesting their energy in other relationships so that their lives can continue. For example, they can be encouraged to keep a journal of their thoughts about the deceased to help them see that by developing new relationships they are not forgetting the person who has died.

Providing time to grieve

There is an expectation in most Western societies that people should 'get over' a major loss in a few months, whereas most experts in grief counselling agree that it generally takes up to two years for a child or an adult to adjust to any major loss. This only applies if individuals are grieving during this time and not avoiding expressing their feelings, in which case it may take much longer.

Providing ongoing support

Children will need continuing support for at least a year following the death and probably longer. Certain times may be particularly difficult for them, such as birthdays, Christmas and the anniversary of the death. Bereavement support groups (discussed later) can be very helpful, so parents and children should be made aware of their existence in the local community.

Interpreting normal behaviour

Children can become frightened by their thoughts and feelings following the death of someone close. It is helpful to be able to explain the grieving process to them, including a discussion of typical reactions, in order to reassure them about the normality of what they are experiencing.

Allowing for individual differences

It is also important to explain to children that the reactions triggered by grief will be different for each person. Their surviving siblings, parents and friends will all be grieving in different ways.

Examining defences and coping styles

Some of the ways in which children (and adults) cope with a bereavement are not healthy because they involve using defences to avoid experiencing the pain of grieving. For example, children who withdraw from contact with friends and family or refuse to talk about or look at photographs of the deceased are using defence mechanisms to avoid facing up to their grief and need help in order to develop more effective coping strategies.

Identifying pathology and referral

A minority of children who are experiencing severe difficulties coping with their loss will need more intensive help. It is therefore important for teachers to be able to recognise this and be prepared to suggest to their colleagues or to parents that professional counselling is required.

WHAT CAN TEACHERS DO TO HELP?

It is clear from the above discussion that a death in the family produces a situation for which children and their parents need a great deal of help, and also that the death of others with whom children have developed close relationships, such as friends, classmates and teachers, can be traumatic for children. Teachers are in the ideal position to provide help in coping with bereavement, both directly to the children concerned and indirectly through their parents (Thornton and Krajewski, 1993). First, teachers have knowledge of child development and are therefore aware of the different levels of understanding of death which children have at different ages. Second, teachers are also experienced observers of children's behaviour and since they see children five days a week are in an excellent position to notice any behavioural changes which may indicate difficulties they are having in coping with a bereavement. Third, teachers have access to information on death and grieving either through PSE curriculum material in their schools or through sources like those referenced in this section. Fourth, teachers will know of, or can find out about, the professional and voluntary help for the bereaved which is available in the local community. Finally, teachers provide a vital link between school and home. They can work closely with parents to ensure that children's needs are met.

However, although teachers are well placed to help children and their parents cope with bereavement this frequently does not happen because death education has such a low profile in most schools (Leaman, 1995). There has been a lack of training on the topic so most teachers simply do not know enough about the grieving process and how to help children cope with it. The following sections provide some guidelines for helping children adjust to their loss.

Guidelines for working with bereaved children

Charkow (1998) considers that teachers have three key functions with bereaved children:

- to help children feel safe and secure and to acknowledge the reality of the death;
- to provide an environment in which children can express their feelings;
- to provide appropriate curricular materials and learning opportunities for effective death education to take place.

Specific guidelines for teachers in working with bereaved children individually, or during class teaching about grief and bereavement, include:

- deal with death in an open and sensitive manner in order to provide a good model to pupils;
- anticipate and be aware of changes in behaviour, such as depression and lack of concentration, following bereavement;
- ensure that all pupils receive death education through the PSE or tutorial programmes;
- discuss death in terms that children can understand;
- provide children with information about death and grief suitable for their developmental level;
- encourage the adoption of healthy and effective coping strategies;
- encourage bereaved children to express feelings verbally, through writing, drama or art work;
- ensure there are places to which children can go when they become upset;
- refer children to staff with particular expertise in coping with loss;
- promote constructive attitudes and approaches to bereaved pupils from their classmates;
- be prepared to deal with the occasional pupil who will make cruel remarks;
- take advantage of in-service training on death and bereavement;
- create links with the bereaved child's parents.

Guidelines for working with parents

In addition to what teachers of bereaved children do at school they can be an invaluable support and resource for parents (Hornby, 2000). Guidelines for teachers in working with parents of children who have been bereaved are outlined below.

Two-way communication

Keeping open channels of communication between school and home by such means as phone contacts, meetings and notes sent home is the most important thing teachers can do to help parents. In this way concerns which either teachers or parents have about how children are coping can be shared and strategies for helping children can be agreed.

Providing guidance

Teachers can provide invaluable guidance to parents based on their knowledge of child development and of the effects of bereavement on children. Their knowledge of the children concerned and the working relationship they have established with the parents place them in an excellent position to provide this guidance. Teachers can recommend to parents books about how to help children cope with their grief, such as those by Dyregrov (1991). They can also recommend books written for parents who have lost a child, such as the powerful and moving book by Schiff (1977) and that by Rando (1988). In addition, they can suggest to parents books on death for surviving siblings to read (see Ordal, 1984).

Providing counselling

Teachers can provide supportive counselling to parents in order to help them cope with the effects of the loss on themselves and other family members. Mainly, what parents need is someone who can listen in order to help them clarify their thoughts and feelings and to help them decide what to do about the various problems they face. Most teachers do not have the time or skills to take on intensive or long-term counselling of parents. However, even a brief session in which parents are encouraged to open up and can see the value of counselling can make them more likely to agree to being referred to sources of more specialised counselling and support.

Referring parents on to other sources of counselling and support

Teachers can help by making parents aware of the counselling services available in their community, particularly any that offer specialised help for people who have been bereaved. A very important source of support for parents and other members of families who have suffered a death are the bereavement groups that are now available in most communities. Such groups can help participants gain hope, feel less isolated, develop feelings of fellowship, get information on other sources of help and develop support networks (Hopmeyer and Werk, 1993). Often the most valuable things which people report gaining from participating in these groups are a feeling of not being alone in their grief and the opportunity to share thoughts and feelings with others who understand. Some groups are peer led, others are co-led by a professional and a peer facilitator. They can be ongoing and open to new participants at any time or alternatively involve a predetermined number of meetings, in which case they may be closed to new participants once they have begun. Whatever the organisation, such groups can be an important source of support for the bereaved.

Further reading

Dyregrov, A. (1991) *Grief in Children: A Handbook for Adults*. London: Jessica Kingsley.
Hornby, G. (2000) *Improving Parental Involvement*. London: Cassell.
Papadatou, D. and Papadatos, C. (eds) (1991) *Children and Death*. New York: Hemisphere.
Webb, N. B. (1993) *Helping Bereaved Children: A Handbook for Practitioners*. New York: Guilford.
Worden, W. (1996) *Children and Grief*. New York: Guilford.

References

Allan, J. (1988) *Inscapes of the Child's World: Jungian Counseling in Schools and Clinics*. Dallas, TX: Spring.
Allan, J. and Bertoia, J. (1992) *Written Paths to Healing: Education and Jungian Child Counseling*. Dallas, TX: Spring.
Branwhite, T. (1994) Bullying and student distress: Beneath the tip of the iceberg. *Educational Psychology*, 14, 1, 59–71.
Charkow, W. B. (1998) Inviting children to grieve. *Professional School Counselling*, 2, 2, 117–122.
Dyregrov, A. (1991) *Grief in Children: A Handbook for Adults*. London: Jessica Kingsley.
Hopmeyer, E. and Werk, A. (1993) A comparative study of four family bereavement groups. *Groupwork*, 6, 2, 107–121.
Hornby, G. (1994) *Counselling in Child Disability*. London: Chapman and Hall.
Hornby, G. (2000) *Improving Parental Involvement*. London: Cassell.
Kubler-Ross, E. (1969) *On Death and Dying*. New York: Macmillan.
Leaman, O. (1995) *Death and Loss: Compassionate Approaches in the Classroom*. London: Cassell.

Moore, M. and Carr, A. (2000) Depression and grief. In A. Carr (ed.) *What Works with Children and Adolescents? A Critical Review of Psychological Interventions with Children, Adolescents and their Families*, 203–232. London: Routledge.

Morgan, S. R. (1985) *Children in Crisis: A Team Approach in the Schools*. London: Taylor and Francis.

Ordal, C. C. (1984) Death as seen in books suitable for young children. *Omega: Journal of Death and Dying*, 14, 249–277.

Rando, T. A. (1988) *How to Go on Living When Someone You Love Dies*. Boston, MA: Lexingham.

Rutter, M. (1966) *Children of Sick Parents*. London: Oxford University Press.

Schiff, H. S. (1977) *The Bereaved Parent*. New York: Crown.

Thornton, C. and Krajewski, J. (1993) Death education for teachers. *Intervention in School and Clinic*, 29, 1, 31–35.

Webb, N. B. (1993) *Helping Bereaved Children: A Handbook for Practitioners*. New York: Guilford.

Worden, W. (1996) *Children and Grief*. New York: Guilford.

18 Child abuse and neglect

> Sally was sexually abused by her stepfather from the age of 3 until she was 14 years old, at which time she disclosed the abuse and was placed into the care of the local authority. After a long and traumatic court case, her stepfather was sent to prison for a number of years and her mother refused to have any further contact with her. Sally received ongoing counselling, but foster placements rarely lasted because of her challenging behaviour. At times, her emotions became so unbearable that she would deliberately harm herself. This led to short periods of more intensive treatment in a mental health adolescent unit. Sally was bright and talented, but her education was severely disrupted. She moved school frequently and her attendance was poor. When in school, teachers found her behaviour very difficult to manage.

Child abuse and neglect can take many different forms, from frightening children by yelling at them to severe acts of assault or sexual abuse. Whatever form it takes, however, it can cause considerable psychological harm. The abuse of children is often secretive and this means that it may go on undetected for years, causing serious long-term emotional damage. Teachers have regular day-to-day contact with children, so if the problem of child abuse and neglect is to be tackled successfully, they must listen to children, be alert to the signs of abuse and be aware of its effects. In addition, they have a legal obligation to instigate child protection procedures in cases where abuse or neglect is suspected.

Definitions

Child abuse in the UK is determined according to Department of Health (1991) guidelines, where it is referred to as that which causes 'actual or likely harm to the child'. However, it is difficult to obtain a universal definition because what one person considers harmful another may not. For this reason, some authorities (e.g. Skuse and Bentovim, 1994) have suggested that definitions should focus on the central feature of child abuse – the adult's abuse of power and control, which is present whatever form the abuse takes. When considering any form of child abuse or neglect, the normal parenting practices within the prevailing culture should be take into account. Whilst children frequently experience more than one form of abuse and there is considerable overlap of the different types, child abuse is usually categorised as either physical, sexual, emotional abuse or neglect. Each category is defined in the Department of Health (1991) guidelines, para. 6.40, and these definitions are presented below.

Physical abuse is defined as: 'actual or likely physical injury to a child, or failure to prevent physical injury (or suffering) to a child'. It includes punching, beating, kicking, biting, burning and shaking, as well as deliberate poisoning and suffocation. In the majority of cases it is the result of discipline or physical punishment that has gone too far.

Within the guidelines sexual abuse is defined as 'actual or likely sexual exploitation of a child or adolescent'. It involves the use of children for the sexual stimulation of adults and covers participation in any sexual activity by a dependent, developmentally immature child who is unable to understand the nature of the activity.

Emotional abuse is defined as 'actual or likely severe adverse effect on the emotional and behavioural development of a child caused by persistent or severe emotional ill-treatment or rejection'. It is more difficult to detect and it often exists alongside other forms of abuse. Generally, it is a failure to provide an emotionally satisfying environment in which the child can thrive and develop (Blumenthal, 1994). Habitual criticism, threat and ridicule, as well as rejection and withdrawal from a parental role, are typical features.

Within the guidelines neglect is defined as 'persistent or severe neglect or the failure to protect a child from exposure to any kind of danger, or extreme failure to carry out important aspects of care, resulting in significant impairment of the child's health or development'. It is the failure to provide for children's basic physical, educational and emotional needs, including their developmental needs. It might include, for example, a delay in seeking health care, inadequate supervision, keeping a child off school for no reason or allowing a child to take drugs or alcohol.

Features

The signs of physical abuse and neglect may seem obvious. Professionals, however, must be cautious, as most of the signs of abuse, taken in isolation, can be indications of other difficulties. It is vital that the whole picture is taken into account, together with any information from the child or the teacher's knowledge of the family's circumstances (David, 1993).

Physical abuse

Most healthy children have bruises from time to time, but particular injuries, such as cigarette burns and bite marks, for example, are rarely caused accidentally and should always be a cause for concern. Children who are physically abused often have behavioural problems. They may be overcompliant, seek constant attention or react angrily and aggressively.

Neglect

A child who is neglected may be underweight, dirty or often hungry. Lack of stimulation may cause delayed development, such as speech impairment. Self-stimulatory behaviours, such as head banging, are common. There tends to be a lack of attention to safety and frequent attendance at hospital is common. Supervision of young children may be inappropriately delegated to children a few years older or children may be left in the home for long periods without supervision. When these children are ill parents tend not to seek medical help. Older children often have educational problems and problems of school attendance, either because it is not enforced or because children are deliberately kept off school. For this reason, these families are often well known to education welfare services. It is important to monitor suspected cases, rather than jump to conclusions, and to discuss them with other professionals, such as health visitors, school doctors or social workers to get their perspective. Neglected children are frequently physically abused as well.

Sexual abuse

With children who have been sexually abused behavioural difficulties may be the only indication that something is wrong, although sexually precocious or explicit behaviour, lack of friends, lack of participation in school activities, frequent absence from school, running away from home, depression and eating problems are also common. Caution must be applied as again these symptoms may be due to other factors.

Emotional abuse

Any form of abuse may be accompanied by emotional abuse. It can include verbal threats and put-downs, belittling and scapegoating, which can cause as much distress and as much harm as physical abuse. Parents may use extreme forms of punishment, such as confining children in cupboards. It exists to some degree in all forms of maltreatment. It has consequences for children's mental or emotional functioning and may lead to anxiety, depression, withdrawal, aggression or delayed development.

Associated disorders

Studies indicate that children who experience abuse are at much greater risk of significant emotional problems that can become pervasive and chronic in later life. Associated disorders include:

- anxiety disorders
- depression
- deliberate self-harm and suicidal ideas
- post-traumatic stress disorder
- eating disorders
- conduct disorders and ADHD
- alcohol and drug abuse.

Of children who are physically abused, for example, about a third have a disruptive disorder, such as ADHD or conduct disorder, about a quarter suffer mood disorders, and over a half have an anxiety disorder (Flisher *et al.*, 1997). Girls who have been sexually abused tend to develop emotional problems, whilst boys tend to exhibit more suicidal tendencies. Depression and abuse of drugs or alcohol are particularly common amongst those who have been both physically and sexually abused. Many abused children may experience considerable stress, but post-traumatic stress disorder (see Chapter 19) is more likely to occur where the abuse is chronic and it is more common among sexually abused girls (Wolfe *et al.*, 1994). Children who experience routine violence are more likely to be involved in violent delinquent behaviour. However, it is also important to recognise that many children who are abused do not grow up to be abusive adults and that many other factors play a part in this process.

Incidence

In England alone, in 1991, 45,200 children were placed on the at-risk register (Creighton, 1992) and, in the UK, about 4 per cent of children up to the age of 12 are brought to the attention of professional agencies each year because of suspected abuse. Figures for both the USA and UK indicate that the number of children abused is increasing each year. Child abuse or neglect can affect any child, regardless of age, social status or ethnicity. In one retrospective study, a history of physical abuse was reported by about 31 per cent of males and 21 per cent of females, whilst sexual abuse was reported by 20 per cent of females and between 3 and 11 per cent of males (Finkelor, 1994). Similar rates have been found in all Western countries, suggesting that child abuse is a significant problem. Cases of physical abuse have always predominated, followed by sexual abuse, neglect and then emotional abuse (Creighton, 1992). In 1991, for example, physical abuse formed about 20 per cent of the total number of cases, sexual abuse and neglect each formed about 12 per cent, whilst emotional abuse formed about 6 per cent of the total.

Causes

No single cause can explain child abuse and it is very difficult to predict which families are likely to be involved. Given the right conditions – the complex interaction of individual, family, community and cultural factors – it is likely that any family could be affected. Despite this, a typical picture emerges of parents who find parenting stressful, express little affection for their child and are isolated from the wider community. The major risk factors are concerned with social deprivation, stressful life events, parenting practices, abuser characteristics, characteristics of the child and family support, as well as some cultural factors. These are outlined briefly below.

Social deprivation

Overall, child abuse is more common among the poor and disadvantaged, where deprivation creates an additional stress on families. Low income and social isolation, for example, may mean that parents find it difficult to provide suitable childcare or safety precautions.

Stressful life events

High levels of stress increase the risk of child abuse. Coping with a new baby or a difficult adolescent, for example, can create added pressures. Child abuse is often related to marital conflict and violence and unless such underlying stress factors are addressed it is likely that it will reoccur. Children living with a single parent and those living in large families are at significantly greater risk of both physical abuse and neglect. Children are more vulnerable to sexual abuse where they live with a stepfather, have lived for a period without their mother or have a poor relationship with their mother, as well as where they have few friends. These children often have no one to confide in or to support or reassure them. This means that it is easier for the abuser to keep it a secret.

Parenting practices

Abusive parents often lack basic parenting skills. Parents who lack psychological maturity, such as young mothers, may have little concept of the basic requirements of childcare and may react negatively, for example, to crying. For some parents the line between child abuse and discipline is confusing. Their attitude to behaviour tends to be rigid and inflexible and expectations of children unrealistically high. When parents lack experience and guidance and are also faced with overwhelming stress, they do not know how to cope and are likely to respond emotionally and impulsively.

Abuser characteristics

Most children are abused by a parent or someone known to them, such as a foster parent, baby-sitter, relative or friend. Psychotic illness, drug abuse and parental depression place children at increased risk. Other factors, such as learning difficulties, may also prevent parents from fulfilling their role. Whilst there appears to be a link between those who were sexually abused as children and those who go on to abuse others, this is not thought to be inevitable. They are, however, more likely to have significant social deficits and their sexual interests may become confused with their need for emotional closeness.

Child characteristics

Certain characteristics, such as prematurity, low birth weight, prolonged crying, demanding behaviour in a young child or oppositional behaviour in older children, may put them at greater risk. Children with a chronic illness or disability that places high demands on families are also at increased risk. Such characteristics, however, may play a role in continuing or escalating the situation unintentionally, rather than causing the problem.

Family support

Families are frequently socially isolated and lack support, in the form of extended family, neighbours, community, as well as support agencies, which increases the risk of abuse.

Cultural factors

Child abuse is also often influenced by cultural factors. For example, men are often portrayed as powerful and women as passive. This is ingrained from an early age and is thought to be the basis for some men's need to maintain control and power in a relationship.

Protective factors

Abused children may constantly be subjected to unpleasant events, such as unfriendliness, criticism and a chaotic lifestyle, as well as more dramatic events, such as seeing their mother being hit by their father, which are beyond their control. They learn to deal with these situations in many different ways and some show remarkable resilience despite such adversity. A positive self-esteem is the best protective factor. Given care and protection, appropriate opportunities and a positive relationship with at least one significant adult, many children are able to recover from abusive experiences and live normal lives as adults.

Effects

Child abuse and neglect affects different children in different ways. The effects will depend on the relationship of the abuser to the child, the nature of the abuse, the children's age and development, as well as the frequency and duration of the abuse. Whilst the effects of emotional or long-standing neglect are often less evident than those of physical abuse, the long-term consequences on social, emotional, cognitive and behavioural development may be far reaching and profound. Some children seem to cope well despite such adversity. Those who are able to tell someone, be believed and supported and told they are not to blame are less likely to suffer serious long-term effects. For a more detailed summary of the effects of maltreatment the reader is referred to Corby (1993). Abuse can result in wide-ranging problems that can be physical, behavioural, psychological and social in nature.

Physical problems

Those who have been physically abused may show evidence of physical injuries, such as bruises, burns or broken bones. Neglected children can also suffer physical health problems, such as limited growth, impaired cognitive and psychomotor development and delayed language development. Emotional abuse can cause failure to thrive, short stature and developmental delay. Younger neglected children often show regressive and somatic signs of distress, such as sleep problems, bed wetting, headaches, stomachaches, diarrhoea and ulcers. In addition, the physical health of children who have been sexually abused may be affected by urinary problems, gynaecological problems, sexually transmitted diseases and pregnancy.

Behavioural problems

Regardless of the type of abuse, there is a tendency for the behaviour of these children to be either withdrawn or aggressive. Neglected young children, for example, may alternate between undisciplined activity and extreme passivity (Crittenden and Ainsworth, 1989). They may show little persistence and enthusiasm, poor impulse control and can be excessively clingy. The effects, however, are often more striking as children get older and school-age children may show signs of conduct disorder (see Chapter 3). Older boys tend to be more aggressive with peers, whilst girls tend to be more passive, withdrawn and low in self-esteem (McCloskey *et al.*, 1995). Younger children who have been sexually abused commonly show regressive behaviour, as in bed wetting, whilst older children often show acting out behaviours, delinquency, drug use, promiscuity or self-destructive behaviour. In addition to this, they often show age-inappropriate sexual behaviour and attempt to sexualise interpersonal relationships. This can be very difficult to deal with, particularly in a school setting.

Psychological problems

Regardless of the type of abuse, there is a tendency for school-age children to lack positive beliefs about themselves and for their self-esteem to be low. They may have a great sense of self-blame and inferiority. The powerlessness and betrayal that are typical of their circumstances make it easier for them to blame themselves. The lives of abused children are often characterised by emotional turmoil and this makes it difficult for them to learn how to regulate their emotions like other children. They tend, therefore, to inhibit their feelings. As they get older this becomes more of a problem and can be associated with depression and anxiety, as well as aggression and acting out behaviour. Sexual abuse can have profound short- and long-term effects upon emotional adjustment and may be a precursor to serious mental illness.

Social problems

The characteristics of aggression, impulsive behaviour and distrust in children who have been abused make it difficult for them to form relationships. They often alternate between aggressor and victim and lack social skills and sensitivity to others, making them unpopular with their peers and their teachers. In particular, those who have been physically abused tend to be more physically and verbally aggressive towards their peers whilst those who have been neglected tend to withdraw from, or avoid peer interactions. Sexually abused children, on the other hand, tend to be anxious, inattentive and unpopular.

Treatment

With the provision of adequate care, dramatic improvements can be achieved in the developmental attainments of children, their behaviour and social adjustment. However, removal from the family can create more distress for children and may have undesired side effects (Melton, 1990). This often places social workers in a difficult position. Harm may be minimised if separation of children from their parents is managed correctly as part of a long-term treatment plan that includes rehabilitation of the family. This will depend on the motivation of parents and an assessment of interactions within the family. The interests of children and families are best served by close co-operation and communication between all the professionals involved. The role that teachers can play is discussed more fully in the final section of this chapter.

Child abuse is an issue for the whole family and the best outcome is achieved when intervention is focused on parent–child relationships, but the child may need to undergo individual therapy first. Individual therapy may be used to help children address their feelings and resolve conflicts. This can be a long and painful process which, in severe cases, may go on for years. Creative therapies may be used where children have difficulties expressing themselves verbally, for example, play therapy may be used for younger children. A focused casework approach can then be used to address issues with the family as a whole and family therapy may be helpful to address the relationships within the family when the child has undergone sufficient individual work.

Course and outcome

Whilst many adults with histories of maltreatment lead productive and satisfying lives, others continue to show signs of serious psychological distress and disturbance. Two-thirds of those who develop symptoms in relation to sexual abuse, for example, recover significantly during the first twelve to eighteen months following the abuse, but the possibility of delayed symptoms is increasingly recognised (Kendall-Tackett *et al.*, 1993). Whilst there is a connection between children who have been abused and those who become abusive adults, it is important to note that the majority of abused children do not become abusive adults. The positive factors within their lives, including positive school influences, are often able to counterbalance the negative effects of abuse.

WHAT CAN TEACHERS DO TO HELP?

Teachers have a key role to play in the prevention of child abuse and in the identification and protection of those at risk. A positive school experience can also be influential in helping to counteract the negative effects of abuse on some children so it is important that consideration is given to providing effective support in school for children who have been abused.

Prevention

There are a number of ways in which teachers can contribute to the prevention of child abuse: by developing a positive school ethos, through the delivery of a PSE programme that focuses on personal safety and future parenting, and by directing vulnerable parents to appropriate resources within the community.

School ethos

For some children schools are threatening places, but there is a lot that teachers can do to make schools safer for children. Most importantly, the ethos of the school needs to encompass values that reflect the importance of respecting and helping others. It is important that teachers listen to the children in their care and are able to provide the support and guidance that the children need. Some vulnerable children, for example, may be bullied by others. It is important therefore that school policies on behaviour and anti-bullying are formulated and implemented and that all teachers promote a non-violent ethos. They may need to reflect on their own practices as to whether they may be considered non-abusive. This is discussed in more detail in Chapter 15, which is devoted to bullying.

PSE programmes

Schools can also play a major role in promoting the safety of children by providing a comprehensive personal safety programme within the framework of the PSE curriculum. In addition, the school can have a long-term impact through incorporating comprehensive parenting programmes within the school curriculum for secondary children. The PSE programme is therefore critical in preventing future abuse by teaching children:

- how to recognise and avoid abusive situations;
- where to seek help when they are in danger of being abused;
- to develop positive mental health so they become non-abusive adults;
- the social skills for developing positive non-abusive relationships with others;
- the knowledge, attitudes and skills necessary for them to develop into non-abusive parents in the future.

Support for parents

Effective prevention is likely to require long-term commitment and to include social and educational support for parents. Strategies may be directed at the total population, for example, where all young children are reviewed at intervals through health visitors, or directed at those at risk, such as the poorest, most vulnerable families and those with the least support. This might include, for example, the provision of local authority nurseries for children in need, or courses on parenting skills. Teachers may be involved in, or at least should be aware of initiatives, such as Sure Start, within their local area so they can direct parents to appropriate resources. Parents most at risk of maltreating their children may be suspicious of the involvement of external agencies or those in authority and may need a lot of encouragement to engage in these types of programmes.

Identification and protection of children at risk

Intervention may also be aimed at preventing reoccurrence of abuse and minimising harm. This involves the identification of suspected child abuse and the reporting of cases by professionals, including teachers. All public inquiry reports on child abuse cases highlight the need for interprofessional communication and co-operation as a vital ingredient in effective child protection work. In the past, little attention has been given to the potential role that teachers may play in child protection. However, with their close daily contact with children, they are ideally placed to spot the signs of abuse and to know about children and their families. Whilst teachers may rightly feel that their primary task is that of education, they are also concerned with child welfare and the recognition of child abuse is one of teachers' pastoral duties. Many teachers, however, fear this responsibility and are concerned about their lack of training for this task. They may be worried, for example, that such action may not be in the best interests of the child. The dilemmas for teachers are discussed more fully in David (1993) and Braun (1991).

Recent concerns about child abuse have led to a lot of advice, guidance and instructions to all professionals, including teachers, from both central and local government. This guidance emphasises the need for a multi-agency response. At a local level, all areas have an Area Child Protection Committee (ACPC) that provides a joint forum for developing, monitoring and reviewing child protection policies. The committee establishes guidelines for all professionals for the prevention, management and monitoring of child abuse, as well as being responsible for interagency training and reviewing of cases. It is also able to provide training for teachers. Others who can provide teachers with support and advice include education welfare officers, educational psychologists, school nurses, school medical officers and advisory teachers for child protection within the LEA.

Recognition of those at risk

For the period 1988–1990 schools initiated just under 10 per cent of all cases of child abuse, second only to social services (Creighton, 1992). Teachers may notice a child who always seems to have some bruises or injuries, especially if they get progressively worse. They may notice a child who is too compliant, demanding constant attention or a sudden change in behaviour that indicates that the child is unhappy. By making a regular note of children's appearance or behaviour, they may also be able to detect a pattern. Teachers have the advantage of being skilled in observation and having extensive experience of normal child development.

Where children are already on the Child Protection Register, teachers should be alert to signs of distress and significant changes in behaviour. It is vital not to jump to conclusions. Suspicions should be discussed with others, particularly those with pastoral responsibility to help substantiate abuse. It may be appropriate to do nothing except make a careful record of what has occurred and to monitor children's progress. On the other hand, if other factors also indicate abuse, it is helpful to contact social services to discuss the case informally to help decide whether there are grounds for further action. It is essential that professionals take the time to assess whether sufficient facts are available to intervene before any steps are taken. This process is facilitated where the designated child protection teacher within the school has a good working relationship with social service staff. This can provide the breathing space required for a reasoned decision to be made. In this way, the teacher involved, who may have limited experience of child abuse, can feel supported. Teaching staff should also be aware of the far-reaching implications that an inaccurate assessment of abuse can have for the family involved.

Reporting suspected cases of abuse

Teachers are under obligation to report evidence of abuse and neglect to social services, who will then instigate an assessment. Child protection guidelines issued by the DFE (1995) state that all staff should be alert to signs of abuse and know who they should report concerns to, and that all schools should:

- have a designated member of staff, with appropriate training, responsible for co-ordinating action and liaising with other agencies;
- be aware of the child protection procedures established by the ACPC;
- have procedures for handling cases of suspected abuse.

It is very important that all teachers are aware of the procedures, have ongoing training and know what course of action to take. Where teachers are alleged to have abused children in their care, child protection procedures should be followed, as with other cases. Where parents themselves admit to abusing their children and ask teachers not to tell, they are obliged to respond by contacting the appropriate authorities. This may be a cry for help and they may be doing the family a disservice by not acting.

The most important factor is to ensure children's safety. Children may need to be taken to hospital, in which case parents should be informed without discussion about the cause of the injury. Teachers who are attentive and listen to children in their care are highly likely to be the ones that children choose to go to for help. Where sexual abuse has been disclosed they should acknowledge how difficult it must be for children to tell them, but also inform them that they will need to discuss it with other professionals in order to support them. The way in which disclosure is handled is vital as this can have a lasting impact on children. The temptation may be to question them, not only causing them more distress, but also possibly prejudicing further investigation as this is not part of teachers' role (Maher, 1987). Listening and focusing on how children feel at this point can be helpful. It is vital that the member of staff, as a person they trust, support children through the investigation process (Furniss,

1991). In turn, teachers themselves may require support from other school staff or social workers during this period, as it can be a harrowing and lengthy process.

Once the referral has been passed to social services, an experienced social worker will be allocated and an investigation initiated immediately. The social worker will involve the police, other professionals, parents or carers and the child, and they will then set up a child protection case conference. Most concerns are investigated within twenty-four hours of receiving the report and often within a few hours. Investigations are carried out in the strictest of confidence.

Involvement in case conferences

No one professional group can deal with child abuse alone. Teachers have been criticised in some child abuse inquiries for inadequate communication within and between schools and with other agencies, as well as for inadequate record keeping, and lack of awareness of potential cases. The child protection case conference is the central focus of child abuse management and the forum in which professionals from different agencies exchange information about the child and his or her family. The purpose of the case conference is to share information, decide if there is cause for concern, identify sources and level of risk and decide action to be taken. Recommendations may also be made to the local authority to instigate legal proceedings or for the police to pursue an investigation. The school should send someone who has a thorough knowledge of the child and his or her circumstances. In the past, for example, exclusion of the class teacher from discussion with other agencies has been highlighted as unhelpful. Teachers have a unique knowledge of children, knowledge of non-abused children with whom to compare, as well as training in child development, and they should feel confident in the contribution they are able to make to the conference. However, child protection case conferences can be daunting and it may be difficult for teachers to challenge the views of social workers. For these reasons, it may be helpful for teachers with little experience to have training and to be accompanied by a more experienced member of staff.

Where a decision is made to place the child on the Child Protection Register, a child protection plan will be formulated and a key worker (a social worker) appointed. The child protection plan must be reviewed every six months. However, any concerned professionals may ask the local authority to call a review if they believe that children are not adequately protected. Details of the procedures for case conferences are provided by Blumenthal (1994) and readers are also referred to their own local ACPC guidelines. Typically, the LEA also has an advisory teacher for child protection issues, who can be consulted.

Monitoring and recording

Schools have been criticised in child abuse inquiries for the paucity of information in children's records, such as failure to record discussions with other agencies and to note relevant social factors. All staff will need to be aware of children who require careful monitoring and the help being provided for them under the child protection plan. Children on the Child Protection Register or showing suspected signs of abuse should be monitored carefully. It can be helpful to have a locally agreed system of monitoring to give teachers confidence. Detailed written records of significant events and communications affecting any child at risk must be made. Teachers may, in some circumstances, be required to provide evidence in court in cases of child abuse. It is important for accounts to be as factual as possible and a distinction made between fact, observation, allegation and opinion (DFE, 1995). The focus should be on educational progress, behaviour and relationships with peers and family. In addition, health concerns, contact with the family, information about siblings and views from colleagues may also be needed. This information is confidential and should be available on a 'need to know' basis. Records should be kept securely by the designated member of staff within the school.

Supporting abused and neglected children

For many children facing distress school is their only form of stability and support. Teachers, however, may be concerned about how they can support abused and neglected children, who often have a wide range of needs and difficulties. These children frequently stand out in school as those with the most severe and wide-ranging problems. They often have great difficulty forming relationships and may require the support of teachers in helping them build relationships with their peers. Those who suffer neglect are highly dependent on teachers for support and nurture so this relationship can make all the difference (Erickson *et al.*, 1989). They also often exhibit behavioural difficulties that can be addressed by supporting them with an individual education plan or a pastoral support programme (DfEE, 1999). More detailed advice on addressing behavioural difficulties, particularly conduct disorder, is provided in Chapter 3.

Addressing educational needs

As well as difficulties in relationships with peers and teachers, children who have been abused also tend to have significant learning difficulties. Low educational aspirations, lack of language stimulation, lack of encouragement to learn and lack of recognition of strengths and achievements by parents all militate against academic achievement. Living in a world that lacks predictability raises anxiety and discourages belief in one's own competence, which in turn inhibits intellectual development and learning. These children therefore face considerable challenges once they enter school. Most have difficulty completing schoolwork, lack initiative, lack concentration and are over-reliant on teachers for help, as well as exhibiting aggressive or withdrawn behaviour (Erickson *et al.*, 1989). These difficulties should be addressed through the learning support department within the school and through provision of an IEP. Difficulties may be such that they warrant the child having a formal SEN assessment. Parents should be encouraged to be involved, as they should with all educational matters concerning their children, despite the fact that professionals may consider that they are neglectful or abusive.

These children may withdraw from school activities and are excluded from school more often than their non-abused peers. Their behavioural difficulties may be significant so referral to the educational psychologist may be appropriate. School attendance problems are common and may need to be addressed through a referral to the school's education welfare officer. They also tend to move home more often with consequent disruption to their education, in which case education welfare officers may be able to provide some form of support.

Further reading

Blyth, E. and Cooper, H. (eds) (1999) Schools and child protection. In the Violence Against Children Study Group, *Children, Child Abuse and Child Protection*, 115–128. Chichester: John Wiley & Sons.

Corby, B. (1993) *Child Abuse: Towards a Knowledge Base*. Buckingham: The Open University Press.

David, T. (1993) *Child Protection and Early Years Teachers: Coping with Child Abuse*. Buckingham: The Open University Press.

Department for Education (1995) *Protecting Children from Abuse: The Role of the Education Service, Circular 10/95*. London: Department for Education.

Department of Health (1991) *Working Together under the Children Act 1989: A Guide to Arrangements for Interagency Cooperation for the Protection of Children from Abuse*. London: HMSO.

Maher, P. (ed.) (1987) *Child Abuse: The Educational Perspective*. Oxford: Basil Blackwell.

References

Blumenthal, I. (1994) *Child Abuse: A Handbook for Health Care Professionals*. London: Edward Arnold.

Braun, D. (1991) Responding to child abuse: Dilemmas of protection. *Pastoral Care in Education*, June, 17–19.

Corby, B. (1993) *Child Abuse: Towards a Knowledge Base*. Buckingham: The Open University Press.

Creighton, S. J. (1992) *Child Abuse Trends in England and Wales 1988–1990*. London: National Society for the Prevention of Cruelty to Children.

Crittenden, P. M. and Ainsworth, M. (1989) Attachment and child abuse. In Cicchetti, D. and Carlson, V. (eds) *Child Maltreatment: Theory and Research on the Causes and Consequences of Child Abuse and Neglect*, 432–463. New York: Cambridge University Press.

David, T. (1993) *Child Protection and Early Years Teachers: Coping with Child Abuse*. Buckingham: The Open University Press.

Department for Education (1995) *Protecting Children from Abuse: The Role of the Education Service, Circular 10/95*. London: Department for Education.

Department for Education and Employment (1999) *Social Inclusion: Pupil Support (Circular 10/99)*. London: DfEE.

Department of Health (1991) *Working Together under the Children Act 1989: A Guide to Arrangements for Interagency Cooperation for the Protection of Children from Abuse*. London: HMSO.

Erickson, M. F., Egeland, B. and Pianta, R. (1989) The effects of maltreatment on the development of young children. In Cicchetti, D. and Carlson, V. (eds) *Child Maltreatment: Theory and Research on the Causes and Consequences of Child Abuse and Neglect*, 647–684. New York: Cambridge University Press.

Finkelor, D. (1994) The international epidemiology of child sexual abuse. *Child Abuse and Neglect*, 18, 409–417.

Flisher, A. J., Kramer, R. A., Hoven, C. W., Greenwald, S., Alegria, M., Bird, H. R., Canino, G., Connell, R. and Moore, R. E. (1997) Psychosocial characteristics of physically abused children and adolescents. *Journal of American Academy of Child and Adolescent Psychiatry*, 36, 123–131.

Furniss, T. (1991) *The Multi-professional Handbook of Child Sexual Abuse: Integrated Management, Therapy and Legal Intervention*. London: Routledge.

Kendall-Tackett, K. A., Williams, L. M. and Finkelhor, D. (1993) The impact of sexual abuse on children: A review and synthesis of recent empirical studies. *Psychological Bulletin*, 113, 164–180.

Maher, P. (ed.) (1987) *Child Abuse: The Educational Perspective*. Oxford: Basil Blackwell.

McCloskey, L., Figueredo, A. and Koss, M. (1995) The effects of systematic family violence on children's mental health. *Child Development*, 66, 1239–1261.

Melton, G. B. (1990) Child protection: Making a bad situation worse. *Contemporary Psychology*, 35, 213–214.

Skuse, A. and Bentovim, D. (1994) Physical and emotional maltreatment. In Rutter, M., Taylor, E. and Hersov, L. (eds) *Child and Adolescent Psychiatry: Modern Approaches (Third edition)*, 209–229. Oxford: Blackwell.

Wolfe, D. A., Sas, L. and Wekerle, C. (1994) Factors associated with the development of post-traumatic stress disorder among child victims of sexual abuse. *Child Abuse and Neglect*, 18, 37–50.

19 Post-traumatic stress

At 7 years of age Gemma was involved in a serious car accident with her parents and her little sister. It took some time before the ambulance arrived at the scene of the accident and Gemma was found unhurt but huddled in the back of the car. Her mother had been knocked unconscious and her father had received serious injuries. For some months afterwards Gemma had nightmares about the incident. She became irritable and had temper tantrums. She lost interest in activities she previously enjoyed, even refusing to play with her friends. She became reluctant to go to school and when she did go she appeared preoccupied a lot of the time and found it difficult to concentrate on her work.

Teachers need to know how to work therapeutically with children who have experienced trauma. With the recent influx of refugees into the UK from war-torn countries, it is likely that many teachers may be faced with children who have been traumatised, without ever having had any training in how to handle this. Much, however, has been learnt about the impact of traumatic events on children in recent decades from disasters, such as the sinking of the *Herald of Free Enterprise*. Three different types of stress reaction have been noted in children: there may be a period of adaptation to stressful life events or life changes; there may be an immediate reaction to an exceptional stress, such as an earthquake or a serious accident, which usually lasts only hours or days; or there may be a delayed and/or protracted response to a traumatic event. The last type constitutes post-traumatic stress disorder (PTSD) and it is with this that we mainly concern ourselves here. PTSD, therefore, tends to occur after a one-off traumatic event, such as a natural disaster or a severe car accident, rather than from long-term stress due, for example, to prolonged marital discord or sexual abuse. It is increasingly recognised that PTSD can occur in children. Their reaction to stress varies and, whilst in some children reactions may be devastating, other children show extraordinary resilience.

It is unclear whether PTSD is an anxiety disorder or a separate disorder in its own right. However, it differs from other anxiety disorders in that it is associated with a specific event, in the way that it affects the child's view of safety and the greater generalisation of fear (Yule, 1994), so for these reasons a separate chapter is devoted to it here.

Diagnosis

The diagnostic criteria for PTSD, as given in DSM-IV (American Psychiatric Association, 1994), include:

- Experience of, or witness to, an event that involved actual or threatened death or serious injury to self or others, in which the individual experienced intense fear, helplessness or horror.
- Persistent re-experiencing of the event through one or more of the following:
  - recurrent and intrusive recollections of the event;
  - recurrent distressing dreams of the event;
  - acting or feeling as if the traumatic event were recurring;
  - intense psychological distress or physiological reaction on exposure to cues that represent or resemble an aspect of the traumatic event.
- Persistent avoidance of stimuli associated with the trauma and numbing of general responsiveness, as indicated by three or more of the following:
  - efforts to avoid thoughts, feelings or conversations associated with the trauma;
  - efforts to avoid activities, places or people that arouse recollections of the trauma;
  - inability to recall an important aspect of the trauma;
  - markedly diminished interest or participation in significant activities;
  - feelings of detachment or estrangement from others;
  - a restricted range of feelings;
  - a sense of a foreshortened future.
- Persistent symptoms of increased arousal that were not present before the trauma, as indicated by two or more of the following:
  - difficulty falling or staying asleep;
  - irritability or outbursts of anger;
  - difficulty concentrating;
  - being overvigilant;
  - an exaggerated startle response.

Symptoms must last for more than one month and cause significant distress or impairment, such as socially and academically. The disorder may be acute (last less than three months) or chronic (last more than three months). Onset of the disorder may also be delayed and can begin as long as six months after the traumatic event.

Differential diagnosis

Care must be taken with the diagnosis of PTSD as it is possible that some symptoms may not be due to the trauma. PTSD can be confused with obsessive–compulsive disorder (see Chapter 11) because of the intrusive thoughts associated with the disorder, but the latter can easily be distinguished as these thoughts are not related to a specific traumatic event. In addition, the flashbacks experienced in PTSD must be distinguished from perceptual disturbances seen in other mental disorders, such as schizophrenia, substance-related disorders and some general medical conditions.

Features

The essential feature of PTSD is the development of characteristic symptoms following a psychologically distressing event that is outside the range of normal human experience, not including bereavement or chronic illness. Typically, the event is experienced with intense fear, terror and helplessness. Extreme traumatic events that might give rise to PTSD include disaster, war, a major accident, physical assault or extreme violence, as well as some extreme incidences of physical and sexual abuse, but it can also occur after life-threatening illness and medical procedures. When someone is killed suddenly in tragic circumstances, such as a car accident, the effects on those bereaved can be just as severe as those bereaved by disaster and they may show symptoms of PTSD. Children in hospital with serious injuries or illness are at increased risk, as are also refugees from war-torn countries. Children who witness extreme domestic violence may also suffer from PTSD, as do many severely abused children. Most research, however, has been done on PTSD connected with disasters (e.g. Capewell, 1993; Duggan and Gunn, 1995; Yule, 1994; Yule *et al.*, 1990; Yule and Williams, 1990). In addition, Goodyer (1990) has examined the impact of war on children.

PTSD can occur at any age and symptoms usually begin within the first three months of the trauma. It is important to note, however, that there can be a considerable delay, even of months or years. Depression and anxiety may be apparent in the first six months, whereas the symptoms of PTSD may not be evident until later. This delayed effect can lead to a lack of recognition of the problems, many of which are unlikely to be resolved spontaneously. Whilst fear, which may be expressed as agitated and disorganised behaviour in children, may become an integral part of children's functioning, the main features of PTSD are the re-experiencing of the trauma, avoidance of traumatic reminders and numbing of general responsiveness, as well as marked symptoms of anxiety or increased arousal.

Re-experiencing the trauma

In the days and weeks following the traumatic event, images of the incident may keep recurring or children may experience life-like dreams in which the event is re-enacted. In rare cases, the event is relived for several hours or even days. Whilst older children tend to experience flashbacks and the emotions associated with them, it is common for young children to experience nightmares and to re-enact the event through their behaviour, repeatedly drawing pictures of what happened or acting it out in play. Children need to go over and over the event in their minds. Whilst some symptoms, such as anxiety, sleeplessness and irritability, tend to decrease within months, preoccupation with the event tends to remain and this can cause children to become increasingly withdrawn and isolated.

Avoidance of reminders

Exposure to a situation that resembles the event or one that provides a trigger, such as an anniversary, can lead children to become intensely psychologically distressed. Typically, there is a great fear of objects or events directly connected to the trauma. Individuals with PTSD often deliberately avoid things associated with the event and can even develop amnesia. This can affect children's social lives and, if insensitively handled, can lead to conflict with teachers or peers and adversely affect their relationships. Whilst general anxiety and depression tend to diminish over time, specific fears and the avoidance reaction can persist. Studies have shown that avoidance is still often present two years after the event (Duggan and Gunn, 1995).

Anxiety, arousal and lack of general responsiveness

The symptoms of anxiety and increased arousal may include difficulty getting to sleep, increased vigilance and an exaggerated startle response, and, in some cases, irritability, outbursts of anger or difficulty concentrating or completing tasks. Children who have experienced a traumatic event can become very safety conscious and very alert to the dangers in the environment. At the same time, there is often a general lack of responsiveness that usually begins soon after the traumatic event. Children may lack interest in activities they previously enjoyed, they may feel estranged or detached from others or their ability to feel emotions may be diminished. It is, however, often difficult to identify these signs in children who are often well behaved, so they may go unnoticed by teachers and others. In addition, affected children frequently cannot see a future for themselves. As a consequence of these difficulties, children with PTSD can find schoolwork particularly difficult. They may, for example, have memory problems when it comes to mastering new tasks and remembering old ones.

Physical symptoms and behaviour

Children may develop physical symptoms, such as stomachaches and headaches. They may feel very guilty at surviving an event that others did not. Despair and hopelessness, self-destructive behaviour, social withdrawal, impaired relationships or even a change in personality may occur. It is generally agreed that pre-school children react differently to stress, although it is not known whether they are more greatly affected than older children. They may regress developmentally and display behaviour that is inappropriate for their age. They may also show antisocial behaviour and become aggressive both at home and at school.

Associated disorders

There is evidence to suggest that exposure to extreme stress increases the risk of developing other disorders. Anxiety disorders and substance abuse, as well as depression, for example, are common (Bolton *et al.*, 2000). In adolescents, in particular, there are high rates of depression, suicidal thoughts and overdose in the year after the traumatic event, as well as anxiety symptoms. It is not known to what extent these symptoms precede or follow the onset of PTSD.

Incidence

There is little information about the incidence of PTSD and rates are not available for children in the UK, but the disorder is thought to be more common than was first believed. An overall lifetime incidence rate of between 1 and 14 per cent has been indicated, whilst in the USA, an incidence rate of 5 to 10 per cent has been found (Kessler *et al.*, 1996). Elevated rates, however, are found in certain populations, such as those from areas of social unrest, for example the Kosovan refugees. Studies suggest that about 30 to 40 per cent of children who have been involved in disasters have the disorder (Fletcher, 1996). There is also some evidence that PTSD may be increasing (Amaya-Jackson and March, 1995).

Risk factors

Similar traumas can have very different effects on different children. Anyone can develop PTSD, but it is more common and the symptoms are likely to be more severe in those closest to the event and when the event itself was of a severe nature (Pynoos *et al.*, 1987). Those directly experiencing pain or coming very close to death therefore tend to be the worst affected. The strongest predictor of PTSD in children is the threat to their life, although family reactions to the disaster also contribute (Green *et al.*, 1991). Families who do not share their experiences with each other may have more difficulty adjusting in the long term, a negative family reaction may help maintain the disorder. Children may be able to cope with stress better if they have a supportive relationship with at least one parent and a cohesive family and support from a wider social network of peers and teachers. Lack of such support is likely to impair resilience. The course of the disorder will also depend on the age of the child. How trauma is experienced will depend on the child's developmental level since the child's ability to process information cognitively and emotionally is vital to adjustment (Yule, 1994). Different responses may also reflect differences in temperament, personality or genetic predisposition. Social support, family history, childhood experiences and the presence of other mental disorders can influence the development of PTSD. However, it can also be found in individuals with no predisposing factors, particularly if the trauma is extreme. The children most affected tend to be those who already have anxiety-related problems. There are conflicting findings on whether gender is a risk factor, but, in general, females seem to be more vulnerable than males.

Treatment

PTSD often goes unrecognised and untreated. It is difficult for children, especially young children, to report their feelings. They need to be carefully assessed using reports from teachers and parents, as well as their own accounts. Parents, however, may be unaware of children's distress, as many children do not tell their parents because they do not want to upset them. Children need to be asked about their specific fears, their thoughts and about avoidance behaviour. With specific questions, children as young as 3 are likely to be able to give some account of the event. When devising a treatment plan, account must also be taken of children's educational and social needs, as well as their health needs, and this should involve teachers and social workers. While it is important to recognise and treat PTSD symptoms early, it is also important to realise that this often has to be done in the context of the child's or the family's other problems.

In the aftermath of a traumatic event practical issues may need to be attended to first. This will be the case, for example, where a child has been orphaned or received serious injuries. In addition to formal treatment interventions for PTSD, family and social support is important. This more informal support can be a key factor in protecting children against the adverse effects of stress so social support networks for children should not, for this reason, be left to chance, and teachers can have a role to play in this. It is important to consider both the immediate and more long-term needs of children. Crisis intervention can be used to deal with the immediate aftermath of the disaster, but some children may require more long-term treatment, such as individual therapy, cognitive therapy or support groups. These are outlined briefly below.

Crisis intervention

Interviewing children as soon as practical after the event can be helpful because they rarely speak spontaneously about their experiences (Pynoos and Eth, 1986). Children generally do want and need to share their thoughts, feelings and fears and they gain a great sense of relief when taken through the incident in detail. They may be frightened and even fear that they are going mad. Reassurance that these are normal reactions to traumatic events can help them greatly. Intervention at this point can prevent long-term difficulties and more deep-seated problems. It is important, however, to use debriefings cautiously since children will adjust at different rates to their experiences (Yule, 1994).

Individual therapy

Individual therapy can be helpful in dealing with intrusive thoughts and avoidance behaviour in a safe and supportive environment. The child is encouraged to relive the event and at same time, with support, manage his or her distress. The aim of therapy is to help children express feelings and establish coping strategies. Children who have PTSD may require intensive individual therapy in order to explore their memories of and feelings about the event. Techniques, such as play therapy, drama therapy or art therapy, may be used to facilitate this process. Family therapy and group therapy may also be useful and sleep problems may be helped with relaxation techniques.

Cognitive therapy

A number of cognitive approaches can be useful with children. Triggers can be identified and addressed through relaxation and other anxiety-reducing techniques. Gradual exposure to fearful situations, for example, can be helpful to overcome avoidance behaviour (see Chapter 6 for more detail on this form of intervention). Other techniques, such as challenging irrational thoughts, may also be used.

Support groups

Group discussions with fellow victims can be very beneficial and may provide children with the only opportunity they get to go over the event and express their feelings. Whether the traumatic event involved them or not, those close to children, such as parents and teachers, may need help to acknowledge what has happened. If they feel that the event should not be talked about or they themselves are frightened, children can often sense this. Under these circumstances it is impossible for the child to deal with his or her own experiences and feelings.

Course and outcome

The course of PTSD depends on the age and developmental stage of children at the time of the trauma and the nature of the trauma. There have been very few systematic long-term studies of the effects on children. Symptoms do tend to decline over time, but for a significant number of children symptoms continue for more than a year. Complete recovery occurs in about half of those affected within three months, but many others have persistent symptoms for longer than a year after the trauma. In some disaster studies, for example, ten months to a year after the event 30 to 40 per cent of individuals still had substantial symptoms and significant impairment (La Greca *et al.*, 1996; Raphael, 1986). The more severe the trauma the more likely it is that effects will last for six months to a year or more. Children's reactions to major stresses can last for many years and be quite disabling. PTSD can become a chronic disorder with remissions and relapses that last for decades (Fletcher, 1996). Other factors that influence the course of the disorder include the amount of trauma during and after the event, the individual's characteristics, major life stresses, family reactions, social support and coping strategies (La Greca *et al.*, 1996).

WHAT CAN TEACHERS DO TO HELP?

There are a number of things that schools can do to help children cope with trauma. According to Capewell (1993), these include:

- having policies and plans in place for dealing with emergencies, such as a major local disaster;
- preparing pupils through programmes within the normal curriculum in which they are taught coping strategies, such as stress management and coping with bereavement;
- training all teachers to recognise and support pupils who experience trauma.

Whilst the strategies and interventions below are discussed mainly with reference to major disasters, the principles underlying them may also be applied to personal tragedies and serious accidents.

Managing a major local disaster

There is a lot that services and professionals, including schools and teachers, can do to minimise the impact of disasters or trauma on children. A lot has been learnt from disasters that have occurred in recent years. There is, however, still a need for training and general education about the impact of disasters and how a wide range of organisations and professionals can co-operate to offer constructive help. Social and mental health services have a recognised role to play, but support potentially involves a whole range of workers, including teachers (Department of Health, 1991). Schools, in conjunction with other services, must therefore plan ahead to ensure that the effects of a major crisis on the children and young people in their charge, and also their staff and the wider community, are minimised (Yule and Gold, 1993).

A great variety of skills need to be deployed in the aftermath of a disaster so teachers should be aware of sources of help available and the procedures for accessing them. These may include, for example, mental health services, youth services, social services and voluntary agencies, as well as educational professionals, such as the educational psychologist and the school's education welfare officer. In some areas, crisis services have been set up specifically to deal with local disasters. Social services usually provide a co-ordinating service and advice and support to victims and a team of social workers is usually set up in the week following a disaster (Newburn, 1993). It is crucial that all professionals know how the expertise available can be effectively and efficiently deployed. In the event of a local disaster, which can raise a wide and complex range of emotions, close liaison between services is essential so professionals need to be able to appreciate what others can offer. Teachers, for example, are not trained in dealing with the emotional aspects of trauma and they will need support from health and social services colleagues. Only by working collaboratively can the more long-term consequences of trauma be avoided.

The aftermath of a disaster

Capewell (1993) suggests that, when helping children and young people following a disaster, it is important to:

- find out who is involved and assume that the impact is wider than anticipated;
- create environments that are familiar to children so they feel safe enough to discuss their experiences;
- offer help and do not wait for children to ask for help or demonstrate their need for help by their behaviour;
- deal with one's own emotions first before trying to support children;
- help families and groups of children to support each other;
- include children in the rituals of the community (e.g. attendance at funerals);
- help those children less involved to support their friends;
- be prepared to consult with or refer to other professionals and offer support when it is needed, even when treatment is being received from elsewhere.

Providing information

It is important that all those involved, including children, are kept informed about what is happening. Survivors need this sort of information to help them get over the tragedy. Schools, for example, could provide information through assemblies or through a newsletter. A telephone help line, which is usually set up by social services, is a common method of providing information. However, if the disaster is school related, this responsibility may fall on the school. The media can also be used to help pass on information to others.

Providing support for children

Although it has only recently been recognised, children, even very young children, are profoundly affected by disasters. It is easy for them to be overlooked, as they often do not readily confide their thoughts to parents and teachers and this means that the extent of their distress is often underestimated. Children may require practical as well as psychological support in the immediate aftermath. They are unlikely to ask for help themselves and it is important that this is not left to chance. Knowing something of the signs and symptoms of PTSD can be helpful, as this facilitates understanding of children's difficulties and the importance of reassuring them that their experiences are normal given the circumstances. Teachers can also play a role helping children and their parents by encouraging them to seek expert help when it is needed.

Children's thoughts may be dominated by their experiences and they may feel a compelling need to talk. It is important that this is recognised and that they are allowed to do this in a safe and familiar environment, not just in a formal counselling or therapy setting. This may require teachers to abandon their formal teaching role for a temporary period and to use listening skills to allow children to share their experiences and feelings. Children differ in their cognitive awareness and it is always a good strategy to get them to repeat back what you have discussed to check that they fully understand. Creative ways may be used to help them with this process, such as writing their thoughts down, drawing pictures, or writing poetry. As they develop they may need to go over the event again so as to gain a deeper level of understanding. This can help them make sense of their emotions, piece together the experience, facilitate self-help and mitigate against any long-term impact. At the same time, however, it is important for teachers to recognise when children require more formal treatment and for them to acknowledge when they feel out of their depth.

Providing opportunities for children to share their experiences

Sharing experiences and feelings with other victims is an important part of the process of healing for children. The use of groups has proved helpful, but it is important to remember that the degree of trauma experienced by children will be different and that those not affected may not understand the distress of others. This may include the parents of children, who may not recognise their child's level of distress and who may prefer to brush the incident aside. Teachers may need to help parents deal with their own anxieties. The school setting may therefore provide some children with the only opportunity they get to share their experiences and their feelings. Group experiences could be deliberately structured into the school day and support from mental health professionals, experienced at facilitating groups of this nature, obtained. Providing a relaxed and informal atmosphere in a familiar setting for some children can be more beneficial than formal counselling with someone they do not know.

Staff support

It is important for teachers to have an awareness of what they are likely to confront in a disaster situation. Their knowledge of the children and the day-to-day skills they normally use in their work are invaluable under these circumstances. An initial feeling of helplessness is normal. This work is emotionally and physically demanding and to avoid them becoming victims of the disaster themselves it is important that they are adequately supervised. It can be difficult for some professionals to recognise or admit that they too are distressed as they may feel that they are expected to be able to cope. The event may raise personal issues, such as past bereavements, for some people. Effects on those offering support to victims can be dramatic – some professionals have described it as a life-changing event. For this reason, it is important that teachers get sufficient support from social services and mental health professionals and work closely with them. Staff can also be supported through the offer of counselling from someone with experience from outside the school.

Early identification and referral

There is a natural tendency in adults to be overprotective towards children who have experienced trauma, but this is often more about protecting themselves. This can lead to a resistance to formal treatment. Social workers offering support following a local disaster, for example, have been known to be rejected by schools because of their focus on exams (Newburn, 1993). It is important to find ways of allowing children to express their feelings in safety so formal treatment must be provided where it is needed. Teachers need to be alert to the signs and symptoms of PTSD. Children's reactions can be delayed so teachers need to be vigilant for some time after, when children are known to have experienced a traumatic event. Home–school liaison is important in ensuring that teachers are informed of any events outside of school that might affect children in this way. Children and their parents, who may be reluctant, should then be encouraged to access expert help when it is required.

Supporting children who have experienced trauma in school

The impact of trauma on children can be tremendous and it can affect all aspects of their lives – their family life, relationships with peers and their schoolwork. It is important that teachers recognise that children who have experienced trauma may experience a number of difficulties in school and that extra support may need to be provided, albeit perhaps for a temporary period.

School attainment

It is highly likely that children's school attainment will be adversely affected by trauma, although this can be prevented if children are given community support and time to talk about their experiences (Martin and Little, 1986). In addition, if it occurs at a crucial time, such as during GCSE examinations, it can have long-term consequences. Some children may require time off school to recover, whilst others may be extremely anxious and refuse to go to school. They may fear that another disaster may beset their family whilst they are away so it may be difficult for them to leave the home. Younger children, particularly, may demonstrate their anxiety in this way. It is important that they are encouraged to return to school as soon as possible otherwise this can lead to more long-term entrenched problems that are difficult to treat, such as school refusal (see Chapter 6). Children are likely to be totally preoccupied with the event, to the extent that they have little motivation or concentration for their schoolwork. In conjunction with this, disrupted patterns of sleep can make them feel tired and exacerbate their inability to concentrate.

Practical suggestions for parents, such as playing music or reading a story to children to get them to sleep, can be helpful. Bad dreams can be retold during the day when they can be given a happy ending. Lack of interest and motivation forms a major part of depression (see Chapter 8) and children should be monitored carefully. If their interest does not return after a short time, parents should be encouraged to seek specialist help to prevent more entrenched difficulties.

Associations with the trauma may directly affect aspects of children's school lives, but if recognised these can usually be avoided. A stark example was provided in the *Herald of Free Enterprise* disaster (Yule, 1990) in which a boy's GCSE coursework was destroyed. Despite his difficulty concentrating, the school had not considered that forcing him to redo this work, which he now associated with the event, might cause him to become emotionally distressed.

Behavioural difficulties

The period of instability that a trauma often creates can lead to behavioural difficulties. Adolescents, especially, may cover up their concerns by creating conflict. With acknowledgement of their underlying difficulties and sensitive handling, these problems can be alleviated in time. It can be helpful, for example, to provide a trusted member of staff for children to go to during times when they are finding it difficult to cope and are experiencing difficulties.

Relationship difficulties

Symptoms, such as mood swings and irritability, can have a knock-on effect for normal relationships and this can lead to children becoming withdrawn and isolated if it is not dealt with in the early stages. Peers may feel excluded or resentful that those affected are unable to share their thoughts with them (Newburn, 1993). Peers are often afraid to approach friends who have experienced a traumatic event for fear of upsetting them and consequently the child affected can feel rejected. Teachers can help by encouraging them to listen and provide support.

Further reading

Department of Health (1991) *Disasters: Planning for a Caring Response*. London: HMSO.

Perrin, S., Smith, P. and Yule, W. (2000) Practitioner review: The assessment and treatment of post-traumatic stress disorder in children and adolescents. *Journal of Child Psychology and Psychiatry*, 41, 3, 277–289.

Raphael, B. (1986) *When Disaster Strikes: A Handbook for the Caring Professions*. London: Hutchinson.

Yule, W. and Gold, A. (1993) *Wise before the Event: Coping with Crises in Schools*. London: Calouste Gulbenkian Foundation.

References

Amaya-Jackson, L. and March, J. S. (1995) Post-traumatic stress disorder. In March, J. S. (ed.) *Anxiety Disorders in Children and Adolescents*, 276–300. New York: Guilford.

American Psychiatric Association (1994) *Diagnostic and Statistical Manual of Mental Disorders (Fourth edition)*. Washington, DC: American Psychiatric Association.

Bolton, D., O'Ryan, D., Udwin, O., Boyle, S. and Yule, W. (2000) The long-term psychological effects of a disaster experienced in adolescence: II. General psychopathology. *Journal of Child Psychology and Psychiatry*, 41, 4, 513–523.

Capewell, E. (1993) Responding to the needs of young people after Hungerford. In Newburn, T. (ed.) *Working with Disaster: Social Welfare Interventions During and After Tragedy*, 105–118. Harlow: Longman.

Department of Health (1991) *Disasters: Planning for a Caring Response*. London: HMSO.

Duggan, C. and Gunn, J. (1995) Medium term course of disaster victims: A naturalistic follow-up. *British Journal of Psychiatry*, 167, 228–232.

Fletcher, K. E. (1996) Childhood post-traumatic stress disorder. In Marsh, E. J. and Barkely, R. A. (eds) *Child Psychopathology*, 242–276. New York: Guilford.

Goodyer, I. M. (1990) *Life Experiences, Development and Child Psychopathology*. Chichester: John Wiley & Sons.

Green, B. L., Korol, M., Grace, M. C., Vary, M. G., Leonard, A. C., Gleser, G. C. and Smitson-Cohen, S. (1991) Children and disaster: Age, gender and parental effects of PTSD symptoms. *Journal of American Academy of Child Psychiatry*, 30, 945–951.

Kessler, R. C., Sonnega, A., Bromet, E., Hughes, M. and Nelson, C. B. (1996) Post-traumatic stress disorder in the National Comorbidity Survey. *Archives of General Psychiatry*, 52, 1048–1060.

La Greca, A. M., Silverman, W. K., Vernberg, E. M. and Prinstein, M. J. (1996) Symptoms of post-traumatic stress in children after Hurricane Andrew: A prospective study. *Journal of Consulting and Clinical Psychology*, 64, 712–723.

Martin, S. and Little, B. (1986) The effects of a natural disaster on academic abilities and social behaviour of school children. *British Columbian Journal of Special Education*, 10, 167–182.

Newburn, T. (1993) *Making a Difference? Social Work after Hillsborough*. London: National Institute for Social Work.

Pynoos, R. S. and Eth, S. (1986) Witness to violence: The child interview. *Journal of American Academy of Child Psychiatry*, 25, 306–319.

Pynoos, R. S., Frederick, C., Nader, K., Arroyo, W., Steinberg, A., Eth, S., Nunez, F. and Fairbanks, L. (1987) Life threat and post-traumatic stress in school-age children. *Archives of General Psychiatry*, 44, 1057–1063.

Raphael, B. (1986) *When Disaster Strikes: A Handbook for the Caring Professions*. London: Hutchinson.

Yule, W. (1990) The effects of disasters on children. *Bereavement Care*, 9, 1, Spring.

Yule, W. (1994) Post-traumatic stress disorders. In Rutter, M., Taylor, E. and Hersov, L. (eds) *Child and Adolescent Psychiatry: Modern Approaches (Third edition)*, 392–406. Oxford: Blackwell.

Yule, W. and Gold, A. (1993) *Wise before the Event: Coping with Crises in Schools*. London: Calouste Gulbenkian Foundation.

Yule, W. and Williams, R. (1990) Post-traumatic stress reactions in children. *Journal of Traumatic Stress*, 3, 279–295.

Yule, W., Udwin, O. and Murdoch, K. (1990) The 'Jupiter' sinking: Effects on children's fears, depression and anxiety. *Journal of Child Psychology and Psychiatry*, 31, 1051–1061.

Part IV

Promoting mental health and services for children

20 Mental health services for children and adolescents

Mental illness is one of five key areas of health concern identified by the government. In a handbook focused specifically on child and adolescent mental health (Department of Health, 1995) mental health problems were noted to affect many or all aspects of children's lives. All those in direct contact with children, including teachers, were considered to have a part to play in addressing mental health problems and in the promotion of mental well-being. The need for a core of locally based specialist Child and Adolescent Mental Health Services (CAMHS) was also highlighted. Specialist CAMHS, however, have been found to be patchy, underfunded and their effectiveness sometimes inhibited by the lack of co-ordination between agencies (Mental Health Foundation, 1999). The skills and knowledge of mental health specialists therefore need to be passed on to those working on a daily basis with children, while CAMHS engage in more consultation and partnership with other professionals.

The present context

Concerns about discrepancies in working practices between CAMHS across the country have recently been raised (Audit Commission, 1999) and this has led to the introduction of the HAS model (NHS Health Advisory Service, 1995), which has now become a widely accepted model for CAMHS delivery. This is a strategic approach based on four tiers of service delivery which were described in Chapter 1. The main aim of the model is to provide a comprehensive service for children, adolescents and their families and to encourage the development of support and training for professionals working directly with children. In this way, it is hoped that some mental health difficulties may be addressed in the community by other professionals thereby preventing the need for referral to specialist services. The need for close working relationships between all the agencies involved so that an effective and efficient service is provided to children and their families was also recommended.

At the present time, many changes are taking place within CAMHS. An overview of services has been provided here, but it is important to recognise that services will vary widely from one area of the country to another. The staffing, the client group, referral and access to services, the services offered, treatment approaches and liaison with educational professionals are discussed below.

Staffing

CAMHS usually comprise multi-disciplinary teams that enable them to offer a holistic approach to children's problems. Staffing typically includes a number of health professionals, for example child and adolescent psychiatrists, clinical psychologists, community psychiatric nurses, child psychotherapists, as well as other specialist therapists, such as drama therapists, art therapists, occupational therapists and family therapists. The mix of professionals, however, varies considerably across the country and often does not reflect local needs (Audit Commission, 1999). Some teams, for example, lack specialists, such as clinical psychologists, that are normally an integral part of the CAMHS team. Where residential and day treatment facilities, as well as outpatient facilities, are available, some staff may work solely within the community setting, some solely within a specialist unit, whilst others may work across both settings.

In some cases, professionals from other agencies, such as social workers and specialist teachers, are included within the team. Until the late 1980s CAMHS teams were often established within Child Guidance Centres, which had a tradition of being multi-agency. Pressure on resources, however, has meant that, in many areas, social services and education have withdrawn staff from these teams and this has created further inconsistencies in CAMHS across the country. There is a duty to provide education for children attending day or residential treatment facilities. In some areas, therefore, specialist teachers still form part of the CAMHS team. Such teachers usually fall under the auspices of the Special Educational Needs Support Service or the Hospital and Home Tuition Service with the LEA. They can be a useful contact for mainstream teachers as they have usually had experience of working in mainstream schools and are therefore able to understand the difficulties and constraints on teachers working within this setting. A specialist teacher within the CAMHS team can greatly facilitate collaborative work with schools and other educational professionals and raise the awareness of non-educational professionals within the mental health team with regard to educational issues.

The client group

Many CAMHS operate within the age range from birth up to 16 years of age, but there can be some variation in this and again there have been found to be inconsistencies across the country (Audit Commission, 1999). Generally, those over 16 are referred to adult services, although, in some cases, the age limit is as low as 14. Some services are more flexible and will see young people over 16 who have accessed the service previously. Within other services, whether a youngster is seen by child or adult services may depend on the youngster's level of maturity rather than their chronological age.

Over the last fifty years the work of CAMHS has changed considerably and they are no longer concerned solely with children and young people who have serious mental illness. An increased understanding of mental health and child development has led to a broader view of mental health so services now work with a wide range of children's emotional, behavioural and developmental problems. The topics covered in this handbook illustrate the many and varied problems they may help to address. This has resulted in their work overlapping considerably with the work of other professionals – hence the need for them to work more closely with other agencies. In some cases, for example, education psychology services work closely with the CAMHS team and they may even undertake joint work, which facilitates understanding of each other's roles. More recently, a broader focus on mental health has meant that CAMHS have also become involved in work with a more preventative focus.

Referral and access to services

In contrast to other health service provision, CAMHS often adopt a policy that any professionals or agencies involved directly with children and their families can refer to their services. However, a wide variation exists across services, and in some cases referral is limited to GPs only (Audit Commission, 1999). The majority of referrals are commonly made by GPs, although a range of health professionals, such as paediatricians, can usually refer. Typically, some referrals are also made by field social workers. Thus, whilst teachers concerned about children's behaviour and their academic attainment should consult their educational psychologist in the first instance, they can also encourage parents to seek help through their GP. The educational psychologist acts as a filter to prevent inundation of referrals, as services tend to be overloaded with cases. Some educational psychologists will work with families where children have mental health problems, whilst others may refer such cases directly to the local CAMHS. In some areas, Education Welfare Service staff can also refer. Self-referrals, especially from young people or parents who have had previous contact with the service, may also be accepted. In cases where professionals other than GPs refer, CAMHS are usually obliged to notify the child's GP. Referrals are usually expected to be made in writing to a central base and as much information provided as possible. Even when telephone referrals are accepted (sometimes in special cases) professionals are usually expected to follow this up with a letter that includes more detailed information. If referral is considered urgent this can usually be specified on the referral form or letter. It is helpful for teachers, who generally know the children and the family well, to provide the educational psychologist with as much information as possible.

Parental permission for referral is essential, since this is considered a necessary prerequisite for an effective working relationship and treatment is rendered ineffectual without it. Whilst the school may feel that a mental health problem may underlie children's difficulties, the family may perceive the problem as entirely school related and therefore refuse to access CAMHS. This can be a significant obstacle to effective treatment and can leave teachers feeling helpless and ineffective. Children may not accept responsibility for their behaviour and teachers and parents may want children to change, whilst they themselves see nothing wrong with their behaviour. The motivation to change, however, is considered critical for treatment to be effective. Under such circumstances, it is easy, but not helpful, to blame the child and the family and it is not uncommon for schools to exclude children until they have agreed to seek help (Carrick and Hodgson, 1999). This places unrealistic expectations on CAMHS and generally renders any treatment ineffective. It can be more productive for teachers to seek support through consultation with CAMHS and schools should see this as a way forward in such circumstances.

Specialist CAMHS are often seen as remote and inaccessible by other professionals (Carrick and Hodgson, 1999). There is a great demand for CAMHS and there are often long waiting lists. Like other services, they do not have unlimited resources and it is inevitable that this limits the number of children that can be seen and how quickly they can respond. In some areas children have to wait more than six months or even over a year to be seen (Audit Commission, 1999). By this time, difficulties may have become too entrenched or the situation may have broken down altogether. This can leave teachers feeling helpless and ineffective. With the introduction of the HAS model, teachers may find it easier to seek consultation and support from the CAMHS in these circumstances. Similarly, where teachers are unclear about the appropriateness of referrals, it can be helpful for teachers to have the opportunity to discuss cases with the CAMHS team to assess their appropriateness since this can prevent time being spent on inappropriate referrals. Having a named contact within the local service could facilitate this process. In addition, a mental health co-ordinator could be appointed by the school to act as a central point for teachers who have concerns about pupils' mental well-being (WHO *et al.*, 1993). A co-ordinator could get to know the work of the local mental health team in more depth and act as a personal link with the service. Such a person could have a role in enhancing teachers' knowledge about the work of CAMHS, as well as ensuring that referrals were appropriate. This is discussed more fully at the end of this chapter.

Services offered

There is a wide variation in the services offered by CAMHS throughout the country, particularly for adolescents (Audit Commission, 1999), but services may include:

- outpatient clinics;
- day and residential treatment facilities;
- specialist educational support;
- consultation, support and training for other professionals.

Outpatient clinics

The vast majority of services only run outpatient clinics, which usually operate from health authority premises, such as health centres and GP surgeries in local areas. Children and their families are usually seen at the clinic closest to their home. The teams in these areas are in the best position to help families as they will be aware of other facilities in the local area to which they may direct families for other forms of support. A range of treatment approaches (discussed next) may be offered on an outpatient basis and children and their families may be seen at different intervals depending on the nature of their difficulties. Some may be seen only once, whilst others with more intractable problems may be seen on a regular basis for a few years.

Day and residential facilities

Day and residential treatment facilities are highly specialised services and are usually only provided on a regional basis. The number of day treatment facilities has increased over the years and residential placement has become less common. Day facilities may be an integral part of a residential unit with children mixing during the day or they may be separate entities with purpose-built premises. Children may attend every day or for certain days of the week and the programme usually runs from 9 a.m. to 5 p.m. each day. Some units are open at weekends, whilst others only open in emergencies. They may cater for any number of children, up to about forty. There are often separate child and adolescent units. Whether younger teenagers attend the children's unit or the adolescent unit often depends on the maturity of the child, the type of problems he or she is experiencing and the mix of each group at the time, rather than chronological age. Individuals are seldom admitted for residential or day treatment without being seen in an outpatient clinic first. However, where the referrer makes a specific request for residential placement to be considered this may be taken into account. Day or residential treatment is generally considered where:

- more intensive therapy is needed;
- a more detailed assessment is required;
- it is helpful to break a cycle or pattern of behaviour;
- a break from negative circumstances may be beneficial;
- the degree of psychiatric disorder is such that children cannot be contained in the community.

The focus nowadays tends to be on short-term psychiatric care, providing a thorough assessment, crisis resolution and the treatment of acute symptoms of disorder (Hersov, 1994). Day treatment lessens the danger of mutual rejection and scapegoating by the family, as well as providing a more normal existence for the child. Residential treatment is often only reserved for those more seriously disturbed with recognised mental illness, such as schizophrenia and severe depression. Where residential placement is deemed necessary, however, a gradual planned move to day provision and then to outpatient support is common. Whilst the length of stay can range from a few months to several years, a long stay makes it more difficult for children to reintegrate into their normal community setting. A lot of time is usually taken to introduce children and families to day and residential units as it is important that they understand the commitment they are making and that their fears about attendance are allayed. It can be quite a threatening process for both parents and children. Attendance is voluntary and a lot of emphasis is placed on children's willingness to attend, especially in the case of adolescents.

Specialist educational support

The LEA has a duty to provide education for children attending a psychiatric unit on a daily basis. This is usually done through an attached school unit, although, in practice, the number of hours of education children receive varies tremendously. Some units operate more or less a normal school day, with therapeutic activities taking place outside of normal school hours, whilst others intersperse therapeutic activities throughout the school day. Specialist teachers within the unit usually liaise closely with relevant mainstream school staff to maintain continuity of education and the more information and resources mainstream teachers can provide to support their work the easier it will be for children to reintegrate back into their normal school setting. Having educational support in a small-group setting within the unit can provide children with the opportunity they need to become re-motivated and for them to catch up with work they may have missed. Children who attend the unit part time will usually be expected to attend their mainstream school for the remaining time. Whilst this may not be an ideal arrangement from an educational perspective, it is usually in the best interests of the child. In order to be effective this requires careful negotiation between mainstream schoolteachers and CAMHS team staff. Children's educational and therapeutic needs have to be taken into account, although at this stage, their therapeutic needs are likely to take precedence.

Consultation, support and training

Not all children who need help are able to receive it from specialist services. In fact, 90 per cent of children with mental health problems may not be seen by CAMHS. This means that it is important that professionals working directly with children and their families get training, support and consultation from these services so that they are able to identify and support children with mental health problems (Carrick and Hodgson, 1999). The aim of consultation is to help professionals gain insight and understanding and to provide a different perspective on the problem. For teachers who are open to new ways of working, this form of support can be most valuable. The amount of time psychiatrists spend in consultation with other professionals, however, varies (Audit Commission, 1999). Some child psychiatrists, for example, often provide valuable consultation work in special schools for pupils with EBD, whereas others have very little time for consultation. With the introduction of the HAS model, there may be more formal structures in place to facilitate this type of work.

Treatment approaches

Typically, an initial assessment of the problem may be conducted by any member of the CAMHS team. A community psychiatric nurse and a social worker, for example, may see the child and his or her family on the first occasion, although a psychiatrist will see them if a formal request for a psychiatric assessment has been made. The team may consult with other professionals involved with children and their families at this stage and this may obviate the need for psychiatric intervention. Once direct involvement of the CAMHS team has been agreed, a thorough assessment of the problem is then undertaken. This usually involves interviewing the whole family so that problems can be understood within the context of the family, so that the team can assess how family relationships contribute to children's difficulties and so that they can determine the best approach to treatment. Occasionally other professionals are invited to the first meeting if it is thought that this will be beneficial.

More recently, CAMHS have tended to move away from a medical model, which focuses on children as having inherent difficulties, to a more holistic view of problems, although in some services an emphasis on diagnosis and treatment still remains. Educational and social difficulties may therefore be addressed as an integral part of the treatment plan, and this has facilitated their work with other agencies. Currently a large and diverse number of treatments for children and families exist. There is rarely one specific type of treatment for a particular problem and the approach chosen will also depend on clinicians' and the family's preferences. Treatment may be focused on individuals, groups, families, or on the wider community. Nowadays it is common practice to combine two or more interventions. A brief summary of general approaches to treatment is provided below, but within each of these approaches many different variations also exist.

Psychodynamic

A psychodynamic approach focuses on underlying conflicts and helping children to develop an awareness of unconscious factors that may be contributing to their problem. In this way conflicts may be resolved and children helped to develop more effective ways of coping.

Behavioural

Within behavioural interventions the focus is on re-educating children through techniques such as positive reinforcement, modelling and systematic desensitisation. The focus may also be placed on changing children's environments by working with parents and teachers.

Cognitive

A cognitive approach focuses on addressing the deficits and distortions in children's thinking, such as irrational beliefs and interpretations. Once identified, such beliefs can be challenged and the child encouraged to see things differently.

Client centred

A client-centred approach focuses on the therapist establishing an unconditional, non-judgemental relationship with the child. The therapist then works with the child to clarify and resolve the child's thoughts and feelings.

Family

Family approaches assume that the problem is determined by factors within the family and disturbance in family relationships. Different types of family therapy exist and they may focus on family interaction, communication, dynamics or boundaries, depending on the type of approach.

Biological

Medical models assume that problems result from biological impairment or dysfunction and rely primarily on medication or other biological approaches, such as the use of Ritalin for ADHD or anti-depressants in the treatment of depression.

Residential and day treatment programmes

Where day and residential units exist they usually have to meet the needs of children with a wide variety of problems. An individual treatment programme is usually provided for each child using the wide range of expertise within the team, although psychiatric nurses generally form the core staff, alongside specialist teachers where they are employed. The treatment programme may consist of a combination of any of the types of therapy described previously, but in addition, day-to-day interactions between children and between staff and children provide opportunities for therapeutic intervention. Typically, for example, a community meeting involving staff and students is held each day. Within the meeting, issues ranging from the day's activities, to concerns about a child harming him- or herself, may be raised by staff or students and these are discussed. Special meetings may also be held to address urgent matters. It is through this process that youngsters are helped by others to face issues and deal with their behaviour. More personal and emotive issues touched on within the meeting can then be taken to individual therapy sessions for more detailed exploration. Children with specific difficulties, such as severe school refusal, may be expected to attend their mainstream school as part of their treatment programme. This requires very close co-operation between teachers and unit staff, along with the pupils and their parents, so that a jointly agreed action plan is developed.

Liaison and collaborative working with teachers

In the majority of cases children with mental health problems will also have learning difficulties, albeit sometimes for a temporary period, and children's educational needs will need to be addressed through close liaison between mental health professionals and teachers. Problems may be exhibited at school as well as within the home environment and the reasons may be complex. For this reason, treatment may be focused on the wider community, including schools, as well as directly on children and their families. Generally, a treatment programme is agreed with the child and his or her family and a contract drawn up which is regularly reviewed. Teachers, where relevant, may be asked to be involved in meetings with the family or to attend more formal case conferences. These meetings can provide school staff with an opportunity to find out about the progress of pupils and to raise any concerns they may have. It is important that someone who knows the child well attends. As conferences can feel threatening to inexperienced teachers, it is also probably best that someone with experience in liaising with outside agencies, such as the SENCO or a designated mental health co-ordinator from within the school (as discussed earlier), also attends. The conference should be seen as an opportunity for a two-way exchange of information. It is important to remember that children's therapeutic needs are likely to take precedence over their educational needs, but at the same time it can be helpful to remind the CAMHS team of the educational issues. As far as possible, following more intensive treatment, return to school should be planned with the child, the family and the mental health team. Close liaison is required between the mental health staff and teachers to facilitate this process. If teachers are uncertain how to support children on their return to school, this should be discussed with the team. It is important that everyone is clear about what is expected and that the school endeavours to provide whatever support is required.

The underlying principles and ways of working within CAMHS are fundamentally very different from those within education. Without an understanding of this, barriers between professionals can be created and different perspectives and opinions can be a significant obstacle to collaborative working (Carrick and Hodgson, 1999). There are a number of potential conflict areas. First, there is often an expectation that CAMHS can produce rapid and dramatic changes in individuals and that they will return to school with the problem 'solved'. The reality, however, is that dealing with the underlying causes of behaviour takes a long time. Many children require ongoing support and it is unlikely that they can cope effectively in school without adapting the environment in some way or providing them with some form of extra support. This may require teachers to change their behaviour and the way in which they work with such children.

Second, treatment is voluntary, except in exceptional circumstances when the Mental Health Act (Department of Health and Social Security, 1983) is applied. This is in direct contrast to education, where there is a legal obligation to ensure that children go to school. Consent to treatment is important in establishing children's motivation to change and it is essential if treatment is to be effective, particularly with adolescents, but it can create tension between educational and mental health professionals. Even young people under the age of 16 may have the right to seek or refuse psychiatric treatment, without parental consent. Although every effort is normally made to involve parents in treatment, it is the responsibility of the doctor offering the treatment to form a judgement of the young person's capacity to understand the issues concerning consent to treatment (Wolkind, 1994). There is evidence that the majority of adolescents do understand these issues and that if they disagree with their parents' views or refuse to allow them to be consulted, they will probably be capable of giving informed consent. Psychiatrists placed in this position, however, usually seek legal advice before proceeding.

Third, mental health workers are working primarily for the well-being of individual children and their families. Teachers, on the other hand, whilst wishing to do the best for the child, also have the well-being of other pupils to consider. This can cause friction as mental health professionals may wish the child to be treated in ways that are inconsistent with normal school procedure or require additional resources. In these situations it is important that a compromise is negotiated.

Fourth, the CAMHS team will work with whatever the family presents, despite the fact that other professionals may hold a different view of the problem, as this is an important part of the process of engagement. It can therefore sometimes feel to teachers as if the team are listening to the family and not listening to their perspective. It is helpful to understand that this is part of the engagement process and teachers should avoid becoming defensive. Finally, because they tend to work with very difficult cases, CAMHS often employ indirect and unusual approaches that are sometimes at odds with the ways that other services work and hence are difficult for other professionals to understand. A child's hyperactive behaviour, for example, may be framed as natural curiosity enabling the parents to adopt a more positive response, which in turn will have a positive effect on the child's behaviour. If teachers are to understand such approaches they need to be open minded and good communication and liaison with the mental health team are required.

The role of the school mental health co-ordinator

CAMHS are often criticised for being inaccessible to schools because teachers are rarely able to refer pupils directly for treatment and because teachers often lack understanding of their working practices. However, appointment of a mental health co-ordinator within the school, who could act as a focal point for access to services in the local area, could facilitate this process (WHO *et al.*, 1993). A co-ordinator would have the responsibility for building a personal relationship with professionals in the local mental health team so that s/he develops an understanding of the work of the team and so that advice and support is readily available through him or her for all school staff. The co-ordinator could, for example, spend time observing the team's ways of working so that he or she is fully aware of the services they offer and their working practices. A co-ordinator could also facilitate joint training sessions with school staff, thereby raising the awareness of teachers. This would be consistent with good working practice commensurate with the effective operation of Tier 2 of the model of CAMHS delivery. By sharing experiences in this way teachers would have a better understanding of the work of such services and a greater awareness of how they too can help pupils and families by addressing mental health problems more effectively.

Further reading

Department of Health (1995) *A Handbook on Child and Adolescent Mental Health.* London: HMSO.

Mental Health Foundation (1999) *Bright Futures: Promoting Children and Young People's Mental Health.* London: The Mental Health Foundation.

Steinberg, D. (1986) *The Adolescent Unit: Work and Teamwork in Adolescent Psychiatry.* Chichester: John Wiley & Sons.

References

Audit Commission (1999) *With Children in Mind: Child and Adolescent Mental Health Services.* Abingdon: Audit Commission Publications.

Carrick, A. and Hodgson, S. (1999) Children's Mental Health Services: How should they look? *Young Minds Magazine*, 41, 12–13.

Department of Health (1995) *A Handbook on Child and Adolescent Mental Health.* London: HMSO.

Department of Health and Social Security (1983) *The Mental Health Act. Memorandum on parts I–IV, VIII–X.* London: HMSO.

Hersov, L. (1994) Inpatient and day-hospital units. In Rutter, M., Taylor, E. and Hersov, L. (eds) *Child and Adolescent Psychiatry: Modern Approaches (Third edition)*. Oxford: Blackwell Science.

Mental Health Foundation (1999) *Bright Futures: Promoting Children and Young People's Mental Health.* London: The Mental Health Foundation.

NHS Health Advisory Service (1995) *Child and Adolescent Mental Health Team Services. Together We Stand: The Commissioning, Role and Management of Child and Adolescent Mental Health Services.* London: HMSO.

WHO, CEC and CE (1993) *The European Network of Health Promoting Schools: Resource Manual.* Copenhagen: WHO Regional Office for Europe.

Wolkind, S. (1994) Legal aspects of child care. In Rutter, M., Taylor, E. and Hersov, L. (eds) *Child and Adolescent Psychiatry: Modern Approaches* (Third edition), 1089–1102. Oxford: Blackwell.

21 Promoting mental health in schools

Specialist mental health services are inundated with referrals and find it difficult to cope with the increasing demand for services for children and adolescents. There is an urgent need to focus resources on the promotion of mental well-being and the prevention of children's mental health difficulties. Schools provide an ideal setting for this as they allow regular access to all children, which means that teachers can implement preventative strategies that avoid stigmatising those children who are vulnerable to mental health problems. The recent focus on performance indicators and academic targets in schools, however, has made this more difficult.

Many mental health problems cannot be solved quickly so schools may need to provide ongoing support for some children on a long-term basis. Teachers cannot be expected to solve all pupils' problems or to take them on alone. They must be aware of their limitations and know when they should refer children to more specialist services. Despite this, there is a lot that teachers can do to make the school environment more therapeutic and to make pupils' lives more positive. The Mental Health Foundation (1999) refers to schools which promote children's and young people's mental well-being as having the key characteristics of:

- a committed senior management team that focus on creating a climate based on trust, integrity, democracy, equality of opportunity, within which each child is valued regardless of ability;
- a culture that values teachers, non-teaching staff and all those involved in the care and supervision of pupils;
- whole-school policies for important issues, such as behaviour and bullying, that are clearly set out and accepted and implemented throughout the school.

What is needed is a whole-school approach to the promotion of positive mental health. This involves having in place programmes for prevention of mental health problems, procedures for identification of disorders and strategies for intervention to remedy the various problems likely to be encountered in schools. This requires schools to have a clear policy and a comprehensive set of procedures for addressing mental health issues. The various elements of such policy and procedures are outlined in the model presented in Figure 21.1. This sets out a framework which provides guidance on the development of procedures for identification, prevention and intervention for mental health issues in schools. There are four levels in the model, each of which focuses on different aspects of school policy and procedures. These are:

- school ethos: which encompasses values shared by all staff;
- whole-school organisation: which comprises a range of school policies;
- pastoral provision: which is concerned with procedures in place throughout the school;
- classroom practice: which involves the practical strategies used by teachers;

School ethos

School ethos is a broad term used to describe the curricular and organisational features of the school which communicate certain values to the school community and thereby help to promote the development of fundamental values in children. Research shows that effective schools implement early intervention, promote pupils' self-esteem, provide personal support, counselling and guidance, teach life and social skills, actively involve

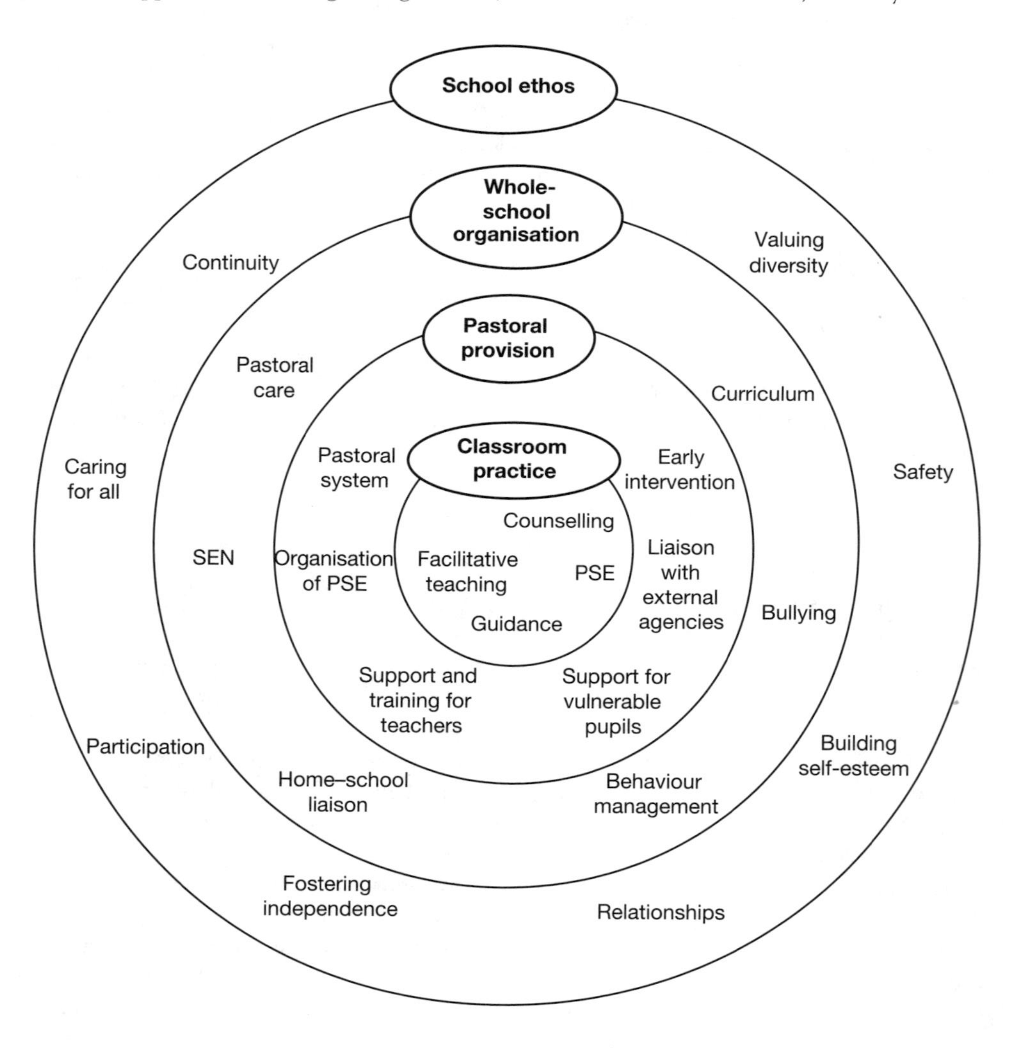

Figure 21.1 Framework for promoting mental health in schools

pupils and parents and establish a positive school climate (Rutter *et al.*, 1998). Many schools identify a set of core value statements as a guide to planning all aspects of the educational process. This can be crucially important to the overall functioning of the school, as long as all staff share these values. The school ethos encompasses a number of aspects, including building pupils' self-esteem, developing a sense of community, teaching children to co-operate and to help others, focusing on their moral development and teaching pupils to take responsibility and to participate in decision making.

As part of the school ethos a commitment to equal opportunities creates an atmosphere in which all pupils and staff are encouraged to value each other for the contribution they are able to make, whatever their difficulties, personality, appearance, race or gender. Although value statements about equal opportunities may not change the attitudes or behaviour of chronically disruptive students, they may positively influence other students. The school ethos is therefore important in what it conveys to children and young people. With a positive, caring ethos in place the school can create a safer and more productive learning environment for its pupils.

Increasing emphasis on academic achievement in schools in recent years and the need for schools to compete in league tables of performance indicators, however, are likely to have a dramatic impact on children's well-being. This makes the overall ethos and value system of the school increasingly important. Building pupils' self-esteem and focusing on relationships, as well as a sense of permanency, safety and belonging for pupils, are important. By paying attention to such factors, teachers can create a climate that is more, rather than less, therapeutic for all pupils.

Caring for all

An essential aspect of the school ethos is the extent to which the school communicates that all its pupils are valuable. It is important that children with difficulties are seen to be in need of help rather than as problems to be got rid of. A useful indicator of this is the number of pupils who are excluded each year, which is known to vary widely between schools in similar catchment areas. The reasons for this variation can usually be traced back to differences in school ethos which have led to some schools having more effective procedures for coping with troublesome pupils than others (Parsons, 1999).

Valuing diversity

Another key aspect of school ethos is the extent to which the diversity of pupils who make up the school's population is valued (Weare, 2000). Having an equal opportunities policy helps pupils to learn to value others from different backgrounds to their own. For example, they need to learn to appreciate what pupils from different ethnic groups can contribute to the education of all pupils. Beyond this, children need to learn to value having children with various special needs in the school. Having children with SEN, such as physical disabilities, learning difficulties and sensory impairments, in mainstream classrooms can have a positive impact on the other pupils, particularly in the learning of social skills. In order for this to happen teachers need to communicate positive attitudes about children with SEN to their classes and establish such things as buddy schemes to help other pupils to develop similar attitudes along with the social skills required for helping such children.

It is a much greater challenge for teachers and pupils to value the contribution of children whose special needs are due to emotional and behavioural disorders or other mental health problems. However, this is important if the school is to establish effective procedures for helping such pupils.

Building self-esteem

A common feature of children and young people with mental health problems is their low level of self-esteem. The development of positive self-esteem is important for the healthy development of children and schools have a fundamental role to play in this (Rutter *et al.*, 1998). Achievement at school is based on the accomplishment of a variety of academic tasks. An inability to achieve well in these tasks can have negative consequences for children's self-esteem. Continually being placed in situations where they experience failure, for example, can have disastrous consequences for them. On the other hand, there are many ways in which teachers can have a positive influence on the self-esteem of their pupils. This can be achieved, for example, through the liberal use of praise rather than chastisement and the fostering of co-operation rather than competition amongst pupils (Johnson and Johnson, 1999).

Relationships

Good relationships between teachers and pupils are paramount in providing an effective environment in which pupils can grow emotionally and socially. Research studies have shown that greater cognitive and affective achievement is associated with more cohesiveness and less tension within classrooms and that schools in which there are poor relationships tend to lead to depression and absenteeism in teachers and pupils (Weare, 2000). Children need to feel valued and accepted for who they are so that they can be themselves and do not have to put up a front. Within such an environment they are able to be open and honest about their difficulties. In many schools, however, because of the constraints on teachers, interaction between students and teachers tends to take place at a superficial level. Also, some children have a particular difficulty with authority figures, which is usually something that they have learnt from their families. A greater priority needs to be given to developing good relationships among pupils and teachers. Opportunities should be provided within the curriculum for pupils to develop social skills. Group work, for example, can be beneficial as an integral part of many lessons. In addition, teachers themselves should provide positive role models in their relationships with pupils and other teachers. Procedures should therefore be in place for teachers to deal with potential differences with colleagues and pupils in constructive ways (Hall and Hall, 1988).

Safety

It is important that children feel physically and emotionally safe in the school setting. This is especially important for vulnerable pupils since they may find it difficult to learn and may be less open and honest when they feel insecure. Having whole-school policies in place for dealing with disruptive behaviour and bullying, for example, is important. Having clear expectations and boundaries as well as an agreed set of school rules is essential. It is important that any form of threatening behaviour is dealt with swiftly and effectively. Aggressive behaviour, even if not directed at them, can make vulnerable children feel threatened and uncomfortable and this may make them withdraw (Peterson and Skiba, 2000). Children often complain, for example, that teachers shout at them. It is important that teachers are approachable and that children feel able to talk to someone in the school when they have difficulties. The pastoral system, discussed later in this chapter, therefore provides another important aspect of safety for pupils.

Continuity

A sense of permanency needs to be established for children to feel secure within the school setting. In primary schools, where children usually remain with one teacher throughout the year, continuity is established and a sense of permanency is easier to achieve, but it is also an important consideration in secondary schools. There are, therefore, grounds for maintaining this approach, as far as possible, beyond the primary years. It is advantageous for the same form tutor to take the form throughout their secondary years or for heads of year, or their equivalent, to move up with the year group. This can help ensure continuity and therefore some sense of permanence for pupils. For many pupils a constantly changing timetable can be an unsettling and unhelpful experience. Having a well-structured timetable and established procedures for providing pastoral care can provide vulnerable pupils with a sense of security.

Participation

The Elton Report (DES, 1989) concluded that the most effective schools are those that have created a positive atmosphere based on a sense of community and shared values. Effective participation is facilitated when the role of the headteacher is seen as being the leader of a staff team which consult pupils and parents about the running of the school (Weare, 2000). It is important that children feel that the school belongs to them and that it is a community in which they feel they belong. Teachers can reinforce this in practical ways, for example, by displaying pupils' work and by allowing them as much say as possible in the running of the school, as in student councils. Pupils are more likely to comply with rules which they view as important and that they have had some role in developing themselves.

Fostering independence

An important role of schools is to empower pupils to be independent. Research shows that more effective learning takes place when pupils are encouraged to think for themselves and are allowed to be as independent as is appropriate for their age (Weare, 2000). They should be given as much responsibility as possible within the classroom and in the school as a whole. Providing structured opportunities for students to share their views also helps, as does giving them opportunities to make decisions. The extent to which this can be done will vary with the maturity of the child, but it is especially important in the teenage years that young people have opportunities to make decisions in supportive environments so that they can learn to accept the consequences of the choices that they make.

Whole-school organisation

The second level of the framework is set within the values established by the school ethos at the first level described above. This level of the model focuses on the need to develop clear policy and procedures in key areas of school functioning, including pastoral care, the curriculum, pupils with SEN, home–school liaison, behaviour management and bullying.

Pastoral care

Pastoral care is that part of the school's role which is concerned with providing help in the areas of personal, social and moral development, educational guidance and vocational guidance. Government policy in the UK states that pastoral care should be a central feature of the education offered to all young people. Also, that PSE is required to be an explicit part of a school's curriculum policy, both within and outside the formal timetable. It is also considered to be the responsibility of all teachers and to be equally important in all phases of education (National Curriculum Council, 1989).

It is therefore essential that schools have a comprehensive policy and well-established procedures for delivering effective pastoral care (Calvert and Henderson, 1998). These will include the means for ensuring that all staff know of their pastoral responsibilities and of the strategies available for fulfilling these responsibilities. Pastoral strategies are the means by which the pastoral care provided by the school is dispensed to students. There are three major pastoral strategies: counselling, guidance and PSE. These pastoral strategies are at the centre of the school's pastoral care provision. The implementation of these strategies is discussed later in the chapter.

Curriculum

In order to facilitate the development of positive mental health in pupils it is important that the school curriculum strikes a balance between academic content and a focus on personal, social and moral development. This has become more difficult in recent years because of the emphasis which has been placed on academic goals by such things as the introduction of Standard Assessment Tests and the publication of league tables of academic test and examination results. The increased focus on academic goals has led to reduced emphasis on the role of the school with regard to pupils' personal, social and moral development. This is short sighted and will in the long term be counterproductive for two reasons. First, if schools do not pay sufficient attention to the development of a moral code and personal, social and vocational skills then societal costs for such things as delinquency, unemployment and mental health problems will increase in the future. Second, it is clear from the school effectiveness literature that schools which optimise academic success are ones which manage to maintain a strong emphasis on the personal and social development of their pupils.

Therefore, it is essential that a balance is maintained in the curriculum between academic goals and pupils' personal, social and moral development (Best, 2000). It is important therefore for the school curriculum to address directly the promotion of mental health, the prevention of mental health problems and the learning of coping strategies for dealing with mental health disorders. This should be implemented by means of input within the different subjects of the National Curriculum as well as being specifically addressed within the school's PSE programme, as discussed later in this chapter.

SEN

Schools need to have a policy for the education of children with SEN which embodies procedures linked together in a whole-school approach. This involves having procedures for the identification and assessment of SEN, for designing and reviewing IEPs and for collaboration with parents and specialists. Schools' policies and procedures for SEN need to take into account the requirements of the Code of Practice for SEN (DFE, 1994) which provides comprehensive guidance on establishing a whole-school approach to SEN. This is important since, as discussed in Chapter 14, children with SEN are at a greater risk of developing mental health problems than other pupils.

Home–school liaison

An important function of the pastoral system is also to liaise with pupils' parents. Parental attitudes are a key factor in children's education and in their mental well-being. Parental involvement is positively associated with student success, higher attendance rates and less exclusion, as well as greater teacher satisfaction and an improved school climate in general (Hornby, 2000). Links with home are an important factor in understanding children's behaviour and may also give indications as to the most useful approach to take when pupils are having difficulties. Background information can be vital in building a whole picture of children's circumstances. Parental involvement promotes a healthy learning environment and a healthy emotional climate by providing the opportunity to establish mutual goals between parents and teachers and by developing strategies and activities that can be implemented both within the home and the school setting.

Many parents with children who have mental health problems feel that they are left to cope alone. They are often frustrated and at their wits' end. They feel that they know their children well, yet professionals do not sufficiently take their views into account. Greater co-operation between parents and professionals in this area is therefore required. Parents have their own ideas about what is helpful for their children and these should not be dismissed. Strategies can be used to encourage parental involvement at a variety of levels (Hornby, 2000). This may include, for example, parenting skills classes, stressing learning at home, increased communication between parents and teachers, providing opportunities for volunteering to assist in school activities and involvement in decision making. All strategies for encouraging parental involvement help by increasing parent–school collaboration, promotion of healthy child development and providing a safe school community (Peterson and Skiba, 2000). It is therefore essential that schools develop comprehensive policies and effective procedures for home–school liaison.

Behaviour management

Mental health difficulties in children may manifest themselves in the form of difficult and challenging behaviour that is very difficult to deal with in the school setting, in contrast to the therapeutic setting where more one-to-one work is possible and where there is usually more support available to staff. It therefore needs to be recognised that dealing with such children is extremely challenging for teachers so the need for effective behaviour management strategies is paramount. However, it is easy for children with behaviour problems to be cast as scapegoats for inadequacies of the system or individual teachers. It can be far easier to evict children who are a problem for someone else to deal with, or to expect a head of year to work miracles without addressing the classroom environment, but this is not the answer. Whilst children may require individual treatment, effort also needs to be put into improving behaviour management in the classroom and throughout the school.

Schools should have behaviour policies that are known to all school staff, pupils and parents. These should focus on encouraging positive behaviour as well as spelling out sanctions and setting clear boundaries. Policies should be agreed by all staff and made known to all pupils otherwise it is unlikely that they will be adhered to. Policies and procedures need to be clear and understood by all. They should be an integral part of induction for new teachers entering the school since effective classroom management strategies need to be adopted by all teachers (Charlton and David, 1993; O'Brien, 1998). Mechanistic, behavioural strategies alone, however, are insufficient as different pupils respond to different strategies and different strategies suit different teachers. It is important to recognise the need to take into account the individual nature of children's problems and the fact that teachers need to develop their own style of management. It is not as clear cut as applying a set of rules. Children need to be taught to be tolerant of others and their differences. Whilst children usually have a very strong sense of what is fair, the reality is that pupils are all individuals with their own particular characteristics, so classroom management strategies need to take account of this. Thus, for example, an awareness of the fact that a child's grandmother died recently may quite rightly affect a teacher's response to his or her uncharacteristically difficult behaviour. This further illustrates the importance of teachers getting to know the children in their care, and their parents, so that they are aware of children's circumstances and their likely response in stressful situations.

Bullying

It is important for schools to address the issue of bullying since it can lead to more serious mental health difficulties for victims who are vulnerable. All schools are legally required to have an anti-bullying policy, which should form part of an overall policy on behaviour. All teachers and non-teaching staff should be aware of the procedures in place within their school to deal with bullying incidents when they are encountered (Jenner and Greetham, 1995). It is important to apply clear rules that are backed by appropriate sanctions, as well as having systems in place to support victims. Teachers need to be aware of systems that might inadvertently maintain bullying and they need to focus on developing positive relationships, promoting co-operation and non-violent resolution of conflicts amongst their pupils. Recent interest has focused on developing schemes in school such as peer support, befriending and peer mediation as approaches to bullying and these can be incorporated into a whole-school approach (Smith, 2000).

It is important that the policy encourages all teachers to take responsibility for bullying and procedures are in place so that incidents are dealt with quickly, consistently and effectively. In order to achieve this it is helpful for teachers to be taught about the underlying causes and psychology of bullying, how to identify incidents of concern, as well as techniques to maintain control within the classroom. They also need to provide good role models. Further to addressing bullying, schools need to have policies and procedures in place which promote non-violent means of resolving conflicts; therefore teachers need to be adept at de-escalating conflict situations within the classroom (Peterson and Skiba, 2000).

Pastoral provision

The third level of the framework is set within the values established by the school ethos at the first level and the policies and procedures established by the whole-school organisation at the second level. This level of the model focuses on the need to develop effective provision of pastoral care within schools, which involves having effective pastoral systems, early intervention, support for vulnerable pupils, and organisation of PSE, as well as support and training for teachers.

The school's pastoral provision encompasses the structure of the pastoral network, staff expertise and the different methods through which PSE is provided. This pastoral provision is set within the context of the whole-school experience that has an impact through school policies on such things as curriculum, SEN, parental involvement and behaviour management.

Pastoral support is an important means of reducing distress, isolation and helplessness for students who are attempting to cope with some form of interpersonal problem, since good teaching and management in itself may not be enough to assist all students to succeed. Teachers may be concerned that they have limited opportunities and resources for providing effective personal support for pupils in the present educational climate. When individuals have pressing concerns they may need to be provided with individual time and support to address these. It is important to provide children and young people with opportunities to talk about their concerns and aspirations. Such opportunities should be provided as an integral part of the pastoral system, through the form tutor and PSE time. Teachers need to adopt a sensitive approach to ensure that more withdrawn and vulnerable children are able to access such opportunities effectively.

Pastoral system

The way that the pastoral system is set up is important in helping pupils to settle into the school environment and to help them address any difficulties they may encounter. It is important that it is not seen as a discipline system (as is often the case) but is more supportive in its nature. Pastoral support plans (DfEE, 1999) can provide a framework for developing a positive way of helping pupils cope with their problems and for supporting them in school. The form of support given to pupils needs careful consideration. Adolescents especially may not perceive teachers as supportive, so they may not confide in them. More emphasis might need to be placed in schools on teacher qualities, such as setting a good example, being friendly, listening, staying calm, giving encouragement and dealing fairly with problems of greatest importance to students. Alternatively, students might need to be directed to other forms of support outside of the school, such as youth counselling services.

Early intervention

An essential remit of an effective pastoral system in schools is to identify problems early. By intervening early with children's worries and providing support at this stage it is likely that more serious mental health problems can be averted (Rutter *et al.*, 1998). Raising the awareness of teachers of potential problem situations in this respect is therefore important. Some schools adopt an approach in which all children are screened at an early age for social and emotional difficulties, including poor self-esteem and difficulty mixing with their peer group or relating to adults. The Code of Practice for SEN (DFE, 1994) provides a framework for identification, assessment and provision of support for pupils at different stages.

With more serious problems teachers may need to give consideration to the tension between early identification and the possibility of labelling children at an early age and the effect that this itself may have on their development. It is important that learning difficulties, as well as emotional and social difficulties, are picked up early so as to prevent secondary mental health problems. The role of the new learning mentors and other support staff in schools may be helpful in making sure that pupils are progressing and not feeling that they are failures. If learning difficulties are picked up early, intervention can prevent the development of low self-esteem which otherwise could become ingrained and lead to more long-term difficulties, such as conduct disorder.

Support for vulnerable pupils

There may be particular times when pupils feel vulnerable and it is part of the pastoral team's role to recognise this and put in place support for these pupils. It is important to recognise that children may be particularly vulnerable to mental health problems at certain periods of their life and that there are particular stages in education that can be potentially damaging. Providing support at these times is very important. Thus, support for vulnerable pupils at the transition between primary and secondary school can avert some difficulties. Activities provided to help new pupils to get to know the school and their teachers and to make friends can make this a less threatening experience for many children. These types of programmes are already in place in some areas through the Education Welfare Service. Examinations can also be particularly stressful so extra support may be needed for some pupils at these times. Vulnerable pupils can be selected for group work around these and other relevant issues in order to help them cope.

Organisation of PSE

A PSE programme, which also includes moral and vocational education, is an essential part of the pastoral care provision of every school. There are three ways in which PSE can be carried out in schools. First, PSE can be infused into all subjects across the curriculum so that all teachers cover aspects of PSE as part of their subject teaching. For example, mathematics teachers will cover budgeting, social studies teachers will address the issue of discrimination and science teachers will cover sex education. Second, PSE can be included in the tutorial work programme; that is, form tutors teach it to their tutor groups, along with other activities, during form periods. Third, PSE can be taught as a separate subject on the school's curriculum and is taught by form tutors or by heads of year, or by some combination of these. In most schools nearly all teachers are involved in teaching aspects of PSE so they all need to develop the skills necessary for using the teaching methods, such as developmental group work, which are used in PSE programmes.

The content of PSE programmes varies from school to school. Many schools use published materials such as *Active Tutorial Work* (Baldwin and Wells, 1979). Some schools have developed and use their own materials and others use a combination of their own and published materials. Both primary and secondary school programmes need to address aspects of moral education as well as personal and social development. This may be done in separate lessons of religious education. In addition, secondary school PSE programmes also need to address vocational development and careers education.

Support and training for teachers

Whilst a lot of emphasis has been placed on the role that teachers can play in preventing mental health problems here, it is unrealistic to expect them to be able to achieve this alone and it is important that they get adequate support. Working with emotionally disturbed children can be particularly stressful and challenging as it can involve high levels of emotion and this can lead to stress (Hanko, 1993). This is recognised as an important issue in working with emotionally disturbed young people in therapeutic settings, where staff supervision and regular staff support meetings are typically provided. Similarly, support can be provided for teachers through teacher support groups, supervision, training and links with external agencies. It is important for teachers to have supervision and to know when to pass things on. This can take the form of support groups within the school, where teachers are able to share with others the difficulties they have encountered, as well as their successes. This can be a particularly valuable form of support if an external facilitator is appointed so that maximum benefit and positive outcomes are maintained. It can give teachers the confidence needed in their approach when dealing with pupils' mental health problems.

Training in behaviour management techniques is helpful, but insufficient alone as the underlying causes of behaviour are important to address if any long-term impact on children's behaviour is to be achieved. Teachers need to have a deep understanding of behaviour and mental health problems and what may underlie them. Difficult behaviour, for example, may be a cover-up for other difficulties that are either too painful or too embarrassing for pupils to discuss. Children who fail academically may cope in school by being disruptive, thus raising their status in the eyes of their peers and, concomitantly, especially in adolescents, raising their self-esteem. In these circumstances situations are likely to escalate because pupils find it too difficult to back down. Teachers need to be trained to handle such situations and, in the presence of an empathetic, non-judgemental listener, pupils may be able to address their true difficulties. An awareness of child development and group dynamics when dealing with mental health problems in children can also be important. Training in brief therapy (De Shazer *et al.*, 1986) can be helpful in solving problems in difficult cases, as can also techniques based on systemic approaches that have been shown to be effective with challenging cases (Dowling and Osborne, 1994).

Liaison with external agencies

Teachers often have limited training, time and resources with which to identify, address and monitor pupils' mental health difficulties, or to deliver an appropriate and effective quality of counselling for distressed students or their parents (Branwhite, 1994). Pastoral staff are frequently required to carry out a full timetable of teaching commitments themselves. For this reason, in many cases teachers may need to refer pupils and their parents to other agencies, such as the Educational Psychology Service or CAMHS. These services can also offer helpful consultation, support and training. Other agencies, such as the Youth Service and the School Health Service, are able to provide support to schools and to help with pupils' problems at an early stage. The youth counselling service, for example, can offer an alternative when pupils are unwilling to discuss their problems with school staff or parents and this can provide them with the opportunity to talk that they need. It is important to remember that not all approaches suit all individuals and a range of opportunities need to be provided for children to address their problems effectively. Where parents or pupils are reluctant to discuss their difficulties with school staff, who they often see as authority figures, they may be willing to talk to other professionals without connections to education.

Classroom practice

The fourth level of the framework is set within the values established by the school ethos at the first level, the policies and procedures established by the whole-school organisation at the second level and the systems for effective provision of pastoral care at the third level. This level of the model focuses on the need to develop effective classroom practice for promoting the development of children's mental health. This practice needs to be based on a thorough understanding of children's development and the mental health problems to which they are susceptible. Classroom practices for promoting mental health focus on the use of facilitative teaching strategies, as well as what teachers can do in terms of teaching PSE and providing guidance and counselling for students.

Facilitative teaching

A key factor in promoting children's mental health in schools is the rapport which teachers develop with their pupils. This involves teachers in implementing constructive relationships with pupils, which are part of the schools' ethos as described above. It also involves them in using lots of encouragement and rewards in order to motive pupils as well as fair and consistent enforcement of sanctions to set limits and reduce inappropriate behaviour. In addition, it involves teachers using strategies which promote a healthy atmosphere in the classroom and encourage pupils to help one another, such as peer tutoring and co-operative learning (Johnson and Johnson, 1999).

PSE

Teachers have an important role to play in providing children and young people with opportunities for PSE. Opportunities for them to talk about their feelings should be structured into the school day. Circle Time (DfEE, 1999; Mosely, 1996), an increasingly popular technique now used in many schools, is one example of how this might be achieved. It is important to ensure that all pupils, including the most vulnerable, have an opportunity to share their feelings and their views. In this way pupils can be taught how to become emotionally literate (Goleman, 1998), as well as preventing emotions being built up with the potential for later problems. This type of approach can give them self-confidence and enhance their self-esteem. It is also valuable in promoting social skills, such as co-operation and listening to others. Nurture groups (DfEE, 1999) and peer support (Cowie and Wallace, 2000) are also examples of approaches that might be adopted to help provide opportunities for pupils to develop emotionally and socially. PSE can be taught as a separate subject, as well as through relevant parts of subjects in the National Curriculum, and is the responsibility of all teachers (Weare, 2000).

Guidance

Guidance involves helping students individually or in small groups with making personal, educational or vocational choices. It is considered that four levels of guidance need to be in place in schools. The first level involves the provision of information by classroom teachers as part of a wide range of subjects in the curriculum in order to provide pupils with the knowledge needed to make personal, educational and vocational choices. The second level involves the use of guidance by form tutors in order to help pupils make personal, educational and vocational choices. This can be provided individually or as part of the school's PSE programme. The third level is individual or small-group guidance available from a trained specialist within the school. This could be a careers officer or guidance counsellor, head of year or house, or a senior teacher who has a pastoral leadership role within the school. The fourth level involves referral procedures to help pupils access agencies outside the school, such as careers services or job placement agencies.

All teachers need to have a basic knowledge of guidance, sufficient to fulfil their roles as classroom teachers and form tutors at the first and second levels. In addition, at least one member of staff should have had further training in order to provide intensive guidance at the third level and to know which agencies to refer pupils to outside the school at the fourth level. This member of staff should also act as a resource to other teachers in the school.

Counselling

The term counselling is often misused within educational circles. It may be used to describe a friendly chat, giving advice or information, or even telling pupils what to do. Whilst these may, in different circumstances, all constitute valid forms of helping, they are not counselling. The British Association for Counselling (1991: 1) states that 'Counselling is the skilled and principled use of a relationship to facilitate self-knowledge, emotional acceptance and growth, and the optimal development of personal resources.' This is a useful approach to adopt when pupils have emotional and family problems. Effective intervention at this stage can help prevent more serious mental health problems from developing. It requires training and, whilst all teachers cannot be expected to be trained counsellors, they can be trained to use counselling skills to advantage both in and outside of the classroom. Some teachers may have no difficulty adopting this type of approach when they encounter pupils with mental health problems, whilst others, who are more used to giving advice or telling students what to do, will find it more difficult.

A key aspect of counselling for classroom teachers is the use of active listening skills. Weare (2000: 89) suggests that 'listening is the single best way to help those in emotional difficulties'. Active listening involves establishing a relationship based on empathy, genuineness and respect (Rogers, 1961) and using skills, such as maintaining eye contact and appropriate use of body language, in addition to reflecting and summarising thoughts and feelings (Hornby, 1994).

Counselling is most effective when it is an integral part of a whole-school approach to pastoral care alongside the provision of guidance and PSE. Counselling in schools involves helping students individually or in small groups to deal with the concerns or difficulties they are experiencing. It is considered that four levels of counselling need to be in place in schools (Hamblin, 1993; Lang, 1993). The first level involves the use of counselling skills in the classroom in order to provide a positive learning environment and promote high levels of pupil self-esteem. Within the classroom situation, where it is easy for pupils to lose face in front of their peers and for them to feel a sense of failure, counselling skills can be used to convey acceptance and belonging and this can have a vital impact on vulnerable pupils. The second level involves the use of counselling skills by the form tutor in order to help pupils solve day-to-day problems, as well as the use of counselling skills to facilitate group activities as part of the school's PSE programme. This can include group activities that are conducted in order to focus on pupils' long-term development and the formation of constructive relationships with pupils in the classroom. The third level is the individual or small-group counselling available from a trained specialist within the school. This could be a counsellor, head of year or house, or a senior teacher who has a pastoral leadership role within the school. The fourth level involves referral procedures to help pupils access professionals outside the school, such as psychologists and psychiatrists, for specialist counselling help.

All teachers need to develop basic counselling skills, sufficient to fulfil their roles as classroom teachers and form tutors at the first two levels. In addition, at least one member of staff should have had further training in counselling in order to provide intensive counselling at the third level and to know when and where to refer pupils for specialist help outside the school at the fourth level. This member of staff should also provide training, supervision and support to teachers in their work at the first and second levels.

Further reading

Best, R. (ed.) (2000) *Education for Spiritual, Moral, Social and Cultural Development*. London: Continuum.

Calvert, M. and Henderson, J. (1998) *Managing Pastoral Care*. London: Cassell.

Cooper, P., Smith, C. and Upton, G. (1994) *Emotional and Behavioural Difficulties: Theory to Practice*. London: Routledge.

Hamblin, D. (1993) *The Teacher and Counselling*. Hemel Hempstead: Simon and Schuster.

Mental Health Foundation (1999) *Bright Futures: Promoting Children and Young People's Mental Health*. London: The Mental Health Foundation.

Weare, K. (2000) *Promoting Mental, Emotional and Social Health*. London: Routledge.

References

Baldwin, J. and Wells, H. (1979) *Active Tutorial Work (Books 1 to 5)*. Oxford: Blackwell.

Best, R. (ed.) (2000) *Education for Spiritual, Moral, Social and Cultural Development*. London: Continuum.

Branwhite, T. (1994) Bullying and student distress: Beneath the tip of the iceberg. *Educational Psychology*, 14, 1, 59–71.

British Association for Counselling (1991) *Code of Ethics and Practice for Counsellors*. Rugby: BAC.

Calvert, M. and Henderson, J. (1998) *Managing Pastoral Care*. London: Cassell.

Charlton, T. and David, K. (1993) *Managing Misbehaviour in Schools (Second edition)*. London: Routledge.

Cowie, H. and Wallace, P. (2000) *Peer Support in Action*. London: Sage.

Department for Education DFE (1994) *The Code of Practice on the Identification and Assessment of Special Educational Needs*. London: HMSO.

Department for Education and Employment (1999) *Social Inclusion: Pupil Support (Circular 10/99)*. London: DfEE.

Department of Education and Science (DES) (1989) *Discipline in Schools: Report of the Committee of Enquiry chaired by Lord Elton* (The Elton Report). London: HMSO.

De Shazer, S., Berg, I. K., Lipchik, E., Nunnally, E., Molnar, A., Gingerich, W. and Weiner, Davis M. (1986) Brief therapy: Focused solution development. *Family Process*, 25, 207–222.

Dowling, E. and Osborne, E. (1994) *The Family and the School: A Joint Systems Approach to Problems with Children (Second edition)*. London: Routledge.

Goleman, D. (1998) *Working with Emotional Intelligence*. London: Bloomsbury.

Hall, E. and Hall, C. (1988) *Human Relations in Education*. London: Routledge.

Hamblin, D. (1993) *The Teacher and Counselling*. Hemel Hempstead: Simon and Schuster.

Hanko, G. (1993) *Special Needs in Ordinary Classrooms*. Hemel Hempstead: Simon and Schuster.

Hornby, G. (1994) *Counselling in Child Disability*. London: Chapman and Hall.

Hornby, G. (2000) *Improving Parental Involvement*. London: Cassell.
Jenner, S. and Greetham, C. (1995) Forming a whole-school anti-bullying policy. *Pastoral Care in Education*, 13, 3, 6–13.
Johnson, D. W. and Johnson, R. T. (1999) *Learning Together and Alone: Co-operative, Competitive and Individualistic Learning (Fifth edition)*. Boston: Allyn and Bacon.
Lang, P. (1993) Counselling in the primary school: An integrated approach. In Bovair, K. and McLaughlin, C. (eds) *Counselling in Schools: A Reader*, 21–35. London: David Fulton.
Mental Health Foundation (1999) *Bright Futures: Promoting Children and Young People's Mental Health*. London: The Mental Health Foundation.
Mosely, J. (1996) *Quality Circle Time*. Cambridge: LDA.
National Curriculum Council (1989) *The National Curriculum and Whole School Curriculum Planning: Preliminary Guidance (Circular Number 6)*. York: National Curriculum Council.
O'Brien, T. (1998) *Promoting Positive Behaviour*. London: David Fulton.
Parsons, C. (1999) *Education, Exclusion and Citizenship*. London: Routledge.
Peterson, R. L. and Skiba, R. (2000) Creating school climates that prevent school violence. *Preventing School Failure*, 44, 3, 122–129.
Rogers, C. (1961) *On Becoming a Person*. London: Constable.
Rutter, M., Giller, H. and Hagell, A. (1998) *Antisocial Behaviour by Young People*. Cambridge: Cambridge University Press.
Smith, P. K. (2000) Bullying and harassment in schools and the rights of children. *Children and Society*, 14, 294–303.
Weare, K. (2000) *Promoting Mental, Emotional and Social Health*. London: Routledge.

Index